Britain in the Middle East

Britain in
the Middle East

1619–1971

ROBERT T. HARRISON

Bloomsbury Academic
An imprint of Bloomsbury Publishing Plc

B L O O M S B U R Y
LONDON · OXFORD · NEW YORK · NEW DELHI · SYDNEY

Bloomsbury Academic

An imprint of Bloomsbury Publishing Plc

50 Bedford Square	1385 Broadway
London	New York
WC1B 3DP	NY 10018
UK	USA

www.bloomsbury.com

BLOOMSBURY and the Diana logo are trademarks of Bloomsbury Publishing Plc

First published 2016

British Library Cataloguing-in-Publication Data
A catalogue record for this book is available from the British Library.

ISBN: HB: 978-1-4725-9072-5
PB: 978-1-4725-9071-8
ePDF: 978-1-4725-9073-2
ePub: 978-1-4725-9074-9

Library of Congress Cataloging-in-Publication Data
Names: Harrison, Robert T., author.
Title: Britain in the Middle East: 1619-1971 / Robert T Harrison.
Description: New York: Bloomsbury Academic, 2016.
Identifiers: LCCN 2015035200| ISBN 9781472590718 (paperback) | ISBN
9781472590725 (hardback)
Subjects: LCSH: Middle East–Foreign relations–Great Britain. | Great
Britain–Foreign relations–Middle East. | BISAC: HISTORY / Middle East /
General. | HISTORY / Europe / Great Britain.
Classification: LCC DS63.2.G7 H37 2016 | DDC 327.4105609/03–dc23 LC record available at
http://lccn.loc.gov/2015035200

Typeset by Deanta Global Publishing Services, Chennai, India
Printed and bound in India

CONTENTS

List of illustrations vi
List of maps vii
Introduction viii

  1   The search for trade: 1555–1763 1

  2   British victory, power, and dominance to 1797 13

  3   Napoleonic wars and regional security 1798–1815 25

  4   Control in the Gulf, Red Sea, and Egypt 1815–41 41

  5   The "Great Game," Afghanistan 1838–42 55

  6   The Crimean War and its impact 1838–58 63

  7   The question of Egypt 1838–79 71

  8   The turning point: Invasion of Egypt 1879–82 85

  9   Aftermath and the imperial scramble 1883–1914 103

10   The Middle East in the Great War 1914–18 121

11   War's aftershock: The watershed 1918–22 141

12   Tenacity enshrined: Holding on 1922–40 155

13   The Middle East in the Second World War 1939–45 169

14   End of the road: Exit from empire 1945–71 189

Conclusion 209
Notes 213
Bibliography 259
Index 267

LIST OF ILLUSTRATIONS

Figure 1   Battle of the Pyramids, July 21, 1798 27

Figure 2   Battle of the Nile, August 1, 1798 27

Figure 3   Henry John Temple, 3rd Viscount
(Lord Palmerston) 47

Figure 4   Colonel Ahmed Urabi, Egypt, 1882 93

Figure 5   British navy at Alexandria, 1882 96

Figure 6   Clashes at Alexandria, June 11, 1882 96

Figure 7   Egyptian artillery at Alexandria 97

Figure 8   British navy bombards Alexandria,
July 11, 1882 98

Figure 9   Battle of Kassassin, August 28, 1882 99

Figure 10 Battle of Tel el-Kabir, September 13, 1882 100

Figure 11 Scottish regiment at the Sphinx, 1882 101

Figure 12 British troops relaxing at the Sphinx, 1882 104

Figure 13 General William Hicks, Sudan, 1883 107

Figure 14 General Charles Gordon, Sudan, 1885 109

Figure 15 General Garnet Wolseley, Egypt and Sudan,
1882–85 110

Figure 16 The Fashoda Incident, 1898 113

Figure 17 Prime Minister David Lloyd George, 1922 128

Figure 18 Colonel T. E. Lawrence "of Arabia," 1918 135

Figure 19 Egyptians demand independence, 1922 149

Figure 20 Roosevelt, Churchill, and Chang Kai Chek,
Cairo, 1943 180

LIST OF MAPS

All maps adapted from Nigel Dalziel, *The Penguin Historical Atlas of the British Empire* (London: Penguin, 2006). Reproduced by permission of Penguin Books Ltd.

Map 1 The Great Game, Russia and British India 57

Map 2 The Ties That Bind: Britain's Steamship Network 76

Map 3 World Wide Web: Telegraphic Communications to 1902 90

Map 4 Egypt and the Route to the East 108

Map 5 Naval Power and Gunboat Diplomacy 119

Map 6 Imperial Defense I: The First World War 125

Map 7 Securing the Canal: The Middle East to 1945 145

Map 8 Imperial Defense II: The Second World War 174

Map 9 The Road to Suez: The Middle East 1945–56 205

INTRODUCTION

Britain maintained a three-and-a-half-century sojourn in the "Greater Middle East" from 1617 to 1971. During that period, the region had evolved into a British sphere, inescapably linked to the security of the entire British Empire. This proved no accident. Individual tradesmen and politicians gave direction and sustainability to the British presence in the Middle East, and once done, there was no turning back. Without such personal direction, Britain's stay in this region would have been as transitory, aimless, and ephemeral as that of the other European powers. This story will examine how that wide-ranging and resilient grip would, instead, grow to protect the vital trade and communication network essential to safeguarding the empire as an integral part of the imperial equation. In time, Britain's tenacious presence would prove a mixed blessing. On the one hand, it has preserved the region's geographical integrity to this day, keeping other Europeans out. At the same time, it set the stage for the region's current political climate and ongoing volatility. Most importantly, its possession allowed Britain great victories for the free world over military dictatorships in two world wars, but the price proved enormous. In the end, it cost Britain control of the region and with it, great power status. In the strangest twist of all, this very important glue of empire would generate its undoing.

This book centers on diplomatic and political history, as well as key, highly influential individuals. It holds to a traditional methodology that will examine how Britain maintained its regional hegemony. The question of "formal" versus "informal" empire in relation to Britain's ability to control such a vast area is a central focus. Whenever possible, Britain tried to avoid formal control as too expensive, forceful, and risky. Britain's conquest of Aden and Egypt proved the exceptions. Instead, successive British governments preferred informal management of the region that included the Ottoman Middle East, Persia, the Gulf Protectorates, and Afghanistan. British representatives handled this region through advice as well as manipulation of elites or native dynasties, a technique most historians have interpreted as cheaper, less intrusive, and more benign. Britain's handling of most of the Middle East proved characteristically more humane and culturally sensitive than that perpetrated by the French in North Africa, Lebanon, and Syria; or that of czarist Russia in Muslim South Asia. Such British management worked well in the Ottoman Empire for over a century. It also proved successful in the Gulf Protectorates, where Britain controlled foreign affairs but took a "hands off" policy on domestic issues. This allowed the friendly sheikdoms and sultanates to remain unmolested. Most of these dynasties continue to the present. Much the same occurred in Jordan following the League of Nations Mandate. Although this approach was tried in Iraq, it suffered mixed results after the termination of the mandate. On the other hand, the so-called benign nature of Britain's informal "guidance" produced a significant and sometimes violent reaction from those who struggled for political control or independence in the face of the more elusive and tenacious grip of informal management. In some cases, the political struggle produced both military and Islamic political parties that exist to this day and challenge the great power dominance of the international system. These parties had emerged to confront and oust the "puppet" native elites together with the British who pulled the strings. This was especially the case in Egypt in 1954 (after so-called formal independence had been granted in 1922), as well as later in Iraq in 1958 and finally in Iran 1952 and 1979.

Whether implemented as a formal or an informal empire, the British presence also endured throughout the region due to the mobile threat of forces from Britain and the empire and the rapid deployment of those naval and military assets throughout the eastern Mediterranean, the Red Sea, the Arabian Sea, the Persian Gulf, and the Indian Ocean. Britain maintained military and naval bases at the Straits of Hormuz, Aden, the Suez Canal, and ultimately at Haifa in Palestine. Moreover, Britain's control of this region had become absolutely essential during the First and Second World Wars. It had turned out to be the key to preserving the empire as well as defeating the enemy. But Britain's tenacious and abuse-ridden manipulation of the region, understood as a wartime expediency, would cost Britain the Middle East. Toward the end of the British stay following the Second World War, the financial condition of the sterling worsened and political stability deteriorated in each location. Britain, always tenacious, simply played a shell game and withdrew from one base to another until not one remained, the last being Aden in 1967. Significantly, this final exit occurred, of course, when all popular trust had disappeared and no empire remained to protect. Though the British presence has now largely vanished from the region, the legacy of Britain's almost forgotten long moment in the Middle East continues to the present.

Britain had come to be in the Middle East through an evolutionary process, its presence there initially the unintended consequence of trade and competition. Three important individuals, however, would provide very determined political direction to all future British actions in the Middle East. Sir Thomas Roe, ambassador to the Mughal court, enforced a fundamental political dimension to the East India Company's earliest trade endeavors in India and Persia. His position gave the company durability and placed it on equal terms with the Mughal and Safavid courts. East India tradesman George Baldwin brought home Egypt's never-to-be-forgotten strategic value to the empire by saving India for the British in 1778. Finally, Foreign

Secretary Lord Palmerston, acting on the precedents of Roe and Baldwin, put into action an official policy of regional control. Britain's empire in the Middle East would never drift thereafter but always maintained a sense of purpose and direction. It would keep all foreigners at bay and provide a secure communication and transportation artery for the empire. No future prime minister or political party would ever find an alternative to this policy. Britain and the empire depended on it. The die had been cast. The Middle East, formally or informally, had become an integral, if not the most important, part of the British Empire, and would remain so until the end.

To begin, British penetration into the region started slowly with the arrival of the English East India Company on the west coast of Mughal India in 1615. From there, the company launched small forays into Safavid Persia, the Persian Gulf, and the Red Sea to trade in wool, silver, silk, and spices in the seventeenth and eighteenth centuries. Although these ventures were marginal in comparison with the company's substantial efforts in India, thanks to Sir Thomas Roe they proved a successful endeavor in the face of stiff Portuguese and Dutch competition as well as conflict with the French in the eighteenth century. Significantly, Britain's role inexorably shifted from trade to one of political power after victories over the French in both the Seven Years' War as well as in India during the war of the American Revolution due to the efforts of George Baldwin. The company and the British government's eventual domination of India resulting from these conflicts would at the same time propel British influence into Persia and the Gulf, Afghanistan, and the Ottoman Empire or the "greater Middle East." In time, some British leaders saw Britain's presence in the region as essential to the maintenance and survival of the British Empire. The Middle East had rapidly become the lynchpin and the lifeline of empire. But not all agreed with this view, and while East India Company merchants like George Baldwin understood this as a reality by the late eighteenth century, many government officials, consuls, and ambassadors did not. French general Napoleon Bonaparte's invasion of Egypt quickly resolved the arguments.

Napoleon's 1798 foray into Egypt compelled Britain to reappraise its position and to thereafter safeguard this region as both the buffer and gateway to India, firmly linking it to trade, transportation, and communication vital to the defense of the empire. Because of the Middle East's enormous size and diversity, it had never occurred to the British to try and conquer the entire region simply because of its strategic position, but rather to develop a formula of informal influence through cultivation, exploitation, and management of native elites (sultans, pashas, or sheiks) to guarantee loyalty to Britain. For the most part, this proved successful. Throughout the nineteenth century, the Ottoman Empire, Persia, Afghanistan, and Britain's Arab Protectorates in the Persian Gulf and the Red Sea emerged as a de facto British security shield against any future European territorial encroachment as well as interdiction points to combat piracy and the slave trade. Skillful use of informal influence served to control this vast region for larger British imperial interests.

But what if the diplomacy of informal empire failed, as in 1840? The government then took the direct approach. Britain occupied Aden, invaded Afghanistan, and subjugated Muhammad Ali's Egypt. Britain's aggressive foreign secretary, Lord Palmerston, now assumed a new and more forceful posture in the Middle East and set the stage for a permanent British presence with the London Treaty of 1840, which assured Egypt to the Ottoman Empire under British guarantee. Because imperial security had become inexorably linked to the Middle East, the British would guard this region at whatever cost, now and in the future. This policy became quickly apparent with even bolder moves. Britain's renewed determination to support the territorial integrity of the Ottoman Empire against Russian expansion brought on the "Eastern Question" and the costly Crimean War in 1854, as well as the Berlin Congress of 1878, which aimed to contain Russia once more. Collision with the French over the Suez Canal in 1869 and a subsequent clash with the Egyptian national movement's alleged threat to British interests, including the route to India, provoked a much-contested seventy-two-year occupation of Egypt in 1882. The invasion of Egypt proved the logical outcome of Palmerston's policies. These actions proved risky enough, but more was to come. Britain would not only defend the Middle East but utilize it as source of strategic offensives against other European interlopers. Britain retook the Sudan in 1898 to checkmate the French in the Upper Nile and opened the twentieth century with the creation of the Kuwait Protectorate to prevent Germany's Berlin–Baghdad railway from reaching the Persian Gulf. As a result, the Middle East not only remained safe in British hands, as did the security of Britain's empire; but, more importantly, the springboard for British offensives.

The First World War tested both that premise and Britain's resolve as never before. Following the maxim that the best defense is a good offense, during the Great War and against vociferous opposition of her French ally, Britain exerted extraordinary military endeavors in Palestine and Mesopotamia. This was done not simply to protect the empire's Middle Eastern sphere as the lifeline to India and the rest of her Asian and Pacific empire or to garner the region's newly discovered oil-rich resources, but to take the war to the enemy on these two fronts and channel another million imperial troops to the trenches in France. This Middle East strategy proved the forefront of British labors from the beginning of the conflict and was not merely an afterthought to German and Turkish aggression in the region. As much as anything, this effort contributed significantly to the final triumph over the central powers. Therefore, Britain would retain those Middle East assets blindly, tenaciously, until the next global conflict. Roe, Baldwin, and Palmerston had set an irreversible path with inevitable consequences.

Moreover, of the treaties made to support the British war effort, the most important involved those devised for the Middle East, such as the

Hussein-McMahon Accords, the Sykes-Picot Agreement, and the Balfour Declaration. These documents, however, worked at cross purposes, generating misunderstandings, broken promises, and more clashes following war's end. Some of the region's most enduring conflicts can be traced directly to these treaties. The creation of the League of Nations British Mandate in Iraq (Mesopotamia) in 1920 provoked a revolution, while Britain's Palestine Mandate propelled an Arab collision with the British-sponsored Jewish settlement or Zionism. The Iraq crisis was settled when Britain installed a Sunni-dominated Arab regime under British influence, but in Palestine, no solution proved viable. Overall, the British had used the Arabs to support their war effort and thus the empire, only to disregard Arab expectations following the war by attempting to utilize the Zionist settlers to protect the Suez Canal and thus imperial security. Imperial necessity, as always, dictated the direction of regional decisions. In short, the British designed each of these wartime agreements to maintain the nation's paramount position in the Middle East following the war.

At the same time, a revolution in Egypt resulted in quasi independence in 1922. Britain, however, had no thought of retreat, and, thereafter, maintained control of the country through "reserved powers," prompting the rise of the Islamic fundamentalist Muslim Brothers to seek the complete removal of British influence. Without the British presence, it seems unlikely this fundamentalist movement would ever have materialized. Noticeably, subsequent Islamist movements that came as spinoffs from the Muslim Brothers did not emerge in a vacuum but always in response to real or perceived British or Western interference in the region. Significantly, that pattern continues. Importantly, the British presence remained intact and steadfast.

The interwar years witnessed increased Jewish immigration to Palestine and more anti-Zionist riots; the loss of British influence in Persia, Afghanistan, and Turkey; and the rise of the Soviet Union and thus the rebirth of the "Eastern Question." Next, Italy's growing military presence in Ethiopia and Libya and ties to Nazi Germany in the 1930s pointed up the state of British vulnerability in the Middle East on the eve of the Second World War. Fearing the worst, Britain abruptly changed course and restricted Jewish immigration to Palestine to garner Arab favor. Imperial necessity as opposed to principle appeared to be the root of this decision. At the same time, Britain secured agreements with Egypt and Iraq to use their military bases, and, in the case of Egypt, to modernize its army and then leave in twenty years. The endeavor in Egypt, however, proved counterproductive. Despite the incredible human and financial losses of the First World War and the increased internal and external stresses the British now faced in the Middle East, no one gave thought to retreat. They had determined to stay the course. The Middle East loomed more important than ever to British purposes.

Despite that importance, a careless disregard of regional sensitivities dogged the British effort throughout the Second World War. First, Britain's abusive management of Egypt's resources in order to protect the Suez Canal against the Axis prompted an increase in the activities of the Muslim Brothers and the birth of the Egyptian nationalist Free Officer Corps, which together would force a British ouster in 1954. Second, in Palestine, continued restrictions on Jewish immigration provoked Zionist extremists (Irgun and Stern Gang) to attack the British during and after the war and force Britain's early removal in 1948. Overall, Britain's shifting policies and hurried exit from Palestine helped generate the bloody and still unresolved Israeli-Palestinian conflict. Finally, in the middle of the conflict, a British engineered coup in Iran (Persia), which created a pliable regime to serve the war effort under the young Reza Shah Pahlavi, ignited two significant political upheavals that have reverberations to this day. As essential as the Middle East would prove to the British war effort, using it without restraint in both world wars came at an enormous cost: Britain would lose the last measures of popular trust and with it the region, the key to empire, and great power status.

Britain's postwar financial collapse served to hasten the protracted and often bloodstained period of retreat from Palestine, Egypt, and finally Aden from 1945 to 1967. Britain's withdrawal from the Kuwait Protectorate in 1961 propelled an immediate Iraqi attack to reclaim disputed territory as well as serving as Saddam Hussein's justification for the 1990 invasion. Britain's honorable withdrawal from the remainder of the Gulf Protectorates by 1971 effectively ended three-and-a-half centuries of imperial dominance in the Middle East.

In all, Britain's legacy in the Middle East remains mixed. On the negative side, Britain's stay in the Middle East, maintained through the use of formal control through armed occupation or informal management by manipulation of elites, provoked popular resentment. The rise of military parties or Islamic extremist groups to remove the British soon materialized. Examples of these political institutions perpetuate the turbulence of today's Middle East landscape, as does the ongoing Arab-Israeli conflict, the direct result of British rule in Palestine. The mechanics of British imperialism reveals the impact of informal management through trade treaties, protectorates, and guardianships as well as formal control, conspicuous outright invasion, or occupation within the region. While these schemes produced benefits for Britain and the all-important security of empire, at the same time, by utilizing native elites through informal or formal means to do their bidding, British authorities undercut cultural accommodation and acquiescence to the desires of subject populations. Power at the top, a poor substitute for mutual respect, never provided a sensitive ear to political discontent or social needs. Except on a very superficial level, Britain felt no obligation to, nor did it, promote democratic processes in the Middle East. It had never been in its interest to do so nor had the British claimed that it was. Therefore, the techniques and the attitudes that kept British authority in place without much popular support only served to promote increased resentment following the Second World War. British management sparked strident anti-British Arab and Jewish nationalism in the case of Palestine and thus the ensuing Arab-Israeli conflict. Moreover, reaction to Britain's administration generated the first Islamic fundamentalist movement to oppose British control as well as quasi-military dictatorships to oust the British in Egypt and Iraq. These morphed into single national parties, which controlled Iraq until 1958 and Egypt until the Arab Spring of 2011. These entities, together with the ongoing feudal dynasties of Jordan and the Gulf, have continued to define the domestic landscape of the modern Middle East as part of the British heritage.

On the positive side, Britain noticeably only established one colony in the Middle East (Aden), and for the most part it directed and defended its sphere informally through treaty protectorates (Gulf States), a guarantorship (Egypt and the Ottoman Empire), and collaborative dynasties (mandates) supported by British military and naval forces when necessary. Trade again loomed large with the discovery of oil in the twentieth century, and thus the region's security became more tightly fastened to British imperial and financial interests, despite two world wars and the loss of India. These important ties survived Britain's final military and political withdrawal from the region, leaving a heritage of ongoing British influence. Significantly, while serving to stimulate trade with the West and protect the route to India, the British sphere in the Middle East significantly retarded the encroachment of rival European powers, helping to guarantee the region's general boundaries to the present. That, along with Britain's century-long effort to interdict the slave trade and piracy in the Persian Gulf and Red Sea, stands as a commendable heritage in the minds of many. In the end, and most importantly, Britain's almost blind determination to control the Middle East rested on the growing belief that it had become integral to the philosophy and essence of empire itself. That belief, if nothing else, sustained the British effort through two world wars and a final victory for the free world. This alone might outweigh the negatives, and though largely ignored, it remains a paramount measure of the British heritage in the Middle East.

CHAPTER ONE

The search for trade: 1555–1763

Established on December 31, 1600, "The Governor and Company of Merchants of London Trading into the East Indies" was granted exclusive rights to trade across the world "beyond the Cape of Bona Esperanza (Good Hope) to the Straits of Magellan." Charter, East India Company.

J. HUREWITZ, *Diplomacy in the Near and Middle East*

In 1619, Sir Thomas Roe, who represented the English crown and the East India Company, signed the first official trade agreement with the Safavid Empire (Persia) granting English merchants the privilege of trading in the Middle East. The efforts leading to this singular event began in the second half of the sixteenth century with the successive efforts of three joint-stock enterprises that held franchises from the English: the Muscovy, Levant, and East India Companies. Based on Venetian explorer Sebastian Cabot's idea of finding a sea route to the East through the northern ocean, 240 London merchants founded the Muscovy Company in 1554 to search for the Northeast Passage to China and the Indies.[1] The company charter had been based on Sir Hugh Willoughby's successful trade expedition the year before to Russia's White Sea port at Archangel. The hazardous voyage resulted in the loss of two of the expedition's three ships. Czar Ivan IV "The Terrible" received the small but determined party at Moscow, and upon acknowledging a letter from Edward VI, granted favorable trade privileges to the adventurous merchants. Another expedition in 1555 bore letters from England's new monarch, Queen Mary, and her husband Philip. Ivan again granted to "them and their successors, forever, very important privileges."[2] This meant direct trade within all of Russia and beyond.

In the absence of any competition, Muscovy Company merchants soon made their way into the Middle East. Successive voyages led southward along the Syrian and Turkish frontier, where the company obtained trade concessions from Persian Governor Abdullah Khan at Shirvan. This became the first English factory (warehouse) in the region. A second route followed the Volga River to Persia and the Caspian Sea. Here, trade in raw silk and other luxury items and the potential for a route to India spurred the company to six expeditions over a nineteen-year period.[3] In 1566, Persian ruler Shah Tahmasp granted a *ferman* (royal decree) to the English for trade and freedom of transit for commerce with India.[4] Banditry and excessive tribal warfare, however, prompted the termination of the Persian enterprise by 1581.[5]

The imminent closure of the Russian route to this promising but dangerous area prompted the creation of the Levant Company in 1581 in order to approach the silk trade from the direction of the Ottoman Empire.[6] The French had been there since 1535, and before the company received its charter, negotiations had to be hammered out with the Ottoman sultan, who in 1580 issued a ferman granting the English a company monopoly with the attendant capitulations (special rights) for the protection of English subjects.[7] This act occurred despite fierce opposition from the French, who had maintained the only European trade monopoly in the empire.[8] The Levant Company later acquired additional political rights to maintain an embassy at Constantinople and consular offices throughout the sultan's realm. Except for one ferman in 1603, which expanded the company's privileges, the company monopoly in the empire remained relatively stable until free-trade pressure at home forced its dissolution by Act of Parliament in 1825.

The East India Company, founded in 1600 as the last of the great companies of the Elizabethan age, followed the Cape route and groped for trade in the Indies and China. In 1615, the company initiated commerce with India and the Persian Gulf, and, after a century, opened direct trade into the Ottoman Empire as well. This company succeeded where others faltered or failed due to one unique feature: More than a simple trading company, it bore the power of the English crown as well. The company, therefore, emerged to become the major political power in India following the Seven Years' War and far surpassed the economic and political strength of the rival Levant Company. In the 1790s, the East India Company negotiated treaties with the Arab sheikdoms along the Red Sea and the Persian Gulf to secure the area as a buffer against French threats to India. From that time until the Sepoy Mutiny in 1857, the company evolved to become a major political player in the affairs of the Middle East.

East India Company and the Persian Gulf

The general European foray into the Indies took place against the background of Europe's political turmoil during the late sixteenth and seventeenth centuries, known as the Age of Religious Wars. The major Catholic powers, Portugal and Spain, were the first to dominate European overseas commerce. Between 1415 and 1560, Portugal had initiated trade to the African coast, the Indian Ocean, the Persian Gulf, and the East Indies, as well as to China and Japan; and by 1560, Spain had both conquered and colonized portions of the Americas and the Philippines.

With the coming of the Protestant Reformation in the sixteenth century, Dutch Calvinists in the Spanish Netherlands found themselves continually at war against their Spanish overlords. Protestant England under Elizabeth I soon entered the fray and struck against Spanish trade in the Americas, which ultimately led to Philip II's failed revenge—the Spanish Armada of 1588. Spain's absorption of the Portuguese Crown in 1580, moreover, made Portugal and her seaborne empire the hapless victim of newly formed Dutch and English trade companies after 1600. Thus, at the beginning of the seventeenth century, Europe's religious and mercantile wars spread to the Indian Ocean, the Persian Gulf, and the South China Sea. Inexorably, the powerful Dutch East India Company seized many Portuguese colonies and strongholds throughout the region and would soon make war on the rival English East India Company as well.

Established on December 31, 1600, "The Governor and Company of Merchants of London Trading into the East Indies" was granted exclusive rights to trade across the world "beyond the Cape of Bona Esperanza (Good Hope) to the Straits of Magellan."[9] The East India Company sought to establish a base for the spice trade in the East Indies from 1600 to 1615. Unfortunately for the Honorable Company, the Portuguese and Dutch had already constructed military bases there, and after several misadventures, numerous company ships were driven out of the Spice Islands (Indonesia) by the very determined naval forces of the Dutch East India Company (VOC).[10] Although the English company refused to quit the Spice Island trade altogether, it reassessed its position in the Indies and thereafter focused on the trade potential offered by the Indian subcontinent—a very fortuitous event for a company deemed the most unlikely to succeed.

India and the territory of the eastern Persian Gulf, meanwhile, had undergone significant political changes on the eve of the English company's arrival. The Portuguese had penetrated the region a century earlier, and in 1510, under Alfonso de Albuquerque, they created a sizable colony on India's west coast at Goa. From there, they captured and fortified all the strategic choke points for trade in the Red Sea, the Indian Ocean, and the Persian Gulf. Thus at Aden, Hormuz, Bahrain, and Ceylon, the Portuguese forced Arab, Indian, and Persian traders to buy letters (*cartezas*) to exercise commerce in their own traditional waters.

In the mid-sixteenth century, however, north and central India had fallen under the domination of the powerful Mughal Empire. Under forceful leaders like Babar, Akbar, and Jahangir, the Mughals would soon expand their state into most of the subcontinent. The Portuguese, who were no match for the Mughal military, stayed on their good side by paying a percentage of their commercial proceeds to the Mughal rulers at Delhi. To the north during this same period, Persia's Safavid Dynasty had revitalized under the energies of Shah Abbas I. He continually waged war with the Portuguese in the Gulf and against his traditional Ottoman rival in the west.[11] Although these were tumultuous times for the English East India Company to seek trade in the region, these various political rivalries oftentimes worked to its advantage.

East India Company fleets made twelve voyages to the Indies from 1600 to 1612, including that of Commander William Hawkins, who brought the first English ship to the fringes of the Mughal Empire at Surat on India's northwest coast in 1608. He delivered a letter from King James I to Mughal Emperor Jahangir, and although he was well received initially, Portuguese intrigues at court forced Hawkins' dismissal in 1611.[12] Attempts to restore relations failed until Thomas Best brought his fleet to Surat in 1612 and negotiated a trade agreement with local authorities. A Mughal ferman quickly followed.[13] Company traders tenuously planted their factory a year later and pursued trade in raw cotton, cotton piece goods, silks, pepper, indigo, and saltpeter destined for England and for resale to Europe.[14]

Maintenance of a permanent Surat factory, however, was to prove anything but a sure thing. A Portuguese naval threat might have materialized at any time from her colony to the south at Goa. Dutch fleets, moreover, already had started active and aggressive probes into the region. Finally, the Mughal Empire could eject any European presence from her coastal territories if necessary. She had chosen not to do so with the Portuguese only because they paid a percentage of their seaborne trading profits to the Mughals, who themselves had little interest in overseas trade.

India and the Persian Gulf also presented immediate concerns of a different sort to the East India Company. The greatest challenge the company faced was in understanding the concept of the ferman used by the great powers of the region. Fermans differed from Western treaties in several important ways: Full power or sovereignty resided in the ruler, who granted certain privileges to a person or office of lower rank (or to a company)—it was never a treaty between equals; it could be revoked at any time and usually had to be renegotiated upon the death of the ruler; and finally, it extended privileges, not rights. In short, a ferman was never intended to convey a sense of permanency or security to the recipient.

The turning point came in 1615, when the company sought permanent trade treaties in India and Persia; its representatives vigorously negotiated in the name of the crown for fermans to place the company on more equal footing in the eyes of the Mughal and Safavid rulers. The English proved surprisingly tough negotiators in both instances, not only for trade but as advocates for equanimity. The individual most responsible for the company's changed status and future success was Sir Thomas Roe, the company's agent to the Mughal court, who also represented the English crown. Roe thoroughly impressed Emperor Jahangir, demanding greater respect for his position as King James' ambassador as well as for the company. His firm negotiating posture and force of personality won the company a remarkable ferman for trade, which endured for the remainder of Mughal history.[15] Roe's diplomatic activity was accompanied by an unrelated though timely demonstration of English naval power, which practically blew a rival Portuguese squadron out of the water at Swally Hole in full view of the Mughal commander and his army. This duly impressed everyone, and the English were there to stay.[16] From this point on, English trade and political power went hand in glove.

The company's administrative expansion throughout the Mughal realm soon produced a triregional apparatus. Although ultimate authority for company decisions resided with the permanent council in London, regional presidencies established at Surat (Bombay after 1687), Calcutta, and Madras handled local issues. Under these presidencies came the agencies and residencies that earmarked the outposts of trade throughout the company's network. The Surat Presidency, situated on India's northwest coast, early on explored the eastern Persian Gulf coast; it reopened the route for trade to Persia in 1615 and ultimately to Basra as well as to Mocha and Suakin on the Red Sea in 1640.[17]

Anxious to extend the Surat trade into Persia, the company factors (merchants), acting against Roe's wishes, sent a delegation to the Persian court to negotiate a ferman. As a result, in 1616, Shah Abbas I granted the company what appeared to be an agreeable ferman allowing universal company trade at any Persian port. He ordered all of his subjects "to kindly receive and entertain the English Frankes or Nation, at what time any of their ships or shipping shall arrive at Jasques (Jask) or any other of the ports in our Kingdom."[18] Roe's objections to this order can be attributed to the fact that he had a much broader political view than the company factors. He knew that Shah Abbas sought a European alliance against the Ottomans and had sent a representative to Spain for that purpose. In Roe's view, such an alliance would give Spain, which now ruled Portugal, a trade monopoly in Persia and would prove counterproductive to English efforts.[19] Roe, in fact, wrote a letter to the shah suggesting that Persian negotiations with Spain were inconsistent with the terms of the ferman: "whereby freedom of trade was guaranteed to all Christian merchants, and hinted that the grant of a monopoly to another nation might oblige the English to resort to arms and so disturb the tranquility of the Gulf."[20] In 1617, while camped on the Ottoman frontier, Abbas received Roe's message. Still in consultation with the English delegation, Shah Abbas toasted King James and recognized him as an elder brother—an equal—and issued a second ferman with expanded privileges.[21] What was the reason for all this generosity? Abbas, though courting the Spanish, still hated the Portuguese and, for all his apparent strength, he needed English firepower to destroy their fortress at the entrance to the Persian Gulf at Hormuz.[22]

In 1618, following a decisive victory over the Ottomans at Tabriz, Abbas revived the issue of company help against the Portuguese.[23] The question "placed the English in a dilemma: to attack two strong fortresses with merchant ships, especially on behalf of a 'heathen' ruler, when the fortresses belonged to a friendly European state—and possibly suffer the fate of Sir Walter Raleigh—or to refuse to lose the silk trade then being built up after so much effort."[24] After some hesitation, the company responded, and a joint Anglo-Persian expedition on April 23, 1622, routed the Portuguese after a two-month siege.[25]

Although the victorious parties split the booty and the company gained its own port, the Persians took most of the treasure; however, they gave the company control of one half of the customs at the port of Bandar Abbas on Persia's south coast.[26] Actually, the company finished with little profit after King James got £10,000 and the Duke of Buckingham, as Lord High Admiral, took £10,000 more.[27] Although the company garnered little from the actual conflict overall, the agreement with the shah provided the foundation for Anglo-Persian commercial relations for the next century.[28] Company factories (warehouses) soon emerged throughout the Persian Empire at Bandar Abbas, Shiraz, and the Safavid capitol at Isfahan. The last factory at Bushire was established in 1763 and remained a British residency until 1947.[29]

In summary, these Mughal and Persian fermans did not merely represent a grant from a superior power to a lesser one, as had been the normal tradition. Rather, at Roe's insistence, they reflected a greater parity based upon the recognition of mutual sovereignty. Thus, Roe, as an ambassador of the crown, had accomplished what his commercial colleagues could not and had successfully elevated these fermans to the status of instruments resembling treaties between equals. As historian H. H. Dodwell concludes, "He had done all that was really necessary, and indirectly had contributed greatly to the establishment of his countrymen's position. His own character raised considerably the reputation of the English at court."[30] If nothing else, this accomplishment represented a significant diplomatic coup in the political economy of the Middle East. This mark of respect remained stamped on subsequent fermans granted to the company for the next 150 years. Roe did not negotiate a formal treaty, something totally alien to Mughal political ideas; rather, the fermans that he did secure placed English trading privileges on a sound basis throughout the empire as well as at Surat. Roe also paved the way for the expansion of English trade with Persia and the Red Sea.[31] More importantly, these agreements had been achieved without the use of force, except against the Portuguese. As one English trader later stated, "We have more courteous use of the common people than they (the Portuguese) ever had, and more respect of the great ones."[32] In short, by 1619, Roe's efforts had helped to establish not just a trade company but a permanent English political presence in India and the Middle East for the next 350 years. Against all odds, there would be no turning back. Roe had achieved the impossible. England's move into the Middle East would now prove irresistible and certain.

Despite this auspicious beginning, the East India Company's first century and a half in the Persian Gulf was characterized by weakness, bare-knuckle survival, and questionable trade practices. First, this result was caused by the company's own decision to devote the majority of its resources to India and less than a tenth of its energies and capital to the Gulf. Second, the Gulf's great powers were a factor: The Ottoman and Persian Empires, powerful Arab sheikdoms, and the rival Dutch East India Company (VOC), as well as the French, all forced the East India Company to assume a lower profile. Almost immediately following the victory at Hormuz, the English company's trade in the Gulf suffered a serious downward spiral lasting several decades. While the first joint-stock enterprise (1613–21) had gained a profit of 87 percent, the profit of next three joint-stock ventures up to 1649 dropped under 20 percent. There were various reasons for this: the corruption of Persian officials, increased Dutch competition, and rival trade "interlopers" from England.[33]

Shah Abbas' death in 1629 came as the first blow to the company because it marked the end of strong central leadership and control. An immediate upswell in corruption among local Persian governors and officials propelled many to ignore the fermans already granted to the company. Shah Abbas' successor, Shah Sufi, reconfirmed the fermans but with strings attached, including an annual tribute.[34] Moreover, stonewalling port officials blocked the company's efforts to regenerate its guaranteed custom duties at Bandar Abbas. "Shah Sufi reconfirmed the fermans to the Company, but at an annual cost of £1,500 in presents. The Company had to buy silk at £60,000 per annum—one-third to be paid in cash and two-thirds in goods. This result did not satisfy the Persians, however, and for the succeeding years, the Company encountered many difficulties with the Persian Government which neither persuasion nor threats could resolve."[35]

Next came the Dutch threat. Three seventeenth-century Anglo-Dutch wars induced the Dutch East India Company to use every conceivable tactic to drive the English from Persia and the Gulf. They sold European goods at cost, bribed Persian officials to accept Dutch goods while blocking the transfer of English commodities, and bought Persian products for more than market value. If these measures failed, they resorted to the use of military force to gain their point. On numerous occasions, Dutch fleets blockaded Persian ports, and in 1645 they attacked the fortress at Qishim to force their demands. Needless to say, the shah yielded and provided them with the right to purchase silk anywhere in the country and to export it duty free, clearly placing English merchants at a tremendous disadvantage since they still paid a 4-percent export duty.[36] Smarting from ill-treatment on all fronts, local English company merchants sought redress through military reprisals, but apart from inadequate naval strength in the Gulf, the company council in London overrode these demands as being too costly and ultimately counterproductive to Persian relations. In the long run, the decision of the London council proved correct.[37] The principles of Sir Thomas Roe continued to guide the London council as the company's political agenda overrode the immediate commercial decisions of those tradesmen on the spot.

Thus, as Dutch trade increased dramatically in Persia and the English situation steadily worsened, the company looked for more favorable opportunities elsewhere and turned its attention to the northern end of the Gulf at Basra under Ottoman jurisdiction. Negotiations began in 1640, but a civil war postponed the factory's opening until 1644. In the same year, the company embarked on an adventure to commence trade between the Gulf and the Arabian coast at Socotra and Mocha.[38] Undeterred, the Dutch remained in hot pursuit. Having cornered the Persian silk trade and India's Coromandel coast by force, they then directed eight warships to "proceed up the Gulf to Bussora, where they almost ruined the English Factory."[39]

The arrival of competitive English companies proved the last straw. Company trade had practically come to a standstill in Persia until the new shah, Sultan Abbas, restored the fermans, removed the 4-percent export tax, and renewed the company's collection of customs at Bandar Abbas.[40] This bright spot quickly evaporated in 1640 with the first appearance of rival English ships under the banner of the Courteen Association, which landed their cargo without payment of customs. The company attacked them as "interlopers" and denounced their charter (granted by Charles I) as illegal and a violation of the charter given to the East India Company.[41] After nine years of fierce rivalry, the two companies reached an agreement, only for this to be followed in 1655 by the specter of more unwanted competition from the merchant adventurers commissioned by England's new ruler, Lord High Protector Oliver Cromwell.[42] Following two years of competition and continued war against the Dutch, the two companies merged.[43] Obviously frightened by the possibility of losing the Gulf trade altogether to the Dutch, first the government of the crown and then Cromwell's protectorate sought redress through these additional mercantile enterprises in order to restore what had once been a very lucrative trade. Despite the rivalry, the additional fusion of new capital and ships into the arena may in fact have given the company new life to survive the worst of times. The last threat of this nature occurred toward the end of the century. A House of Commons resolution in 1693 had affirmed the right of all English companies to trade in the East and elsewhere unless prohibited by parliament. Based on that resolution, "The English Trading Company Trading to the East Indies" was born. The ensuing conflict, which almost destroyed both companies, forced them to arbitrate in 1702 and to merge in 1708 as "The United Company of the Merchants of England Trading in the East Indies."[44] This, notwithstanding, proved another incarnation of the East India Company, which had survived all previous competitors, especially as as result of Roe's politically based fermans. This entity continued to stand the test of time and kept an English presence in the Middle East for centuries to come.

Although relations with Persia remained erratic, the overall status of the company improved in the Gulf throughout the second half of the seventeenth century because of the decline of the Dutch. Several factors contributed to their demise. First, Louis XIV's two Wars of Devolution against the Netherlands inexorably drained Dutch resources. Second, the Dutch East India Company (VOC) squandered its profit margin on excessive military exploits aimed at maintaining monopolies throughout the Indies and the Gulf. This practice proved counterproductive, since the prices for sale to Europe had to be set a year ahead in the VOC's capital at Batavia (Jakarta), allowing no immediate market flexibility for sale to the Continent. The English, by contrast, never set prices until the goods reached London, whereupon they ascertained the European market price for silk, Kirman wool, or spices and sold these for less profit at high volume. Finally, the VOC owned its own ships but never factored in the cost of maintenance, repair, or depreciation for its large fleet, whereas the English company leased its vessels and suffered no depreciation loss. Because the English company operated with more flexibility and on the cheap, its profits steadily rose toward the end of the seventeenth century. Another reason for the company's upswing occurred at the end of the century when, in 1694, Shah Hussain confirmed all the company's former privileges, resembling those Shah Abbas had granted a century earlier.[45]

The dawn of the eighteenth century appeared very upbeat for the English. Dutch power had faded considerably, and with the exception of Goa, the Portuguese had practically disappeared. Although the French had established a factory at Bandar Abbas in 1664, their trade remained negligible.[46] Moreover, company commercial efforts had increased throughout Persia under a stable regime, and while not free of competitors, the English had slowly but steadily gained the upper hand in Gulf trade. But the region had never proved an easy market because of an array of external circumstances far beyond company control, and the next sixty years would offer no exceptions. England (Great Britain after 1708) would be locked in three continental and global wars with France, which spilled over into India and the Gulf. During this period, Arab piracy increased dramatically, and finally, the Afghans invaded Persia.

In the first instance, the War of the Spanish Succession against Louis XIV (1700–14) greatly reduced the number of ships available to the company for use against Gulf pirates. This reduction forced the company in 1704–05 to reject a plea from the shah to aid Persian ports under attack.[47] Although unintended, the response demonstrated remarkable ingratitude in view of the major increase in company trade in silk and Kirman wool from Persia.[48] Without a navy and greatly weakened by these pirate forays, the Persians proved unable to withstand a surprise invasion from Afghanistan in 1721. Other predators were not far behind as both Russia, under Peter the Great, and the Ottomans invaded and divided Persian territory in the north. Overall, these invasions completely paralyzed the trade and left the country in utter chaos for the next decade.[49]

Company personnel also proved culpable of perpetrating some of the trouble in Persia. As before, fermans granted to the English by the shah were not always upheld, and frequently local pashas or governors ignored them altogether. In response, company agents (men on the spot) sometimes acted of their own accord to recapture lost economic and political leverage. But in most cases, seeing the bigger political picture inherited from Sir Thomas Roe, the company council in London or the Bombay Presidency refused to back such efforts, and while the company's message to Persian officials was often divided and unclear, the company survived.[50]

Even more damaging, the company continued to drain silver specie from Persia to meet the demand for silver as a result of its entry into the China tea market. This effect further exacerbated the economic upheaval and breakdown of Persian political authority in the face of piracy's onslaught and the Afghan invasion. Apart from trying to alleviate the country's economic distress, the East India Company abruptly abandoned Persia to embrace safe and stable trade with the Ottoman Empire at Basra, thereby avoiding an equitable solution to the Persian currency problem.[51] The temporary factory established at Basra in 1644 at long last received permanent status as a residency through the Ottoman sultan's ferman, obtained in 1723. This residency soon generated considerable company profits and resulted in a shorter mail route from India to Britain,[52] but it also placed the company squarely within the territorial jurisdiction of the Levant Company, leading to more conflicts in the years ahead.

During this period, the company's penchant for creating more tension and confusion manifested itself. Since it had access to superior naval firepower, its aid was often sought in disputes between rival empires or Arab pirates. It was well-known that the Bombay Presidency and the London council rarely supported such schemes, but local agents or residents implied the possibility of aid as a lever in negotiating a more favorable ferman for the company, only to renege on the arrangement once the deal was signed. As noted, Shah Hussain failed to gain company naval support despite the lucrative fermans granted to the British.[53]

When Persia's new ruler, Nadir Shah, founder of the Qajar Dynasty, reopened the trade routes in the 1730s, he too anticipated company help against both Arab pirates and the Ottomans. Since another war with France (the War of the Austrian Succession, 1740–49) had just commenced, the company again pleaded a lack of ships for Gulf defense. Despite the alleged shortage, the company managed to sell Nadir Shah two older British ships at Surat, which he manned with unreliable Arab sailors who mutinied and stole the fleet in 1740.[54] At another point, when the British refused to aid the Persians in their attack on Basra, Basra's Ottoman governor reversed the situation and seized company ships to defeat Nadir Shah's forces.[55] The shah remained convinced that the British had deliberately supported the Ottomans.[56] Obviously, the company representatives had been playing both sides and got caught. In a vengeful mood until his assassination in 1747, Nadir Shah harried company trade in Persia, believing he had been betrayed. The bitterness, frustration, and corruption that marked the last years of his reign undoubtedly provoked his assassination. But it can be argued that these questionable negotiating tactics might have provoked more than considerable political mischief if Nadir Shah's murder and Persia's subsequent chaos can be remotely attributed to them. At best, such tactics pointed up a form of trade imperialism on the cheap, one awash in deceit. Angered and offended, both the Persians and the Ottomans still held out for the illusion of company assistance in their next go around.

One historian has pointed out that Nadir Shah's rule (1736–47) nonetheless represented a significant watershed in the region, especially for British interests. Not only did he defeat the Afghans and drive out the Ottomans and Russians, but he also captured Oman on the western side of the Gulf and launched a successful invasion of the Mughal Empire in India, leading to its dissolution. His defeat of the Mughals opened the door for the company to expand its economic and political control in India within twenty years. Moreover, the vast quantities of plundered silver and gold thoroughly reinvigorated Gulf trade throughout the second half of the eighteenth century, favorably impacting the company's commercial efforts.[57]

In the years immediately following Nadir's death, however, Persia's return to chaos resulted in the destruction and closure of company factories throughout the country, including Isfahan.[58] The company council at Bandar Abbas wrote the Bombay Presidency on September 8, 1752, detailing the magnitude of the disaster: "This Kingdom is so far from being settled under any regular government, that it is now almost fallen beyond any hopes of recovery."[59] Company efforts, as noted, developed increasingly at Basra, where trade receipts had steadily climbed since 1723. Under stable Ottoman governors, Basra afforded perfect export opportunities for silk and wool, plus the importation of finished woolen products from Britain for trade into northern Persia. Since the Persian capture of Oman, that trade also had been rerouted to Basra. Overall, Basra had risen to second in company trade volume behind Bandar Abbas.[60]

Basra's importance to the company had also been elevated in a noncommercial sense because of the wars with France. Her strategic location at the Gulf's northern end, near the mouth of the Tigris-Euphrates rivers, offered shortened mail route access to Aleppo, Constantinople, and finally London. Typically, news from India to Britain could take nine months following the older Cape route. During the War of the Austrian Succession (1740–49) and the upcoming Seven Years' War (1756–63), valuable wartime dispatches from Britain to India and back remained utterly useless if not received in time. The newer Basra route took only six months.[61] As war drew closer, Basra's company resident received orders on August 8, 1755, from the Court of Directors at Bombay to spy on the French resident, who was himself a spy.[62] Thus, Basra's strategic position suddenly proved imperative to the defense of India. In the years ahead, that role would increase.

Persian affairs, meanwhile, remained confused up to the start of the Seven Years' War. Karim Khan, the new ruler, had been consolidating his power in the face of renewed Arab piracy along the Persian coast after 1750.[63] Still far from completing that job, local governors and coastal pirate sheikhs continued to dominate the political landscape, controlling the territory in and around Bandar Abbas, where Mulla Ali Shah, admiral of the Persian fleet, proclaimed himself governor under Karim Khan. Although the British helped him preserve his fleet against Arab pirates, their lackluster naval support persuaded him in 1752 to ally himself with several of the pirate tribes. Thereafter, he made life so difficult that the agent suggested the company move the factory to Bahrain and seize four Persian ships in compensation for British losses. Bombay rejected this proposal out of hand, fearing endless Persian reprisals.[64] After several years of fruitless discussion on the issue, the French solved the problem during the Seven Years' War with their destruction of the factory at Bandar Abbas on October 13, 1759.[65] The company completely abandoned the location on March 7, 1763, and transferred the factory further north to Bushire as a residency, while the agency itself was relocated at Basra. At that point, the trade stabilized, and the company again had proved a survivor.[66]

With the end of the war came the end of the company's first century and a half in the Gulf. Overall, the company's Gulf representatives, with a political mindset minus much political muscle, had developed into skilled and patient negotiators who wisely sought high trade volume with lower profit margins. They rarely priced themselves out of the market and never demanded a monopoly. Unlike the Portuguese or Dutch, the company had come to trade, not to dominate or colonize. By avoiding political entanglements or military commitments, the company remained aloof from acts of vengeance in this competitive and predatory environment. Although the "Honourable Company" was not always so honorable, fair, or innocent during this period, its reputation was enhanced, and its agents, despite notable exceptions, became trusted and respected as honest and fair dealers.[67] All in all, by capitalizing on their weaknesses, the British both outflanked and outlasted their Portuguese, Dutch, and French rivals. By 1763, the East India Company had emerged not only as the virtual ruler of Mughal India but also as the sole European imperial power in the Gulf. Sir Thomas Roe's vision had created a new a reality and the British were here to stay—for a very long time.

CHAPTER TWO

British victory, power, and dominance to 1797

After Gulf trade collapsed in the 1780s, the Company redoubled its efforts at Mocha and further north to Jedda. In 1789, Mocha's ruler, Abdullah bin Mansur, issued a ferman allowing the Company to purchase 600 bales of coffee annually, free of custom duties as an incentive. Hundreds of camels were necessary to transport the beans from the remote location at Beit el-Fakih, which the British called Beetlefuckee!

INDIA OFFICE RECORDS

Gulf trade and politics to 1780

Britain's global victory over France in the Seven Years' War, accompanied by the East India Company's stunning military successes in India, all but suppressed, for the time being, the French threat to the subcontinent and the Gulf. Sir Thomas Roe's efforts 150 years earlier had prepared the company for its upcoming political role. The virtual collapse of Mughal authority along with the French defeat in 1763 left the company as India's largest landholder, tax collector, and political force. The British government suddenly took a keen interest in India and gave Robert Clive, the man most responsible for company success, the job of reforming corruption.[1] Company employees could no longer engage in lucrative private or "country" trade or collect taxes. Flush with success, however, company employees continued to thwart Clive and his successors for decades on the issue of private trade.[2]

Self-assured and rife with victory, the company developed a more aggressive attitude toward the Gulf, as demonstrated by heightened political and military activities. These activities included meddling with the affairs of the Baghdad Pashalik as well as using naval intervention to support both the Persian and Ottoman Empires against increasing piracy.

First, company agents in the Gulf, without European competitors, sought to improve their economic footing with political intrigue. This development came about after 1763 when Ottoman authority in the Baghdad Pashalik (province) suffered erosion from incompetent Pashas as well as pirate attacks from the tribe of the Kab near Basra.[3] Since the Turks needed East India Company military assistance, its employees attempted to step into the political void to support their own candidate for Pasha, who, as a collaborator, would support local company interests. When the Ottoman sultan failed to support this scheme and nominated his own choice, the local company agents undermined the Ottoman government by attempting to create an independent Pashalik at Basra in 1764, all with company support. This Pashalik was a first, and it had been done to divert the Levant Company's silk and wool trade to that of the East India Company.[4] It may also have been undertaken for a more subtle political reason: to check Russian expansion and influence in the Ottoman Empire. If so, this event could prove to be the genesis of the Eastern Question.

At the same time, the sultan had allowed the British ambassador at Constantinople to appoint the company agent at Basra as a British consul.[5] This novel development provoked a strong reaction from the Levant Company, which had maintained exclusive rights to consular authority throughout the Ottoman Empire. Following an acute clash between the two companies, the East India Council in London backed down and decommissioned the Basra Consulate.[6] Although the power grab had failed, the company's political muscle had been flexed for the first time in the Gulf region.

Next, in order to safeguard its own trade, the company, for the first time, used its naval force, the Bombay Marine, to help the Ottomans and Persians in an attempt to drive Arab pirate fleets from the Gulf. However expensive these forays, Gulf trade, now dominated by British merchants, proved lucrative enough to warrant such action. As noted, in 1763, the Persian ruler, Karim Khan, had granted the company a new factory port at Bushire. Under the terms of the new ferman, he also gave the British the best trade terms ever offered, including the reduction or elimination of tariffs at various Persian ports, the protection of British ships and cargoes wrecked on the coast, the recovery of company debts by local officials, British jurisdiction over company employees in judicial matters, and, above all, an exclusive monopoly for the importation of woolen goods into Persia.[7] Karim Khan made one important stipulation: that the company take part payment in commodities rather than silver specie, "as this will impoverish the kingdom and in the end prejudice trade in general."[8] Unfortunately, the company appeared to take little notice of this salient point. Karim Khan's motive for granting the ferman lay in his inability to deal with a substantial pirate threat to Persia's coastline and merchant shipping from Mir Mahanna, the scourge of Gulf, as well the Kab, whose stronghold on the Shatt al-Arab disrupted Ottoman–Persian trade.[9] He desperately needed British naval power to curtail this growing menace.[10]

Although the company was far more ready to offer aid than it was before, its divided council greatly inhibited effective action. This difference was caused by Persia's recent chaos and poor relations with the company as well as some misgivings among company officials over Karim Khan's authority. One of his greatest detractors, the company agent at Basra, intervened with the London council against the Bombay Presidency's more positive view of Karim Khan. The London council, the Bombay Presidency, and the resident at Bushire were unable to agree on the amount of aid required to support the Persian ruler.[11] He had requested two British ships to back his own vessels and army to destroy Mir Mahanna's force.[12] While it remained in everyone's interest to do so, the company, again operating on the cheap, sent only one small vessel, the *Tartar*, to do the job.[13]

The military engagement commenced in May 1765 with inconclusive results. The Anglo-Persian force destroyed Mir Mahanna's stronghold at Bandar Rig, but the bulk of his naval force eluded the blockade and headed into the open waters of the Gulf.[14] With time on his side, Mir Mahanna grew ever stronger, eventually requiring the company to commission a much more expensive naval and military commitment to contain the threat.[15] British mistrust of Karim Khan and of the Persians in general forced the company to make a calculated mistake, which proved far more costly in the long run and made an enemy of a powerful ruler who would have proven a substantial and beneficial ally.

Better relations with the Ottomans encouraged the company to respond unanimously with a greater naval force to aid against the Kab in 1766.[16] Two additional reasons lay behind the company's action: The Kab presence now threatened the trade and mail route from Basra to Baghdad; moreover, the Kab had seized three British ships, including one under company protection.[17] Four British warships set sail to retaliate in a combined military operation with Ottoman land forces up the Shatt al-Arab waterway.[18] Karim Khan heard of this action and again offered to ally himself with the expedition if the British would help him destroy Mir Mahanna as well. While the company resident at Bushire enthusiastically supported the proposal, the agent at Basra and the Bombay Presidency flatly rejected it.[19] Karim Khan thereafter lost any sense of trust in the British.

The four ships, meanwhile, sailed directly to Basra to engage the Kab. The Ottoman response proved slow and inconsistent, leaving the British naval force alone to do the impossible job of closing the trap. Sheikh Salman, the Kab chief, simply withdrew his small ships and land forces from Ottoman territory eastward into the marshes across the Persian border.

When the Ottomans finally arrived, the decision was made to pursue the Kab into Persia. The difficult six-month campaign was characterized by a lack of coordination and inconclusive engagements.[20] Karim Khan equally detested the Kab, but he viewed this border incursion as an outrage to Persian sovereignty and demanded an immediate withdrawal.[21] When the Anglo-Ottoman force pulled back in September 1766, the British warships repositioned to enforce a two-year blockade against the Kab near Basra. Although the initial expedition had little success, the subsequent blockade with five additional ships demonstrated a greatly intensified British determination to protect their interests in the Gulf.[22]

Political and economic conditions in the Gulf rapidly deteriorated after 1767. Britain's failure to support the Persians had provoked bad relations with Karim Khan, while Ottoman authority at Basra and Baghdad tottered on the brink of collapse despite British efforts. A general increase in piracy resulting from the company's bungled efforts soon hampered British trade at Bushire and Basra. Growing enmity between Karim Khan and the company at last forced the resident, from 1769 to 1775, to abandon the factory at Bushire, leaving Basra, now infested with pirates, the sole center for British trade in the region.[23] Commercial efforts continued at Basra, but trade fell dramatically and finally came to a standstill after a series of disasters, including increased piracy, the corruption of local governors, the plague of 1773, and the Persian invasion of 1775. In that year, the company reluctantly reopened its factory at Bushire.[24] The Persian government might not have been friendly, but at least it was now stable.

Karim Khan's invasion of Basra and Baghdad in 1775 had been launched to settle a number of lingering issues. These included the ill-treatment of Persian pilgrims in Iraq (Turkish Arabia), revenge for old defeats, the extension of Persia's frontier, the seizure of Basra as the gateway to capture Oman, and the thwarting of favored British trade with Basra.[25] The Persian action may have been also tied to a less obvious purpose: to counter British economic practices in the Gulf. The company's relentless drain of silver specie from Persia, despite his earlier warning, probably provoked Karim Khan to follow the earlier example of Nadir Shah and to attack the Ottoman cities of Baghdad and Basra in order to rejuvenate his treasury.[26]

East India directors in London viewed its Gulf prospects as altogether gloomy in 1779 and ordered the Bombay Presidency to close Basra and reduce the factory at Bushire. The Bombay Presidency refused to do so.[27] Bombay's independent decision had been based on the maintenance of secure communications rather than trade. The upcoming war with France (the War of American Independence) necessitated preservation of the speedier Basra–Aleppo mail route to London over the slower Cape run. As a result, the company maintained both Basra and Bushire for security purposes throughout the war.[28]

The destructive Ottoman-Persian War (1775–79), meanwhile, brought about the region's devastation and the Gulf's economic collapse. By the

1780s, the Gulf had become a commercial "Dead Sea," especially for the British. Lacking any sense of responsibility for the region's economic failure, the company simply deserted Gulf trade for expanded opportunities on the south Arabian coast, the Red Sea, and Egypt, as well as in the lucrative China market.[29]

East India Company traders had explored the southwest coast of the Arabian Peninsula (Yemen) for coffee trade with Mocha as early as 1609.[30] This territory had been loosely held under Ottoman authority for a century. A general Ottoman ferman provided the company with its first trade agreement in 1618, but excessive pirate activity soon forced the factory's closure. In 1644, the company embarked on another voyage from Surat to the Red Sea and Mocha to tie the coffee trade to India and the Persian Gulf.[31] This endeavor was apparently short lived, and nothing like it occurred again until 1660–62, when coffee briefly appeared again on the East India shipping lists.[32] Company trade in this region during the seventeenth century proved as difficult and sporadic as it had been in the Gulf because of many of the same factors. These included constant conflict with the Portuguese, competition and warfare with the Dutch and French, unreliable local officials, and the menace of marauding pirates.

After fifty years of relative nonactivity, the company sent two ships, the *Donegal* and the *Blenheim* to reestablish commercial ties with Mocha in 1710.[33] Trade moved into full swing within ten years and remained so until 1828. Over half of the 16,000 bales of coffee sent to Europe in 1723 arrived on English company ships.[34] During this period, the English company representative at Mocha became one of the most politically and financially powerful figures in the country or private trade, dominating the numerous company employees involved in individual trading schemes that purchased coffee and then sold it at much higher prices to the company.[35] This practice remained steady while Mocha continued as the sole source of coffee on the global market, and prices were high. In order to maintain the market price, local Arab authorities exercised every conceivable measure to prevent the removal of coffee plants from the area. Alas, the endeavor proved futile as additional coffee sources evolved in South America, the Caribbean, and Java after 1750, developed from plants smuggled by European traders.[36] Although prices dropped thereafter, Mocha's rulers still kept the inland plant growing location relatively secret.

British trade at Mocha equaled all other competitors combined throughout the eighteenth century, and, as in the Gulf, steady growth of company influence after 1763 spurred a more aggressive attitude toward belligerent or uncooperative local rulers. When the Imam placed a 9 percent tax on all company goods from India, the Bombay council ordered its fleet (the Bombay Marine) to bombard Mocha, an attack that was called off when the ruler backed down.[37] After Gulf trade collapsed in the 1780s, the company redoubled its efforts at Mocha and further north to Jedda. In 1789, Mocha's ruler, Abdullah bin Mansur, issued a ferman allowing the company to purchase 600 bales of coffee annually, free of custom duties, as an incentive. Hundreds of camels were necessary to transport the beans from the remote location at Beit el-Fakih, which the British called *Beetlefuckee*![38] Although this figure reflects a general decline in coffee exports over six decades, this important trade rebounded as evidenced by fierce competition between the Bombay council and company ships (supercargoes) sent directly from London in 1815.[39]

France's entry into the War of American Independence in 1778, meanwhile, had made the region's security a top priority over and above trade. Mocha gained strategic importance in guarding India and later Egypt, especially as a way station on the communications and mail route between London and Bombay,[40] and this importance further increased during the Napoleonic wars (1798–1815). Denoting Mocha's elevated status, the company made it a residency and finally an agency from 1802 to 1830. At the height of this activity in 1828, it became a coaling station for British steam ships on the Suez–Bombay run. Once Egypt had been secured for trade and transport in the 1830s, however, the company abolished the Mocha agency but continued to monitor its trade and political activity from the company's Egyptian agency in Cairo.[41]

Expansion into Egypt—the die is cast: George Baldwin, merchant of empire to 1799

About the time officials showed interest in Egypt, the company itself underwent profound structural and political changes due to the Regulating Act of 1773. The company's tripartite division in India now fell under control of a government-appointed governor-general, who supervised the former independent presidencies and councils of Bombay, Madras, and Calcutta.[42] Under Governor-General Warren Hastings (1772–85), the British dominion of India really emerged as a major political entity. Hastings, operating from Bengal, was in turn responsible to a council at Calcutta, which reported to London. This awkward structure soon proved a source of meddling and intrigue, frustrating Hasting's single-minded attempts at reform.[43] Challenging his efforts, the various presidencies and the council manipulated for power, while illegal private traders eluded Hasting's new laws.[44] Bombay still handled the major share of company trade in the Gulf and the Red Sea, but a shift occurred during this period, giving the governor-general at Bengal much greater weight in trade and political decisions in this region.

Because of the company's turmoil in India, its entry into Egypt proved a long and very tenuous affair, laced with much opposition. Yet the attraction remained constant, since Egypt offered tantalizing prospects for East India Company trade as well as an alternative communications and mail route between Britain and India. Before 1763, neither the East India Company nor the rival Levant Company, which had trade jurisdiction over Ottoman territory including Egypt, viewed any adventure there in a positive light. First, the voyage from Bombay to the Red Sea was impossible during the monsoon season; second, the Ottomans prohibited Christian ships from sailing north of Jedda near the holy cities of Mecca and Medina; third, Egypt suffered internal conflict from Mameluk Beys trying to establish independence from the Porte (the Ottoman government); fourth, plague remained rife in the region and quarantine delays were frequent; and finally, there was little incentive since Britain had secured the Cape of Good Hope while France still controlled the Mediterranean.[45] But pressure mounted on the East India Company to do something, since many of its employees had extended their influence to the Red Sea and Mocha and, throwing caution to the wind, had attempted to export illicit trade through Ottoman Egypt using corrupt Mameluk officials.[46]

Ultimately, Egypt's very instability proved a magnet to East India Company officials in India and London. The Mameluk war of rebellion against Ottoman authority (1760–98) encouraged the Egyptian Beys to pursue their own trade with Europe and India. Ottoman officials feared this Egyptian activity would destroy trade via Syria to the Persian Gulf and Basra and increase the importance of Cairo to the detriment of Constantinople. The company saw it differently. Trade in the Gulf at Basra already had come to a standstill, and the company could redress this result by wrenching new commercial ventures from the control of the Levant Company, which, at any event, had done very little in Egypt.[47]

In 1773, Mameluk ruler Ali Bey, seeking revenue and support, opened the port of Suez and sent a letter of invitation for trade to Warren Hastings, the new governor-general of Bengal.[48] Hastings lost no time in responding. He had already authorized three Bengal merchants to pursue a project to investigate, explore, and chart the waters from the northern Gulf at Basra to the coast of the Red Sea for a new communications route.[49] Unfortunately, the ship was lost with all hands in a massive gale off India's Coramandel Coast the following year.[50] Undeterred, Hastings and his associate James Bruce, who had already been to Egypt, lost no time in negotiating a commercial treaty with Ali Bey's successor, Mohammed Abou Dahab, in 1775. This agreement inspired the confidence of Bengal merchants to begin immediate trade between India and Egypt at Suez.[51] The scheme's very logic found support from those advocating this trade as a prelude to a shorter mail run from London to Bombay, estimated at forty-nine days via Egypt and the Red Sea. This route took eleven days off the Basra–Constantinople route and represented half the time necessary for the Cape run.[52]

This expanded venture, however, faced detractors and diplomatic opposition. Bengal council member Sir Philip Francis protested that British, Europeans, and private traders would profit and the native Bengalis would not, and that it would drain the resources of the country.[53] Francis based this rather disingenuous argument on his personal and political opposition to Hastings as governor-general.[54] Next, Sir Robert Ainslie, newly appointed British ambassador to Constantinople (1776–92), fought the whole idea as dangerous to Anglo-Ottoman relations and an infringement on Levant Company rights, which he also represented.[55] Since his arrival at his new post, Ainslie had been barraged with complaints from the Porte as well as the Sheriff of Mecca, whose highly tariffed trade at Jedda was now bypassed for Suez.[56] In a stern letter to officials in Bengal, Ainslie warned, "Britain has licence to trade at Mocha and Jedda only. Subjects found trading at Suez were liable to have all goods confiscated." Ships carrying company letters only, however, would not be affected.[57] In April 1778, the Bengal government complied with the order, posted the prohibition and requested permission from Bombay to purchase a vessel (a company ship) to take letters to Suez, since they could no longer be trusted to private merchant ships.[58]

The saga continued and so did the problems. Company employees warned officials in London of French intrigues in the region. They did so in order to obtain a British Consul for Egypt and thus a permanent foothold. Their choice fell on George Baldwin, a merchant in the region since 1760. The choice of Baldwin proved a major turning point for British interests in the Middle East. Like Sir Thomas Roe before him, Baldwin added an important dimension by cementing British strategic and political interests in the region with his focus on Egypt, an idea that would save India to the empire in the immediate future. First the Levant and then the East India Company employed him as a packet agent in Cairo in 1775.[59] Baldwin also acted as temporary Consul in 1776 through an appointment of former ambassador John Murray.[60]

Ambassador Ainslie, who represented the Levant Company's interests in the Ottoman Empire, greatly mistrusted the activities of the East India Company in Egypt and particularly Baldwin as its representative. His mistrust may have been exacerbated by the possibility of Baldwin's quasi-consulship. Baldwin's middle-class merchant background also offended the aristocratic Ainslie, whose sensitivities seemed hard-pressed by Baldwin's straightforward communications.[61] On a particular sore point, Baldwin wrote Ainslie that no amount of prohibition from the Ottoman or British governments would stop the East India Company merchants from pushing their goods through Egypt. On this score he appeared quite right, and in December 1778, Ainslie grudgingly communicated this message to Foreign Secretary Lord Weymouth: "Ban will not be sufficient deterrent to Company employees smuggling their fortunes out of India."[62] In the same year, Ainslie wrote Baldwin a conciliatory note, complimenting him for his expeditious handling of British mail and merchandise between Britain and India. He also asked him to forward an urgent dispatch to India to the effect that France had joined the American war against Britain. Baldwin responded that he had his own sources for that information and already had sent this vital message to authorities in Bengal six weeks earlier.[63] Baldwin's tone proved offensive enough to warrant Ainslie's unrelenting opposition and obstruction thereafter.

Despite this drawback, Baldwin survived twenty-three extraordinary years in Egypt (1775–98). He did more to awaken British awareness of Egypt's importance than any single individual. His primary achievement had been to negotiate successfully with Egyptian Mameluk Beys and Arab traders for the quick transmission of merchandise unloaded from British ships at Suez bound for Alexandria and back. At almost no point in his career had these goods been held up or confiscated by banditry or unprincipled Beys.[64] As a hands-on individual, and much out of pocket, he contracted for the dockworkers, camel drivers, and mounted Mameluk guards for protection and speedy delivery. He had a command of Turkish and Arabic common to few Europeans, and he knew whom to bribe and how much the cost of ordinary business was in an anything but ordinary country.[65] The East India Company had been slow to pay Baldwin and already owed him 18,000 Turkish dollars by the end of 1777.[66] His financial survival, therefore, had required him to take a percentage of the profit made from the sale of company or private trade merchandise shipped through Egypt. As usual, Ainslie criticized Baldwin on this account.[67]

France's declaration of war on Britain in 1778, however, elevated Baldwin's role from that of merchant extraordinaire to national hero. Baldwin's timely warning to officials in India provided them with a jump on the French military throughout the country, which served them well for the war's duration. Although France's fortunes in India had plummeted, her interests and influence in Egypt had increased throughout the war. French agents in Egypt had negotiated a trade agreement with another Mameluk leader, Morat Bey, which threatened British interests.[68] Although Ainslie and others downplayed French activities and discouraged British growth in Egypt to pacify Ottoman sensitivities, even Ainslie had to admit the French had received favored treatment from the Porte.[69] British ships and crews had been seized and detained, while French cargo moved to and from Suez or Alexandria unmolested.[70] Ainslie addressed the problem with terse communications to the Porte and the British foreign secretary. His message prompted the Foreign Office to decide in 1779 that a British withdrawal or retreat from Egypt was a mistake.[71] Thereafter, British trade and communications in Egypt remained a vital part of the war effort. Privy Councilor Lord Henry Dundas later wrote: "Communication with Egypt-India saved our national honour."[72] Thanks to Baldwin, despite the numerous British military and naval disasters in America as well as in the Atlantic and Indian Oceans, the British in India held their own and ultimately crushed the French and their Indian allies. In the treaty of 1783, the French regained nothing of their lost Indian possessions. Baldwin, above all, had proved the validity of his view favoring Egypt as the primary communication route between London and Britain's East Indian possessions.[73]

The whole question of communication and trade through Egypt still remained a difficult problem beyond British control because of the unsteady state of the country's political scene. Egypt remained theoretically part of the Ottoman Empire under reforming Sultan Salim III, as it had been since 1517, despite the Mameluk rebellion. Ambassador Ainslie, representing the Foreign Office and the Levant Company, strongly supported that position. But East India Company trade contracts with Egypt had been made with various Mameluk Beys, who rivaled each other for power and, in turn, challenged Ottoman authority, which forbade such trade. France also had developed a growing presence in Egypt and, as part of that thrust, supported Mameluk independence from the Porte.[74] Both the British government and the East India Company needed to find a way to pursue communication and trade through Egypt and, at the same time, guard Egypt's status within the Ottoman Empire, to limit French influence. Doing so was no easy task, and from 1783 to 1798, these two agendas periodically clashed.

The British government needed to establish a permanent Cairo consulate under Ambassador Ainslie to recognize Egypt's connection to the Porte. The choice for consul fell on George Baldwin because of his knowledge of the country as well as his invaluable service to the British cause in India during the war.[75] His selection in 1785 came through Prime Minister William Pitt's colleague and friend, Lord Henry Dundas, who had noted Baldwin's past efforts and extended his patronage to him.[76] His support would prove a valuable asset for Baldwin in the tumultuous years ahead. At the same time, his continued relationship with both companies guaranteed ongoing mail service through Egypt.[77] The new salary scheme paid Baldwin £350 and £500 from the Levant and East India Companies, respectively, plus £400 to deal with the Beys and Arabs. These funds eliminated the necessity for commission or private trade and satisfied the need for a proper consulate in Cairo without funding problems.[78] Baldwin took up the appointment on May 19, 1786.[79]

Baldwin had been a firm believer in a strong British presence in Egypt, but he feared that the country's complex politics could derail the British initiatives. He also knew, despite Ottoman assurances relative to mail delivery through Egypt, the Mameluks would effectively stop it if it were not tied to trade from which they took a percentage. In a series of papers written to government and East India Company officials the year before his appointment, Baldwin argued the case for trade through Egypt as a way to guarantee the communication route.[80] In short, without trade, no movement of mail would be possible. He saw France as the net gainer if British officials stalemated over the question. Baldwin's view was not without merit, and he understood the issue as a race for time. Although some in the British government saw no French threat, French activities in Egypt dramatically increased in 1785. Chevalier de Truguet, attached to the French Embassy at Constantinople, secretly arrived in Egypt to negotiate a series of trade treaties with the Mameluk Beys. These negotiations proved more than trade agreements. On February 7, he signed the convention between France and the government of Egypt, which implied Egypt's independence from Ottoman authority.[81] After the completion of additional agreements,[82] the nature of the treaties were discovered and revealed in November to the outraged sultan.[83]

Baldwin's concern about the French found support, if reluctantly, from Foreign Secretary Lord Carmarthen and Ambassador Ainslie. In May 1785, Carmarthen urged Ainslie to find a way to prevent France from gaining influence in Egyptian or Red Sea affairs.[84] Following six months of correspondence, Ainslie responded with alarm that France's commercial treaty with the Beys sought to separate Egypt from the Porte.[85] Baldwin's consular appointment in 1786 appeared in response to the French move, although Ainslie would have preferred anyone but Baldwin. Throughout the next twelve years, the question of trade in relation to mail via Egypt received no clear definition, but this indecision did not stop Baldwin, who, with Henry Dundas' implied backing, negotiated a commercial treaty with the Mameluk Beys.[86] Thereafter, British packets and mail ran through Egypt with some regularity until Napoleon Bonaparte's invasion of Egypt in 1798.

Foreign Office interest in Egypt began to decline a few years after Baldwin's appointment, while French influence again grew. The British government appeared far more distracted with a development on the Continent: the French Revolution of 1789. Early stages of the revolution through 1791 established France as a constitutional monarchy, which evoked some British sympathy, if not open support. But events in late 1792 and early 1793 brought Britain again into conflict with her old enemy. French Jacobin radicals had overthrown the moderate revolution, ushered in the Reign of Terror and executed King Louis XVI in January 1793. Compared with hostilities in Europe (the War of the First Coalition, 1793–95), British officials in London viewed events in Egypt as a sideshow, despite the steady flow of French agents into Persia, the Gulf, the Red Sea, and Egypt.[87] Obviously, the French were planning something, but neither company agents nor British officials in the region knew exactly what or where, nor were these men on the spot, including Baldwin, able to push the government into concerted action.[88]

Baldwin's trade deals, in fact, had gotten him into trouble with the next foreign secretary, Lord Grenville, who threatened the Cairo consulate with closure in 1792. Henry Dundas, now home secretary and president of the India Board of Control, kept it open another year.[89] He then intervened once again, saved Baldwin, and temporarily restored the position until the foreign secretary terminated the consulate in 1795.[90] Baldwin remained three more years in Egypt as a company agent until illness forced his departure. He also seems to have retained some British consular authority, which he turned over to the Venetian consul, Carlo de Rossetti, in March 1798, just four months prior to the French invasion.[91] If George Baldwin had partially awakened a British awareness of Egypt, Napoleon did the rest. Baldwin, notwithstanding, had driven home the point as no one else that the Middle East, especially Egypt, had become the strategic center of the British Empire. A generation later, the British government would adopt this view as a centerpiece of its foreign policy.

CHAPTER THREE

Napoleonic wars and regional security 1798–1815

British forces now combined with Mameluk and Ottoman troops in combat operations against the French, and in a six month campaign, forced the surrender of six thousand French troops at the Cairo Citadel on June 28. The final capitulation of eight thousand more troops at Alexandria on September 4, 1801 brought the Egyptian campaign to an end as an unqualified British victory.

JOHN MARLOWE, *Perfidious Albion*

French invasion of Egypt (1798–1802) and the British response to secure it

Sir Thomas Roe and George Baldwin had provided, beyond modest trade, both a political and strategic dimension to the British focus in the Middle East. Napoleon's invasion of Egypt would guarantee the future certainty of that position in British foreign policy.

After the collapse of the First Coalition in 1795, France went through a counterrevolution (Thermadorian Reaction) that overthrew Jacobin rule.[1] The new Government of the Directory (1795–99), however, still faced European military opposition and determined to take the offensive.[2] Egypt, as well as territories bordering the Red Sea or the Persian Gulf, could not long escape another all-engulfing European conflict. French troops led by

Napoleon Bonaparte invaded Egypt and convulsed the region like nothing before and directly challenged Britain's dominant position held there since 1763.

Napoleon already had demonstrated a knack for daring and military genius before the invasion of Egypt. As a young artillery commander, he had broken the British navy's siege of Toulon in 1793.[3] Noting his talents, the Government of the Directory promoted him in 1796, whereupon he led the French army to a series of stunning victories over the Austrians, culminating in the Treaty of Campoformio the following year.[4] After this singular success, Napoleon secured command of the French force poised to strike Britain, known as the Army of England. Invading Britain proved an impossible task because of the inability of the weakened French naval command to guarantee a channel crossing.[5]

Napoleon's strategic genius understood Egypt as the jugular vein of the British Empire, even if British officialdom did not yet recognize it. His decision to strike Egypt, as that jugular vein, appeared a realistic alternative to the channel crossing.[6] This idea, however, did not originate with him alone. French agents from Persia to Egypt, including the consul in Cairo, had long since encouraged the government to pursue some form of campaign into the Middle East to dislodge the British and restore French colonial grandeur in India.[7] As noted, British agents in the region had continually warned London that something was brewing but could prove nothing conclusive.[8] The British government, overall, had dismissed these reports as alarmist and took no immediate action. As historian Crane Brinton has noted,

> All through the eighteenth century the French were active in Egypt, more active, indeed, than the English, who were not fully awakened to the critical relation between India and Egypt until Bonaparte's expedition brought it inescapably to their attention.[9]

Napoleon departed Toulon for Egypt on May 19, 1798 with thirteen ships of the line; 400 transports; 35,000 soldiers; 300 assorted scientists, botanists, cartographers, and historians; and two Arabic printing presses.[10] He intended to conquer Egypt as a French colony and as a stepping-stone to British India.[11] Although the British knew some kind of expedition was afoot, a severe storm allowed the French fleet to elude Commander Horatio Nelson's British squadron.[12] Nelson arrived at Alexandria a few days before Napoleon and, finding nothing, headed on for the Levant (Syrian coast), while Napoleon captured Malta and, on July 2, took Alexandria unopposed.[13] After a two-week march, he encountered the main Mameluk force of some 6,000 mounted troops. Napoleon's artillery decimated them at the Battle of the Pyramids on July 21 and took Cairo without opposition three days later (Figure 1).[14] Napoleon's scheme, however, received a setback, as Nelson discovered and destroyed the French fleet at Aboukir Bay on August 1 (the Battle of the Nile) (Figure 2).[15]

FIGURE 1 *Battle of the Pyramids, July 21, 1798. DEA / G. DAGLI ORTI. Getty Images.*

FIGURE 2 *Battle of the Nile, August 1, 1798. PASCAL RONDEAU. Getty Images.*

Despite its isolated position, Napoleon's army, now trapped in Egypt, remained an even more dangerous and resourceful foe, requiring every bit of British ingenuity and force to dislodge it, and without guarantees. While the French continued operations against the Mameluks and pursued their forces all the way to the Upper Nile, Napoleon hoped to dissuade Muslim hostilities and proclaimed himself Islam's true savior and defender of the sultan. His proclamation to the Egyptians published in Alexandria and Cairo declared that he had not come to destroy their religion but to restore their rights and support the Koran as the sultan's true friend.[16]

Napoleon immediately established *divans* (commissions) in Cairo and throughout the country with Egyptian representatives and several French commissioners to govern Egypt.[17] In this way, France's brief occupation of Egypt from 1798 to 1801 awakened the long-dormant spirit of Egyptian nativism, which altered the country's course throughout the nineteenth century.[18] Egyptians at the time, however, had no illusions that Napoleon also ruled their country at gunpoint.[19] French diplomats, moreover, had failed to convince the sultan of Napoleon's sincerity, and on September 9, 1798, the Ottoman Empire declared war on France.[20]

When word of Napoleon's invasion of Egypt reached Europe in mid August, the British responded with a four-fold strategy. First, they organized another alliance with Austria, Russia, and the Ottoman Empire to fight the War of the Second Coalition (1798–1801) to crush French forces on the Continent.[21] Second, an Anglo-Ottoman expedition set sail to strike Napoleon in Egypt.[22] Third, British naval units immediately sealed off the Red Sea at Perim and Aden to prevent any French exit from Egypt into the Indian Ocean.[23] Finally, British agents from India moved to establish dependency treaties with Arab sheikhdoms to keep the French out of the Persian Gulf.[24] Of these four endeavors, only the last two proved completely successful. Significantly, even without an official policy in the midst of an enormous war, the British rushed headlong to the defense of the Middle East, especially Egypt, as the artery of empire.

The British-led coalition against France met with mixed success. An Anglo-Russian force, under the Duke of York, bogged down in the Netherlands and was forced to surrender in October 1799. The Austrian and Russian armies fared better in Switzerland and Italy, but in 1800, the Russians, feeling badly used by their British and Austrian allies, began to pull away from their commitment.[25] Meanwhile, the Ottoman army under British naval escort launched a disastrous attack against the French near Alexandria. Napoleon had just returned from campaigning on the Syrian coast, and although commanding a much smaller force, he again proved his skill. Historian Owen Connelly describes this engagement as an impressive slaughter of the Ottomans, who were cut down before they ever reached the shore.

On July 25, 1799 Napoleon, with 7000 troops, met a Turkish force of 20,000 on the beach at Aboukir. His artillery shattered their ranks; his infantry columns drove in. Behind them came the cavalry of the Gascon Joachim Murat, driving the enemy into the surf, charging, cutting, trampling until the waves frothed with blood. The awed British admiral, Sir Sidney Smith, watching from his flagship, quickly agreed to take the pitiful survivors away.[26]

Following the victory, Napoleon deserted Egypt, army and all, and returned to France to overthrow the Directory and establish his consulate in November 1799.[27] His successive military campaigns in Europe soon turned the tide against the alliance. Already disgruntled, the Russians changed sides, and by 1801, the coalition was in shambles.[28] British officials, meanwhile, had determined that Egypt could not be left to an indefinite French occupation. Although reduced to half its strength through climate and disease, the French army in Egypt remained dangerous and needed containment before Napoleon could send reinforcements.[29] There was no way around it; Britain would have to send its own army to Egypt.

Alexander Dalrymple, an East India Company hydrographer employed by the admiralty, had made the dangers of a French occupation of Egypt crystal clear on the eve of Napoleon's expedition. Echoing the concerns of George Baldwin, he had warned the British government in May 1798 that Egypt was the granary of the Ottoman Empire and a center for Muslims going on the *Haj* (pilgrimage) to Mecca. Most importantly, he spelled out the dire ramifications for India if the French cut a channel from sea to sea. They would control the passage to India, and Dalrymple, as a hydrographer, believed it could be done. He suggested that if the French took Egypt, the British would have to secure a strategic position at the mouth of the Red Sea to prevent enemy ship passage.[30] The government heeded Dalrymple's advice and prepared a military expedition for Egypt, while the East India Company immediately bolstered its defensive position in the Persian Gulf and Red Sea to cut off the French.

Birth and expansion of informal control in the Middle East: No turning back

Rapid expansion of British power and control in India up until 1798 had sparked the development of dependent states and protectorates (lapsed dynasties) that were absorbed into the British Raj. Company officials and the governor-general of India now viewed the Gulf as a strategic buffer guarding this precious resource against the French. Dalrymple's call, coupled with Napoleon's invasion of Egypt, propelled the company to transfer a variation of the Indian protectorate model to the southern Gulf and Red Sea sheikdoms with a series of dependency treaties. Company officials enacted the first treaty with the ruler of Muscat in 1798: "That an English gentleman of respectability, on the part of the Honourable Company, shall always reside at the port of Muscat, and be an Agent through whom all intercourse between the States shall be conducted."[31] This treaty proved the beginning of Britain's strategic domination of the Persian Gulf.

At the mouth of the Red Sea, meanwhile, British agents negotiated a treaty with local Arab leaders in November 1798 to establish a naval base at Perim Island.[32] With Perim under their control, the British could "prevent all communication with the French in Egypt with the Indian Ocean by way of the Red Sea."[33] This endeavor soon required adjustment as the location proved too desolate without water, and, following more negotiations, the entire operation moved to Aden on December 15, 1799.[34] With British control of the Red Sea passage now secured, troops and supplies could be moved into Egypt without delay, and the British invasion of Egypt proved only a matter of time.

Following these negotiations, the admiralty sent Rear-Admiral Sir Home Popham to the Red Sea in 1800 to secure treaties with other Arab sheiks to facilitate the French army's destruction in Egypt.[35] French activities in the region had not been confined to Egypt or the Syrian coast. Their agents had been working at Jedda as well to disrupt British trade and communications. Popham's assignment was to reestablish some degree of British control over the activities of Jedda's ruler, the Sheriff of Mecca. Popham communicated his report to the secret committee of the company: "Jedda has fallen under French influence—French soldiers pretend to be Sheriff's deputies. Only the Ottoman Porte can dispel this." He then suggested that the Ambassador to Constantinople, Lord Elgin, urgently move on the matter.[36] After a further series of meetings with the sheriff, Popham concluded: "The Sheriff is an usurper, patronized by the French, and unlikely to cooperate with the British until the French are driven from Egypt." He then opted to support a palace coup to reinstate the imprisoned former sheriff, Abdella, who had strongly supported British interests. The plot apparently failed.[37]

In the midst of all this activity, Popham also had begun the detailed work of planning for the British invasion of Egypt. He had arranged for the conveyance of British forces from the Mediterranean and the Cape of Good Hope for Sir Ralph Abercromby's Egyptian expedition planned for early 1801.[38] As a precaution, he then ordered additional forces from India.[39] The Indian regiments sailed from Ceylon and Bombay, rendezvoused at Mocha, then departed for Egypt.[40] Meanwhile, Popham's friend, Ali Khan, a relative of the former Sheriff of Mecca, negotiated in Arabia for the expedition's horses and camels.[41]

With everything in readiness, the British invasion commenced. The navy sealed off the Egyptian coast against possible French reinforcements while Abercromby's expeditionary force landed at Aboukir Bay in March. Following months of heavy fighting, the Indian reinforcements arrived in Egypt via the Red Sea. British forces now combined with Mameluk and Ottoman troops in combat operations against the French, and in a six-month campaign, forced the surrender of 6,000 French troops at the Cairo Citadel on June 28. The final capitulation of 8,000 more troops at Alexandria on September 4, 1801, brought the Egyptian campaign to an end as an unqualified British victory.[42] Significantly, the relative importance of Egypt and the Middle East to British policy, although still unofficial, had emerged immensely important and as imperative as the war on the continent.

Although the conflict in Egypt had ceased, the European war continued for another six months amidst heated discussions in Egypt. Contentions arose over the imprisonment of captured French troops and a redistribution of power between the Ottomans and Mameluks, as well as the maintenance of a British presence in Egypt. These lively issues remained unresolved when the Treaty of Amiens, signed between the major powers, cut the debate short in February 1802.[43] Napoleon's old army was repatriated to France, British troops evacuated Egypt in twelve months and Egypt returned to the chaos of former rivalries.[44] As such, the peace provided no sense of satisfaction or unity for British officials, who sharply divided over military and company support of the Mameluks, as opposed to the Foreign Office, who gave lukewarm backing for greater Ottoman control.

On the Continent, the period between February 1802 and May 1803 produced more stress with neither side really trusting the motives and activities of the other. A general breakdown of the peace occurred as France consolidated her Continental position with additional expansion in Italy, the Netherlands and the German states. Britain, meanwhile, responded to another rumored French invasion of Egypt and refused to give up Malta.

In Egypt, the Gulf, and the Red Sea, the situation heated up as well. A relatively unknown figure, Mehmet Ali, had swept aside both Mameluks and Ottomans, filling the power vacuum created by the French and British withdrawal from Egypt. Moreover, British officials and company agents aggressively pursued more treaties to guarantee British hegemony through informal control in the Persian Gulf and the Red Sea in the event of another war with France.

Renewal of hostilities and the War of the Third Coalition 1803–07

International tensions increased at an alarming pace in the spring of 1803. Napoleon had closed Continental markets to British trade, and Russia's new czar, Alexander I, feared growing French influence in the Balkans and opened Russian ports to the British. When the British government offered to leave Malta if the French withdrew from Italy, Napoleon responded with insults. Not surprisingly, Britain declared war in May 1803.[45]

Britain had maintained her position in Malta as a safeguard against another possible French attack on Egypt. But events in Egypt unfolded in a way nobody could have predicted. Following the French and British evacuation, the country had returned to its former state of deterioration, as recorded by one contemporary: "The country fell into a horrifying state of lawlessness and decay. . . . Wild dogs and villains roamed the streets of the cities and no European dared go out at night."[46]

But Egypt's political anarchy had unexpectedly provided an opportunity for Egyptian nativism to gain a focus of power and ascendancy for the first time in centuries. Religious and intellectual leaders expressed a new spirit of self-determination born in the ideology of the French sojourn and in the face of the Ottoman pasha's inability to control rival Mameluk and Turkish factions.[47] All these energies quickly found a new leader.

Mehmet Ali was a captain in the Ottoman army and leader of one of the factions. He had developed a popular movement to oust the corrupt pasha, break the power of the Mameluk Beys and restore order. Considered the founder of modern Egypt, Ali had been born and raised in Albania, the son of a Turkish official. Called to military duties in Egypt in 1798 as part of the Ottoman force sent to repel Napoleon's invasion, he survived the Anglo-Turkish defeat at Aboukir Bay. After British forces withdrew in 1803, Ali seized command of the Albanian contingent of the Ottoman army and set about removing Mameluk and Turkish rivals. Pressure from Egypt's rebellious populace forced Ottoman Sultan Selim III to remove Hursev Pasha as governor and replace him with Mehmet Ali in 1805. Ali had carefully and successfully wedded his ambitions to Egypt's growing nativism in his desire to create a more dynamic Egyptian state.[48] His enlarged and diverse military force of Albanians, Turks, and Egyptians proved invaluable in sustaining him in the renewed international conflict, which again impacted Egypt.[49]

French agents had already resumed activities in the Ottoman Empire and Egypt when hostilities commenced.[50] French action prompted the British government to appoint Major Ernest Missett as head of the British establishment in Egypt to checkmate the activities of the French.[51] At the same time, the East India Company lost no time in choosing Samuel Briggs, a Levant Company representative, as their agent in Alexandria.[52] Missett quickly approved Briggs as provisional vice-consul as well.[53]

Egypt's civil war continued to rage in the midst of these maneuvers, prompting British officialdom to take sides. Both company agents and Missett, representing the War Office, supported the various Mameluk Beys, while the Foreign Office backed the revival of Ottoman authority represented by Egypt's governor, Hursev Pasha. Mehmet Ali was mistakenly viewed as a French agent and, therefore, unworthy of British support on any level.[54] Ali's continued victories over his rivals and the Ottoman sultan's subsequent appointment of him as Egypt's new governor in 1805 left the British stunned.

On February 8 of that year, Samuel Briggs sent a routine message to the British Agent at Cyprus: "Lord Nelson set sail yesterday from Alexandria Harbor with the British squadron to engage the French."[55] Eight months later, Nelson intercepted and destroyed the French fleet at the historic Battle of Trafalgar. That summer, Austria and Russia joined Britain in the War of the Third Coalition (1805–07) against Napoleon, who had recently declared himself emperor.[56] French victories over Austria at Ulm and Austerlitz in the fall and winter of 1805 soon placed Napoleon's influence at the door of the Ottoman Empire.[57] Word of Nelson's victory on October 21, however, had encouraged the Russians to keep fighting. Partly to bolster their defensive position, Russia invaded and occupied the Ottoman territories of Moldavia and Wallachia. Russia's other agenda was to promote the breakup and division of the Ottoman Empire between herself, Britain, and Austria. The sultan's declaration of war against Russia in 1806 now placed the Ottoman Empire and Egypt on the side of Napoleon.[58]

Britain's failure to master informal control of Egypt 1807

From the British perspective, the breakup of the Ottoman Empire was unacceptable and the position of her Russian ally intolerable.[59] Britain somehow had to keep Russia in the war and still protect the territorial integrity of her Ottoman enemy. Ottoman Egypt now loomed as a vital part of that equation, since the British already viewed Egypt's governor, Mehmet Ali, as pro-French and supportive of more French influence or even occupation.[60] Encouraged by Major Missett and Samuel Briggs, the British government decided to invade Egypt, destroy Mehmet Ali and support their own Mameluk client, Elfi Bey.[61] A temporary British occupation would preserve Egypt within the Ottoman fold and out of French hands, guarantee a fresh grain supply to British forces at war in the Iberian peninsula, and, once again, safeguard the gateway to India. For the second time in less than a decade, the British army went to Egypt as its importance to unofficial British policy grew more entrenched each year.

In March 1807, Admiral Charles Collingwood ordered General A. Mackenzie Fraser to lead an expeditionary force of 7,000 to Egypt. Fearing that recent Anglo-Russian attacks against Constantinople might provoke a second French invasion of Egypt, Collingwood opted for the preemptive expedition to support Elfi Bey's forces, now in rebellion against Ali.[62] Urged by the British consul in Cairo to support the Mameluks, Britain clearly backed the losers. As noted, Ali already commanded majority popular support contrary to Missett's information to British authorities.[63] His army had killed Elfi Bey and defeated his followers on March 12, six days before Fraser's unopposed landing at Alexandria. He then persuaded the remaining Mameluks to his cause with future promises of shared governance. Ali now stood ready to face Fraser.

Fraser's force, without Elfi Bey's promised help or food, foraged for supplies in preparation for an attack on Rosetta and Cairo. Fraser's plan met with disaster. His force was much smaller than Napoleon's in 1798, and Ali's army was much larger and better than the Mameluk army Napoleon had defeated. Moreover, Ali's ally, religious leader Umar Makram, rallied the populace to fighting pitch against the British and supplied Rosetta with weapons to thwart Fraser's advance.[64] Generals William Steward and Patrick Wauchope attacked twice on March 31 and were repulsed with heavy casualties and a number of officers captured. Ali counterattacked, encircled Fraser and forced his retreat to Alexandria, where he remained trapped from April to September.

Sensing the magnitude of the disaster, Missett reluctantly sent word of events to British authorities on May 2.[65] Meanwhile, Ali laid siege to Alexandria from August 17 to September 25 but allowed Fraser to receive supplies. In a surprising but revealing gesture, Ali then offered the British both grain and security for their routes to India if they would recognize his independent status in Egypt.[66] Although momentarily at war with the Turks, Britain had no intention of dismantling the Ottoman Empire and, except for the grain, refused the offer. Britain's unofficial management of the Middle East depended on securing informal control of the Ottoman Empire, of which Egypt was a part.

The summer of 1807 brought about a realignment in the international situation. The Russians had suffered two hard-fought winter and summer defeats at Eylau and Friedland, forcing Alexander I to capitulate and sign the Treaty of Tilsit with Napoleon on June 25, which destroyed the Third Coalition.[67] Tilsit guaranteed both parties a sphere of influence in Europe, including a Russian interest in the Balkans and the Straits. British diplomat Robert Adair wrote to the Ottoman Foreign Minister concerning the treaty: "Instead of being a stipulation to prevent the dismemberment of your provinces, [Tilsit] was, in fact, an arrangement to regulate the manner of taking possession of them."[68]

With France and Russia allied, the angered Sultan now retreated from the French alliance and leaned again toward the British. This development undercut the need for Fraser's expedition, which evacuated Egypt in late September after negotiations with Ali.[69] A number of British soldiers' decapitated heads displayed outside the walls of Cairo, however, provided a stark reminder of Britain's failed campaign. This fiasco only drove the Egyptian population and the national cause to further support Mehmet Ali and to greatly mistrust the British, who increasingly backed Egypt's connection to the Ottoman Empire.

Extension of informal control to the Gulf, Red Sea, and Persia 1800–15

Before the 1790s, neither the East India Company nor the British government appeared concerned or knowledgeable about the western side of the Persian Gulf on the Arabian coast. Its waters, riddled with coves and dangerous shoals, remained largely uncharted.[70] One thing was known about the area: It sheltered numerous Arab sheikdoms involved in piracy against the Persians, Ottomans, and British and was thus named the "Pirate Coast." Various Arab tribal confederacies had for decades dominated the region of Muscat, Oman, and the area later known as the Trucial Coast.[71]

At several points in the late eighteenth century, as mentioned, a few tribes had extended their influence across the Gulf to the Persian coast, made life difficult for company traders, and challenged the authority of Persian ruler Karim Khan. Among Khan's reasons for capturing Basra in 1776 had been to use it as a staging area to attack Oman and destroy the pirate threat. Because of the Ottoman-Persian War and the disruption of the Gulf's economy in the 1780s, the company greatly reduced its commercial enterprises and took little interest in the region until the appearance of French agents at the Persian court and at Muscat in the 1790s.[72]

Already aroused by French activities in the Gulf, Napoleon's Egyptian adventure in 1798, as noted, quickly provoked the East India Company to shore up its defense of the Persian Gulf with a dependency treaty establishing a protectorate at Muscat in 1798. This treaty was only a beginning: "The agreement with the Imam of Muscat . . . constituted the first of a series of acts which gradually placed most of the principalities along the eastern and southern laterals of the Arabian Peninsula in varying degrees of dependence on Great Britain."[73] A second treaty with Muscat in 1800 allowed the company to establish a permanent British resident to the exclusion of any other European presence.[74] This provision, of course, had been directly aimed at the French.

Although the military situation on the Continent had deteriorated for Britain with the collapse of the Third Coalition in 1806, the company position had solidified substantially in the Gulf. The British resident at Muscat had signed a *qaulnamah* (agreement) with the sheik of the Trucial Coast, Ibn Saqr of the Qawasim, the most powerful pirate tribe. Besides keeping the French out, the agreement also guaranteed a halt to future pirate attacks on British shipping.[75] In the same year, the sheiks of Oman negotiated a treaty with Captain David Seton of the East India Company to suppress piracy, return stolen ships, and release Indian crews held as slaves.[76] In most cases, a British resident or agent would be recognized as the exclusive European representative.

These treaties were continuously reinforced throughout the nineteenth century to guarantee Britain's strategic protection of the region—but at a price. They certified British control over the sheikhdoms' affairs with other Europeans as well as partial control over their economies, which relied on piracy and the slave trade. Their leadership, corrupt or not or whether popularly supported, eventually fell under British guardianship, which followed a hands-off policy on domestic affairs as long as the rulers supported British interests. This policy fostered some political mischief in the years ahead. In the first instance, the company agreements sought to undermine French penetration in the region, but in a more positive and long-lasting vein, they also slowly curtailed the scourge of piracy and the slave trade. The India Office record states "The wars with France were crucial to development of British policy in the Gulf. They brought into prominence the strategic value of the area in terms both of the sea route to India and of the overland route which was increasingly used during the hostilities as a more speedy and reliable means of communication."[77] Moreover, the anti-pirate campaign between 1806 and 1820 proved that there had been a dramatic change in British interest in the area.

After the French surrender of Egypt in September 1801, Britain's ambassador to Constantinople, Lord Elgin, wrote company officials in London recommending Aden as a future British settlement to safeguard trade and protect the region against future French aggression.[78] Although a treaty had been signed in 1799, Aden's ruler, the Sultan of Lahej, signed a subsequent one in 1802 with special envoy Sir Home Popham to guarantee a more permanent British presence.[79] So important had been this area (later known as Yemen) to trade, communications, and India's strategic defense that more negotiations in the coming decades created dependencies and protectorates among the various Arab tribes surrounding Aden.[80] Ultimately, Aden itself would be forcefully annexed in 1839 as Britain's only formal colony in the Middle East.[81]

Popham's activities continued, meanwhile, based on his authorization from the governor-general of Bengal to negotiate additional British protectorate treaties with Arab sheikdoms along the Red Sea coast. As an enticement, Arab chiefs received open or tariff-free trade with India without custom duties. All former restrictions were eliminated and, importantly, the trade now included military and naval stores. In a huge policy reversal, the British offered to build them ships if necessary.[82] All this activity meant one thing, and one thing only, although no one had yet said so: The British were here to stay.

At the insistence of the Foreign Office, all military and naval equipment thus provided had a specific restriction: It could not be used to foment revolution against legitimate authority or the Ottoman government. Each sheikdom, moreover, now fell under the protective umbrella of the British government, against the French.[83] In order to negotiate the terms of the new protectorates properly, Popham received a trained assistant proficient in Arabic and Persian. No errors could be allowed; the stakes were too high.[84] In the end, these treaties firmly secured Britain's presence in the Red Sea for the remainder of the Napoleonic wars and well into the nineteenth century.

Company relations with Persia had deteriorated badly during the reign of Karim Khan, as noted earlier, and after his death in 1779, Persia suffered more revolution and a war with Russia in 1795. The French government of the directory immediately sent a delegation to the Persian court to promote its union with the Ottoman government in a war against Russia. The mission failed, but Napoleon's subsequent overtures to Persia forced the British government in 1801 to send their own envoy, Sir John Malcolm, to cement a commercial and political alliance with Persia's new ruler, Fateh Ali Khan.[85] Britain had feared either an Afghan or French invasion of India or both. In the event of an Afghan invasion, the agreement committed Persia to attack Afghanistan and to keep the French out of Persia.[86] Britain agreed to assist Persia with military hardware, while Malcolm's commercial negotiations restored all the former company factories throughout the country.[87]

The new Anglo-Persian relationship remained untested until 1805, when Britain's ally, Russia, again invaded Persia. Persia requested British help, but Britain held to the letter of the law, which only called for aid against the Afghans or French. Fateh Ali now turned to Napoleon, who offered an alliance against Russia if Persia invaded British India or permitted the French to attack India through Persian territory. Negotiations fell through in 1807 when Russia signed the Treaty of Tilsit with Napoleon. This treaty threw the Persians, like the Ottomans, back into the British camp. Campbell, representing the Government of Bengal (Government of India), returned to the Persian court to shore up the relationship.[88] Meanwhile, the British government had sent its own envoy from London to the Court at Tehran, causing utter confusion. According to historian C. U. Aitchison, "This led to unseemly complications which had the effect of rendering both governments ridiculous in the eyes of the Persians."[89]

In 1809, Sir Hartford Jones negotiated a second treaty, which prohibited any European army from crossing Persia to attack India and promised British military aid to help Persia against any European invader, including Russia.[90] Jones returned to Britain following the negotiations, and India's governor-general, Lord Minto, now appointed Campbell as envoy to Persia.[91] Two years later, the British government replaced Campbell with its own envoy, Sir Gore Ouseley.[92] In negotiations with Ouseley, Persia annulled all previous alliances with other European states in two subsequent Anglo-Persian treaties signed in 1812 and 1814, respectively.[93]

Britain's debacle at the Persian court on the issue of representation pointed up the confused and hybrid nature of company, Bengal and crown relationships in India, Persia, and the Gulf. Despite the potential for crisis, no unified, definitive, or permanent solution to the comingling of authority emerged in the upcoming century. To solve the immediate problem, however, the crown appointed the envoy to Persia, who reported directly to the British government. The company resident at Bushire now communicated with Bombay on trade matters and with the British envoy at Tehran on political concerns.[94] This novel arrangement came at the insistence of the Bengal government, who "wished to avoid giving the impression that Crown and Company interests were in any way divergent."[95] The solution was short-lived. In 1823, the Government of India sent an envoy to replace the crown representative in Persia. Fateh Ali considered this diplomatic devolution an insult, and, thereafter, relations remained cordial but cool.[96] All this confusion had developed because the importance of the British presence in the Middle East had developed so rapidly that neither Britain nor the Indian government had time to define or settle jurisdictional boundries.

Persia's earlier conflict with Russia, meanwhile, had erupted again, but Britain quickly stepped in and mediated the boundary dispute in 1813.[97] These two empires had to be kept from one another's throats since British treaties with Persia had become imperative to the defense of India, while her renewed alliance with Russia in 1812 was essential to the defeat of Napoleon. In the final years of the Napoleonic conflict, however, officials in London and Bengal began to perceive Russian expansion into Persian and Ottoman domains to be equally as menacing as French aggression had been. It represented a clear threat to British interests in India and the Middle East, and Britain's efforts to checkmate the Russians became known in the nineteenth century as the "Eastern Question" and the "Great Game".

The last phase of the Napoleonic conflict saw imperial France in control of most of Europe through the Continental System, designed to keep out British trade. Britain's counterblockade, the Orders in Council, worked to prevent war supplies or contraband from reaching Napoleon. Although the British effort had been more successful, smuggling was rife, and neither power was able to stop it. In the end, Napoleon's tactical blunders in Spain and Russia proved his undoing.

His decision to replace the Spanish king with his own brother Joseph in 1808 provoked a civil war against the French, known as the Peninsular War or the "Spanish Ulcer." Spanish guerilla fighters now combined with British forces under the Duke of Wellington to fight a bloody and protracted campaign from 1808 to 1814. This campaign encouraged Austria's failed attempt to break from Napoleon's grip in 1809 as well as Alexander I's decision to reject the Continental System and reopen Russian ports to British trade. Napoleon's disastrous campaign to force Russia back into the system in 1812 led to the loss of his *Grande Armée* and subsequent defeat at Leipzig in 1813. The Duke of Wellington, meanwhile, marched his forces across the Pyrenees into France and, together with the Austrians, Prussians, and Russians, forced Napoleon's capitulation in 1814. His escape from exile in Elba and final defeat at Waterloo on June 18, 1815, brought the war to an end and concluded a century of Anglo-French global conflicts.

Although Britain was exhausted from twenty-three years of savage struggle, the termination of hostilities saw it emerge not only as Europe's industrial, commercial, and political leader but also the world's dominant imperial power. Moreover, the conflict had rendered Britain's tactical and commercial presence practically unassailable from Persia to the Red Sea. As for Egypt, she would never be lonely again. Napoleon's invasion together with Mehmet Ali's subsequent rise to power now provoked

British officials to reexamine thoroughly Egypt's strategic value to Britain's ever-growing imperial network, with ominous consequences for the future. Time had arrived for Britain to set in play an official Middle East policy following the lines Sir Thomas Roe and George Baldwin had established. That job rested with Britain's upcoming, single-minded foreign secretary, Lord Palmerston.

CHAPTER FOUR

Control in the Gulf,
Red Sea, and Egypt 1815–41

It is clear that the settlement made by [General] Keir was the right one. A generous and open-handed treatment . . . would go further towards reconciling them to the British Government's determination to stamp out piracy than a settlement dictated in a mood of vindictiveness. Time was to prove him right.

J. B. KELLY, *Britain and the Persian Gulf*

Eradication of piracy and slave trade in the Gulf

Britain and the Government of India continued to face a number of serious challenges stretching from the Persian Gulf to Egypt in the decades immediately following Napoleon's downfall. Piracy and the slave trade, rampant among the tribes of the Gulf and the Red Sea, became tied to the expansionist Wahhabi movement (Islamic reform) under the House of Saud, which soon controlled much of the Arabian Peninsula, including Mecca and Medina. Overall, these activities clearly threatened the peace of the Gulf and the Red Sea, requiring British intervention. In addition, Britain faced another conflict with Egypt. Mehmet Ali's thrust into Syria and Mesopotamia, which undermined Ottoman stability, provoked a determined British response to protect vital imperial trade and communication routes to India, which were already threatened by growing Russian expansion and a renewal of French intrigues. Division between the Foreign Office and the Indian government exacerbated the problems inherent in any attempted solution to terminate the slave trade or curtail Mehmet Ali during this time. Ultimately, Britain's aggressive foreign secretary, Lord Palmerston, would command the direction of British policy in the region and set the stage for a permanent and unalterable British presence in the Middle East well into the twentieth century and the end of empire.

The Congress of Vienna in 1815 acknowledged Britain's continued possession of numerous Dutch and French colonies in the Atlantic and Indian Oceans acquired during the war. The most important included Cape Colony, Ceylon, Indonesia, and several islands off East Africa. Though portions of Indonesia were returned to the Dutch, the British kept the strategic port of Malacca on the Straits and, through the efforts of Sir Stamford Raffles, added Singapore, at the tip of the Malay peninsula, in 1819.[1] These important locations provided increased protection for the routes to India and to the China trade, while the British navy, recently emerged from the French conflict without a serious rival, now connected these far-flung strategic outposts.[2]

Britannia clearly ruled the waves, but her navy had been provided with another formidable challenge. Under pressure from British evangelicals, the All Talents Ministry had outlawed the slave trade in the year following Prime Minister William Pitt's death in 1806, and the Vienna Congress of 1815 followed suit at British insistence.[3] It now remained the task of thinly stretched British naval squadrons to enforce this edict in the Indian and Atlantic Oceans, as well as in the Caribbean.[4] The pirate-infested waters of the Red Sea and the Persian Gulf were assigned to the Government of India and the Bombay Marine.[5]

The Government of India stood more ready, if reluctantly so, to meet this demand after 1815, since it had steadily undergone needed reforms generated by Pitt's India Bill in 1784.[6] This bill had limited the power of the quarrelsome council, created the board of trade and secretary of state for India as cabinet positions in the British government and gave more power to the office of governor-general, who reported directly to the Indian secretary.[7] Imperial apathy, resulting from the loss of the American colonies, had been replaced with imperial pride in the ensuing years, as young, talented, and well-paid civil servants, encouraged through patronage, took up important political positions in the company.[8] As an overdue reform, the company's political activity was separated from its commercial focus so that its agents could not indulge in both.[9] Finally, under Governor-General Richard Wellesley (1793–1805) and his younger brother Arthur (later Duke of Wellington), the company's private army as well as the Bombay Marine had increased both in size and experience to bear the brunt of India's conflicts throughout the Napoleonic wars.[10]

Company officials and the marine's small patrols had been very active in keeping the French from the Gulf during the war, but as it turned out, pirate attacks against British shipping proved a more serious military threat. Company treaties with Muscat and Oman also had been designed to reduce these attacks,[11] but a British military force sufficient to enforce the agreements proved impossible to send to the Gulf while French-inspired conflicts raged in India. Though defeating one pirate fleet in 1806,[12] the Bombay Marine had to settle for a draw against Qasimi pirates three years later.[13] Most importantly, the tribe of the Qawasim had allied with the Wahhabis (Islamic reform movement) under Saud ibn Abdul Aziz, Amir of Najd in north central Arabia. Fighting with the Qawasim proved tough enough, and the Government of India wanted no additional land war with the Wahhabis, who with their allies could muster over one hundred well-armed Arab *dhows* (small ships) against the British in the Gulf and in the Red Sea.[14]

The subcontinent returned to a degree of calm after 1817, leaving the victorious Government of India as its dominant power and freeing the company to pursue the pirate threat and related slave trade throughout the waters surrounding the Arabian Peninsula. In 1819, the Bombay Marine, with 3,000 company troops, joined by ships from the Royal Navy, now embarked on a do-or-die expedition to crush the Qasimi pirates.[15] Aid against the Wahhabis materialized from an unexpected source, Egypt's ruler Mehmet Ali, whose forces decimated Saud's army and his capital at Derayah in 1818.[16] Attempted negotiations with Ali's son, Ibrahim, to unite with the British and crush the Qawasim, however, failed to materialize. The British effort in the Gulf thus proved a solo adventure. Why? British officials exercised no desire or rush to support Ali's ambition, including that of an independent Egypt separate from the Ottoman Empire.

Thus began Britain's longest, most dogged and successful endeavors in the region, the hundred-year effort to suppress piracy and the slave trade. The biggest problem facing the British on the eve of the first expedition, however, appeared to be the lack of clear objectives following a projected victory. India's governor-general at that time, the Marquis of Hastings (1812-23, formerly Lord Moira), wanted no heavy-handed British presence in the Gulf, while Bombay's governor, Evan Nepean, did. Hastings pointedly told Nepean to avoid "all interference in the concerns of the Arab states beyond what may be necessary for effecting the suppression of piracy."[17] Major-General Sir William Grant Keir, meanwhile, launched his campaign in early November 1819 and, following a number of bloody engagements, defeated the Qasimi pirates and their allies in late December. In the final analysis, Keir adhered to the spirit of Hasting's mandate in a series of treaties negotiated with the defeated Gulf sheikhs in January 1820.[18]

Provisions of the General Treaty had been designed specifically to maintain a general peace in the Gulf and the Red Sea and thus prohibited the various tribes from random plunder and piracy against one another without a specific declaration of war. Violations would result in the forfeiture of life and property. Further, ships belonging to the pirate tribes now carried reduced armaments, flew a required flag for identification by British vessels, and bore a register with port clearance from the ruling sheikh, countersigned by a British government representative.[19]

The treaty's more humanitarian terms mandated an end to the slaughter of prisoners, a common practice, as well as the termination of the African slave trade as required by the Congress of Vienna. Any tribe involved in these activities or in continued piracy would face joint military action by the British and the other tribes.[20] Finally, the maritime tribes were permitted to trade at British ports, particularly in India and with neighboring states allied with the British. Although the Government of India had written similar provisions into the earlier Gulf dependency treaties (1799–1806), these were now reinforced and extended over a wider area and would remain so over the next several decades, enforced, when necessary, with additional military muscle.[21] The British had determined to apply informal influence through skillful treaties and a restrained use of force as the best way to secure the Gulf. This equitable approach eventually curtailed piracy and the slave trade.

Keir's lenient and even-handed provisions in the General Treaty remained at odds with the ideas of Bombay Governor Nepean and those of his successor, Lord Elphinstone, who sought greater punishment and control of the Qawasim. He wanted to place British representatives at all ports, create a naval base in the region for search and seizure operations and give friendly and more collaborative sheikhs greater political control over the western Gulf. This last point would have proved the most troublesome: "Elphinstone was prepared to invest the Sultan of Muscat with the suzerainty of the Pirate Coast and to make use of his navy to police the waters of the Gulf."[22] Keir reminded the governor, "If he had replaced the chiefs with his own nominees, the British Government would have been committed to the support of these nominees, and consequently to further interference in the future."[23] The fact that the Government of India, however, would be able to extend and maintain such considerable influence in the Gulf with such minimal efforts over the next century appears to demonstrate the correctness of Keir's approach. Historian J. B. Kelly best sums up his contribution: "It is clear that the settlement made by Keir was the right one. A generous and open-handed treatment . . . would go further towards reconciling them to the British Government's determination to stamp out piracy than a settlement dictated in a mood of vindictiveness. Time was to prove him right."[24]

The final agreement soon included the sheikhs of Oman and the Trucial Coast (former Pirate Coast), and the island of Bahrain.[25] Since Persia claimed Bahrain, the Government of India's recognition of the claim depended on Persian cooperation for a joint expedition to eradicate reported piracy on the Gulf's Persian coast. The shah, Fateh Ali, refused to sanction military action, fearing a British violation of his territorial sovereignty.[26] Keir's careful investigation of alleged Qasimi pirate attacks from Persian coastal territory, moreover, revealed there was no truth to the stories, and the effort was aborted along with recognition of Persia's claim to Bahrain.

That left Bahrain's de facto rulers, the sheikhs of the Al Khalifah dynasty, to sign on to the treaty in February 1820.[27] Two months later, Elphinstone assured the Al Khalifah "that the British Government had no intention of helping the Persians to subdue them, and that the Shah, for his part, could be told that any move by him to enforce his claim to the island, which disturbed the peace of the Gulf and disrupted trade, would be viewed with regret in India."[28]

Kier's expedition and the overall settlement did curtail piracy, but the sanctions failed to retard the slave trade, as more naval engagements and treaties in the following decades testify. First, the Congress of Vienna's call to end the trade was more clearly understood as a European issue that could not be forcibly applied to the Gulf's Arab sheikdoms without serious consequences. Second, the Government of India, with its regional mindset, proved more ready to attack piracy—because it disturbed the tranquility of the Gulf—than the slave trade, then perceived by some British observers as a somewhat benign and normal part of Arab commerce.[29] Third, the centuries-old practice of running slaves through the region was exacerbated by the fact that Muscat, Britain's sometime ally against the Qawasim, maintained a political connection to Zanzibar, one of the largest slave markets on the east African coast. Muscat's ruler, Saiyid Said, moreover, had not signed the General Treaty containing the anti–slave trade provision since it had been primarily directed against the Qasimi pirates and their allies. Finally, the treaty had referred only to kidnapping or seizing slaves from the coast, not to the usual Arab purchases of African slaves at market locations.

From 1820 to 1854, inescapable legal concerns and the region's traditional attitudes conditioned the Indian government's cautious and protracted approach to the slave trade. "Not only had the British authorities in India no desire to interfere with the Arab slave trade, but they took pains to avoid giving the impression of wishing to do so."[30] India's governor-generals and company officials, therefore, ignored the trade at first, but steady pressure from the home government and the company's board of directors in London prodded Indian officials to try to embrace a more enlightened view.[31]

An estimated total of 8,000–10,000 African slaves per year went to Persia, the Ottoman Empire, and India, as well as to European buyers in the area. Since the European Congress had specifically interdicted it, in 1821 the British government targeted the Arab sale of slaves to European or British buyers. The new injunction, known as the Moresby Treaty, also took aim at the Sultan of Muscat as the primary agent of these sales, who reluctantly agreed to the prohibition.[32] This treaty included the Royal Navy's right of search and seizure, but it gave no such authority to the Bombay Marine, which readily patrolled the lanes of the Gulf and the Red Sea. Despite this loophole, the treaty proved the beginning of an effort to attempt to control the slave traffic from east Africa to India. Finally, the company itself was forced to take measures to streamline its organization in the region in order to clarify its position on Gulf affairs and to act with one voice.

"In 1822 . . . the Resident at Bushire took over responsibility for the affairs of the whole of the area and his title was accordingly restyled 'Resident in the Persian Gulf'."[33]

Notwithstanding, further efforts to eradicate or curtail the trade faltered over the next twenty years. The Government of India, in fact, could not even prevent its spread to territories of the Bombay Presidency, much less to Persia or the Ottoman Empire. The British and Indian governments, moreover, remained at odds on the issue throughout this period, India's leaders believing that the suppression of the slave trade would undoubtedly result in an even more bloody return to piracy. Conflicts with Persia and the First Afghan War (1839–41) added to the confusion and seriously distracted the Indian government's feeble attention to the issue. At this juncture, Foreign Office Secretary Lord Palmerston, embroiled with the seizure of Aden in 1839 and the suppression of Mehmet Ali in Egypt in 1840, demanded that Indian officials take a much tougher stand against the Arab slave trade and outlaw it altogether. They refused to do so, having neither the will nor the means to carry it out. Palmerston, however, had determined to tie the final knot in his Eastern policy. "He had already made up his mind to launch a full-scale assault upon the Arab slave trade, and he was not going to be deflected from that course by misgivings about its political consequences . . . let alone to allow such consideration to hamper or frustrate the launching of a crusade against the slave trade."[34]

Though Palmerston soon left his Foreign Office post, his views propelled the British government in 1842 to transfer the responsibility for eliminating the slave trade from the Indian government to the Foreign Office: "This great question being one rather of national than of Indian policy and its decision resting of necessity with Her Majesty's Government exclusively, we have no instruction to address to you on the subject."[35] Palmerston had begun to manifest a single-minded policy for the entire Middle East and would allow no wiggle room for the Indian government to go it alone, even in the Gulf.

A series of treaties negotiated from 1838 to 1853 between the Indian and British governments and the Gulf sheikhdoms, however, demonstrated the difficulties in balancing, managing, or eliminating either of these two traditional enterprises, as illustrated in the following scenario. Ibn Saqr of the Qawasim agreed to stop the slave trade for the second time in 1838 and allow British ships to search his vessels.[36] As efforts to circumscribe this activity mounted, more piracy erupted, requiring the British resident in the Persian Gulf to hammer out the Ten Year Maritime Truce with the sheikhs of Trucial Oman in 1843 to halt increased conflict between the tribes.[37] Once more, Ibn Saqr stopped his piratical activities but again returned to the slave trade until forced, along with five Omani sheikhs and the rulers of Bahrain,[38] to halt and sign another agreement. At last, the British negotiated the Perpetual Treaty of Maritime Truce in 1853 to prevent these same sheikhs, who had just limited their slaving activities, from again resorting

FIGURE 3 *Henry John Temple, 3rd Viscount (Lord Palmerston). Print Collector. Getty Images.*

to piracy.[39] Although the slave trade was not completely eradicated at that time, the perpetual treaty at least pacified the Gulf for the remainder of the century. As one historian notes, "After the Treaty of 1853 with which the *Pax Britannica* truly began, the British inevitably took control of the sea lanes of the Gulf."[40]

The subjugation of Mehmet Ali: Informal influence and Egypt 1827–41

The British and Indian governments had been inching toward a solution to issues in the Gulf when another problem demanded immediate attention. Russia's southern advance into Ottoman and Persian territory before and during the Napoleonic wars had reactivated British concerns over the region's security as the highway to India, this sparked the evolution of the Eastern Question. The Ottoman Empire loomed larger than ever as the key to imperial defense, yet in 1839, all appeared lost in a race against time but

Russia was no longer the immediate threat. Despite numerous treaties and fermans to reinvigorate the Ottoman regime, it appeared doomed to conquest at the hands of the sultan's vassal, Mehmet Ali (Turkish for Muhammed Ali) and his Egyptian empire. This unexpected turn of events prompted Foreign Secretary Lord Palmerston in 1840 to seek an international agreement to stop Ali and preserve Ottoman integrity.

Not since General Fraser's failed expedition during the Napoleonic wars had the British government attempted to confront Mehmet Ali's growing power in Egypt. After defeating Fraser in 1807, Ali had consolidated his position with the Egyptian people and strengthened his ties to the sultan.[41] His evolving relationship with the Ottoman government rested on the basic recognition of Ottoman suzerainty over Egypt as a vassal state, which included regular payment of tribute and important military support for the sultan's wars in Arabia and Greece. Over time, these contributions rendered Ali indispensable to the Ottoman cause.[42] Though juridically tied to the Ottoman Empire, Egypt continually extracted significant internal administrative autonomy from the Ottoman structure as Ali intended. His reign as *Wali* (Governor) not only altered Egypt's internal organization, but its external direction as well, with every action focused on one clearcut goal: political and economic independence from the Ottoman Empire.

As part of that goal, Ali embarked on an ambitious program to reorganize Egypt along more modern lines, including a new constitution, strong central government, taxation reform, bold irrigation projects, industrialization, and a formidable military machine.[43] Egypt's agricultural and industrial base developed dramatically through the increased development of cash crops and textiles protected by an Egyptian state monopoly. Construction of dams, barrages, and canals, moreover, provided thousands of new jobs, as did Ali's 150,000-man military force and the need to supply it. Hundreds of young men sent to Europe provided Egypt with new ideas and technology for Ali's modernization program, as did the additional employment of Europeans to provide expertise and leadership for these new undertakings.[44]

Most notably, Egypt had gained considerable prominence in the international arena through a period of imperial expansion cleverly affixed to Ali's support of the sultan. He first backed the sultan's bid to retake the pilgrimage sites of Mecca and Medina from control of the reformist Wahhabis under Al-Saud. Ali's son, Ibrahim, broke Wahhabi resistance after six years of conflict and conquered Saud's capital at Deraya in eastern Arabia in 1818.[45] Ali next brought the Sudan and its lucrative slave trade under Egyptian control. These two endeavors, however, extended Egyptian hegemony down both sides of the Red Sea, clearly challenging established British trade and security arrangements developed there at the height of the French wars.

Finally, the sultan requested Ali's help against the Greek revolt in 1821.[46] His naval successes in Crete and Cyprus, followed in 1825 by the destruction of Greek resistance on Morea and at Missolonghi, brought a quick response from Britain, Russia, and France, who now took on the Greek struggle against the Ottoman Empire. Britain's purpose in forming this alliance had been twofold: to prevent the Russians from singlehandedly defeating the Ottomans and absorbing the Greek provinces, and to curtail Ali's bid to tie the Greeks to Egypt's economic expansion in the eastern Mediterranean. Ali's policies thus prompted direct European military intervention against Egypt as their combined fleets sunk the Turko-Egyptian navy off Navarino on October 20, 1827.[47] Though distraught over the loss, Ali never looked back. He rebuilt his navy in two years.

Ali continued to nurture increased imperial ambitions and, as a very tough politician, he remained single-minded in the face of his European or Ottoman adversaries. His subsequent expansion into the Ottoman Empire, however, remains the subject of much historical debate. Some historians have suggested that it was prompted either by French-inspired nationalism, the desire to create a greater Islamic nation; internal social pressure; or a plan to absorb all or part of the Ottoman domains.[48] Arab historians at the time suggested that Egyptians, although unimpressed and unmotivated by French revolutionary ideology, without a frame of reference, were indeed awed by French military prowess.[49]

It appears certain that Ali, like the Pashas in Syria and Tunis, had developed a focus of economic monopoly and political power in the midst of Ottoman decline, but in Ali's case, it also produced a very successful if unusual military imperialism that is difficult to explain. In view of his military success and instinct for assimilation, it also seems possible that Mehmet Ali's model for an expanded military and imperial state had been Napoleon's Grand Empire and the Continental System, a context to which Ali had been exposed for fifteen years. Thus, Ali's subsequent strike against sultans Mahmud II and Abdulmecid's territory in Syria as a step toward building his own Egyptian empire might be more clearly comprehended. There are possible truths contained in all of the foregoing views, but historian A. L. Al-Sayyid Marsot has offered the most solid interpretation to date of Ali's expansion. "He regarded military expansion and imperialist designs as essential to his economic development, and his economic development as essential for independence."[50]

Consequently, from 1831 to 1839, Ibrahim led Ali's forces in steady triumph over the Ottoman army in the conquest of Syria, culminating in a major victory at Nezib on June 26, 1839; and within a year, the Egyptian army threatened a coup de grace of the entire Ottoman Empire. A quick surrender of the Ottoman fleet to Ali prompted the desperate sultan to offer him the hereditary rule of Egypt, but as part of an earlier promise, he demanded Syria as well.

The British had been enlarging their own imperial sphere at the time of Ali's expansion and, as noted, had created a series of guardianship-buffer-state and dependency treaties (protectorates) from India outward into the Gulf and the Red Sea toward the Ottoman Empire. These were designed to keep out the French and, after 1815, to check Russian expansion into Southwest Asia and the Middle East. Ali's stunning successes, therefore, increasingly alarmed Foreign Secretary Lord Palmerston, who was vexed over the security of contracts recently concluded with the Ottoman Empire relative to trade and transportation routes to India via Syria and Mesopotamia. In short, Ali's moves had unwittingly placed him in the middle of the complex and volatile Eastern Question, since he now threatened Britain's commercial and strategic foothold in the Ottoman Empire, developed since 1834 to safeguard these routes and thwart Russian expansion in the region.[51]

Palmerston's trade contracts together with the Ottoman ferman had provided Britain with commercial privileges throughout the Ottoman Empire, with the notable exception of Egypt.[52] Negotiations also included the possibility of British steamship operations on the Euphrates to the Gulf based on the 1835 Euphrates Expedition.[53] Sultan Mahmud II accepted this arrangement as vital to Ottoman interests for increased finances, trade, modernization, and protection from Ali, while Britain profited from additional free-trade markets and received assurances of more democratic reform of Ottoman institutions (Tanzimat).[54]

When British and Egyptian interests finally collided in 1840, they represented long-standing differences between Ali and the British Foreign Office and not merely a last-minute confrontation. The Foreign Office always had supported the territorial integrity of the Ottoman regime, which included Egypt. As noted, this support remained a constant to the end of the eighteenth century and throughout the Napoleonic conflict. Neither the Mameluks' nor Ali's lure of guaranteed British mail and trade routes through Egypt to India could push Palmerston or his predecessors to recognize Egypt's independent status and desert the Ottoman cause.

As so often happened, the Indian government and agents of the East India Company rarely saw eye to eye with the Foreign Office and earlier had backed the Mameluks and later Ali in direct opposition to the British government. In fact, Ali had provided undaunted support for the British Euphrates Expedition from 1834 to 1838 and had seen to it that his son, Ibrahim, had supplied the expedition with enough material aid to complete the project.[55] For this support he received high praise from the Indian government including Governor-General Lord Auckland (1835–42), who sent Ali a present of two war elephants with mounted artillery.[56] Moreover, Ali provided the British with coaling stations at Alexandria and Suez for increased steamship runs from the Red Sea to Bombay.[57] Ali's efforts had guaranteed steady, safe, and fast delivery of mail and traffic from London to India via Egypt. The early success of the Peninsular and Oriental Steamship Line (P&O) clearly owed something to Ali's goodwill.[58] Overwhelming evidence suggests that Indian officials and company agents remained very pleased with Ali and supported most of his actions,[59] even including his brief occupation of Aden, staunchly denounced by Palmerston.[60] Much to

Ali's dismay, the British seized Aden in 1839 and forced the evacuation of Egyptian troops.[61] Palmerston obviously had remained unimpressed with the Indian government and the company's favorable assessment of Egypt's ruler. In particular, the greatly weakened company, which in 1840 lost its exclusive trade monopoly in India, was in no position to protest effectively the views of the foreign secretary.

Why did the British support the Ottoman Empire, a clear loser, over Ali, who would have offered much more resistance to Russian expansion in the Middle East? The official British explanation was that free trade into the empire had been tied to Ottoman promises of institutional reform and greater freedom for its people;[62] British officials perceived Ali as a repressive tyrant. The evidence demonstrates, however, that Ali was at least as enlightened as the Ottomans, if not more so. Ali's long-standing friendship with France also raised the specter of eventual French dominance of the region if Egypt gained complete independence or conquered the Ottomans. In the end, the Ottomans needed the British and Ali did not! The Ottoman Empire depended on British support and trade, whereas Ali's monopolies in Egypt, Syria, and Arabia thwarted the now popular imperialism of free trade advocated by Palmerston and his colleagues.[63]

On the west coast of the Arabian Peninsula, Ali's forces dominated Mocha and the coffee trade, invested Yemen and occupied Aden.[64] As noted, the company agent in Cairo, Mr. P. Campbell, had urged Palmerston to allow Ali's control of Aden to protect British interests there, not only as a goodwill gesture but as a secure and frugal investment.[65] Palmerston, however, already had made up his mind. Aden's vital position as a coaling station on the new steamship run from Suez to Bombay, Madras or Calcutta provoked Palmerston to order its seizure as a British colony and for the area's relocated residency.[66] Aden proved no easy location to hold as both Egyptian and Bedouin forces plagued the British there until 1845.[67] British agents also had warned Palmerston that Egypt's pasha was about to invade the Baghdad Pashalik, further exacerbating his dislike of Ali. There was no evidence for this rumor, and the British consul-general in Egypt urged the Foreign Office not to believe it.[68]

Imminent defeat of the Ottoman Empire in 1839, nevertheless, prompted Palmerston to act, and the European powers jointly issued a note at his urging to forbid the sultan from signing any deal with Ali. The London Convention (Treaty) of July 15, 1840, concluded between the Ottoman government and the powers—except France, which had trained Ali's army—offered him the hereditary Pashalik of Egypt but forced him to relinquish any claim to Syria and Mesopotamia.[69] Significantly, it universally applied all Ottoman laws and treaties to Egypt, which broke Ali's state monopolies. This Palmerstonian provision, at last, would provide Britain with free access to Egyptian markets. Ali, angered and desperate, now depended on faltering French support to resist the British and deliberately, if unwisely, allowed the twenty-day acceptance period to lapse, voiding the offer.[70]

The swiftness and clandestine nature of the British action, meanwhile, had caught numerous British and European merchants completely off guard in Egypt. Most had maintained good relations with Ali and complained bitterly to the British government about being placed in peril of life and property. A belated letter of August 11 from the Foreign Office to Mr. T. M. Larking, the British consul in Cairo, warned British subjects to "arrange their affairs without loss of time."[71] A second letter of August 15 urged merchants to be ready for a quick exit "in the present and very serious and menacing situation of affairs."[72] Angry and frustrated, an ad hoc committee of merchants responded to the Foreign Office on the same day: "If the situation is so 'serious and menacing' why hasn't Her Majesty's Government given definite instructions to British subjects in Egypt?"[73] Ironically, only several months earlier, the Indian government had presented Ali Pasha with the gift of an entire botanical garden shipped from the subcontinent with great care and much expense.[74] P&O, moreover, had been in the midst of delicate negotiations with the pasha for additional steamship routes on the Nile at the time of the crisis.[75] The government, obviously, had decided to deal with Ali quietly and quickly, without recourse to public opinion, which generally favored the pasha. This decision left British merchants, P&O officials, company agents, and the Indian government in some consternation over Ali's treatment and mostly in the dark relative to the actions of the British government.

Popular opposition notwithstanding, Admiral Charles Napier directed a joint British, Russian, Austrian, and Ottoman naval squadron to land an Anglo-Turkish force along the Syrian coast to defeat Ibrahim in September.[76] In response, Ali subsequently ordered all company agents and British consular officials to evacuate Egypt. Most resettled in Malta from October 18 to December 21 to conduct operations in exile.[77] True to an earlier promise, however, Ali protected the British mail through Egypt during the ordeal and later received thanks from the company but none from the government.[78] Ibrahim's army, meanwhile, blockaded in Syria, suffered serious losses and faced widespread rebellion of the population against Egyptian rule.[79] France finally withdrew support from Ali and signed Palmerston's pact. Completely isolated, the pasha reluctantly and belatedly received Palmerston's offer delivered at Alexandria by Admiral Napier in November 1840.[80] Safe withdrawal of Egyptian forces from Syria preceded a final Ottoman ferman establishing Mehmet Ali's line as Egypt's hereditary rulers.[81]

Signed on June 1, 1841, the Alexandria Convention allowed Ali to save face and forestalled the Ottoman Empire's probable dissolution. The treaty purposely undercut Ali's bid for sovereignty and circumvented the Egyptian state's high-priced cotton monopoly. Palmerston treated the Ottoman territories as a political and economic whole for the benefit of British free trade, since agreements pertaining to one Ottoman region automatically applied empire-wide for British advantage.[82] This treaty, like those developed earlier in India and the Persian Gulf, made Britain, in effect, the guarantor of the legal apparatus connecting Egypt with the Ottoman Empire and firmly secured Ali's family to Egypt's hereditary pashalik.[83] But it also undermined Egypt's autonomy and gave Britain the legal device and precedent for interference and ultimately Egypt's invasion forty years later.[84]

Britain and the European Concert, which had curtailed nationalism in areas of European interest since 1815, now thwarted whatever hope Ali had planned for independence and expansion. He again became the sultan's vassal, while Britain, ever expanding into Egyptian affairs after 1840, guaranteed the arrangement through the London treaty as a technique of imperial dominance for her own commercial and strategic reasons and as an expanded form of informal influence. In the international arena, Palmerston's five-power pact clearly neutralized growing Russian influence in the Ottoman Empire.[85] It also harnessed independently minded France back into the European Concert and away from from numerous intrigues in Egypt and elsewhere in the region.[86] On the domestic front, however, the London treaty propelled Egypt's native Arab majority on a downward socioeconomic spiral. They had been without political power for centuries under the Ottomans. Their voices never counted in Ottoman affairs, nor would they in future British dealings with Egypt. As pawns in the greater picture, their history, traditions, religious values, economic status, and aspirations continued to be ignored as inconsequential. The harsh impact of informal influence on the native population became clear very quickly.

Importantly, Palmerston's official policy, treating the Middle East as a whole for British economic, communication, and strategic benefit, now became fixed as the guiding principle for British hegemony over the region for the remainder of the nineteenth century and beyond. No future British government, liberal or conservative, would ever find an alternative to Palmerston's formula. For better or worse, the Middle East had become an integral part of the British Empire.

CHAPTER FIVE

The "Great Game,"
Afghanistan 1838–42

*His first few sentences extinguished all hope in the hearts
of listeners regarding the future of the Kabul force.
It was evident that it was annihilated.*

BRIAN FARWELL, *Queen Victoria's Little Wars*

The British government and the Government of India had maintained deep-running and unresolved differences over Mehmet Ali's regional role, the occupation of Aden, and termination of the Arab slave trade. But their points of view proved almost unanimous on one issue: the perceived threat of Russian expansion from the western reaches of the Ottoman Empire to the wilds of Afghanistan. On this question, if nothing else, India's governor-general, Lord Auckland, and Britain's foreign minister, Lord Palmerston, were in perfect agreement. While Palmerston had been dealing with the Egyptian crisis and the seizure of Aden, the tentacles of the so-called "Great Game" had already meandered eastward to the gateway of British India (Map 1). Persia and Afghanistan had become flashpoints for Russian intrigue and presumed expansion. Lacking much credible evidence, both the British and Indian governments understood Russia's ultimate target as India. Their joint decision to checkmate the Russian move in Afghanistan rather than India resulted in the First Afghan War. Ironically, the Russians, the ultimate enemy, remained totally absent from this conflict.

Events leading up to this campaign revealed that the government of Czar Nicholas I had, indeed, gained a measure of influence over Persia because of earlier British debacles and, through this influence, sought to create a sphere of alliances across the border among the divided rulers of Afghanistan. If successful, according to the British view, the Russians would control the highway to India. This notion was a stretch, of course, but the major players responded accordingly. As in the Egyptian affair, Palmerston saw the Russian move as a challenge to his Eastern policy and a threat to Britain's Crown Jewel. Lord Auckland pushed logic a step further and now embraced the forward position that the best defense of India was not at the Indus but in Afghanistan. By 1838, the view had evolved that Persia, Afghanistan, and the Middle Eastern provinces of the Ottoman Empire together represented a contiguous British sphere for the protection of security, trade, and communication to the Indian subcontinent.

The crisis came to a head that same year (1838). Russia supported a Persian attack on Herat in western Afghanistan, while Russian agents urged Kabul's ruler, Dost Mohammed, to seek Persian aid to recapture territory lost to British client Ranjit Singh of the Punjab. Palmerston and Auckland responded quickly but for their own specific reasons. Historian J. H. Waller states,

> He [Palmerston] was convinced that Britain could not compete successfully for influence in Persia. He was therefore all the more determined to act in Afghanistan, a region where he believed the British might have a real chance of prevailing over the Russians. Afghanistan was in any case, for him, just one theatre in the wider struggle with Russia which ran from Europe to India. In contrast, those who governed India (Auckland) were more anxious to impress the peoples of the subcontinent with their ability to vanquish any threat—external or internal—to British pre-eminence in India.[1]

Auckland now took the initiative to use military force to replace Dost Mohammed with former ruler Shah Shujah, a British client, now on the British dole (payroll) in India. An India Office note states "The Governor-General was satisfied that a pressing necessity, as well as every consideration of policy and justice warranted us in espousing the cause of Shah Shujah, 'whose popularity throughout Afghanistan had been proved to his Lordship by the strong and unanimous testimonies of the best authorities.'"[2] Unfortunately, Auckland's view of Britain's client had little basis in fact. Shah Shujah, who proved very unpopular, would be dead within two years—a victim of realpolitik, Afghan style.

In point of fact, the reasons for Auckland's military expedition had unceremoniously evaporated before the incursion began. In 1837, Auckland had dispatched Captain Alexander Burnes to Kabul in order to patch up differences with Dost Mohammed and secure his loyalty to the British. Negotiations stalemated over the return of his lost territories held by British client Ranjit Singh, which Auckland and his advisors interpreted as a pro-Russian stance. India Office records reveal that nothing could have been

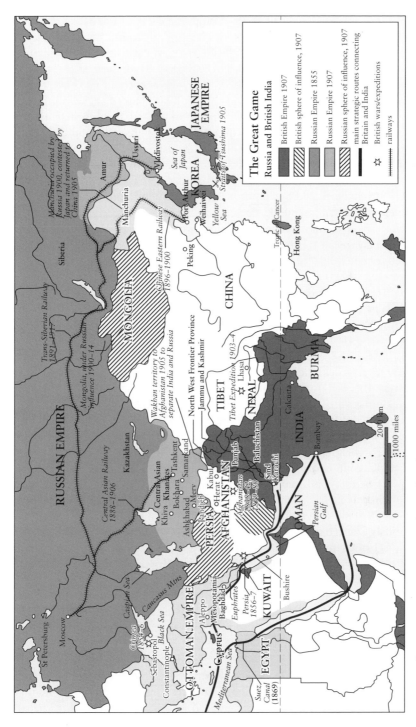

MAP 1 *The Great Game, Russia and British India.*

further from the truth: "The negotiations petered out and Burnes left Kabul with nothing achieved in April 1838, though the Russian Envoy left at about the same time with no more to show for his stay in Kabul than Burnes. . . . On the 1st October 1838, war was declared on Afghanistan."[3]

The Simla Manifesto of October 1, 1838, flew in the face of reality. The Persian and Russian threat had passed, but Auckland could not back down, despite the doubts of his senior military advisor, Sir Henry Fane, commander-in-chief of all Indian forces.[4] Clearly Palmerston and other top British leaders saw the Afghan expedition as part of a much wider picture, and now their focus had fallen on Auckland to fulfill his role in the Great Game for the glory of British India. Such pressure was intolerable. In the weeks before the declaration of war, Palmerston told the British ambassador to Russia that "Auckland has been told to take Afghanistan in hand and make it a British dependency. . . . We have long declined to meddle with the Afghans, but if the Russians try to make them Russian we must take care that they become British."[5] Likewise, on August 26, Palmerston wrote to Sir John Hobhouse, president of the Board of Control for India, proposing the grand strategy. As Waller notes, "He [Palmerston] was in favor of the 'great operation' planned against Afghanistan. Ranjit Singh's forces would 'drive the Persians out of Afghanistan and recognize that country under one chief.' Afghanistan, he was convinced, would make a better buffer than Persia. 'We should have the same kind of geographical pull upon such a state that Russia has upon Persia.'"[6] Likewise, the Foreign Office and the Board of Control for India had supported Auckland's invasion plans in a note sent on August 2.[7]

Despite the fact that on October 24 the secret committee of the East India Company had urged Auckland to make another overture to Dost Mohammed, he delayed. After he received full backing from the British cabinet, Auckland met with his own forward advisors at Simla, who again advocated invasion.[8] Finally, in a note of October 20, 1838, Palmerston attacked Russian moves in Afghanistan, based on outdated information that, nonetheless, reinforced Auckland's decision and provided him with a pretext for war and a commitment to act. An India Office note exclaimed, "But the British Government have learned that Count Simonich . . . strenuously exerted himself to detach the rulers of those Afghan States from all connection with England, and to induce them to place their reliance on Persia in the first instance, and ultimately on Russia"[9] Palmerston's views again carried the day, and Auckland paid the price. Early in 1839, led by General Sir John Kaye, the governor-general's 21,000-strong Army of the Indus, along with 30,000 camp followers, crossed into Afghanistan, into the mountains of the Hindu Kush, and into history: Few survivors returned to tell the tale.

Palmerston and Auckland's objective, if it can be clearly ascertained, was to make Afghanistan a British dependency through the popular and informal client regime of Shujah Shah—at gunpoint. After taking Kandahar in April, the great day came and he entered Kabul, but the cheering crowds failed to materialize. Whatever wisp of popularity Shujah Shah might have had soon evaporated when British advisors assumed control of the government and the country. By any definition of imperialism, this plan was poorly focused and executed. The India Office notes, "The first Afghan War (1838–42) might have ended on the 7th August, 1839, with the entry of Kabul by the expeditionary force . . . It was not therefore surprising that the Afghans, however fond of quarrelling among themselves, were before long thoroughly roused by the occupation of their country by a foreign army and by the spectacle of a puppet King maintained on the throne by British bayonets."[10]

The Army of the Indus, dispersed to several strongholds throughout Afghanistan, had been composed largely of East India Company native recruits (Sepoys) who had no desire to be there in the first place. Leaving Hindustan was a polluting act for Hindus, whereas the army's Muslims resented going to Afghanistan to kill fellow Muslims with whom they had no quarrel.[11] Unfortunately, India's British leaders took little notice of the Sepoy mood. A continuation of that attitude in the years ahead would provoke the Sepoy Mutiny. Although the army's minority of Sikhs, Gurkhas, and Britons had no qualms on this score, they shared a sense of relative unease because of the expedition's obvious unpopularity in a hostile setting. As events quickly revealed, their foreboding had not been misplaced.

Heightened tensions soon exploded into open rebellion when the British violated an agreement and cut previously promised subsidies to the tribal chiefs. On November 1, 1841, rioting erupted in Kabul, and within a month, representative Sir Alexander Burnes and envoy Sir William Macnaghten were murdered. British garrisons came under siege at Kabul, Kandahar, and Ghazni. An attempted withdrawal of the Kabul force to Jellalabad on January 6, 1842, resulted in the complete destruction of the 4,500-strong garrison and 10,000 camp followers. Historian Byron Farwell recounts the episode:

> Seven days later, officers of the 13th Regiment on the walls of the fort at Jellalabad saw a solitary horseman riding slowly towards them from the direction of Kabul. Horse and rider were obviously exhausted, but someone made a signal and the rider replied by waving a soldier's forage cap. The gate was thrown open and several officers rushed out to greet Surgeon William Brydon—the sole Briton to complete the march from Kabul. Henry Havelock, one of the officers who ran out to meet him, wrote: "His first few sentences extinguished all hope in the hearts of listeners regarding the future of the Kabul force. It was evident that it was annihilated."[12]

General Kaye said of the disaster, "There is nothing more remarkable in the history of the world than the awful completeness, the sublime unity of this Caubul tragedy."[13] Two weeks later, the news from Dr. Brydon, now known as the messenger of death, reached Lord Auckland at Calcutta. "The shock, his sister Emily noted, was to age him by ten years."[14] After two months, the horrific message reached Queen Victoria: "When two of her ministers set before the young queen 'the disastrous intelligence from Afghanistan,' she was appalled."[15] And what of Shah Shujah, the "Puppet King"? Without the protection of British troops, he was murdered on April 5, 1842, outside the Citadel-Palace in Kabul, the Bala Hissar, at the hand of his own godson. So much for the Afghan political process.[16]

But the British political process proved little better. The British and Indian governments needed a scapegoat in the wake of a massive public outcry, and Auckland, true to form, stepped to the head of the class. Whether they had had reservations or no, both governments had supported and, in fact, encouraged Auckland's forward policy, but Palmerston, the project's grand architect, the man behind the scenes and Auckland's chief prod, received no public scrutiny. How so? Despite the Afghanistan disaster, the bulk of Palmerston's Eastern policy had succeeded. He had won in Egypt, Syria, and Aden; humiliated Persia; neutralized Russia; and harnessed the slave trade. Few ever associated him with the odium of Afghanistan. Yet, as historian John Waller observed in *Beyond the Khyber Pass*, "Palmerston, chronically obsessed by the Russian threat and a sometimes reckless advocate of a forward-thrusting frontier policy, was probably more deserving of blame."[17] But in the public eye, he was a winner. In the years ahead he would become prime minister. His policy, moreover, would guide British efforts throughout the entire region until the very end.

Auckland, broken and haunted by the Afghan disaster, soon returned to Britain where, fortunately, the public memory was short and forgiving. Appointed Lord of the Admiralty in 1846, he died soon after.[18] He could claim no victories, only the memories, only the nightmares, only Afghanistan. His historical legacy remained that of the culprit and loser, and India paid dearly: "The financial cost of the Afghan experience had also been enormous, and this had to be borne by the East India Company, meaning ultimately, the people of India, not the British government."[19]

Under pressure at home, especially from the aging Duke of Wellington, the Indian government launched a punitive expedition to Afghanistan in late 1842 to settle the score, repair wounded pride, and restore British prestige. Unlike the last venture, they would not attempt to control the land. As a singular act of vengeance, the army destroyed Kabul's grand bazaar and finally withdrew—this time for decades.[20] Ironically, Dost Mohammed soon returned from exile to rule at Kabul until 1863, under an Indian subsidy, to do for the British what they had failed to do for themselves—to guarantee a modicum of informal British control. Afghanistan's rulers, never compliant puppets, offered no guarantees.[21] The future, like the past, would remain uncertain and deadly dangerous. And so, the Great Game continued.

Despite Afghanistan and striking policy differences between the Indian government, the company and the Foreign Office, the British presence in the region had enlarged and evolved into one of political dominance from 1815 to 1842. Thus, the Ottoman Empire, the Arabian Peninsula, Persia, and the Gulf—and, to a degree, Afghanistan—had all emerged in the British mind as a de facto sphere, which inexorably resisted piracy and the slave trade as well as French or Russian territorial encroachment. With the notable exception of Aden, Britain rejected outright colonial acquisition and, instead, managed and defended its sphere through dependency treaties (Gulf states), collaborative dynasties (Muscat), and a guarantorship (Egypt and the Ottoman Empire), supported through international agreement or military force when necessary. Britain had certainly been far more intrusive in Egypt and Afghanistan, but in a broader context, by thwarting more direct European colonialism or expansion, the British had inadvertently ensured the region's boundaries and political integrity for the indefinite future.

Palmerston's golden age vision of free-trade imperialism, in fact, was not free but, more often than not, was paid for and held at gunpoint. Neither the British nor the region's Muslim population ever forgot it. The Russians were not likely to forget it either, and, as it turned out, they were destined to see it again, up close and personal. As noted, the Great Game had not been confined to Afghanistan's rugged terrain, but what was known as the "Eastern Question" had spread across the Middle East lateral of the Ottoman Empire to the Mediterranean and the Balkans. Here, the nineteenth century's cold war was about to erupt again, but this time no one saw it coming.

CHAPTER SIX

The Crimean War and its impact 1838–58

The Crimean War was undoubtedly the worst managed war of the century: logistics, tactics and strategy were all badly handled. On the surface it seems strange that the British, who had so much experience fighting in outlandish parts of the world, should have made such a muddle in the Crimea.

BRIAN FARWELL, *Queen Victoria's Little Wars*

Despite the Afghan fiasco, the British appeared to have tamed the Russian bear with the rest of Europe in tow. As early as 1833, after initial doubts, Palmerston, to the surprise of his colleagues, upheld the Treaty of Unkiar-Skelessi, which allowed the Russians to aid the Ottomans against invasion or revolution and close the Dardanelles to foreign warships.[1] Anglo-Russian understanding on this front led to a uniform view of Ottoman preservation. Historian Roger Bartlett observed, "Russia needed a viable Ottoman Empire and a secure position for itself in the Black Sea. But such a policy needed British help. It was not long before Palmerston began to see advantages for his own strategy in these propositions."[2]

To the astonishment of most, Mehmet Ali's curtailment in 1840 had satisfied both Russian as well as British goals. All this goodwill resulted in the Five Power Straits Convention of 1841, which forbade foreign warships in the Black Sea during peacetime. It undercut the need for the 1833 bilateral agreement and provided security for Russia in the Black Sea.[3] "Russia remained secure unless the Porte was belligerent. This compromise merely delayed a confrontation between Russia and the Western Powers."[4] Yet all appeared well. Unfortunately, events would take an ugly twist.

Continued tensions between Britain and France following the Egyptian settlement opened a window of opportunity for Russian Czar Nicholas I to press his luck and secure a more far-reaching agreement with Britain on his pet passion, the ultimate preservation or dissolution of the Ottoman Empire. A memorandum of understanding was finalized in 1844: "Russia and Great Britain were to maintain the Turkish state as long as possible, and, in case of its impending dissolution, the two parties were to come in advance to an understanding concerning the partitioning of the territories involved and the other problems."[5] More to their liking, the Russians took the idea of partitioning to heart, while the British interpreted the document to support Ottoman territorial integrity as, indeed, Britain always had.

After Russia crushed the Hungarian revolt at Austria's behest in 1849, Nicholas I, in a bravura mood, threatened the Ottomans for yielding to French pressure over control of the holy places in Jerusalem and Bethlehem in 1850. Russian Orthodoxy's collision with French Catholicism in the Middle East now ignited a national cause in both countries. The new French ruler, Napoleon III, threatened the sultan if he backed down under Russian pressure. In October 1853, Nicholas, the avowed protector of Orthodox Christians throughout the Ottoman Empire, sent his army into the Ottoman Danubian principalities facing the Russian border near the Black Sea.

Typically understood as a land grab, among other things, the move possessed a more traditional but often ignored Russian motive: This was an old-fashioned crusade against Islam. Nicholas determined to protect his Orthodox subjects in the Middle East, and the ensuing conflict championed that policy against the Ottomans.[6] He was "uneasy about the sprawling Moslem state which believed in the Koran and oppressed its numerous Orthodox subjects. Once the conflict began, Nicholas I readily proclaimed himself the champion of the Cross against the infidels."[7]

With that in mind, the Crimean War was on, the partition had begun—but Nicholas had misread the British as well as everyone else. Russia's close autocratic partners, Austria and Prussia, denounced the action; Britain and France, usually at odds, now shouldered together; and, at British urging, the Ottomans declared war and proceeded to lose their fleet to the Russians at Sinope in November 1853. Described as a massacre, the battle rallied Britain and France to declare war on Russia in March 1854. Stunned by the quick turn of events and Austria's firm warning to back down, Nicholas realized his complete isolation. Plagued with second thoughts, he withdrew his forces from the principalities that summer and sought pacification; Nicolas Riasanovsky notes, "After the first phases of the controversy . . . the Russian government acted in a conciliatory manner, accepting the so-called Vienna Note as a compromise settlement, evacuating the principalities, and repeatedly seeking peace even after the outbreak of hostilities."[8] There remained no reason to pursue the conflict, but among the allies, the pressure to continue the war proved relentless.

Several factors prodded the allies' decision. Napoleon III needed success abroad to support the prestige of his new regime at home. France may have lost to the British over Egypt in 1840, but this was a new day, and Napoleon III would never be cowed by Nicholas I over the holy places or his other Middle Eastern interests. If Ottoman partition came, it would be on French terms.[9] As for the British, they had just prevented Ottoman dissolution in the Egyptian affair by force of arms and checked the Russian phantom in Afghanistan. And if Palmerston had his way, the British would certainly do so again. Neither their policy nor their commitment had changed. This momentum, further propelled by Britain's fear of Russia, took center stage and energized the public mood: "We should not underestimate the influence of public Russophobia in England, often shared by high officials, which grew especially as Russia's influence in Turkey grew."[10] Thus infected, Britain's ambassador at Constantinople had urged the Ottomans to declare war to "teach the Russians a lesson they would never forget." Palmerston, now home secretary but never quiet on foreign affairs, utilized the public mood for his own ends. Riasanovski observes once more, "But in the case of the Crimean War, some evidence would seem to point to a desire to exploit the popular fervor to serve his ambitious foreign objectives."[11] He made his ideas perfectly clear and "thought this an occasion for blunt speaking to the Russians. He favored the survival of the Ottoman Empire, contending that its existence served British interests better than any likely successor or successors. As in the later 1830s, he argued that Russia would back down if firmly opposed."[12] But by mid-1854 no one was willing to let the Russians back down or Nicholas to save face, especially the British.

All the above factors certainly determined a course of action, but at this juncture there seemed nothing that diplomacy could not resolve, in view of Russia's retreat and bid for compromise. It appears something else had entered the picture that especially stiffened British resolve enough to override diplomatic channels and reinvigorate the dogs of war. But what? What in fact sparked this war, which need not have happened? At that very critical moment, a series of secret dispatches arrived at the British Foreign Office from their agent, Mr. Johnson, in Tehran. They revealed the existence of a secret treaty signed in 1854 between the Russians and the Persians for an invasion of the Ottoman Baghdad Pashalik (Iraq) and a separate attack on India. Such a plan, if carried out, would have wreaked havoc on the British. Agent Johnson had interpreted Russia as the mastermind and major player. These projected invasions on the entire British sphere from the Middle East to India, thus identified, made Britain all the more determined to crush the Russians militarily. Following the war, on June 14, 1862, Johnson's successor, Mr. C. Alison, sent the treaty's summary contents to British foreign secretary Lord Earl Russell: "My Lord, I have the honor to transmit translation of a draft of a Secret Treaty between Persia and Russia, proposed during the Crimean War. . . . The drafts differ in that in two of them the Persians undertake to invade the Pashalik of Baghdad, and in the third to march to India, a scheme so constantly upper most in their minds. He [Johnson] appears to have thought that Russia was the most earnest of the 2 negotiating Powers, whereas in these Papers Persia seems to be the more active."[13]

As foreign secretary during the Crimean War, Lord Russell would have read Johnson's original dispatches first hand and presumably shared this damning material with most of the cabinet, including Palmerston. One can only imagine the Cabinet's consternation and outrage at these revelations, coming as they did at the start of the Crimean War. Apart from seeking compromise with the Russians, in point of fact, the British redoubled their war efforts with a vengeance when an angry Palmerston became prime minister in January 1855. Rather than seek a solution to the conflict, he avoided peace talks and pursued this miserable war with grim determination before and after enemy forces were crushed at Sevastopol on September 11, 1855, and continuing until Russia's capitulation in January 1856. Even then, Palmerston finalized the peace terms only reluctantly, and in a letter to Queen Victoria he regretted that he had to stop short: "To have continued the war long enough for these purposes would have required greater endurance than was possessed by your Majesty's Allies, and might possibly have exhausted the good-will of your Majesty's own subjects."[14]

To some historians and contemporaries, Palmerston's attitude remains a mystery. "But Palmerston's reluctance to contemplate an early peace may still seem surprising, especially given British suspicions of her ally, France."[15] Following the peace his attitude remained obdurate. "Elsewhere in private he did not pretend that the peace was satisfactory: it was at best 'satisfactory for the present.'"[16] It remains probable that the Johnson dispatches—if he knew of them, and it seems certain that he did—played more than a small part in Palmerston's surprising attitude and the severity of the peace terms he imposed on the Russians.

According to Riasanovski, the Treaty of Paris, as it was, signed March 30, 1856, had a devastating impact on Russia's territorial ambitions: "Russia ceded to Turkey the mouth of the Danube . . . and accepted the neutralization of the Black Sea. . . . Further, Russia gave up its claims to a protectorate over the Orthodox in the Ottoman Empire."[17] Notably, "The Treaty of Paris marked a striking decline of the Russian position in southeastern Europe and the Near East, indeed in the world at large."[18] In the end, Britain had crushed the czar's holy war against Islam in the West, while the czar's joint effort with Persia in the East simply fizzled. Now contained and humiliated, the Russian menace east and west on Britain's sphere vanished. Again, Palmerston had succeeded, but at a great price; yet despite the obstacles, he had not pursued his war aims in vain.

In fact, from the beginning, this had not been an easy war to pursue. One historian notes, "The Crimean War was undoubtedly the worst managed war of the century: logistics, tactics and strategy were all badly handled. On the surface it seems strange that the British, who had so much experience fighting in outlandish parts of the world, should have made such a muddle in the Crimea."[19] Early on, the British fleet and supply transports at anchor near the Crimean peninsula suffered a severe winter pounding, sinking, or wrecking many of the ships and supplies. Short rations, near starvation and disease plagued many of the 30,000 fighting men, who were already unfit. The leaders proved incompetent, and most of the general staff, who had not fought since Waterloo, led troops who had never seen battle. Despite victories at the battles of Alma, Balaclava, and Inkerman, demoralizing and costly stalemate became the order of the day, culminating in the long siege at the Russian fortress at Sevastopol. Even the great Charge of the Light Brigade had been a mistake and took the lives of half that valiant force.

The French had supplied more troops to the war effort and, along with their Ottoman and later Sardinian allies, inflicted as much or more harm on the Russians than did the British. In truth, Britain's best troops, those from India, had for the most part not been sent until late in the war. Fresh regiments raised to meet a recent French invasion scare at home instead had been mustered along with the French to stop the Russians in the Crimea. Most of these raw recruits had no fighting experience whatsoever except in the streets of industrial Britain's great slums. Doubtless, their courage exceeded their manifest inexperience, resulting in greater slaughter. But their uniforms had been brilliant. It has been suggested that this was the best-dressed bad army in British history.

The individual most responsible for this fiasco was Lord Raglan and a class system that kept him in place. How could this happen? Historian Byron Farwell observes that the best senior officers from India, who knew how to fight, were not allowed to exercise their skills in the Crimea. The commander, Lord Raglan, detested the Indian officers but had not seen action since Waterloo and had never commanded troops before.[20]

Officers and men sent to the Crimea "were not those experienced in fighting Asiatics in the tangled jungles of Burma, the rocky mountain passes of Afghanistan or on India's hot, dusty plains."[21] In 1855, Palmerston overrode this situation and ordered Indian army units into the faraway conflict. Somehow, Britain's parade-ground army survived until reinforcements arrived and, along with their allies, won the Crimea. Lack of supplies and the death of Czar Nicholas I helped defeat the Russians, who in the end fared worse than did the British.

When the dust settled on the Crimean War, it again proved the obvious. Britain would flex its military muscle to make a point: Afghanistan to the farthest reaches of the Ottoman Empire remained unmistakably a private British preserve. To nail the point, Britain used force to crush adversaries, real or imagined, on four occasions from 1838 to 1856—in Aden, Afghanistan, Egypt, and the Crimea. Even when the cause of war had passed, as in Afghanistan and the Crimea, Britain eschewed the diplomatic options and went for the jugular, with mixed and sometimes catastrophic results. The entire region, again convulsed in Europe's power struggles, had become a titanic football arena for the major powers in the Great Game. Palmerston, who determined the British must win, whatever the cost, set the tone for British policy for the remainder of the century and beyond. No future prime minister, Tory-conservative or Whig-liberal, could escape this reality or the consequences, like it or not. The die had been cast, and the Eastern Question, settled for the moment, remained deceptively deadly as ever.

According to historian Orlando Figes, this war was much bigger and more important than most remember: "The losses were immense—at least three-quarters of a million soldiers killed." Moreover, and most ominously, it changed the region forever. "It opened the Muslim world of the Ottoman Empire to Western armies and technologies . . . and sparked an Islamic reaction against the West which continues to this day."[22]

The last casualty

The Crimean War produced one final and unanticipated casualty: Company control in British India. Less than a year after Crimea, the bloody Sepoy Mutiny erupted in India. Although numerous causes have been identified, generally since 1815 the Government of India, including cautious company officials, under pressure from home, had increasingly ignored or swept aside time-honored Hindu and Muslim religious customs and economic traditions.[23] Pressure to civilize and Christianize had become the fashion. A few examples illustrate the problem: Though understandable but perceived as an assault on Hinduism, new directives saw *tughee* (a murder cult) abolished and *suttee* (widow burning) outlawed. At the juncture where economics and religion intertwined, dislocation occurred as cheap manufactured British imports undercut the weaver caste's position in Hindu society.

Trouble in the military propelled by the Crimean War, however, provided the fatal spark. Indian troops (Sepoys), against their will and religion, had been thrust into combat on foreign soil at the behest of the company. It was Afghanistan all over again, and the company had learned nothing. Recently threatened with a free trip to the Crimea like their many compatriots, Indian troops in Bengal, already disaffected, rioted upon hearing that their bullet cartridges had been coated with pig and beef grease—a flagrant violation of Hindu and Muslim laws.[24] This proved to be the final straw. Clearly, the British had become equal-opportunity offenders. This final, insensitive blunder, although quickly retracted, at last resulted in payback time—the mutiny was on. The clash began with a revolt against the British garrison at Meerut in north India on May 10, 1857, and, shortly afterward, the capture of nearby Delhi. It lasted over a year and ended with the fall of Gwalior in June 1858. Company officials had received numerous warnings in the form of increased military turbulence and discontent for several months prior to the outbreak of hostilities. When the conflict erupted, however, they were stunned and unable to react, having sent most of their force to the Crimea. "The bulk of the mutiny progressed with the sieges at Delhi, Kanput and Lucknow and fierce fighting throughout central India in 1858. The hotly contested conflict ended with a finale of bloody reprisals."[25]

This religious and national revolt among Hindus and Muslims in the military led to the death of thousands of British and Indian soldiers as well as civilians in 1857–58. Britain's control of India nearly toppled. It was a clear warning to back off. But the arrival of fresh troops from Britain and the Crimea saved the day. One witness exclaimed, "When Havelock's Highlanders poured into the Residency, 'the state of joyful confusion and excitement was beyond all comparison . . . thanking God that they had come in time to save them from the fate of those at Cawnpore'."[26]

The British officers' decision to execute reprisals only exacerbated mutual hatred and disgust even after the butchery had halted. Major Garnet Wolseley, who later fought in Egypt and the Sudan, exclaimed, "I never before had seen the dead piled up, one above the other in tiers, in order to clear a passage through a mass of slain."[27] Field-Marshal Frederick Roberts lamented, "It was a sickening sight."[28]

Suddenly it was over. Exhausted and bewildered, the British slowly and cautiously regained their composure and reaffirmed their grip over the land. In the end, however, it appeared Her Majesty's Government had learned very little. Structural changes resulted, but the "We know best" attitude remained. As a result of the mutiny, in 1858, after two centuries, the operations of the Honourable East India Company came to an inglorious end. The company was out and the newly reconstituted Government of India, or the *Raj*, gained sole control of the country. Fresh civil servants from Britain replaced all former company administrators. Viceroys replaced the former governor-generals, and a new secretary of state for India sat in the cabinet. A select group of elite native rulers loyal to the British acted as an advising council to the administration. Most importantly, from this time on, India's British rulers could no longer be found among the masses but, instead, removed to the hill stations scattered throughout the country. The British had, in effect, created their own ruling caste. The cultures, thus separated, generated aloofness, greater mistrust, and a very uncertain future. Still, one fateful point had won the government's attention; British civil servants were scrupulously to avoid interference with India's religions, customs, and traditions, at least for the indefinite future. Notably, the British government of India's formal control immediately replaced the old company's informal management; the company was dissolved, the last casualty of the Crimean War.

CHAPTER SEVEN

The question of Egypt 1838–79

All classes whether Turks, or Arabs, not only feel, but do not hesitate to say openly that the prosperity of Egypt has died with Muhammad Ali. . . . In truth my Lord, it cannot be denied that Muhammad Ali, notwithstanding all his faults was a great man.

TOM LITTLE, *Modern Egypt*

Subjugation of Ali's Egypt: Shock of informal influence

British attitudes reminiscent of those that had provoked the Sepoy Mutiny had been apparent in the Middle East since 1838, but their application appeared more obtuse. With the exception of Aden, Britain's only colony in this region, Palmerston and company had projected influence on the wider area more or less indirectly through agreements with the Ottomans. In the long run, the London treaty, which assured the entirety of the Middle East and kept Egypt in the Ottoman Empire under British guarantee, propelled the British to invade Egypt within forty years. Palmerston's treaty cemented Britain to the Middle East and the Middle East to the empire as nothing before, with consequencial certainty until the end of empire.

In the immediate case of Ali's Egypt, the application of informal influence through the treaty impacted the country in short order. The abrupt results proved anything but benign. Here, one important piece of the equation remained: the reaction and sensibilities of the region's majority Arab inhabitants, who had remained submissive, silent, and without political power for generations under Ottoman rule. Like those of India, their voices rarely counted in Ottoman or British affairs, nor were they consulted. As pawns in the greater picture, their history, traditions, religious values, economic status, and aspirations had been and continued to to be ignored as inconsequential.

Sometimes spurred by force of arms, British intrusions into the Middle East and their debilitating effect more often came through abstract and innocuous treaties. These treaties between political elites took no account of or responsibility for the impact on the general population. As legal instruments, they projected the same British attitudes that provoked the Indian mutiny. They reflected political decisions, pure and simple. The human element remained unimportant to the larger picture since treaties never weighed the social and economic repercussions on the sultan's subjects. In the case of Egypt, Ali had disrupted the Ottoman process for decades until the British restored it through the informal influence of the London treaty. As a result, many of the same issues that would envelop India appeared over time to ignite resentment, resistance, and bloody revolution in these uncharted waters.

The problems began with the treaty of 1841, and Egypt was the flashpoint. As noted, the British treaty with Ali had closely resembled those with the Indian states and the Persian Gulf sheikdoms, but, unlike those agreements, this was Palmerston's unique masterpiece, and he left no loose strings. He tied Egypt and her pashalik legally to the Ottoman Empire and the sultan, armed with five-power support under British guarantee. In the world of treaty making, it did not get any better. The Ottoman Empire had been secured—all of it.[1] From an historical perspective, this pact proved monumental, with major ramifications for the British, the region and the further development of imperialism. Planned or not, the treaty drew Britain ever deeper into Egyptian affairs as a permanent stakeholder and offered a cover for future informal guidance or downright meddling.[2] By curtailing Egypt's political sovereignty, it provided the British with a juridical precedent for interference and, in the years ahead, outright invasion.[3]

On the human level, however, the pact proved immediately devastating. Britain's free-trade commercial advantage undercut Egypt's industrial base and propelled its imminent collapse. Historian Arthur Goldschmidt Jr. writes in *Modern Egypt* that Palmerston's commercial pact with the Ottomans impacted Egypt: "By limiting protective duties on manifactured goods imported into Ottoman territories . . . enabled cheap British manifactures to undercut the local handicrafts, thereby weakening and destroying industries."[4] Al-Sayyid Marsot states that the reduction of the 150,000-man Egyptian army to a tenth of its full strength destroyed much of Egypt's fledgling economy. "In brief, all the war-related industries, which frequently have been the start of many countries on the path to industrialization, came to a resounding halt when the Egyptian army was legally curtailed to 18,000 men."[5]

When all was said and done, a return to agriculture remained viable if unsatisfactory alternative for most of this labor force. On the other hand, buoyed by the recent victory, British manufacturers rejoiced, motivated by transparent self-interest rather than self-restraint. British officials promoted the idea that "Egypt was to be an agricultural country and to export her raw materials to Europe, where they were to be manufactured and sold back to Egypt as finished products. The commercial bias against Muhammad Ali (Turkish: Mehmet) was made clear by British Consul Charles Murray, who believed that Egypt would gain by destroying industries and importing all her manufactures from Europe."[6] This idea proved very convenient for everyone except the Egyptians. Egypt's cotton industry, early on, presented an irresistible target. Long-stem cotton, as always, provided one of the Nile valley's most dominant crops and was the crop of choice for European and especially British mills. Before 1841, Ali could sell to the highest bidder, but after the treaty, Britain trashed his monopoly and quickly dominated the market.[7] Faced with a reduced market and stiff British competition, Egypt's textile industry simply imploded.

The social downside was immediate and far-reaching. Overall, tens of thousands of displaced craftsmen and weavers from the numerous small industries as well as an equal number from the defunct military now fell into an economic wasteland. In order to support Egypt's revitalized agriculture, in the absence of options, some doubtless returned to low-pay farming, or worse, to *corvee* (forced) labor—a grim and humiliating prospect. On the surface, however, the agricultural push looked promising under British prodding. The cotton crop increased by one-third and revenues tripled, while steam-pump irrigation, reopened canals, and other schemes enhanced the Nile valley's year-round fertility and production.[8] Yet agriculture's expansive thrust offered no substitute for lost higher-wage jobs but instead only widened the arena of grinding, back-breaking poverty. Here, *fallahin* (peasants) carried the burden of manual labor with minimum pay, while small farmers, lacking titles to the land, bore the load of increased taxation. Some who tried to return to direct farming found resistance from Egypt's fragile land-allotment system, shared by 80 percent of the country's more than five million people.[9] Adding insult but surprising no one, cash crop prices plunged dramatically when the British replaced Ali's monopoly with their own, forcing many into subsistence farming.[10]

Besides those who suffered the most obvious deprivations, upper-echelon army officers and the young intelligentsia angrily saw their lives turned around as well. Ali had elevated a substantial number of native Egyptians into the upper ranks of his military, but when the treaty downsized the army, it also turned over the power of appointing officers to the Ottoman sultan. His subsequent mandate drove native officers from the commissioned ranks and placed the reduced army under the command of Circassians and Turks, who owed their loyalty to the sultan as much as to Egypt's pasha. Thereafter, resistance to foreigners in the army remained a call to arms for nativism, a slap in the face to Ottoman rule, and fertile ground for insurrection. "Thereafter the struggle of the Egyptian people was directed toward the elimination of the foreigners, and it was logical—however incoherent the events themselves might appear—that Egypt's first revolt . . . should try to secure the Egyptianization of the army."[11]

The general unhappiness pervading the land, following the British intrusion, proved particularly acute among Egypt's young intellectuals. Ali had originally recruited 339 young men from traditional Koranic schools for a European and principally French education. Hundreds more who remained in Egypt were trained in new secular state schools under French tutelage. Together, these young professionals, technocrats, and administrators slowly began to transform the country into a semimodern industrial society according to the pasha's vision. Whether Ali was modern enough to embrace some of their new ideas remains a question. Goldschmidt recounts an incident of a student who told the pasha he had studied "civil administration" in Europe. Ali responded: "You are not entering the administration. It is I who govern. Go to the Citadel and translate gunnery manuals."[12] As things went, the advice proved more than rhetorical. When the British attempted to turn Egypt into a glorified vegetable garden, the intelligentsia were left high and dry, thwarted in mid-career and their modernization ventures suspended.[13] In time, these Westernized Egyptians laid the foundation for the country's increased national spirit and subsequent societal reforms. Exposed to and transformed by constitutional and democratic ideals, they began to direct their energies against both pashas and Europeans. They, along with their military counterparts, who trained for ambitious and now eliminated positions, saw their expectations dashed. Removed from the focus of power by hated foreign influence, many soon filled the ranks of Egypt's educational system and produced an angry new generation whose sense of betrayal, like that of those in the army, erupted into revolution.[14] Unconcerned, both the British and Ottomans remained oblivious to the turn of events these social forces would unleash. All in all, when applied countrywide, the treaty's effect revealed no subtleties and spared few Egyptians. ·

Neither was there anything subtle about the punishing impact of Palmerston's free-trade imperialism when applied to the person of Ali himself. Intentional or not, it had been brutal. But was he down for the count? Some believe he simply lost heart and gave up after 1841 in the face of the British onslaught.[15] Others maintain that until 1849, as long as Ali lived, he contrived various means to curtail the treaty's impact and to stymie British and other European efforts to circumvent his monopolies.[16] Whatever the case, P. J. Cain and A. G. Hopkins in *British Imperialism* suggest it was all over but the shouting: "Mohammed Ali's chances of achieving economic independence disappeared. State monopolies were destroyed, military expansion was checked and Egypt's rulers were forced to rely increasingly on internal taxation and foreign borrowing."[17] Ali, in fact, had never borrowed from the Europeans. He had known better and had foreseen the potential disasters that subsequently befell Egypt and sought every means to avoid them. Goldschmidt notes once more,

> He refused to borrow money from the European bankers to finance his westernizing reforms. He blocked numerous schemes to cut a canal from the Mediterranean to the Red Sea, fearing that it would someday prove as dangerous to Egypt as possession of the Bosporus and the Dardanelles had become for his Ottoman overlords. He was sure that Britain would eventually seize this proposed maritime canal across the Isthmus of Suez.[18]

Instead, he tried to find a way to keep the country intact by "establishing a well-oiled and efficient administrative machinery that would survive his demise."[19] But he also faced one certainty on the personal level: His successors would succumb to the flood. "Ibrahim is old and sick, Abbas is indolent, and then children will rule Egypt. How will they keep Egypt?"[20] When Mehmet Ali died on August 2, 1849, the flood, indeed, came. His fears were not misplaced. His children and grandchildren proved unable to stem the tide of Europeans, with their investments, their loans, and their canal schemes. This last item, which the pasha most dreaded, was Egypt's undoing. Not only would the British seize any future canal, they would take the country as well. "He had refused to consider such a project because he believed it would incite the occupation of Egypt by Britain, and in this he proved prophetic."[21] William Gladstone himself echoed these very sentiments a decade later when the canal was first proposed: "It is England and no foreign country, that would obtain the command of it."[22] Yet Ali, for all of his resistance to the British, in the final analysis had won their respect. Officials of the East India Company and the Indian government already believed it, and finally the British government had to concede that Ali was a uniquely remarkable and admirable figure. British Consul Murray wrote to Palmerston: "The prosperity of Egypt has died with Muhammad Ali. . . . In truth my Lord, it cannot be denied that Muhammad Ali, notwithstanding all his faults was a great man."[23]

Ibrahim, the heir apparent, died a month before the old pasha, and Ali's successors, Abbas (1849–54) and Said (1854–63), simply proved no match for the avalanche of foreign newcomers. Foreigners quickly replaced Egyptians on numerous technical projects first begun under Ali, while others seized the maritime and commercial opportunities that European steamship and railway companies now offered. Foreign investors closely followed the technicians, especially in the urban centers. By 1850, Alexandria boasted a European population over 6,000, whose wealth and influence far exceeded its numbers. One Westerner observed: "Alexandria was well on its way to becoming a European city, more akin to Marseilles, Genoa or Barcelona than to Cairo."[24] Greeks and Italians constituted the foreign majority, followed by Armenian, Syrian, and Lebanese minorities, who immigrated to Alexandria, Port Said, and Suez in the mid-nineteenth century. Here, Muslims

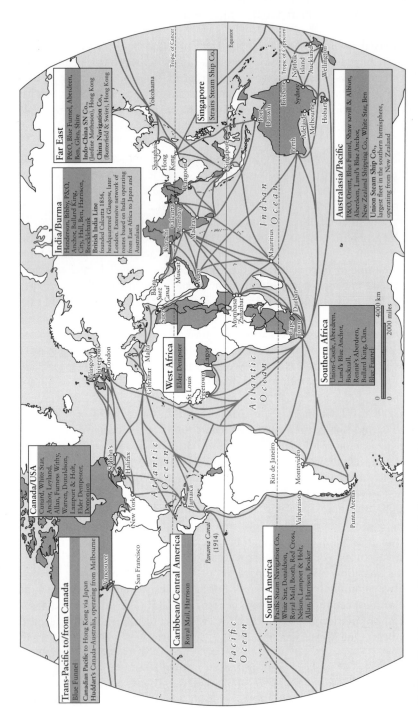

Trans-Pacific to/from Canada
Blue Funnel
Canadian Pacific to Hong Kong via Japan
Huddart's Canada–Australia, operating from Melbourne

Canada/USA
Cunard, White Star,
Anchor, Leyland,
Allan, Furness Withy,
Warren, Donaldson,
Lamport & Holt,
Elder Dempster,
Dominion

Caribbean/Central America
Royal Mail, Harrison

South America
Pacific Steam Navigation Co.,
White Star, Donaldson,
Royal Mail, Booth, Red Cross,
Nelson, Lamport & Holt,
Allan, Harrison, Booker

West Africa
Elder Dempster

Southern Africa
Union-Castle, Aberdeen,
Lund's Blue Anchor,
Bucknall,
Rennie's Aberdeen,
Bullard King, Clan,
Blue Funnel

India/Burma
Henderson, Bibby, P&O,
Anchor, Bullard King,
City, Hall, Ben, Harrison,
Brocklebank
British India Line
founded Calcutta 1856,
headquartered Glasgow, later
London. Extensive network of
routes based on India operating
from East Africa to Japan and
Australasia

Far East
P&O, Blue Funnel, Aberdeen,
Ben, Glen, Shire
Indo-China SN Co.,
(Jardine Matheson), Hong Kong
China Navigation Co.,
Butterfield & Swire, Hong Kong

Singapore
Straits Steam Ship Co.

Australasia/Pacific
P&O, Orient, Blue Funnel, Shaw savill & Albion,
Aberdeen, Lund's Blue Anchor,
New Zealand Shipping Co., White Star, Ben
Union Steam Ship Co.,
largest fleet in the southern hemisphere,
operating from New Zealand

MAP 2 *The Ties That Bind: Britain's Steamship Network.*

represented a shrinking majority amidst this newly expanded population of Eastern Orthodox and other Christians.

One additional element added insult to injury: Besides replacing Egyptians on numerous skilled jobs, many of the new foreigners paid no taxes because of special legal privileges known as capitulations. These extraterritorial benefits had been based on earlier treaties between the sultan and the European state governments. They guaranteed immunity from Ottoman law and taxation and later were applied to European Christian communities throughout Ottoman domains. Backed up by the treaty, Ali and his successors reluctantly decreed Europeans and other foreigners exempt from Egyptian state taxation. As a result, Egypt could tax neither foreign workers nor large foreign-owned estates in the Nile valley, while native farmers and laborers, however harshly taxed, could never make up the difference. The result was increased government shortfalls, which proved a growing menace to the state's stability. On a more personal and confrontational level, capitulations also exempted foreigners from criminal law procedures in Egyptian courts, whereas natives received severe punishment for similar offenses. Public awareness of this two-tier legal system more than outraged the general populace, causing hot-blooded resentment of foreigners and their protected status.[25]

To compensate in part for the loss of taxable land under the capitulatory system, Abbas and Said took what appeared to be a positive step toward improving the lot of Egyptians themselves. It ultimately backfired. Unlike Ali, they granted land titles to native farmers, who quickly succumbed to the pressures of increased taxation. In turn, based on the sale of their crops at monopolistic low prices, the farmers borrowed from unscrupulous foreign moneylenders. Overnight, indebtedness to foreign usurers forced many to sell their small land parcels to a growing foreign landed aristocracy of Turks, Armenians and Greeks, who left the natives on the land as virtual serfs, subject to forced labor and the whip.[26] Ali, shrewd as he was, must have sensed such an outcome and avoided ever taking that first step.

Despite these internal problems, which were unknown or ignored by those outside, Egypt had now became the destination for thousands of Europeans who either came to live and work or to transit through to other far-flung locales. To meet that urgent need, the British readily multiplied their steamship connections to Alexandria, to Egypt's Nile coast, and finally to Suez via canals and overland routes. There they joined Red Sea vessels on the continued journey to India, Australia, and the Far East. From 1847 to 1857, tonnage of coal stores grew dramatically at Alexandria, Suez, and Aden spurred by increased mail, passengers, troops, and supplies.[27] East India Company agents in Egypt literally labored to the point of collapse to meet the demands of this commercial and transportation explosion.[28] To facilitate this expansion, Englishman George Stevens contracted with Ali's successor and grandson, Abbas Pasha, in 1850 to build Egypt's first railroad, the Cairo–Alexandria line. Seven years later, under Said Pasha, the all-important connection to Suez on the Red Sea was finished.[29] From 1863 to 1883, British railroads grew from 245 miles to 1,000. At long last, George Baldwin's vision had become a reality: In the wake of the Crimean War and Sepoy Mutiny, Egypt now proved the heart of Britain's defense of India and the Far East, the linchpin of the transportation and communication revolution and the key to empire.

But Baldwin's dream, now reinvigorated by Palmerston's treaty, was Egypt's nightmare, and the nightmare had just begun. She had become far too vital to take for granted. If anything, Britain's thrust through Egypt to crush the Indian mutiny proved that. Could word of the mutiny spread and provoke revolt for similar reasons elsewhere, perhaps Egypt? Apparently the British thought so, and as a precaution, Indian viceroy Lord Canning ordered destroyed all company letters covering the dates of the mutiny sent from India to their various agents, including those in Egypt.[30]

But the immediate threat to British interests in Egypt materialized from a different source. During the years that Britain and France had fought together in the Crimea and the British had crushed a mutiny in India, a lone Frenchman, Ferdinand de Lesseps, proposed to construct a canal at the Suez Isthmus. Cooperation with France over Crimea was one thing—there would be none when it came to Egypt. Anglo-French rivalries and canal building in Egypt were nothing new. But at long last, these elements came together and provoked new challenges and unforeseen consequences for a British government determined to maintain Egypt's treaty-bound status quo. How far might Britain's informal control of Egypt be stretched and still remain viable?

Among other things, renewed British and French competition in Egypt would certainly put the treaty's elasticity to the test and continued to generate the greatest political changes in Egypt after 1841. Anglo-French rivalry had been an old story.[31] In France's case, her activities in Egypt can be traced to Louis XIV's projected canal scheme in 1665 and again in 1685.[32] Having failed, French efforts reemerged during the American War of Independence. Thanks to George Baldwin, the British finally awakened, somewhat belatedly, both to the French threat and to Egypt's potential for British commerce. Napoleon's invasion of Egypt six months after Baldwin's departure left no doubts. Even Britain's slowest politicians could put this one together. Miscalculations at the Suez Isthmus by Napoleon's surveyors, however, appeared to lay the canal scheme to rest—for the time being.

But this did not deter the Anglo-French collision in Egypt, which continued unabated throughout the reign of Mehmet Ali. Once again, the French gained the upper hand, supporting Ali's bid for independence. As such, France's impact increasingly surpassed that of any European power through control of Egypt's educational system and, above all, the development of Ali's military. Ali's French-sponsored military effort almost trashed the Ottoman Empire, and with it, a century of British regional security. As noted, Palmerston's treaty saved the day at the expense of Egypt's sovereignty, but the French remained—and they still dreamed of canals. The British dreamed too—of building railroads. They were good at it.

Ali, as noted, had feared the canal as a means of British control, but, ironically, it was the French who built it and the British who tried to stop it, and for good reason. By 1859, Britain had cornered the lion's share of Egypt's commercial activity and dominated the maritime traffic to and from Egypt as well as the overland railway system from the Red Sea to the Mediterranean.[33] But Britain's self-assured success proved ephemeral. Count Henri de Saint-Simon had renewed the French dream and in 1846 promoted a canal to upgrade Europe's Asiatic trade and to improve Egypt's general condition. A subsequent survey corrected the miscalculation at the Suez Isthmus, reinvigorated the project, and brought the French and British to loggerheads.[34] Saint-Simon's initiative prompted the British to outflank the French, gain a concession from Abbas in 1850 to jump start their railway projects, and secure British domination by 1859.[35] The effort failed: In a decade, the French had their canal.

Ferdinand de Lesseps, a boyhood friend of the new ruler Said Pasha, now championed Saint-Simon's canal cause, and on November 30, 1854, he gained a similar concession for his project. The *Compagnie Universelle du Canal Maritime de Suez* was now in business under de Lesseps's directorship.[36] The overgenerous terms gave 75 percent profits to shareholders, 10 percent to promoters, and 15 percent to Egypt's government. Egyptian corvee (forced) labor would provide four-fifths of all work. Mineral rights to adjacent land went to the company for ninety-nine years.[37] The British cried foul and, thanks to the Treaty of 1841, they insisted on Sultan Abdulmecid's required ferman for an international project that was not just an Egyptian matter but an Ottoman one as well.[38] This demand proved easier said than done. Since Britain and France now supported the Ottomans in Crimea, he wanted to offend neither and, therefore, did nothing.

In 1855, Palmerston, treaty maker and now prime minister, jumped into the fray. Already angered by a badly managed war in the Crimea and revelations of the secret Russo-Persian threat to Baghdad and India, he assailed the beleaguered director, de Lesseps. "I do not hesitate to point out to you my apprehensions; they consist first, in the fear of seeing the commercial and maritime relations of Great Britain upset by the opening of a new route which, while giving passage to the navigation of all countries, will take away the advantages we possess at the present time."[39] Despite Palmerston's uncommon candor, de Lesseps plunged ahead. In the years immediately following, the British attacked the project from every conceivable direction. They outlined the loss of Egyptian jobs on the railway and the detriment to Egypt's economy.[40] When they denounced the immoral use of corvee labor and again insisted on the sultan's ferman, the arguments turned against them. De Lesseps retorted that the British themselves had used corvee labor to construct their railroad.[41] Meanwhile, young William Gladstone, in parliament, argued that the British had never obtained a ferman but only the pasha's concession. He assailed the British argument as pure hypocrisy and insisted the canal would some day prove an asset to the security of Britain's empire. But he had more to say, much more. In his speech to Commons on June 1, 1858, he supported a view with important implications for the future of his own political actions in the region: "What is the power that would really possess the canal if it were opened? . . . It is England and no foreign country, that would obtain the command of it."[42]

Gladstone lost the vote, but the Foreign Office, at long last, exposed its fundamental objection, with a document revealing the canal's primary threat to British interests. Entitled "Insuperable Objections of Her Majesty's Government to the Projected Suez Canal," it pointed up the danger of French-held fortifications along the Egyptian coast, rendering the canal a French waterway. Most importantly, "The Suez Canal once made, Egypt is completely separated from Turkey and may declare its independence whenever it pleases."[43] This was the heart of the matter and of Palmerston's original fear. It would dismantle the Ottoman Empire, unravelling the treaty and, thus, Britain's informal grip on Egypt. Palmerston's anxiety proved well-founded, as events soon revealed.

Khedive Ismail: The Suez Canal and the failed dream, moving toward formal control

Despite continued British roadblocks, work on the canal, considered the greatest engineering achievement of the century, was completed on March 14, 1869, during Gladstone's first ministry, one year before the Franco-Prussian War and a year behind schedule. The efforts of Ismail Pasha, Egypt's ruler since 1863, were crucial to its success. He had overcome more British obstacles, gained the sultan's ferman, and at last, greatly relieved, directed the canal's opening with great exuberance. One historian recounts,

> On November 17, 1869 the inauguration was celebrated with oriental magnificence. Distinguished guests from all parts of the world were entertained at the Khedive's expense. The Empress Eugenie . . . was there together with royalty including Emperor Franz Joseph, Prince Frederick William of Prussia, and Prince Henry of the Netherlands. The British government was represented by Sir Henry G. Elliot, the new Ambassador at Constantinople.[44]

Almost overnight, the completed canal had rendered the British railway to Suez obsolete and would all but destroy the lucrative transit trade along with thousands of Egyptian jobs. Britain's frustration and arrogant snub at the project was obvious—a lowly ambassador amidst all that European royalty. But the snub proved more than symbolic. Although Britain's anger was understandable, her vindictive demands plunged Egypt into serious debt before the canal opened. "The Company should abandon its claim to free labour and that all lands on the banks of the Canal should be relinquished by the Company. Egypt was to pay £3,360,000 in compensation to the Company."[45] By the time of the ceremony, Egypt's total debt to European bankers exceeded £8,000,000.

Ismail quickly vindicated British concerns as he, like Ali, doggedly pursued Egypt's full sovereignty supported by military expansion and internal modernization. But unlike the old pasha, he borrowed from the Europeans to achieve it. Ismail's imperial ambitions provided increased spending for military adventurism. Positions again multiplied in the Egyptian army for lower-level officers, particularly those from the fallahin class. He hired British and American staff officers to train his enlarged army of 40,000 for campaigns in the south and east to create an Egyptian-African empire.[46] As a clear challenge to British interests, these thrusts extended Egypt's hegemony over much of the Sudan to the Nile's source and from the Red Sea to the Ethiopian highlands. Khedival appointees Samuel Baker, and General Charles "Chinese" Gordon took the Sudan, crippled the slave trade, and extended Egyptian authority into equatorial Africa. In recognition, Ismail named Gordon governor-general of the Sudan. In contrast, according to General Charles P. Stone, an American and Ismail's military chief of staff, the American-led Ethiopian campaign failed because of incompetency among the Turko-Circassian field commanders. During this campaign, known mostly for its disasters, an Egyptian lieutenant, Ahmed Urabi, became a hero by rescuing his battalion under siege.[47] His soldiers never forgot, and neither would the Egyptian people: He soon emerged to lead Egypt's national revolution.

Empire building and modernization cost money, a lot of money, and of course it came from more loans. To his credit, a considerable portion of Ismail's efforts and financial agreements had been successfully directed to lay the foundation and infrastructure for the modern Egyptian state, a truly remarkable achievement for which he has received little notice. Projects for Egypt's progress included more irrigation canals, new shipping docks at Alexandria and Suez, telegraph and rail lines, the Egyptian museum, the National Library and the beautification of Cairo. The London *Times* reported in January 1876 that "She has advanced as much in seventy years as other countries have in five hundred."[48] As Goldschmidt recounts, "These expenditures helped to make Egypt more autonomous and, in the eyes of nineteenth-century Europeans, more 'civilized'."[49]

Just as the British had warned, however, Egypt was inching away from Ottoman rule. The canal had liberated the Egyptian spirit and encouraged Ismail to grow more politically independent. He purchased fermans from the Porte for greater autonomy and the title of Khedive (Viceroy). In 1873, he negotiated expanded self-government for Egypt, including hereditary rights to rule the Sudan, in a bid for empire reminiscent of Ali.[50] Ismail could now enact internal Egyptian laws and decrees and secure independent contracts with the Europeans without the sultan's signature.[51] Egypt's treaty-bound connection to the Porte practically unraveled to that of a legal fiction, yet full independence proved as elusive to Ismail as it had to Ali. As he lessened the sultan's yoke through more tribute, he shackled himself ever tighter to the Europeans with more loans. Significantly, neither could Ismail escape the all-encompassing Palmerston treaty. It was a race against time, and Ismail lost.

In 1875, a great depression struck Europe and areas of European global hegemony, including the Ottoman Empire and Egypt. It quickly stalled Ismail's expansionist and modernization efforts and called into question his deficit spending and spiraling indebtedness. The wolves were soon at the door, as historian Eric Hobsbawm suggests: "It mobilized those militant consortia of foreign bondholders or governments acting for their investors, which were to turn nominally independent governments into virtual or actual protectorates and colonies of the European Powers—as in Egypt and Turkey after 1876."[52] In November 1875, sensing both Egypt's weakness and a strategic target of opportunity, Prime Minister Benjamin Disraeli quickly and quietly purchased Ismail's one untouched asset, his 44 percent Suez Canal shares, for £4,000,000.[53] Disraeli's move stole the march on the French and calmed the fears of British bondholders. Despite earlier anti-canal hysteria, Britain now accounted for 80 percent of traffic on the canal, which had become the vital, strategic link to India's imperial defense and beyond.[54] Purchasing the stock proved a masterful coup. Britain's hold on Egypt now became somewhat more than "informal," but it failed to solve Ismail's indebtedness, now at over £90,000,000.[55]

Ismail looked for a bailout and requested British financial advice. The end result of that process produced the Anglo-French Dual Control of Egypt's finances—a process that pleased nobody and angered everyone. Controllers Sir Rivers Wilson and M. de Blignieres now became part of the Egyptian government, including the Ministries of Finance and Public Works. "To all appearances, Ismail was now a prisoner in the hands of his predators. Wilson and de Blignieres, for all intents and purposes, were representatives of the British and French governments."[56] Ismail bemoaned, "My country is no longer in Africa; we are now part of Europe."[57] Egypt's own finance minister, Ismail Sadiq, protested the move. He soon disappeared, the presumed victim of khedival agents.[58] Egypt thus inched from informal influence to more formal management through the inclusion of the Europeans in Ismail's cabinet. Once this occurred, there was no turning back.

From 1877 to 1879, the situation spun out of control. Nubar Pasha, an Armenian Christian and Egypt's sometime premier, walked a thin line to balance the khedive's destructive ambition against the predatory appetites of the Europeans. His controversial decision to blunt European interference and favor their debts over Egyptian loans during a period when Egypt suffered crop failure, starvation, and diminished tax returns proved disastrous. On Nubar's advice, the government repudiated its debt (Mukabala) to native landholders, halted military wages, and again reduced the army to 18,000, while Europeans in Egypt's employ remained untouched and untaxed. As before, the crushing taxes fell on Egypt's farmers. As Sayyid-Marsot recounts: "Alien residents in Egypt were not taxed, merely because they refused to pay taxes; thus the burden of taxation fell on the unhappy fallahin who had to pay the exorbitant sums necessary to satisfy the bondholders."[59]

As usual, British representatives in Egypt appeared detached from the public mood and, indeed, oblivious to the unfolding human outrage—that is, until that outrage confronted them head-on. In March 1879, an angry army mob, forced to retire on half pay, physically attacked British Controller Wilson and Minister Nubar Pasha. Before the dust had settled, Egyptians from the wealthy and intellectual classes openly demanded a government responsible to the people. In a last-ditch effort to appease popular sentiment, Ismail fired the hated foreigners from his cabinet and convened a native assembly. Minus democratic motives, Ismail decreed a popular election to placate the growing national element that hated his absolutism almost as much as it did the Europeans. But it was too late. French financiers feared a declaration of bankruptcy. Already stunned and believing France was about to take Egypt to secure its interests, Britain launched a preemptive strike to prevent this threat, real or imagined. German Chancellor Otto von Bismarck, always the French nemesis, now joined Disraeli to lobby the Ottoman sultan to remove Ismail. On June 26, 1879, the Porte, in a telegram, deposed the "out of control" khedive, adding that "his continuance in office would aggravate the present disorders" and that his son, Tewfiq would replace him.[60] According to Sayyid-Marsot, "This was the second, and more important, act of intervention by the Powers; it sowed the seeds of trouble to come, for, as Salisbury prophesied, 'after having a Khedive deposed the character of non-intervention is not easy to retain'."[61]

Presumably, the British government had never intended to control Egypt outright, and a change in khedives would permit continuation of informal management, and, as always, preserve Ottoman integrity. Disraeli's Foreign Minister, Lord Salisbury, stated as much in July 1879: "The only form of control we have is that which is called moral influence, which in practice is a combination of menace, objurgation, and worry. In this we are still supreme and have many modes of applying it."[62] But another more aggressive current in British policy proved available if informal influence failed. Just three months later, on October 16, 1879, correspondence between Disraeli, Salisbury, and Britain's consul in Egypt, Edward Malet, revealed that, if necessary, Britain would divide the Ottoman Empire and Egypt with the European powers and, of course, take the choicest parts. In Egypt, this arrangement would have placed all coastal areas, telegraphic and transportation facilities, much of the Nile Valley and finally the Suez Canal under British control.[63] But the situation had not come to that—not yet.

Informal control with a new and amenable khedive had settled the matter, or so everyone thought. Regardless of what the British might do, there remained the assumption that Britain would take some form of action to further cement her rights under the cover of Palmerston's masterpiece, the London treaty.

Egyptians understandably viewed the situation in a different light. Here, Britain's pretense at nonintervention had failed to carry the day. In a single stroke, the British had destroyed Ismail's vision of a sovereign Egypt and collided head-on with the country's fully charged native, antiforeign populist elements. To the surprise of no one, except British observers, Egyptian constitutionalists and nationalists, enlivened by Ismail's dismissal, now rushed to fill the power vacuum to challenge Khedive Tewfiq, perceived as a British puppet. Fully energized, Egypt's disparate factions would move from social and political trauma to unified resistance and revolution within eighteen months. Years earlier, Lord Palmerston had thoughtfully predicted that the Suez Canal would doom Egypt to foreign occupation, and now a confrontation was clearly at hand. Yet neither Prime Minister Disraeli nor his successor, Gladstone, saw it coming as late as 1881, as the latter's evaluation of the Egyptian national movement suggested: "The most efficient of alien governments can never be an altogether satisfactory substitute for the least efficient of native administrations."[64]

But events that had long been unfolding caused a clash between Britain and Egypt. The long arm of Lord Palmerston's Middle East policy, in effect for forty years, now came to dictate events. By summer's end 1882, Britain had invaded Egypt and left the nationalist-populist-inspired movement in ruins. Evolving international alignments, alleged chaos in Egypt, and bondholders' anxieties fueled the crisis. Above all, the canal's strategic placement astride the crossroads of the British Empire, now threatened by a weakened khedivate under Palmerston's treaty guarantee, elevated the tension and propelled events to an inescapable and bloody finale. Alas, the British were about to push Egypt from informal influence into the grip of formal control—at the point of a gun.

CHAPTER EIGHT

The turning point: Invasion of Egypt 1879–82

Gladstone's action in Egypt is the most puzzling aspect of his policy. For the occupation and ultimate annexation of Egypt were contrary to his intention as well as contradictory of his principles . . . he desired to encourage and not repress national movements whenever they manifested themselves. The Egyptian adventure, therefore, violated the fundamental principles of his policy.

J. L. GARVIN, *The Life of Joseph Chamberlain*

Gladstone and Disraeli: A clash of views on the Ottoman Empire and Egypt

Britain's invasion of Egypt in 1882 was no accident, as has been normally understood, but was preplanned. The endurance of Palmerston's Middle Eastern and Egyptian policy made invasion a certainty, and it fell to Britain's antiexpansionist prime minister, William Gladstone, to fulfill that guiding principle. Britain's two leading political protagonists, the conservative Benjamin Disraeli, an imperialist, and anti-imperialist William Ewart Gladstone, head of the Liberal Party, had rarely agreed on anything—and particularly on the Eastern Question. While Gladstone disdained the Ottoman Empire, Disraeli fought to support it as the premier defense of Britain's Middle Eastern sphere and, of course, India.[1]

Disraeli had recently backed the Ottomans to prevent further Russian intrusions into the Balkans and Middle East during the 1877 Russo-Turkish War. Disraeli viewed Ottoman atrocities against the Bulgarians in 1876 (Bulgarian Massacres), which justified the Russian invasion, as a mere pretext for czarist expansion. In 1878, at the Berlin Congress, he called on German Chancellor Otto von Bismarck to support him to reverse Russian gains. It worked, and the Russians again backed down. Next, he upheld Egypt's tie to the Ottomans to prevent any future French encroachment and dislocation of Egypt—always a French goal. Keeping Egypt in the fold proved complicated, but again, along with Bismarck, he engineered the removal of Khedive Ismail in 1879 and replaced him with the more pliable Tewfiq. So far so good. His Eastern policy appeared intact. He had gambled and won, but, as noted earlier, had these efforts failed, he was prepared to permit the partition of the Ottoman Empire and Egypt between the Concert of Europe powers, (often referred to as the Powers) provided Britain got the choicest parts.[2] Had his efforts misfired or had the Egyptian revolution occurred during his administration, the history of the Middle East might have been far different. The Powers could have divided the Ottoman Empire into colonies, not unlike the partition of Africa in the 1880s.

Gladstone, on the other hand, appeared at odds with everything Disraeli stood for. He hated the Ottomans and supported Egypt's incipient national movement. In the 1879–80 election campaign, he attacked Disraeli in a fiery pamphlet entitled *Bulgarian Horrors and the Question of the East*, which sold 200,000 copies.[3] In reality, no one had known the actual situation in Bulgaria, which probably saw as many Muslims as Christians killed.[4] Disraeli's policies, however, proved vulnerable, and Gladstone made great political gain from the general public agitation over Disraeli's alleged sellout of the Bulgarians at the 1878 Berlin Congress.[5] Gladstone's Midlothian campaign and election year speeches, barbed with moral wrath, assaulted the barely defensible position of Disraeli, who, known as the "Most Christian Turk," stubbornly defended the Ottoman Empire. In the end, Gladstone won the election, but after two years he would reverse his position to support that very empire he so disdained.

Political slogans were one thing, political reality another. As an idealist who hated Ottoman rule, Gladstone would be compelled, nonetheless, to preserve Egypt within that empire by armed invasion for the sake of legal rectitude as stipulated in the 1840 London Treaty. He would guarantee Egypt's tie to the Porte as Disraeli had done before him. Most importantly, in view of his legal position, Gladstone would never support Egypt's national movement to the point of independence. Gladstone's bewildered trade secretary, Joseph Chamberlain, bemoaned, "In imperial policy on the Nile . . . the ministry formed to reverse Disraeli's policy became his executors by an irony of contradiction seldom seen."[6] Irony yes, but, nevertheless, a certainty.

When Tewfiq was installed as khedive in 1879, he returned the controllers, who soon decreed that 66 percent of Egypt's revenues fund the debt to the Europeans. This tactless move throttled the country's economy and halved Egypt's military. The action drove most fallahin from upper-echelon army positions now almost exclusively controlled by Turko-Circassian officers, which, in turn, provoked Colonel Ahmed Urabi's army revolt and the first stage of Egypt's revolution.[7]

It seemed certain that Egypt's diverse political factions would never come together on anything, but Tewfiq's policies guaranteed the impossible. Before coming to power he had promised constitutionalism and reform, then named imminent constitutionalist Sherif Pasha to lead the government.[8] Things appeared hopeful until Tewfiq's formal installation. Thereafter, he rejected the constitution, routed its supporters and fired Sherif Pasha. He exiled popular Muslim reformer ad-Din al-Afghani, then turned on the army. He reduced it from 18,000 to 12,000 and, with that, eliminated most of the fallahin class from higher rank. Adding insult, the controllers persuaded him to sell Egypt's remaining 15 percent profit from the Suez Canal and, with it, the last vestige of the nation's pride.

At that point, the country exploded. After years of growing alienation, Tewfiq had provided reformers, clerics, and constitutionalists—as well as farmers and the army—with a common cause. In May 1880, Colonel Ahmed Urabi, hero of the Ethiopian War, led the charge in a direct confrontation with the khedive. He hand-delivered army petitions to Tewfiq to protest discriminatory law against fallahin soldiers for upper-rank promotion.[9] Although not a grand event, the point was taken, controlled anger and all. The army's downtrodden fallahin had spoken, but, as it turned out, this bold move invigorated Egypt's civil and reforming leadership as well. They gathered strength on Urabi's coattails and within months united with him.

Fearful and resentful, Tewfiq struck back and on February 8, 1881, ordered his Turko-Circassian officers to carry out assassinations and arrest Urabi for court martial and exile. Assuming this was a death sentence, Urabi's regiment surrounded the proceedings and liberated their commander. Tewfiq's actions thus further galvanized the national factions around Urabi, who had come to embody the populist movement.

On September 9, with 2,500 troops, eighteen heavy guns, and a new mandate, the colonel again confronted the khedive along with Controller Auckland Colvin, past Controller Sir Evelyn Baring (Lord Cromer) and Tewfiq's military chief of staff, General Stone (Figure 4). The Palace Troops mutinied and joined Urabi, who, as nominal leader of the nationalist movement (Al-Hizb, Al-Watani) demanded Tewfiq radically alter and democratize the government. Urabi's agenda included the creation of a national parliament, the reform of Tewfiq's ministry and the restoration of the army to full legal strength.[10] Al-Sayyid Marsot observes in *Egypt and Cromer* that "Urabi logged demands that were couched in the tone of a nationalist reformer, a 'delegate of the people' as he called himself, rather than in the tone of an insurgent army officer who wished to save his neck."[11] Noting the full extent of Urabi's support, Tewfiq reluctantly acquiesced.

On September 14, five days after that seminal event, Sherif Pasha formed a new cabinet. In the fall of 1881, an Egyptian assembly (parliament) was created by popular vote, packed with Urabi supporters.[12] Urabi, however, stepped out of the limelight, took no government post, and returned to military obscurity. Nevertheless, as the country's singular hero, he soon would be thrust to the forefront of Egyptian politics. British and French ineptitude would see to that.

Astounded, Egyptians and Europeans now witnessed what appeared to be a bloodless revolution and the birth of constitutionalism in Egypt. "The incident had caught the imagination of thousands of Egyptians and was sympathetically regarded by not a few Europeans living in the land. . . . Muslims, Jews, and Christians—whose home was Egypt, were also united by what seemed the dawn of a new liberation of the new Egyptian spirit."[13] Wilfrid S. Blunt, British poet and nationalist sympathizer, exclaimed: "All Egypt woke next morning to learn that not merely a revolt but a revolution had been effected."[14] British Controller Colvin surprisingly supported the action and suggested that "The movement though in its origin anti-Turk is in itself an Egyptian national movement. . . . Furthermore, what gives a show of justification to the recent conduct of the army, and gains them support among great numbers of the more respectable Egyptians is that there is a great deal of truth in their complaints."[15] General enthusiasm quickly spread to the British capital. Foreign secretary Lord Granville stamped his approval in a message of November 4 to Britain's consul in Egypt, Edward Malet. "The Government of England would run counter to its most cherished traditions of natural history, were it to entertain a desire to diminish that liberty or to tamper with the institutions to which it has given birth."[16]

But what of Gladstone, whose support of nationalism was well-known? As leader of the Liberal Party and staunch anti-imperialist, his view of the Egyptian situation should have been predictable, but it was not. Despite his sympathy for Egypt's national movement, his comment of November 5, 1881, suggested something more ominous. He insisted on "the tie which binds Egypt to the Porte" and that "anarchy would not be permitted in Egypt."[17]

Recent European history had taught Gladstone that nationalism's goal was inevitably independence, which he routinely supported. But independence in Egypt's case would almost certainly bring in the French or the other powers, or so he thought. He faced trouble enough in the region having just concluded the Second Afghan War. But more was to come. In May 1881, the French stunned everyone and seized the Ottoman province of Tunis, which aroused much of the Muslim world in "a stroke altering the whole complexion of Mediterranean politics from Gibraltar to the Levant."[18] Gladstone could not and would not let the French gain a foothold in Egypt.

For Britain as well as the prime minister, the stakes were simply too high. First, 88 percent of all British shipping now used the Suez Canal route to India and beyond.[19] "The situation of Egypt on the most direct maritime route between England and her Indian possessions and the Australian colonies give to this country a special interest in Egyptian affairs."[20] In truth, Egypt had become the jugular vein of the British Empire, as Gladstone himself had predicted years earlier. Second, the transportation revolution created by the canal had generated the concept of territorial empire into one of flesh and blood for millions of working-class Britons, who, since the 1867 Reform Bill, had obtained the vote. Friends and family, drawn much closer throughout the empire by this technological achievement, voted to support an empire that had suddenly become popular and personal.[21] Gladstone could not afford to ignore the emotions of his electorate. Thus, Britain's continued dominance over the canal remained essential Gladstonian policy.

Third, European and British investments as well as contracts in Egypt depended on legal protection. Such protection was only afforded while Egypt remained tied to the Ottoman Empire as guaranteed by the international treaty of 1840: "Which further provides that the administration of the country shall devolve on the descendents of Mehemet Ali . . . Its prosperity cannot be affected without involving the material welfare of many British subjects."[22]

Finally, H. C. G. Matthew reveals in *The Gladstone Diaries* that over one-third of the prime minister's personal investments were in Egyptian bonds. These were not just any bonds but were based on specific repayment of khedival loans to the Ottoman government. "Gladstone's bondholdings in Egypt-had 2 Egyptian Tribute loans 'Turkish loans guaranteed by the Egyptian Tribute paid annually to the Porte by the Khedive out of Egyptian revenues.'"[23] Matthew's observation on this score is most important: "To have over a third of a portfolio invested in stock dependent on the credit of a regime whose deceit, untrustworthiness, and immorality he had so frequently denounced was hardly rational, unless he presupposed that external action would in the last resort require the Sultan and the Khedive to honour the loan."[24]

In the final analysis, an independent Egypt free from Ottoman jurisdiction or under foreign domination would prove unthinkable, if not catastrophic. Not surprisingly, Gladstone insisted on that tie that bound Egypt to the Porte. Everything depended on it. Within months, increased British and French pressure on the Egyptians only radicalized the national movement, which forced down bond values and assured intervention.

Bondholders' anxieties were one thing, but stress over French actions provoked another strand in British thinking equally dangerous to Egypt's national movement. Together, these two issues would turn the revolution on its head and provoke an armed invasion that would destroy the national movement. As noted, France occupied Tunis in May 1881. Although the move

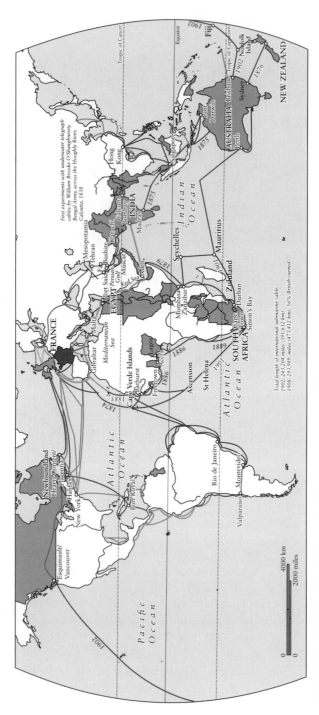

MAP 3 *World Wide Web: Telegraphic Communications to 1902.*

had no direct impact on Egypt, it quickly spawned a British reaction that did. There could be no retreat. Palmerston's treay rendered this inevitable, and it triggered a series of actions. Foreign undersecretary Sir Charles Dilke records the government's ominous response to the French move:

> On May 12th (1881—the very date on which the French Expeditionary Force constrained the Bey of Tunis to accept French suzerainty) steps were taken on behalf of Lord Hartington, Lord Granville, and myself to see whether, now that France had knocked another bit out of the bottom of the Ottoman Empire by her attack on Tunis, we ought to try to get any compensation in Egypt for ourselves. Hartington was to consult the India Office upon the question and I wrote to Sir Edward Hertslet, asking him to consider how we stood with reference to the dispatch(sic) of troops through Egypt in the event of (1) a rising in India, (2) an invasion of India by Russia.[25]

Although this cabinet discussion did not reflect an official British position, it did project a mood or tone on the part of some in the government in favor of increasing Britain's influence and posture in Egypt. Egypt had become the key to quick and decisive British action to counter active French rivalry, another Indian mutiny or a renewal of the Great Game with Russia. Significantly, these talks of greater control in Egypt transpired some five months before the national revolution erupted. Thus, the revolution, when it did occur, only exacerbated the tension and served to unify the British position as a whole.

Dilke also reveals that those discussions proved the start of an ongoing "Committee to consider the affairs of Egypt," which convened at the Foreign Office on July 28 and continued to the end of 1881.[26] Although the committee members themselves—Dilke, civil servant Sir Julian Pauncefote, Egyptian consul Sir Edward Malet and former controller Sir Rivers Wilson— were not top-level officials, they were highly influential. As a group, they spun the interpretation of events in Egypt that was so critical during the decision-making process. Pauncefote, a water rights legal expert, had astutely observed (and then persuaded Gladstone) that without an international treaty, use of the Suez Canal was legally valid only within the Ottoman structure—a critical point, indeed.[27] As Dilke reveals, "My own endeavors on this Committee were directed against increasing internationality in Egypt, as I thought the Governments of England and France would be driven sooner or later to occupy the country with a joint force."[28] As such, the committee represented a single opinion only, but a powerful one, which upheld British authority in Egypt and the use of force to secure it.

Egypt's revolution, meanwhile, gained widespread popularity. Though nationalist and antiforeign in sentiment, it remained constitutionally driven. Throughout the process, one subtle and inescapable fact had emerged: Urabi and the military were steadily gaining influence, while Khedive Tewfiq was losing it by the day. Yet Tewfiq's position remained essential to European and British control. While some in Britain and Europe rejoiced at events in Egypt, the question of just how far the khedive's power might slip proved downright unnerving to French premier Leon Gambetta. During the fall of 1881, which witnessed the creation of Egypt's first elected assembly, Granville sent Dilke as Britain's trade representative to meet with Gambetta. The premier had taken a hard line against the Egyptian nationalists to protect French bondholders. Granville tied the success of a free-trade agreement to that of diplomatic unity on the Egyptian question. To no one's great surprise, an Anglo-French joint note in support of the khedive appeared on January 4, 1882, and, with it, an implied warning for the nationalists to back off.[29] "The English and French Governments consider the maintenance of His Highness on the throne, on the terms laid down by the Sultan's Firmans, and officially recognized by the two Governments, as alone able to guarantee for the present and the future good order and general prosperity in Egypt, in which England and France are equally interested."[30] The note not only proclaimed support for the khedive but "for the maintenance of order and the general security of Egypt."[31] Granville assured Gladstone that Egypt's new-found liberties would not be harmed: "We wish to maintain the connection of the Porte with Egypt as far as is compatible with the liberties which have been accorded to Egypt."[32] Gladstone had accepted the note's premise. It harnessed the nationalist's activities under the khedivate. However important nationalism had been to Liberal doctrine, the security of Britain's empire came first. Urabi and his followers had to work within the durable Palmerstonian structure, a system lacking any democratic sympathies, or face the consequences. That message was clear enough. Just as clearly, the note proved a mistake. It backfired, creating the opposite of the desired effect.

Urabi and the revolution 1882

British and French leaders, still oblivious to popular sentiment, badly miscalculated Egyptian reaction to the note. Decades of European interference had taken its toll as outrage quickly spread throughout the Nile valley. Rather than strengthen the khedive, the note further removed the populace from whatever loyalties remained for Tewfiq and propelled the revolution along a more determined and decidedly anti-European course. The flood of public anger soon thrust Urabi into the cabinet as war minister and forced moderate Prime Minister Sherif Pasha's resignation for the more radical leadership of al-Afghani disciple Sami al-Barudi.[33]

Soon afterwards, in mid-January, a battle ensued in the Egyptian assembly over the budget. It was always the budget. For the Egyptians, it was a question of survival. For the British, it revealed crisis management at its worst. The controllers still demanded 66 percent of all revenues to pay the Europeans, which left little to run the country. The nationalists, equally determined, demanded a reduction of the debt collection, which would allow a revenue increase for domestic relief and restoration of the army to legitimate levels— a longtime Urabi promise to the fallahin soldiery. At home, Gladstone urged compromise to avoid conflict. In Egypt, British consul Edward Malet offered no concessions and gave no quarter. He rejected all compromise, conflict be damned. On January 16, Gladstone notified Malet's superior, Foreign Secretary Granville, that "I suppose we ought to make our way to a part concession."[34] A day later and more worried, he told Granville, "I see Malet says he gave the President of the Notables no encouragement as to a compromise, and perhaps the matter was not ripe for it. But if they admit in good faith the international engagements, as a preliminary, might not a compromise then be considered."[35] For Gladstone, the leading Liberal figure of his day, the political embarrassment was unbearable: "Think of Bismarck and the Turk fighting the battle of representative government against us."[36] But Gladstone had approved the note in the first place—there was no turning back. The old political warrior instinctively knew where all this conflict was headed. And he was right.

On February 7, the Egyptian assembly ousted the controllers and seized the budget—all of it.[37] For Urabi and his followers as well, there was no turning back. As a portent of things to come, in response, the British War Office ordered an immediate assessment of Egypt's military capabilities.[38] The moment of truth had arrived all too swiftly.

FIGURE 4 *Colonel Ahmed Urabi, Egypt, 1882. Print Collector. Getty Images.*

Just two weeks following the notorious budget crisis, a strange thing happened in the land of the Nile. At a state banquet in Cairo, timed with George Washington's birthday, dignitaries, including Urabi, gathered to hear keynote speaker Ferdinand de Lesseps. Chief of Staff General Stone, an American who detested the British, sensed the ripeness of the moment and toasted Washington's memory. Since many Egyptians saw Urabi as the Washington of Egypt, the implication was clear. The British were not amused. In fact, they had just labeled Urabi a military dictator. Most that evening rejected the British accusation—Urabi was a national leader, yes, but a dictator, never. Moreover, they already suspected what the British were up to—a reason for intervention.[39]

But British public opinion and the international community would never condone such action for the sake of bondholders or even the Suez Canal, unless threatened. Nor would they support such an outlandish move, especially from a Liberal government or Gladstone in particular. But they might back the effort for a truly righteous cause: the salvation of Egypt's liberties.

Recent events in Egypt carefully played into this scenario. Over the previous several months, the nationalist slogan "Egypt for the Egyptians" had permeated the land with an intensely patriotic fervor. Further, the joint note magnified the army's role as Egypt's protector, as did Urabi's courageous if naive response to its implied threat: "Let them come; every man, woman, and child in Egypt will fight them."[40] Malet observed in the face of all this popular zeal that the military had seized the government and communicated as much to Gladstone.[41] Adding insult, the Ottoman sultan, irked by the snub represented by the joint note, aided the nationalist cause and declared Urabi a pasha.[42] The assembly's ensuing budget battle and Urabi's popular recognition as Egypt's George Washington proved enough. Although not much, it was all the British needed, and they ran with it.

Trade secretary Joseph Chamberlain first pressed the idea of Urabi's military dictatorship when he sensed the colonel could not be guided.[43] When Urabi became Minister of War in January 1882, Chamberlain quickly marked him as a betrayer of the revolution and demanded intervention, justifiable to a Liberal conscience, for "the liberties of the Egyptian people,"[44] a theme Gladstone could live with: "Our purpose will be to put down tyranny and to favor law and freedom."[45] Gladstone then turned up the rhetoric and condemned Urabi as an "usurper and dictator, who betrayed the true aspirations off Egyptian liberty."[46] Before parliament, he proclaimed Urabi "a military usurper of Egypt's liberties," and compared him to the worst villain of all, Cromwell.[47] The London treaty had certainly dictated this ridiculous Urabi posture, and then Gladstone, who saw no alternative, talked himself into believing it.

Such accusations were disseminated throughout the spring of 1882 in order to separate Urabi, whom the British could not control, from the constitutional revolution, which the Liberals vowed to support. As such, the campaign to secure the khedivate as well as the canal and bondholders' interests was elevated to that of saving the newly-won freedoms of the Egyptian people. Thus, an altruistic goal supported by everyone was rescued from the jaws of the mundane, supported by none. The public-relations value was incalculable, but was it true? Was Urabi a dictator leading Egypt to independence? The answer is an unqualified no.

Unquestionably, Urabi and the national movement reflected a more purely provincial leadership and perceived issues from an Egyptian perspective. Its leaders never appreciated the complexities or dangers inherent in the enlarged international arena or its power to destroy their movement. As such, Urabi never possessed the sophistication necessary to distinguish between freedom from foreign interference, for which he fought for most of his career, and Egypt's political independence. At no time, however, did he attempt to remove the khedive or declare independence. But as Britain mounted pressure against him that spring, he was pushed toward the latter with all its incomprehensible and dire consequences.

An attempt to assassinate the colonel in April, in part backed by Malet, forced Sami al-Barudi's resignation and catapulted Urabi to the forefront as Egypt's de facto political leader.[48] Gladstone now determined on a show of force to cow Urabi. Admiralty Secretary Lord Northbrook ordered Admiral Beauchamp Seymour's naval squadron to Alexandria. France's new premier, M. de Freycinet, not wishing to be outflanked, dispatched a French flotilla as well. They arrived together at the ancient harbor on May 15 (Figure 5). Despite the increased political tension, Egypt at the time appeared peaceful to most foreign observers, except the British. Their pessimistic views, however, received no backing on the ground, even from the French. Historian A. Schloch observed that both French and German representatives in Egypt saw everything running smoothly without any reason for intervention. The public debt was paid and even had a surplus, while international engagements and the "verdicts of the Mixed Courts were executed without delay. Yet, British spokesmen, Malet and Colvin, reported that anarchy and terrorism reigned in Egypt and forced this view on the British public and government." [49]

Urabi again guaranteed full respect for all international laws and obligations.[50] Gladstone, however, remained unmoved, and Granville, not wishing to act militarily with the French, hatched one more plot with Malet to remove Urabi on May 25.[51] Instead, it precipitated another uprising to support the colonel, who took virtual control of the country four days later. While Egypt's assembly heartily approved the move, Gladstone condemned him as an "usurper and dictator." On June 1, he proclaimed in parliament that "Arabi had thrown off the mask," and resolutely justified sending the British fleet—three weeks after the fact.[52] In short, the ill-advised attempts to remove Urabi and shore up Tewfiq only emasculated the khedive's authority and bolstered Urabi's. With only themselves to blame, Gladstone and company now faced a product of their own creation—an independent

FIGURE 5 *British navy at Alexandria, 1882. DEA PICTURE LIBRARY. Getty Images.*

FIGURE 6 *Clashes at Alexandria, June 11, 1882. DEA PICTURE LIBRARY. Getty Images.*

Egyptian government and a volatile situation at Alexandria. The explosion came swiftly.

On June 11, a bloody riot erupted in the city when a Greek merchant killed an Egyptian donkey boy. Egyptians armed with canes and clubs scrambled to the scene and beat to death some fifty Europeans, mostly Maltese Greeks, and injured hundreds, including the British consul.

Citywide destruction quickly followed.[53] British officials serving as press agents, however, deliberately sensationalized the riot into a "Massacre of Christians by Moslem fanatics," but omitted the important fact that secretly armed Greek merchants had shot and killed hundreds of Egyptians.[54]

Alas, the government had struck again. This time, the Foreign Office and the Admiralty were implicated. In the weeks before the riots, Alexandria's British consul, Mr. Cookson, had conspired with Admiral Seymour to arm the city's Maltese Greeks with British rifles. When European and American consuls made the astonishing discovery on June 9, they condemned the clandestine operation. On the morning of the riots, the consuls met in special session and unanimously declared "that arming the Greeks was a most dangerous course and likely at any moment in itself to cause a collision."[55] British customs controller at Alexandria, Baron de Kusel, revealed this declaration in his diary and in a special report to parliament.[56] As might be expected, the riots created a general panic. Thus, the specter of terrified Europeans throughout Egypt, crowding trains for Alexandria and the safety of their ships, projected an atmosphere ripe for British intervention.[57]

The government wasted no time, condemned Urabi for the riots and demanded reparations as well as intervention.[58] As it turned out, Urabi had

FIGURE 7 *Egyptian artillery at Alexandria. DEA / G. DE VECCHI. Getty Images.*

been at Cairo with Ottoman dignitaries during the incident.[59] It did not matter. After the riots, the public mood in Britain swung dramatically in favor of intervention. Urabi had to be removed and Egypt saved. It was time to act. Gladstone belatedly looked to the international community for support, and on June 22, the European powers met at the conference at Constantinople. Gladstone met with disappointment. Neither the Powers nor the Ottomans ever backed the British view of Egypt's situation or demands for immediate intervention.[60] The British position proved too transparent. Britain's final offer, to intervene at the behest of the Powers, was prompted by a new a sense of urgency—on July 1, the conference prepared to offer Urabi de jure recognition. Three days later, on July 3, in desperation and unknown to the Powers, the government ordered Seymour to prepare for the bombardment of Alexandria and commissioned General Garnet Wolesley to raise an invasion force for the Suez Canal.[61]

The great deception: Bombardment of Alexandria, invasion at Suez Canal, and defeat of Urabi

Yet no reason for war existed. At Alexandria, General Stone mused, "Admiral Seymour will finally bombard Alexandria; and that if he cannot find a pretext he will make one."[62] He did not have to; the government did it for him. On July 1, Northbrook privately communicated to Granville: "I do not see the (Egyptian) gun emplacements at Alexandria as presenting any real danger where they are, but if we want to bring on a fight we can instruct B. Seymour to require the guns be dismantled."[63] Granville embraced Northbrook's contrived threat and on July 3 ordered Seymour to require that Urabi halt work on the fortifications overlooking the fleet.[64] Next, he directed Seymour to demand Urabi "dismantle" or "surrender" the batteries within twenty-four hours or face a bombardment mandated in "self-defense."[65] Gladstone ultimately justified the action based on

FIGURE 8 *British navy bombards Alexandria, July 11, 1882. DEA / G. DE VECCHI. Getty Images.*

FIGURE 9 *Battle of Kassassin, August 28, 1882. Universal History Archive. Getty Images.*

the threat of the Egyptian guns to the fleet, despite his admission that evidence from naval intelligence failed to support it.[66] After wrestling with his conscience and legal ambiguities, Gladstone approved the preemptive strike on July 9.[67] Seymour never acted alone, as some later maintained, but in response to orders from the top down. Alexandria's bombardment was no mistake or accident. At the very least, it provided the contrived excuse, a *casus belli*, to unleash the power of the British lion before Egypt's independence materialized. France, meanwhile, threatened with the new Triple Alliance at home, now wavered on the Egyptian issue.

When Seymour issued an ultimatum designed to be rejected, Urabi promptly obliged, and the French fleet promptly withdrew.[68] In quick response, at 7:00 a.m. on July 11, Seymour ordered the British squadron to open fire against the Egyptian batteries (Figure 8).[69] Ten steam-powered warrior-class ironclads fought for ten and a half hours against eight harbor forts manned with obsolete artillery. As expected, they proved no match for Seymour's modern guns.[70] Resistance slowly crumbled, and by sunset it was over. Seymour counted his losses at five dead, twenty-eight wounded. Egyptian casualty estimates ranged from 550 killed and wounded to figures exceeding 2,000.[71] Admiral Sir Arthur Wilson, then a young lieutenant, made this observation at the time: "Until their heavy guns were actually capsized or disabled they made a very good fight of it. They had in reality no chance of success from the very commencement, as only a few of their guns could penetrate the armor of the ironclads, even under the most favorable circumstances."[72] As British naval historian Sir William Clowes

FIGURE 10 *Battle of Tel el-Kabir, September 13, 1882. Culture Club. Getty Images.*

recounted: "Let it be admitted that the bombardment of Alexandria was no very brilliant or dangerous exploit. The place was not a Toulon or a Cherbourg, its defenders were, for the most part, not highly trained; five-sixths of its guns were obsolete."[73] In the end, it proved no contest.

But something had gone terribly wrong. Much of the city had suffered devastation as well. The British blamed Urabi, but eyewitnesses blamed the British "for the death of hundreds of Egyptian women and children who perished in the bombardment and in the panic flight from the hastily bombarded town."[74] As a young British ordinance officer observed, "Our gunnery during the bombardment had not been very good, and the town appeared to me to have suffered more from the misses than the forts had from the hits."[75]

Regardless, the British condemned Urabi for the city's destruction and used this argument to justify General Wolseley's already-planned invasion, which was launched in August. For his part, Wolseley referred to the episode as "that silly and criminal bombardment of Alexandria which Northbrook and the Admiralty concocted."[76] Gladstone still maintained, to anyone who would listen, that the British goal was "to save constitutionalism and the true revolution from the grip of Urabi the usurper and dictator."[77] So Wolseley's army marched on to save Egypt from Urabi's anarchy but landed at the Suez Canal instead, so as to rescue it from Egyptian forces about to destroy it.[78] The landing proved easy—no Egyptians were there.[79] Ferdinand de Lesseps had persuaded Urabi to spare the canal, which became Wolseley's opportunity to seize it.[80] Urabi's small force got to the canal too late and, on September 13, at the Battle of Tel el-Kabir, was overwhelmed by Wolseley's 40,000 crack troops (Figure 10).[81]

In the end, Urabi was tried for treason and exiled to Ceylon.[82] The khedive's tie to the Porte was now preserved under British maintenance as were the Suez Canal, bondholders' interests and Gladstone's portfolio.[83]

FIGURE 11 *Scottish regiment at the Sphinx, 1882. Pascal Sebah. Getty Images.*

France, as usual, got nothing. In the end, Britain rescued Egypt from the jaws of independence, restored "khedival constitutionalism" and remained to guarantee Egypt's "liberties" for the next seventy-two years. Britain's occupation of Egypt removed all the ambiguities and illusions of informal management as the country fell under the grip of formal control.[84]

While Sir Thomas Roe and George Baldwin had laid out a political and strategic role for Britain's presence in the Middle East, Palmerston brought this position into focus as official British dogma. Clearly, Palmerston's London treaty to manage the Middle East had emerged as a formidable foreign policy doctrine, powerful enough to redirect Gladstone's Liberal instincts to take Egypt and for future prime ministers to hold the region for the next century. The invasion of Egypt proved a seminal event for Britain that in the end would unknowingly have a global impact with dire consequences for Britain, the Middle East, and the empire.

CHAPTER NINE

Aftermath and the imperial scramble 1883–1914

Granville promised withdrawal in a circular to the Powers, and the promise was repeated 66 times between 1882 and 1922. But the condition was never fulfilled to British satisfaction.

A. J. P. TAYLOR, *The Struggle for Mastery in Europe, 1848–1919*

Once formal control through occupation had been established, the British found it impossible to reverse the process and return Egypt to informal management. As a result, no one foresaw a 72-year protracted occupation. The British saw this intervention as a short-term affair to rebuild self-governing autonomy for khedival Egypt. None in the cabinet, including Gladstone, envisioned a British presence of more than six months to a year to return Egypt to its condition before the Urabi revolt.[1] Gladstone's memorandum of September 15, 1882 specified a quick withdrawal of most British troops and the return of Egypt as a neutral under Ottoman suzerainty. His note also urged the immediate enhancement of local government and neutralization of the Suez Canal, minus fortifications.[2] Gladstone wanted no protectorate in Egypt, as his communication to Granville clearly stated: "We have now reached a point at which to some extent the choice lies between more intervention and less; and the question is fully raised whether we are to try to prepare Egypt for a self-governing future. I believe our choice has been made."[3] Most members of the cabinet who pressed for the restoration of Egypt's liberties also called for Britain's immediate withdrawal. Chamberlain anticipated a "British evacuation of Egypt in a

FIGURE 12 *British troops relaxing at the Sphinx, 1882. Otto Herschan. Getty Images.*

year or two at the outside,"[4] and declared that "With the tribunals reformed and remodeled and justice generally administered both to European and natives alike, and with the public service thrown open freely to every native of merit and capacity—we shall have secured Egypt for the Egyptians; and we shall retire having accomplished our task."[5] After four months, however, no appreciable movement appeared relative to Egypt's liberties or Britain's withdrawal. In response to parliamentary critics, in early January 1883 Granville revealed for the first time his government's vacillation on the issue. His reply to Lord Salisbury, a principal critic, offered no assurances: "I am asked to state the exact date of the withdrawal of the troops. . . . We shall not keep our troops in Egypt any longer than is necessary . . . until there is a reasonable expectation of a stable, a permanent, and a beneficial Government being established in Egypt,"[6]

A certain unreality pervaded the government's position. The British had taken Egypt by force but could find no simple means of withdrawal. One opposition member succinctly summarized the problem: "The facts were on record, and if it were an honour to the Liberal Party to go to Egypt and suppress whatever there was of free institutions, then by all means let them have the credit."[7] Truly, Gladstone and the cabinet had managed to deceive themselves that they, as knights-errant, acted as saviors of Egyptian constitutionalism. They had fought to secure the country's liberties from the grip of Urabi's tyranny in order to restore popular self-government under the khedive. But that analysis had missed the mark. With Urabi's destruction, Britain also had crushed the very soul of Egypt's democracy, since the spirit that spawned its constitutional vitality and popular assembly had become one with Urabi's nationalism and did not exist apart from it. Egypt's constitutional dream perished with Urabi in the sands of Tel el-Kabir. The London *Times* correspondent MacKenzie Wallace nailed the problem squarely: "The common theory, for which I suspect some of our diplomatic agents are responsible, that he (Urabi) was merely a military adventurer without any kind of popular support, and that the solution of the Egyptian question consisted simply in having him and a few of his accomplices shot or hanged, is now found to be utterly untenable."[8]

Meanwhile, khedival constitutionalism, clearly a contradiction in terms, reemerged as before—a lifeless corpse—and the new British presence soon eroded what little remained of that. Palmerston's 1840 treaty, now imposed through force, disallowed a free or democratized Egypt. Britain never permitted it. As a result, Britain's so-called reform of postwar Egypt's political structure only further diminished her dispirited institutions. Ongoing plans for the emasculated country's economic and political restoration saw Britain emerge as the indispensable tutor and Egypt the subservient pupil—and so it remained. In sum, when the Liberals destroyed Urabi, they exterminated popular government in Egypt—for the duration. Unfortunately, without a fully revived democracy to guarantee order and stability, the canal would never be secure, and the British could never leave. Finally, the defeat of General William Hicks by Muhammad Ahmed, known as the Mahdi, in the Sudan in November 1883 sealed the fate of the withdrawal. A greater British military presence now proved essential to do for Egypt what she could no longer do for herself. In the end, as historian A. J. P. Taylor observed, "Granville promised withdrawal in a circular to the Powers, and the promise was repeated 66 times between 1882 and 1922. But the condition was never fulfilled to British satisfaction."[9]

The Egyptian campaign, inherently different from others during the period, had been directed toward the Urabist movement's utter annihilation. Britain had thrust an overwhelming force to crush this, the first Muslim and national insurgency since the Indian mutiny. Why? Urabi represented an intolerable attitude that, if unchecked, could undermine British dominance over subject populations throughout strategic Muslim areas within her sphere. The government, ergo, took no chances. Forty thousand British and Indian troops far surpassed the tactical requirements to dispatch Urabi's force of half that number. Ultimately, his movement was eradicated, his army scattered and his name forbidden to the tongues of Egyptians for generations. More important, the British were out to prove an unequivocal point to everyone concerned and did so with India's Muslim regiments. On July 31, Indian secretary Lord Hartington expounded the government's position to Commons:

It was impossible to separate the interest of the people and the interest of the Government of India. . . . That the Government of India were, in fact, interested in the suppression of the military adventurer in Egypt, who proclaimed himself a hero to the Mohammedan world. . . . It is important that we should be able to proclaim to the world that we could trust our Mohammedan and Hindu troops, and that they were not merely a garrison of India, but form part of the forces of the Crown, and are able to support the policy of this country, at any rate in all cases in which the interests of India are concerned.[10]

As a result, after fighting at Tel el-Kabir, a predominantly Muslim force of Bengal Lancers was sent to invest Cairo in full view of its astonished inhabitants. The symbolism proved vital: A Muslim army loyal to the crown was willing to fight Britain's enemies—including, if necessary, fellow Muslims.[11] More to the point, Islam and revolution were bad bedfellows and would be dealt with anywhere the British held sway. As a warning, it proved both a powerful missive and a vast overstatement, which ultimately faltered.

General Charles Gordon, former governor of the Sudan, first raised the unnerving specter of future revolts: "As for Urabi, whatever may become of him individually, he will live for centuries in the people. They will never be 'your obedient servants' again."[12] In truly prophetic fashion, this celebrated Victorian hero soon would meet his own end against a subsequent Muslim uprising in the Sudan.

In fact, the threat of expanded Muslim resistance had already surfaced during the Urabi revolt. Not surprisingly, it also had been directed at the British, according to Egypt's Ottoman representative, Dervish Pasha. Britain's ambassador to Constantinople, Lord Dufferin, had received this intelligence and wrote to Granville and expounded on Urabi's wider influence in nurturing an Islamic League in Tunis, Algeria, and the Sudan with a substantial military force.[13]

Little is known of the Islamic Union, Urabi's involvement, or its exaggerated effectiveness and strength. In all probability, it did suggest an enlarged regional response to Western and chiefly British encroachment. As such, it only reinforced Britain's growing paranoia of the Muslim world as a monolithic threat to British interests everywhere. One thing was certain; several thousand Sudanese Muslims had indeed rallied to Urabi's call for war and died together with their Egyptian compatriots at Tel el-Kabir, "fighting bravely, hand to hand, with the British."[14] Was this battle indicative of more to come—had the British action unleashed a wider conflict? To their dismay, they soon discovered just that.

Britain's push into Egypt had provoked a situation further up the Nile requiring serious attention—the revolt of Muhammad Ahmed, known as the Mahdi, the "Expected One," in the Sudan. After the collapse of Khedive Ismail's Egyptian empire, nothing had stood between a politically divided Egypt, a fragmented Sudan and this emergent desert prophet except Urabi. Therefore, Britain's destruction of the Colonel Urabi realized wider implications, which were ignored. Urabi had been a secular national leader, but the Mahdi proved altogether different—an uncompromising Muslim zealot with a broader and more elusive agenda.

How had the Mahdi become so powerful? In the process of subjugating Urabi, the British had settled one problem, but they had unleashed another even less understood; they had tarnished the credibility of the Ottoman sultan in the eyes of the Muslim world. He had failed to defend sacred Muslim soil from the ravages of the infidel British, and thus had forsaken his role as Deputy of God and Defender of Islam. In response, the Mahdi stepped into the void. Muhammad Ahmed assumed the Prophet's mantle, asserted the sultan's prerogatives, and waged holy war in the Sudan against the British as well as Egyptians under their authority.

This totally unanticipated turn of events left the British stunned and ill prepared to rally a defense of Egypt's Sudanese provinces. As a result, Gladstone's government performed poorly throughout the affair. Under the watchful eye of Sir Evelyn Baring (Lord Cromer, known in Egypt as "Lord Overbearing"), Egypt's new governor-general, the British had disbanded Egypt's army after Urabi's fall. Thus, it fell to an almost unknown Indian officer, General William Hicks, to defeat the Mahdi and rescue the Sudan (Figure 13). Short of funds, equipment, or an army and minus government support, Hicks mustered a ragtag and poorly prepared force "of prisoners, pensioned officers, and mercenaries" to do the impossible.[15] British officials in Egypt, including Cromer, who saw the upcoming campaign as an

FIGURE 13 *General William Hicks, Sudan, 1883. DEA / G. DAGLI ORTI. Getty Images.*

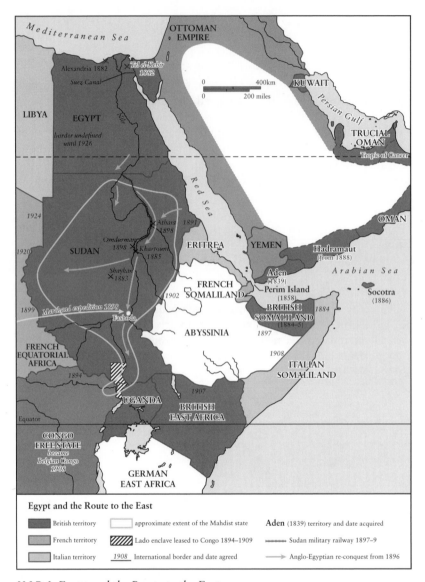

MAP 4 *Egypt and the Route to the East.*

unfolding disaster, were soon vindicated. "On 8 September, 1883, Hicks Pasha with 10,000 men marched out of Omdurman against the Mahdi. The news reached London on 22 November, 1883 that the entire expedition had been annihilated."[16] With the arrival of that news, Britain's announced military withdrawal from Cairo was canceled—permanently.[17]

The grave situation quickly worsened. Not only had the Mahdi massacred Hicks's troops, but his Dervish forces now possessed their weapons and prepared to march on the Sudan's capital at Khartoum. On January 18, 1884, General Charles Gordon was sent to evacuate the Sudan, or so everyone thought. Gordon instead rallied the Egyptian garrisons to defend Khartoum. When he became hopelessly trapped, both the British and Egyptian public rose to his defense. They demanded Gladstone send a relief expedition to prevent the inevitable slaughter. True to form, Gladstone hesitated. Delayed by further political wrangling, General Wolseley's expedition did not arrive at the outskirts of Khartoum until January 24, 1885—two days too late. In the city's smoldering ruins, Gordon and Khartoum's defenders already lay dead. Historian A. L. Al-Sayyid-Marsot notes the consequences for Prime Minister Gladstone:

> While indecision tore the cabinet apart, news of Gordon's death reached England on February 5, 1885. As Gordon, who was a public hero, could not be massacred with impunity like the unknown Hicks, a public outcry was made, and directed against Gladstone. The Queen rebuked him in an open telegram, the populace hissed him in the streets, the music-hall acts dubbed him M.O.G.—for the Grand Old Man had now become the Murderer of Gordon.[18]

As a result, the British abandoned the Sudan to its fate for a time but continued in Egypt as both liberators and now self-appointed protectors.

FIGURE 14 *General Charles Gordon, Sudan, 1885. DEA / G. DAGLI ORTI. Getty Images.*

FIGURE 15 *General Garnet Wolseley, Egypt and Sudan, 1882–85. De Agostini Picture Library. Getty Images.*

Five months after Khartoum, the Mahdi had died and, because of public outrage, so did Gladstone's government—the final victim of the affair.

In all, Britain's intervention had exposed treacherous currents in these uncharted waters. Urabi's revolution, a menacing Muslim league, the Mahdi's religious insurrection, and a hostile Egyptian populace offered a profound security challenge at best. Together, they warned of impending trauma for a government prone to ignore all but its own self-interest. As a final, unexpected jolt, shock waves from Egypt ultimately reached Britain's Crown Jewel. In 1885, India's Muslim and Hindu leaders, inspired by events in Egypt, initiated their own independence movement—the Indian National Congress. Consequently, India's connection to Egypt, envisioned for security, proved more precarious than anything the British had ever imagined.

Gladstone's deception in launching the invasion while the Constantinople Conference convened clearly undermined Britain's credibility among the powers. While Britain understood the occupation as preserving Egypt to the Ottoman Empire, the Europeans perceived the British claim to be a legal fiction and Egypt nothing less than a veiled protectorate. Hence, the gap widened between the Europeans and the British, who found themselves not so splendidly isolated in the coming decades. One historian observes,

> Although Britain appeared to restore normal relations with the Powers and the Ottomans after intervention, the assumption proved wrong. Britain's military occupation of Egypt in 1882, purportedly temporary, had no standing in international law, no formal recognition from the European powers, and no formal acknowledgement from Egypt's internationally recognized suzerain, the Ottoman Empire.[19]

Outraged by Britain's refusal to reinstate the Dual Control, France renounced her former alliance and vehemently opposed the British occupation. Germany's initial support of Britain, as reported to Granville, proved illusory as well.[20] Although Bismarck had earlier urged Britain "to take Egypt," he had done so to break the Anglo-French entente. Alas, Gladstone inexorably did Bismarck's work for him. In a letter to Granville, the chancellor's son, Prince Bismarck, now expressed Germany's reluctance to support Britain. He cited his government's mistrust of Gladstone and fear of alienating the other powers.[21] In the end, Britain's occupation not only separated her from France but left both isolated in the face of a new threat: the German-led Triple Alliance of 1882.

The strangest twist of all, however, befell the historic Anglo-Ottoman relationship. Unlike Palmerston and Disraeli, Gladstone abhorred the Ottoman government. As a result, the Porte's self-appointed deliverer had deliberately excluded Ottoman participation throughout the Egyptian affair. First, the joint note had circumvented the sultan's authority. Second, British restrictions placed on the use of Ottoman troops in Egypt compelled the sultan to refuse the offer as too humiliating. Finally, the occupation continued without Ottoman sanction on any level. Although the sultan and his successors helplessly acquiesced, they never forgot these affronts to their authority. Consequently, in the decades up until the First World War, the Ottomans drifted further from the British economic and military domain and ever closer to Germany and the Triple Alliance.

Overall, the period from 1882 to 1910 witnessed the greatest imperial surge in history—a direct consequence of Britain's intervention. Gladstone's attempt to preserve Ottoman territorial integrity had, in fact, derailed the century-old Anglo-Ottoman tie, essential to past security. Cairo soon replaced Constantinople as the hub of Britain's Middle Eastern and imperial defense, permanently keeping the British in Egypt. Whether the British fully realized their situation or not, the powers presently took full advantage of the possibilities offered by the occupation. In essence, Gladstone's Egyptian fiasco had precipitated the birth of neoimperialism by jolting the powers toward a reawakened territorial expansion throughout the globe. Now hamstrung in Egypt, Britain could offer few serious obstacles or challenges to French, German, Belgian, or Italian colonial adventures in Africa, the Pacific, or the Middle East. Although Britain remained militarily and economically supreme, the Egyptian affair had denuded her political and diplomatic capital. France and Germany determined to keep it that way and labored to hold Britain hostage in Egypt while dividing much of the Dark Continent between them. France absorbed most of North Africa (later French Equatorial Africa), while Germany seized colonies in Southwest and strategic East Africa. Meanwhile, Belgium carved a sphere in the Congo, Italy penetrated Eritrea and Somaliland to gain Indian Ocean and Red Sea ports, and Britain created the Uganda Protectorate to checkmate both.

France and Germany, however, the major players, were not congenial rivals but bitter enemies and had been so since the Franco-Prussian War of 1870. In 1892–93, France achieved a diplomatic revolution by forging a dualentente with Russia in a direct challenge to Germany and the Triple Alliance. From this date on, any overseas imperial clash could provoke a crisis and bring on a general European war. Such clashes were frequent and escalated dramatically up until 1914.

Though Britain remained aloof from either alliance, she was not immune from collisions with France, Germany, or Russia and the sporadic threats of war—all of which transpired in 1898. That year witnessed Britain's reconquest of the Sudan, a clash with the French at Fashoda, renewed nationalism in Egypt, and a check of Russian and German expansion to the Persian Gulf. All these events had been tied to new and more aggressive reason for protecting Britain's Middle East assets via Palmerstonian doctrine: to launch offensives to keep other Europeans out. As the wave of the future, Britain would utilize this daring and costly strategy in the two upcoming world conflicts.

Sudan and Gordon, the French and Fashoda

It had been eleven years since Gordon's death, and the time had come to set things right. Motives for the Sudan's reconquest proved numerous. Legally, this was still Egyptian territory held in trust for the Ottoman sultan as per the conquests of Mehmet Ali and Khedive Ismail. Moreover, Egypt's treasury, almost solvent, might be used for the campaign and thus spare the British taxpayer, or so everyone thought.[22] In addition, young British officers now in Egypt urged the campaign to avenge Gordon's death. What sparked the melee, however, was an event that had nothing to do with avenging Gordon. Word received in 1896 asserted that a French contingent had deployed to the Nile's upper reaches in southern Sudan.[23] This news provoked Prime Minister Lord Salisbury and the Conservative government to take quick and decisive action to retake the Sudan and, above all, stop the French. "Thus the Cabinet's decision to re-conquer the Sudan was a deliberate act of policy and the campaign did not begin haphazardly like so many of Britain's small

FIGURE 16 *The Fashoda Incident, 1898. Leemage. Getty Images.*

wars."[24] Egypt's legal claim to this territory proved Britain's tool of choice to reconquer the province and drive out the interlopers. It also proved the source of trouble in Egypt following the campaign.

In the spring of 1896, General Horatio Herbert Kitchener, Egypt's Sirdar, (commander-in-chief of the Egyptian army) crossed Egypt's southern border with a predominantly Egyptian force newly mustered for the occasion. After a year and a half of fighting and railway building, he remained 500 miles from the fortified Dervish capital at Omdurman and nearby Khartoum. Finally, in January 1898, he received permission to move further south. He now raced ahead with one eye on the Sudan and the other on the French. On September 2, his enlarged army of 22,000 Egyptian and 8,200 British troops faced the Mahdi's successor, the Khalifa, and 50,000 Dervish fighters between Omdurman and the Nile.[25] Several skirmishes, including one involving a young Lancer, Winston Churchill, drew on the main Dervish attack.[26] The climax came quickly. After a furious charge against Anglo-Egyptian positions, maxim guns and Nile gunboat artillery, 11,000 Dervish lay dead. British and Egyptian casualties stood at nearly 500, small in comparison to enemy losses, but deadly enough.[27] Kitchener's force then took Omdurman and Khartoum in rapid succession. Suddenly, it was over. At last, Gordon had been avenged. The Sudan—or most of it—had been retaken.

But that exhilarating moment had been tarnished before the fact when Prime Minister Salisbury's note of August 2 reached Cromer in Cairo: "Her Majesty's Government have decided that at Khartoum the British and Egyptian flags should be hoisted side by side . . . to emphasize the fact that Her Majesty's Government consider that they have a predominant voice in all matters connected with the Soudan."[28]

Salisbury would have his way. Hence, on September 3, Egypt's banner and the Union Jack flew together above Khartoum. Although meant to forewarn the French, it infuriated the Egyptians. They understood at last who ruled Egypt and, now, the Sudan. This pointless humiliation spelled trouble.

Within a few days, the British were also furious but for a different reason. News had reached the Foreign Office that on September 1, a French force had intersected the Nile at Fashoda, some 400 miles south of Khartoum—one day before the victory at Omdurman. Salisbury heatedly responded, "The former territories of the Khalifa had passed to Britain and Egypt 'by right of conquest'; this right was not 'open to discussion'."[29] At Fashoda, Captain J. B. Marchand with seven Frenchmen and 120 Senegalese riflemen made their own statement and waited for reinforcements. They never arrived, but Kitchener did on September 19, backed by elements of the Anglo-Egyptian army that had just taken the Sudan.[30] Thus ensued a classic imperial standoff that could lead to war. To avoid an incident, Kitchener raised the Egyptian flag alone to allow time for diplomacy to settle the matter. Egypt and the Sudan were perceived as vulnerable without control of the Upper Nile, and Fashoda, as part of the Sudan, guaranteed that control. France had arguments but no army; Britain had the army and, therefore, needed no arguments—time was on its side. Britain's ambassador to Paris, Sir Edmund Monson, offered France no concessions: "I said to His Excellency that I must tell him very frankly that the situation on the Upper Nile is a dangerous one. . . . I was right that I should state to him categorically that they would not consent to a compromise on this point."[31] The French hoped to negotiate, but some in Salisbury's cabinet demanded war to deal with the French for good and all to settle this century-old rivalry. Britain immediately bolstered her Mediterranean fleet to take on the French and her Russian ally as the two protagonists drew to the brink of conflict with widening potential.[32] But Salisbury wanted no war, only Fashoda, and Queen Victoria backed him. She had just celebrated her Diamond Jubilee. Her empire covered a fourth of the globe, and she would have her way. The cabinet hawks backed down, and, minus supplies, Marchand backed out. He left Fashoda at the end of October. Four days after the fact, on November 3, 1898, embarrassed by the obvious, the French government ordered his official withdrawal.[33] Cooler heads soon prevailed in both governments, and in March 1899 an Anglo-French declaration divided portions of the greater Sudan between them. Basically, France got the desert, a lot of it, and Britain took the Nile basin and with it, Fashoda.[34]

But this did not end the matter. Battered and shaken by the Boer War (1899–1901) and Queen Victoria's death in 1901, Britain needed a friend, as did France, who faced increased hostility from her powerful German neighbor. At last, in 1904, both countries buried long-held animosities and signed the Entente Cordiale for mutual advantage. This agreement did not come a moment too soon. In 1905, France collided with Germany in the First Moroccan Crisis, while her Russian ally suffered catastrophic defeat in the Russo-Japanese War. Fearful of greater dangers, Britain, France, and Russia drew closer and forged the Triple Entente in 1907 for collective defense. In all, the world had changed, and the great British Empire, now at its height, seemed somehow less secure, prompting Britain to grasp her far-flung domains, including Egypt, ever more tightly.

All this proved bad news for the Egyptians who also needed a friend and had hoped to use the French lever to oust the British. It was not to be. When Britain decided to retake the Sudan and curtail the French, they did so by utilizing Egypt's claim to the territory, itself won through right of earlier Egyptian conquests. Without this tool, the British action would have been without merit, legal, or otherwise. Moreover, Egyptians comprised the bulk of the campaign's fighting force in 1896–98, while Egypt's treasury provided about £1,500,000 to support the effort.[35] In the end, the Egyptians knew they had been cheated. Historian Muhammad Zayid writes in *Egypt's Struggle for Independence*, "They felt they were deceived by the British government. Though they had supplied the main body of the army, plus the greater part of the expenses and the historical title for the conquest of the Sudan, the actual control of the Sudan was to be vested in a British Governor-General."[36] Adding insult, Egypt's victorious army was shortly reduced by half, presumably a disposable threat to British security.[37]

Whatever political capital and goodwill the British had accumulated in Egypt through their efforts in public health, education, agriculture, and financial security they needlessly squandered by these thoughtless decisions. It remained an occupation, lest anyone forget, and no one did. Tension grew and, with it, a revitalized national movement, financed by Tewfiq's successor, Khedive Abbas, and led by fiery orator Mustafa Kamil. Both had counted on French support, which, in the end, faltered after Fashoda and faded entirely with the Dual Entente.[38] The movement continued nonetheless and proved at once both popular but divided. Some elements supported wider pro-Ottoman and pan-Islamic goals, while others backed an exclusively Egyptian agenda, but together they agreed: Britain must go. Its leaders attacked the

British in speeches and the press, until 1906, when two incidents ruptured what remained of Britain's fragile relations with Egypt.

First came the Taba affair, in which the Ottomans built a fort in Egyptian territory guaranteed by Britain, in the Sinai near the Gulf of Aqaba. The majority of Egypt's nationalists, with pan-Islamic sympathies, supported the Ottoman move as a challenge to the British. Other nationalists viewed the fort as an infringement of Egypt's sovereignty, the British and Ottomans be damned. The nationalist cause was clearly divided when Khedive Abbas solicited British support to thwart the Ottomans, while Kamil backed the Ottoman claim as part of his greater pan-Islamic vision. Ultimately, a British naval force and a subsequent demarcation line settled the dispute between the British and Ottomans but not between the two nationalist groups. They nevertheless soon found common cause in a second, more disturbing incident involving the British.[39]

With tensions already high, a British military court executed four farmers from Dinshaway, a Nile delta village, for the alleged murder of a British soldier. This brutal act galvanized every Egyptian, of whatever political and religious persuasion, in a way not seen since 1882 to demand a British ouster.[40] In consequence, Cromer resigned in 1907, nationalist anti-British parties proliferated and new leaders emerged, including Said Zaghlul, future champion of Egyptian independence. International and domestic pressure demanded withdrawal or radical change. Elections in Britain again carried the Liberals to power. They replaced Cromer with Sir Eldon Gorst to reform British administration in a country now more vital than ever to British imperial security.[41] Since reform proved no substitute for withdrawal, tension, nationalism, and repression escalated in Egypt up until the eve of the First World War.

The Kuwait "protectorate" 1898–1914

While the Europeans busily divided Africa, the British received another jolt when the Russians proposed a railway to the Persian Gulf in 1898. Russia and the Eastern Question had emerged again, and the British, as usual, determined to prevent it by any means available, including through support for a similar German scheme.[42] This had been "old school" thinking, but some in the government saw the newer and greater threat as German rather than Russian. "Joseph Chamberlain, for instance, successfully mobilized opinion against his cabinet colleagues and the War Office when they were tempted to welcome the German-inspired Berlin to Baghdad Railway as a potential obstacle to Russian penetration of the Middle East."[43] It soon became clear that either power on the Gulf could menace what the British had come to perceive as their private preserve. An Admiralty communication to the Foreign Office stated, "It would be a great blow to our prestige in the Gulf were any other Power allowed to acquire the Port of Kuwait."[44] Their decision to roadblock both projects resulted in the creation of the Kuwait Protectorate, the obvious terminus of any projected railway to the Gulf.

After negotiations with Britain's resident in the Persian Gulf, Colonel M. J. Meade, Sheikh Mubarak of Kuwait signed an agreement on January 23, 1899, making the Sheikhdom a British protectorate.[45] Final approval came from the Government of India and the Foreign Office. Two clauses proved significant. One bound the sheikh not to receive the representatives of any foreign power, which was standard, but the second committed the British government to protect his family's property in the Ottoman Empire, since the Ottomans still claimed jurisdiction over Kuwait.[46] According to the Porte's view, Kuwait had been and remained part of the Ottoman province of Iraq (Mesopotamia or the Baghdad Pashalik). Significantly, remnants of that dispute continue to the present. Almost at once, the British realized the potential for greater conflict. They had committed to protect the sheikhdom from the "Turks, Germans, and Russians, but also from Rival Arab Sheikhdoms including the Saudis, who were about to invade Kuwait in 1900."[47] Fortunately, the threat dissipated. After further discussions with the British, Mubarak developed better relations with the Ottoman government, whom he recognized as quasi-sovereign, and the British protectorate remained informal rather than formal. To ensure his commitment, Britain, under top-secret conditions, pledged him an annual subsidy.[48] From 1880 to 1892, such agreements had already been reached between Britain and the other Gulf sheikhdoms at Bahrain, Qatar, Muscat, Aden, and the Red Sea.[49] One basic difference separated Kuwait from the others: "All Turkish claims to Bahrain (etc.), which are under the protection of the Queen of England, are totally inadmissable."[50] Yet at Kuwait, a double jurisdiction might be recognized. Lord Landsdowne, Salisbury's foreign secretary and former Indian viceroy, urged a much stronger political stance. On March 21, 1902, he indicated that he had no wish to make the Persian Gulf into "a British lake", but that Britain should be understood as the "predominate Power in Southern Persia and the Persian Gulf."[51]

Meanwhile, the Russian project had folded, but the Germans, together with the Ottoman government, continued to press their efforts. Despite Landsdowne's stance, certain ambiguities lingered relative to Kuwait's status, but the British prepared to defend Kuwait and, whatever the case, to "shoot first and ask questions later."[52] Germany stated that the formal protectorate was a violation of the 1878 Treaty of Berlin.[53] The British responded that they never intended "formal" status but would defend the sheikh if the Turks forced the issue.[54] Formal or informal, the British would protect Mubarak's sheikhdom and, thereby, their own position in the Gulf. To drive home the point, Britain sent Political Agent Major S. B. Knox to Kuwait in 1905, "whose right to be there was absolute." In order to avoid conflict, however, "he was withdrawn periodically so as not to offend the Porte."[55] In short, Britain's legal position was so obscure they were not sure what to do.

One thing was not obscure: German determination to complete the Berlin to Baghdad Railway with extensions to Basra and the Gulf, regardless of British obstacles. Ironically, the German scheme had been based on the 1835 British Euphrates Expedition, a venture ultimately abandoned in the 1880s because of the expenses of the Egyptian campaign.[56] An Indian Office note stated "That is where the Germans stepped in since the British had alienated the Turkish Government. From 1888 to 1903 the Germans secured Concessions for the enterprise."[57]

Now desperate, the government looked to options other than force. One way to control or restrict the project was to buy into it. In June 1906, Lord Landsdowne offered such a scheme to the Germans. Britain, France, and Germany would each have 25 percent of the shares; the remainder would be divided between 15 percent to minor nations and 10 percent to the Anatolian Railway Company.[58] Indian secretary Viscount Morley shared a similar view. "If we hold ourselves aloof and take no part in the railway, the line will be completed, at any rate to Baghdad without us. Our refusal or unwillingness to participate in the line will lead to ill-feeling against us, and to the consequent detriment of our trade in those parts."[59] Both the British press and the Board of Trade, however, turned against the scheme, stating that "It would destroy the virtual British trade monopoly in the region."[60] The government withdrew its support. Again, on December 18, the very resourceful Indian secretary warned the government that the railway would be completed, and if Britain was not involved it would be a disaster. "Best thing is to control the waterways—secure monopoly of river traffic south of Baghdad on Tigris and Euphrates. No need to get involved with the RR at all. If you control the outlets—you control the traffic, without the heavy investment. If not, then need to control southern links of the RR."[61]

After six more years and the German project dragging, the British negotiated a convention with the Ottomans in May 1913, which gave the British position some protection. First, the British no longer recognized Ottoman suzerainty or sovereignty over Kuwait. "But as the important thing is the rights actually secured for Koweit and renounced by Turkey in the rest of the Convention. . . . That Koweit 'est un caza autonome de l'Empire Ottoman'" (an autonomous Ottoman province).[62] The second article of the convention prohibited Ottoman interference with Kuwait's internal or foreign affairs. The third specified that if the railway terminus was to end at Kuwait, it could only do so on conditions agreed to by the British government—so the terminus could not fall into foreign hands. Articles 10–13 evicted the Turks completely from Qatar and Bahrain.[63]

In early 1914, Britain and Germany reached their own agreement—for the moment. "In the event, the slow progress made by the Baghdad railway lowered anxiety levels in the Foreign Office. . . . The outcome, the Anglo-German convention of 1914, was a satisfactory compromise which confirmed Britain's position in Mesopotamia and the Persian Gulf."[64] Thereafter, the strange sight of Kuwaiti, British, and Ottoman flags all fluttering over the

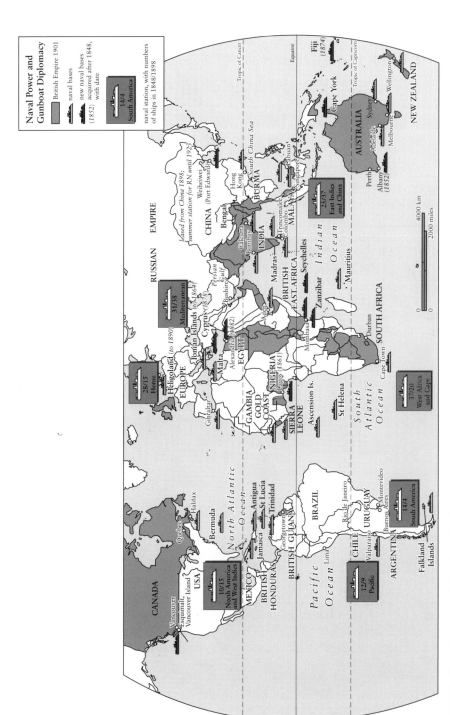

MAP 5 *Naval Power and Gunboat Diplomacy.*

tiny Persian Gulf sheikhdom ceased. In the end, the railway never made it to the Gulf, and the Ottoman banner disappeared from Kuwait forever.

Toward the end of the First World War, an article appeared in the October 1917 edition of the British *Quarterly Review* and was reprinted for limited circulation by the Government of India. It provided an alarming summary of prewar German plans and goals relative to the Middle East based on the German literature then available. It revealed why the British might have reacted to the Berlin to Baghdad Railway with such an emotional and determined response. An India Office abridged version reviews its salient points. "The first is occupied with the subject of a central European agglomerate stretching from the Baltic and the North Sea to Constantinople, and thence dominating Asia to the Suez Canal and the Persian Gulf . . . as a wedge to split the British Empire." Moreover, this is where "England's supremacy and the Pax Britannica must be broken."[65] This could all be accomplished with the completion of the Berlin to Baghdad Railway to the Gulf.

The article furnished British analysts with a somber reminder of their apprehensions of German intentions, justified their prewar posture in the Gulf, and offered a reason for doggedly pursuing the Palestinian and Mesopotamian campaigns in the First World War. Through the well-developed techniques of informal influence and formal control, the British maintained the greater Middle East, from Egypt to Afghanistan, as their sphere and theirs alone, and they planned to keep it that way—by whatever means. Palmerston had set the stage for that determined British stance over half a century earlier. It remained unchallenged and unassailable to date. The Great War would test that resolve.

CHAPTER TEN

The Middle East in the Great War 1914–18

It was at the behest of the Bureau that Colonel T. E. Lawrence came to Hussein's camp in June. On July 6, 1917 Lawrence and Feisal, in command of Arab forces, crossed 200 miles of desert, "The Anvil of God", and took the strategic Turkish fortress at Aqaba on the Red Sea -an extraordinary feat.

INDIA OFFICE NOTE ON HEJAZ REVOLT, AUGUST 31, 1918

Few expected a major European or global war to erupt in 1914, but signs were plentiful that even one crisis among many might evade control of the major European powers and lead to conflict. Fewer still believed that such strife, if it did occur, would envelop the Middle East, much less the globe. Europe had experienced only short or regionally confined wars from 1815 to 1914, and little evidence suggested any believed a future scenario would prove different.

But circumstances had changed, and stresses on the "old order" had multiplied dramatically from 1900 to 1914. First, the creation of the Triple Alliance in 1882 and the Triple Entente in 1907 meant that a small European conflict might quickly generate into a general European war. Second, imperialism, or the extension of national rivalries overseas, practically assured that such a struggle would envelope the globe. Finally, the evolution of large standing armies and the Industrial Revolution's new weaponry would most certainly render such a war catastrophic.

As the old century closed, overseas tensions mounted alarmingly with the second Sudan war, the Fashoda Incident, the Kuwait crisis, and the Spanish-American War. Britain's struggle in South Africa and the Russo-Japanese War opened the new century with even bloodier conflicts. Moreover, the First and Second Moroccan Crises of 1905 and 1911 brought mortal enemies France and Germany once more to the brink.

In the Balkans, a new and more violent nationalism erupted and threatened to draw in the major powers. The Bosnian Annexation Crisis of 1909 saw Austria-Hungary absorb Bosnia, thwarting Greater Serbian aspirations, and outraging Russian pan-Slavists. The fragile government of Czar Nicholas II could not and would not suffer another humiliation. New nation-states Serbia, Bulgaria, Romania, and Greece—emancipated from Ottoman control—now fought each other and against their former Ottoman overlord in the Balkan Wars of 1912 and 1913. As part of those struggles, some aligned with either of the major alliances through the client-state system to settle old scores and pursue greater national goals. While Bulgaria and the Ottoman Empire drew closer to Germany and the Triple Alliance, many in Serbia sought Russian support to avenge 1909. One irrational act by a client-state could bring down the house of cards and unleash the unthinkable. Nonetheless, most felt secure that the alliance system, designed to prevent a war, would prevail and that diplomacy in the end would save the day. Such had been the case with almost every crisis, despite the saber rattling. They were wrong.

On June 28, 1914, everything changed when a Bosnian-Serb nationalist assassinated Austrian Archduke Franz Ferdinand on a state visit to Bosnia's capital, Sarajevo. This was Saint Vitus Day in the Serbian Orthodox calendar, the anniversary of Greater Serbia's defeat and loss of independence to the Ottomans centuries earlier. For many Serbs, it was a day of revenge and restoration of Greater Serbia; for the Archduke, a bad day for a state visit; and for the rest, a long march into the abyss.

Two communications failures rendered the alliance system's defensive posture useless. First, Serbia never warned their Russian ally of the assassination plot, or the czar would have intervened to prevent it. Next, the Austrians, with Germany's blank check, sent an ultimatum to Serbia, silenced contact with Berlin to prevent objections and then declared war on Serbia on July 28. Faced with a *fait accompli*, Russia mobilized for war, first against Austria, then Germany. Now threatened with a two-front conflict, Germany declared war against Russia on August 1, and on France on August 3. In order to defeat France before Russia could fully mobilize, Germany on August 4 launched the Schlieffen Plan through neutral Belgium to attack the French. Still uncommitted, Britain now jumped into the fray against Germany to defend Belgian neutrality, which had been under British guarantee since 1839. On the eve of Britain's August 4 ultimatum to Germany, Foreign Secretary Lord Grey somberly uttered what many had now come to realize: "The lights are going out all over

Europe. We shall not see them lit again in our lifetime."[1] The First World War had begun.

· Within two months, the war's deadly tentacles had crept into the Middle East. On November 5, Britain declared war on the Ottoman Empire. "If Britain needed any additional stimulus to take action, the Ottoman Sultan/ Caliph provided it nine days later, on 14 November, when he declared a *jihad* against the Allies."[2] Egypt and the Suez Canal would inevitably face a German-led Turkish attack.

Apart from her superior naval strength, Britain stood unprepared for a serious war on the continent, much less the Middle East. Britain's 100,000-man army, the "Old Contemptibles", was dwarfed by the millions under arms among the rest of the major powers. When George V went to war, however, he did so "in the name of his people everywhere"—Australians, New Zealanders, Canadians, Africans, and the regiments of British India. They all could count on free travel to France, Gallipoli, Mesopotamia, or Egypt, courtesy of His Majesty's Government.

Although the German thrust into France proved unstoppable despite British and Belgian resistance, a quick reversal of fortune at the First Battle of the Marne on September 8–9 stalled the German offensive. The French held, forcing both sides to stretch their lines from the Alps to the channel over the next several months. Offensives appeared paralyzed by the fact that weapons created for attack could be used for defense as well, resulting in horrendous casualties. This was the Western Front. Here, military planners proved totally perplexed and unable to regain mobility. This impasse completely dispelled any notion the war would be over by Christmas, unless won by the Germans, whose victory against the Russians now seemed inevitable.

A Russian offensive into East Prussia had promised success, until German generals Paul von Hindenburg and Eric Ludendorff all but destroyed the Russian army at Tannenburg on August 26. If Russia collapsed, the German army on the Eastern Front could quickly pour into the West, overwhelm the French before British reinforcements arrived, and win the war.

None saw this eventuality more clearly than Britain's pugnacious Admiralty Secretary, Winston Churchill, who determined to keep the Russians in the war by supplying them through the Ottoman-controlled Dardanelles and Black Sea—the genesis of the Gallipoli Campaign. Churchill, like Palmerston, saw the Middle East as the launch pad for victory. The French understood this all too clearly and, discerning that Britain had wider imperial aims in the region, forced the issue. The British decided to assuage the French before the campaign with preliminary deliberations to share the Middle Eastern portions of the Ottoman Empire with the French and the Russians. Although the diplomacy was not finalized until the subsequent Sykes-Picot Agreement of 1916, these preliminaries, for the British at least, generated an enlarged strategy to defeat the Ottomans through Mesopotamia and Palestine. Fortunately for the Entente powers, Britain's long-contested hegemony in the Middle East would prove a deciding factor in winning the twentieth century's first great global conflict.

For now, imperial troops would have to handle most of the Gallipoli operation, since few British units could be spared from the Western Front. In January 1915, just prior to the campaign, a vanguard of this force arrived in Egypt and thwarted an Ottoman attempt to capture the Suez Canal.

If Ottoman failure at the canal assured some degree of British success, then British failures at Gallipoli throughout 1915 provided the Ottomans with a measure of hope. For the first time, a Muslim force led by a Muslim, Mustafa Kamel (Ataturk), defeated a coalition of Western forces. An imperial army comprised of Australians and New Zealanders (ANZACs), Indians, and smaller numbers of British and French troops was plagued from the beginning by uneven coordination and communication. Lack of naval support, determined Turkish opposition, and the valiant exploits of Kamel to rally his troops resulted in 250,000 Allied casualties from February 1915 to January 1916. Although suffering equally, the Ottomans held their positions. In the end, the venture's greatest success was its evacuation.[3] This debacle left Gallipoli's Field Commander Ian Hamilton disgraced, Admiralty Secretary Churchill without a job, and Lord Asquith's government permanently weakened. Following the war, Kamel, hero of the affair, became first president of the Turkish Republic.

War in the Middle East: Britain defends its sphere—defense to offense

Many commanders at the time and later historians considered Britain's Middle Eastern campaign a sideshow. As noted, however, British officials understood it as an outgrowth of a larger strategy. They aimed to crush the Ottomans and divide the Middle East to keep Russia in the war, thwart German expansion, and preserve the British Empire. In addition, they would secure the newly discovered oil-rich region of southern Persia and the Gulf, essential to Britain's modern oil-dependent dreadnought fleet. Operations in the Middle East, which consequently utilized 1,000,000 troops, involved the cooperation of the Foreign Office, War Office, Admiralty, and the Government of India—no easy task, considering the personalities and institutions involved. The complex diplomatic and political decisions made in conjunction with the campaign ultimately generated more uncertainty, mistrust and upheaval than the war.

The first of many contradictory British political decisions came with a promise to keep Egypt out of the war. When the war arrived at Egypt's doorstep, however, the British quickly removed the country from Ottoman control to that of a British protectorate.[4] Next, they pressured the khedive to declare war on Germany (August 5) to provide the British use of all military

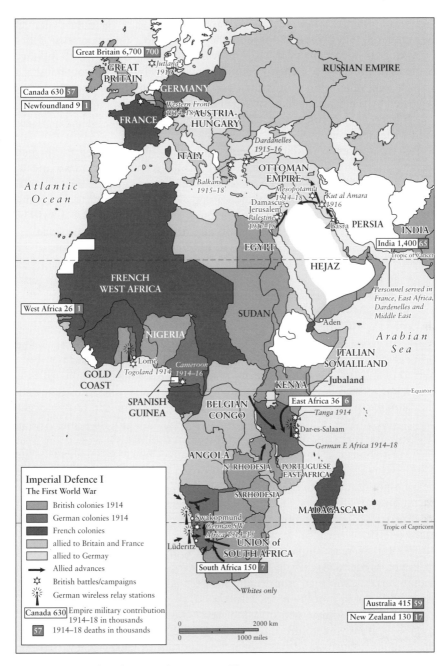

MAP 6 *Imperial Defense I: The First World War.*

facilities.[5] Finally, when Britain declared war against the Ottomans on November 5, they promised not to further compromise Egyptian sensitivities by asking them to fight their Muslim overlord, the sultan. Britain's military commander in Egypt, General John Maxwell, declared, "Recognizing the respect and veneration with which the Sultan, in his religious capacity, is regarded by the Mahomedans of Egypt, Great Britain takes upon herself the sole burden of the present war, without calling upon the Egyptian people for aid therein."[6]

But the Ottoman onslaught arrived too quickly and forced the British in one "magic moment" to declare Egypt's khedive the new sultan and to order Egypt's army to stop the attackers at the Suez Canal. Thus, units of the small, poorly trained, and underequipped force saw immediate action. Egypt's artillery units rolled to the defense of the canal in January 1915 and engaged in a fierce battle to cut off an Ottoman column near Ismaelia.[7] Units of Britain's imperial army arrived in Egypt just in time to counter the Ottoman force of 20,000 and support the Egyptians near the canal.[8] An Egyptian rifle regiment's surprisingly tenacious defense in the southern Sinai produced more casualties the following month.

Together, ANZACs, India's Muslim regiments, and a small Egyptian force thwarted the Ottoman effort for the time being but proved only the beginning of the offensive. Meanwhile, the Ottoman call for jihad had obviously fallen on deaf ears. "Their appeal had little effect, especially among Arabs, whose hatred of the Turks was as great or greater than their dislike of the Allies."[9] It did not matter: The Ottomans had won at Gallipoli, and, thus renewed, they could now prepare for another invasion of the canal. In response, the British presently redoubled their efforts in Egypt, Mesopotamia, and Arabia to crush the Turks and reclaim their prestige in the Muslim world.

At British urging, Egypt called all army reserves in 1916 again to face the Turkish threat. The Egyptian government used physical force to recruit her peasant population into the newly formed Auxiliary Corps and forced labor battalions. Their loyalty remained steadfast, despite misgivings and harsh treatment.[10] Egypt's decision and the devotion of her forces to fight the war alongside British troops, however, came from love of country, now under attack, rather than support of Britain. Britain's new commander-in-chief in Egypt, General Archibald Murray, however, believed his ANZACs and Indian forces, exhausted from Gallipoli, were at that moment inadequate to stop the Turks or mount an offensive.

Although the threatened invasion never materialized, he called for and received a greatly expanded Egyptian force of 200,000 for the regular army, the Auxiliary Corps, and the Camel Transportation Corps. They, together with their British and imperial army counterparts, fought in the Sinai in 1916 and in the 1917–18 Palestinian Campaign. They took heavy casualties, and, unlike Lawrence and the Arabs, their efforts received no credit for the campaign's ultimate success. Overall, their endeavors remain absent from the historical record.[11]

Moreover, 125,000, recruited for the Labor Corps unarmed army, supported imperial troops in Syria; another 10,463 served with the British on the Somme; and 8,230 more backed the Mesopotamian Campaign.[12] According to British sources, the labor force produced one of the war's great tactical and technical feats. According to Major E. P. Newman, who served in Egypt at the time, "They took a considerable part in the construction of the military railway across the Sinai desert, one the greatest achievements of the war . . . so that no man can say that these Egyptians did not pull their weight."[13]

Thousands of Egypt's young men never returned from these conflicts near and far. Many resented the British for betraying their promise not to fight this European war with Egypt's blood and for giving them no credit when they did.[14] Colonel P. G. Elgood, who served with the British throughout the ordeal, lamented, "The truth is that the promise was made without thought of the future. . . . In this instance it would have been more honourable to confess later the undertaking given to Egypt under the proclamation could not be carried out, and a frank admission to that effect might have saved Egypt to the Empire."[15]

Elgood further bemoaned that the "Egyptians had been stripped of their illusions and despoiled of their rights and property. Their manpower, crops, and animals were seized for the war effort, and territorial sovereignty usurped."[16] Major Newman also shared many of the same sentiments: "The Egyptian army was ready to do anything or go anywhere we wanted. . . . They did a great deal of valuable work, which was never recognized, and they have been denied that share in the glory of victory which would have meant so much to them."[17]

In the end, British indifference and contradictory policies would propel Egypt to rebel against the protectorate under the forceful leadership of Said Zaghlul after the war.

Despite these unfortunate policy decisions, the campaign gained momentum, crossed the canal, and pushed through the Sinai, railway and all. General Murray's forces took Arish on the Palestine border by late 1916, but failure to capture Gaza in early 1917 resulted in Murray's removal. David Lloyd George, Britain's new prime minister, ordered General Edmund Allenby to replace him. Lloyd George needed a victory and, like Churchill, he chose the Middle East as the perfect location to launch offensives. Allenby's arrival quickly added renewed vigor to the British thrust.

While the Palestine Campaign regrouped, the British effort in Mesopotamia faced disaster. If the Palestinian theater began slowly and then escalated, the Government of India's Mesopotamian effort proved the reverse. On the surface, this initially successful campaign appeared unessential to the overall British task. British-led Indian troops easily moved northward in November 1914, took the port of Basra, and secured the oil pipelines of the Anglo-Persian Oil Company. Some military historians suggest that is where they should have remained. "They were in a good position to protect

ABONNEMENTS
Trois mois Six mois Un an
FRANCE & COLONIES
4 fr.   7 fr. 50   14 fr.
UNION POSTALE
6 fr.   12 fr.   22 fr.

Le Petit Journal
— *illustré* —

PARAISSANT LE DIMANCHE
33ᵉ Année · N° 1621
On s'abonne dans tous
les bureaux de poste
Les Manuscrits ne sont pas rendus

Pendant la Conférence

Sous le ciel bleu de la Côte d'Azur, dans l'adorable décor de Cannes, où l'éternel
printemps incite à la conciliation, M. Aristide Briand rencontre encore une fois M. Lloyd
George et les deux hommes d'État discutent le projet de reconstitution de l'Europe.

FIGURE 17 *Prime Minister David Lloyd George, 1922. Leemage. Getty Images.*

the oil installations, and no worthwhile military objectives lay beyond this
point. It would have been far better for all concerned had they remained
content to stay were they were."[18] But the British objective had not been
purely military. The German government had recently discovered what the
Government of India had already known, relative to the region's resources
and their potential for war development. German views published in the
Hamburger *Fremdemblatt* on December 3, 1915 and circulated to the British
cabinet on December 27 stated that "Germany's survival and future lies in
the East, in Asia Minor, Syria, Mesopotamia, Palestine. Must be opened
by RR and capital—Done for Turkey with Germany's help. At Ninevah
traversed by Baghdad RR, lies one of the greatest oil fields in the world, in
Tamers are great copper fields. Near Babylon, cotton and wheat—greatest
in the world."[19]

Hence, General Sir John Nixon, in charge of the campaign, had divided
his force after Basra and pressed up the Tigris to Amara and along the
Euphrates to Nasiriya. He captured both by the end of July 1915. While the
Government of India urged Nixon to continue, British officials in London
hesitated. With Gallipoli stalemated, they needed a victory, but was this

force large enough to do the job? Their indecision allowed Nixon time to believe both parties had agreed on his offensive. His assignment had been to encourage local Arab tribes to revolt and harass the Turks, as the victorious army proceeded to Baghdad and the ultimate prize, the northern oil fields.

The Arab revolt never materialized and, stymied by blistering summer heat, meager supplies, poor transportation, and inadequate manpower, the offensive stalled. Meanwhile, in late September 1915, Nixon's subordinate, General Charles Townshend, captured Kut, halfway to Baghdad. So far, Ottoman resistance had been minimal. That alone had encouraged Nixon and most fellow officers to assume that a clean sweep of Mesopotamia was possible. This notion would quickly change. A view offered at the time suggested that a "British-led Indian force was far superior in open field tactics to a defensive minded Ottoman army of greater numbers. But if the Ottomans had time to think, they could defend a position indefinitely."[20] Another illusion focused on Baghdad's capture. "Key to success is to take Baghdad since the Turks hold it as a strong position. If British take Baghdad the Turks will have to disperse their forces. British can hold Baghdad with 2000 troops and use the rest for attack."[21]

If Townshend shared these overly optimistic views he did not show it. He very reluctantly and cautiously led his 12,000 troops to within twenty miles of Baghdad. At that point, he hit a stone wall—the moment of truth had arrived. On November 22, 20,000 German-led Turkish defenders, who refused to be outflanked, inflicted heavy casualties on Townshend.[22] While Townshend regrouped at Kut, those defensive-minded Turks suddenly took the offensive, pursued and surrounded Townshend's force, and cut it off until the spring of 1916. Nixon tried and failed to break the siege at Kut with Indian reinforcements. Starvation set in, and on April 29, 1916, Townshend and 10,000 defenders surrendered.[23] Of that number, only 3,000 survived the war.[24] "The fall of Kut, if hardly a major setback to British arms, sent shock waves all the way to Whitehall. Coming so soon after the abandonment of Gallipoli, this further humiliation at Turkish hands appeared inexcusable."[25] Britain's reputation in the Muslim world had suffered irreparable damage. As a result, the British government relieved the Government of India from any further responsibility for this campaign.

On the Western Front, meanwhile, the Battle at Verdun and Britain's Somme offensive in 1916 produced casualties in excess of 2,000,000, all to no avail. Spring brought on the greatly awaited dreadnought confrontation between Germany and Britain. The resultant Battle of Jutland proved frustratingly inconclusive. Although the British lost more tonnage, they claimed victory because the German fleet fled to port for the duration of the war. Russia's Brussilov offensive on the Eastern Front, a welcome surprise, overwhelmed the Austro-Hungarian army and encouraged the Allies. But the arrival of German reinforcements reversed that success and turned it into a devastating rout. Once more, Russia faced collapse. Thus, the Allies ended 1916 with a sense of increased desperation.

As noted earlier, Prime Minister Lloyd George needed a victory some-where, anywhere to boost sagging British morale. With that in mind, he relieved Murray for Allenby in Palestine and replaced Nixon with General F. S. Maude to handle the task in Mesopotamia. The Middle Eastern theater had suddenly acquired a new sense of urgency and commitment. Lloyd George, following Churchill and Palmerston, saw the Middle East, with its promise of flexibility and mobility, no longer as just an artery of empire but as the key to destroying the enemy and winning the war. Thereafter, the British feverishly rebuilt port facilities at Basra and added gunboats with heavier artillery as well as airplanes to spot enemy movements.[26] Maude, now confident, launched a second offensive in December 1916, this time with sufficient Indian forces to do the job.

Diplomacy British style: The McMahon–Hussein correspondence and the diplomatic efforts of Sir Mark Sykes

If the exotic military conflicts in the Middle East have been obscured by time, the diplomatic and political decisions that accompanied them have not. On this score, policies made in London, Paris, Cairo, and Delhi, conducted without a central focus or unified goal, on the whole proved dangerously conflicted and contradictory. Promises made for an Arab state; for French, British, and Russian spheres; as well as for a Jewish homeland confused the endeavor and still haunt the landscape. While it remains easy to blame British policy makers, it must be remembered that these decisions were made at various times in the midst of a war for survival, in the absence of any certainties. They evolved in stages during the conflict and from individual representatives of different institutions and regions, without the luxury of time or cool, coordinated analysis. As such, the 1915 McMahon–Hussein correspondence, the Sykes-Picot Agreement of 1916, and the 1917 Balfour Declaration presented no single plan for the Middle East but piecemeal, fragmented formulas, tailor-made for postwar conflict. But why so many agreements to cover this single region? In classic Palmerstonian fashion, the British saw the Middle East as the catalyst for victory and to holding it as essential for the future. Each agreement had that in mind.

When the British declared Egypt a protectorate in 1914, the title of governor-general, held by General Kitchener, changed to that of high commissioner and was bestowed on Sir Henry McMahon. With Kitchener off to head Britain's military effort as war secretary, McMahon remained in Cairo to decide, as it turned out, not only Egypt's role in the conflict but that of the region's Arabs. This proved no easy task, nor was it anticipated. The British had repulsed one Ottoman attack at the canal and were stalemated at Gallipoli when McMahon received an unexpected proposal on July 14, 1915, from Sherif Hussein of Mecca. He would join forces with the British and lead the Arabs in revolt against the Turks, but only under certain conditions: "Arab state to be created and independence of Arab countries bounded on the north . . . up to the border of Persia; On the east by the border of Persia up to the Gulf of Basra; on the South by the Indian Ocean . . . on the West by the Red Sea, the Mediterranean Sea up to Mersina. England to approve of the proclamation of an Arab Khalifate of Islam."[27]

Anxious to support an Arab revolt, McMahon and other British officials quickly agreed to the substance of the proposal, especially the last line. As guardian of Mecca, Hussein's claim to the caliphate appeared genuine enough. It also would serve British purposes to counter the Ottoman sultan's call for jihad. Hussein's proposed boundaries were another matter. They included almost all of what is today the Arab Middle East: Palestine, Lebanon, Iraq, Jordan, Arabia, the Gulf States, and most of Syria. McMahon and his cartographers took three months to analyze it and then responded with a modified proposal on October 24: "I am confident you will receive (this) with satisfaction . . . we accept those limits and boundaries and, in regard to those portions of the territories therein in which Great Britain is free to act without detriment to the interests of her ally, France. . . . Great Britain is prepared to recognize and support the independence of the Arabs within the territories included in the limits and boundaries proposed by the Sheriff of Mecca."[28]

Thus, McMahon excluded western Syria or Lebanon, where France had an interest; and the Gulf sheikdoms, already British protectorates. Whether Palestine was separate or part of Syria determined if it might or might not have been included in the proposed Arab state. British analysts were divided on the issue. Some understood Palestine to be part of Syria before the mandates and therefore excluded.[29] Others maintained, however, that Hussein understood McMahon's letter to include Palestine. "It would appear from the King's reception of H.M.G's message that he believed that Palestine had been assigned to the Arabs by Sir H. McMahon's letter of 24 October, 1915, and that whatever the Special Regime there foreshadowed by the message might be, he understood that it would not be in derogation of his sovereignty."[30] Issues surrounding the correspondence became so complex and contentious following the war that in 1940 the Foreign Office decided to settle the matter. It collected some 30 unpublished documents from 1915 to 1939 regarding various aspects of the Hussein-McMahon correspondence and how these items were being interpreted, and 14 translated letters from Hussein to McMahon and vice versa from 1915 to 1916.[31] In the end, nothing was settled and the issues remained.

Whatever Hussein thought he had obtained in Syria was soon compromised under the Sykes-Picot Agreement (1916), as was his claim to Palestine by the Balfour Declaration (1917). Unaware of the small print and of conflicting British promises, Hussein plunged ahead with his war against the Turks. In June 1916, he launched the Arab revolt, first in the Hejaz in western Arabia. "By the end of September forces of Arab tribesmen captured Mecca, Jedda and Taif, but Medina remained in Turkish control."[32] Later, accompanied by T. E. Lawrence, Arab forces moved to the east of Allenby's Palestine campaign and pursued guerilla attacks on Turkish supply lines.

In the summer of 1915, at the height of the Gallipoli campaign, the Foreign Office sent Lt. Colonel Sir Mark Sykes, a Turkish expert, to evaluate the military and political situation in the Middle East. He traveled from India to the Mediterranean and met with Indian government officials as well as political and religious leaders in the Arab world, including Egypt. His sometimes astounding, if simplistic, observations included a general strategy on how to defeat the Turks, divide the spoils between the Entente powers, and settle with the Arabs following the conflict. Some of his recommendations became policy and were included in the Sykes-Picot Agreement, which bears his name.

First of all he felt the Indian government's campaign in Mesopotamia was inadequate, if not inept. He recommended a far larger force to complete the effort successfully. His views, written on November 15, 1915, obviously carried some weight, since Lloyd George followed that course of action in early 1917. He believed that Indian Muslims, unlike the Arabs, were more susceptible to Ottoman political propaganda, since their religious training was inferior to that of the Arabs. He sensed this because the Young Turk Movement and its Committee of Union and Progress had dissuaded many Indian Muslims from the British cause and to the banner of the Ottoman sultan. He sharply condemned the Indian government for this failure and recommended an overhaul in its thinking.[33]

In the Arab world, he urged the independence of the Hejaz under the Sheriff of Mecca to "stimulate an Arab demand for the 'Caliphate of the Sheriff'." The note he wrote in 1915 revealed the germ of his later agreement with the French consul at Damascus, François Picot. "British internal and external protectorate over an area in southern Syria and Mesopotamia in agreement with France and Russia. Declaration of French internal and external protectorate in area north of the British area . . . permitting the use of British, French, Russian, or Italian troops anywhere."[34]

Sykes already knew of Hussein's correspondence with McMahon and supported some of his proposals. Earlier, in conversations with Egypt's sultan, he suggested that Hussein as caliph should have pronounced that title on the sultan to give it legitimacy. "Title of Sultan is artificial since it was bestowed by a Christian Power. Sherif of Mecca as Caliph should bestow title of Sultan on him."[35] Sykes reluctantly agreed with one Arab pan-Islamic leader, Sheikh Reshid Rida, who "believed in setting up independent Arab Caliphate under the Sherif of Mecca with political jurisdiction over Arabia, Syria and Mesopotamia" to replace Turkey if it falls.[36]

Finally, in meeting with Egyptian constitutional leader, Said Zaghlul, in August 1915, Sykes received an earful. Zaghlul expressed the opinion "that to those of advanced views the declaration of a Protectorate had come as a heartbreaking blow, inasmuch as it put an end to the theory that the occupation was not a permanent institution."[37] In unconscious arrogance, Sykes contended that "he (Zaghlul), however, agreed that the idea of an absolutely independent Egypt was not one which could be entertained, and that for purposes of defense, finance, and foreign relations must always depend on some other power."[38] Sykes further maintained that Zaghlul rejected the views of the Committee of Union and Progress but also "that no Enlightened Egyptian including Zaghlul take any steps to counteract such propaganda."[39] Sykes obviously failed to ask himself why any enlightened Egyptian would want to do the British a favor. Zaghlul never forgot that encounter and soon after the war, defied Sykes's dictum and pursued the unthinkable.

Sykes's overall observations and recommendations had been geared to pursue a strategy that would counter Young Turk propaganda aimed at rousing the Muslim world against the British. He sought "to propagandize Islam in a definite and offensive manner—attacking the enemy on the score of injustice, crime, unorthodoxy, and hypocrisy (sic) in our own press, in native press, and leaflets."[40] This immediate and momentary aim to destabilize the Ottoman regime, however, at once resulted in greater and more serious ramifications for the entire region well into the future.

McMahon and Sykes both represented the Foreign Office, but each in their own way pursued different agendas and interests. The Hussein–McMahon correspondence appears first to have been designed to get and then keep the Arabs in the war against the Turks. Thus, McMahon, as Egypt's high commissioner, reached his agreement with Hussein from a regional, and oftentimes critical, wartime perspective. As such, he supported the creation or outline of an independent Arab state that Hussein, Sheriff of Mecca, and his family, the Hashemites, were to rule under British tutelage or informal management.[41] Those who championed this scheme also envisioned the Arab state as a means of guaranteeing informal control of the region in the future through a British-friendly dynasty, albeit that the projected French sphere would be quite small and confined to Syrian coastal areas west of Damascus. In short, the influence of European spheres proved minimal in this projected agreement.

Mark Sykes, with a broader mandate, saw any proposed Arab state as a means to counter the Ottomans and therefore envisioned a much wider role for the British, French, and Russians in line with specific Foreign Office interests. The Sykes initiative had developed as an outgrowth of preliminary discussions about the division of the Middle East, based on Churchill's proposed Gallipoli campaign in late 1914. The French objected to Gallipoli on the grounds that it would delete forces from the Western Front and that Britain would utilize the campaign to extend its empire in the Middle East. The Foreign Office silenced this criticism and proposed to share any future spoils with the French and Russians. The outline of that proposal remained sufficiently vague until Sykes, sent to the Middle East by the Foreign Office, wrote his report on November 15, 1915. His goal was to create British, French, and Russian spheres to displace the Ottoman Empire in the Middle East, once and for all. Therefore, his support of Hussein's Arab state was limited to the Hejaz alone and, though subsequently enlarged for the sake of political expediency, remained of secondary importance to the Allied spheres.[42] The final arrangements in Sykes-Picot appear to be a compromise between the Arab state projected in Hussein–McMahon and Sykes's emphasis on the role of allied spheres.

At last, after many months of political wrangling in London, between May 9 and May 16, 1916, Mark Sykes and François Picot finalized an agreement, coordinated with Russian representative Sergei Sazanov.[43] "Plan envisioned an Arab confederation in which France would have economic priority in the north and Britain in the south. France, in an area along the Syrian coast, and Britain at the head of the Persian Gulf. . . . Britain took the ports of Haifa and Acre in Palestine, and Mosul fell with the French region of economic priority . . . as did Damascus."[44]

Moreover, Russia would gain "control over the Ottoman provinces Erzurum, Trebizond, Van and Bitlis."[45] David Fromkin, in his now famous work *A Peace to End all Peace*, views the arrangement somewhat differently. "In the end Sykes and Picot obtained what they wanted from one another: France was to rule a Greater Lebanon and to exert an exclusive influence over the rest of Syria. Sykes succeeded in giving, and Picot succeeded in taking, a sphere of French influence that extended to Mosul. Basra and Baghdad, the two Mesopotamian provinces, were to go to Britain."[46] Palestine remained a thorn, but since Britain obtained Haifa and Acre, they also received a "territorial belt on which to construct a railroad from there to Mesopotamia, while the rest of the country was to fall under some sort of international administration."[47] Still, each party—the British, French, and Sherif Hussein— claimed Palestine. Following the war, the League of Nations placed the disputed territory under a British mandate, after which some British officials likely regretted not having turned it over to the French or Hussein in the first place. In the end, Russia, which was torn by the Bolshevik Revolution and had abandoned the war in November 1917, got nothing, while Hussein, who now made war on the Turks, was told nothing.

For his part, Sykes, more anti-Turk than pro-Arab, wanted to eradicate the rest of the Ottoman Empire from the map. "Only solution is one that involves partition or spheres of influence on those already adopted by Russo- Franco-British agreements. The only satisfactory solution is the reduction of the Ottoman Empire to such a political non-entity that it shall be worth nobody's while to tamper with it."[48]

Allenby did not arrive in Palestine until June 1917, and the Turks still held Gaza. To everyone's surprise, especially the Turks, he captured Beersheba instead. Now surrounded, Gaza's defenders deserted the city, leaving Allenby to take it in November. He then proceeded northward to capture Jerusalem on December 9 as a "Christmas present for the British people." Part of the reason for his success lay in the Arab revolt, which pinned down Turkish reinforcements east of Allenby's expeditionary force.

By the end of 1916, Hussein had divided command with his sons, Sherifs Feisal and Abdulla, and together with 21,000 troops continued to attack Medina and destroy the Turkish railway near Yanbu on the Red Sea.[49] During the first six months of 1917, in conjunction with British forces in Palestine, they extended their operations.[50] Britain's newly created Arab Bureau in Cairo coordinated much of this effort. It was at the behest of the bureau that Colonel T. E. Lawrence (Figure 18) came to Hussein's camp in June. On July 6, 1917, Lawrence and Feisal, in command of Arab forces, crossed 200 miles of desert, "The Anvil of God," and took the strategic Turkish fortress at Aqaba on the Red Sea—an extraordinary feat.[51] The legend of Lawrence of Arabia was born. After two months, Feisal again took the offensive. "By this time (October 17), Feisal held the area of Trans-Jordan near Petra and the Turks could not dislodge him."[52] Meanwhile, because of sickness, starvation, and Arab attacks, the Turks were now desperate to evacuate Medina and its 11,000 survivors. On the eve of Jerusalem's fall to Allenby, Turkish governor Fakhri Pasha sent a cryptic note to Jamal I, Medina's commander-in-chief: "The Fourth Age was dawning." It was based on an old tradition that the end of the Third Age signaled the end of the Ottoman Empire.[53]

FIGURE 18 *Colonel T. E. Lawrence "of Arabia," 1918. DEA / G. NIMATALLAH. Getty Images.*

By the end of 1917, the old prophecy appeared only too true. "Overall, the Arabs had engaged the Turks 54 times by the end of 1917. Turkish casualties 3400 killed, 757 wounded, 6766 prisoners. They had lost 44 guns (artillery), 11 machine guns, 2417 rifles. 42 attacks on RR—destroyed 7 engines, 3 wagons, 7,770 rails, 34 bridges and 16 culverts."[54] Now desperate, the Germans tried to rebuild Arab-Turkish relations and started their own Arab Bureau at Damascus for that purpose. This effort, like the Damascus-Hejaz Railway, came to a dead end at the edge of the desert.[55] While Allenby's force and Arab guerrillas pursued the Turks through Palestine and Syria, General Maude regained the initiative in Mesopotamia.

Maude and his greatly enlarged force from India regained Kut in February 1917 and proceeded north with a four-to-one manpower advantage. He overwhelmed Baghdad on March 11 and proceeded to take as much of the country as possible, since the Sykes-Picot Agreement had awarded this territory to the British.[56] Taking the land was one thing, but controlling it was another.

Discussions that year focused on postwar occupation and on how and by whom this would be handled in view of presumed British manpower shortages to cover this vast area. London had rejected the idea of Indian administrators as an affront to the Arab population and, instead, recommended a most bizarre scheme—to send in the Japanese. Japan had the army, the administrators, and the money and had proven a good ally in the Pacific against the Germans. The reaction from India was swift. "This suggestion was soundly rejected by the India Office and the Government of India. Although the war was still on the big question why eliminate the Germans and substitute them with the Japanese even though their help and financial assistance could prove valuable. It would cause great resentment in the Arab Muslim world."[57] This was an understatement.

The Mesopotamian campaign proceeded slowly after Baghdad because of the intense summer heat's early arrival in 1917 and the removal of British forces to the Western Front in 1918. The fact remains that it moved ahead nonetheless, despite criticism that it drained resources from more important operations. It did so because of the determined efforts of Lord Curzon, former viceroy of India and now a member of Lloyd George's war cabinet. He believed in the empire and advocated its defense. The Germans took great interest in Curzon's views, as revealed in a German document of October 1916. He saw that the British Empire, especially India, was at once the world's largest Muslim empire and that its prestige needed to be regained and maintained in Asia. As Curzon concluded, "Thus the war in Mesopotamia between the Turks and the British is essential for British survival," and Britain must "control Tigris-Euphrates navigation" and "dominate the oil deposits."[58] At Curzon's urging, despite misgivings and manpower shortages, the Mesopotamian expedition plunged northward along the Tigris and Euphrates. On the eve of Turkey's capitulation on October 31, 1918, the expedition arrived at the doorstep of Mosul and the oil fields, now Britain's by right of conquest.[59] In short, this campaign, though obscure and derided, was a success, although its value proved other than military.

The same cannot be said of the Palestinian campaign. Despite heroes like Allenby, Lawrence, and Feisal; the ANZAC units, the Australian Light Horse; mounted Arab warriors; and a string of exotic victories, political intrigue, and betrayal soon obscured the entire effort. In early 1918, Allenby moved to dislodge the Turks at Amman, while from Petra, Feisal "struck at an area near the Dead Sea and inflicted losses on the Turks in lightening type attacks."[60] Their joint effort in March 1918 drove the Turks from Trans-Jordan. The campaign had gone well, very well, when bewilderment hit the Anglo–Arab alliance.

Russia, now out of the war, had just signed the Treaty of Brest-Litovsk with Germany (March 1918), releasing a million German soldiers to the 1918 spring offensive in the West, which could promise victory to the Germans. At the same time, Russia's new Bolshevik leaders also published details of Sykes-Picot and the Balfour Declaration to inflame the Arabs. The effect was immediate: King Hussein sent two letters to Egypt's new high commissioner, Sir Reginald Wingate. He hinted at suicide over the Balfour Declaration and the Sykes-Picot Agreement, either of which would render him unable to vindicate his revolt before the Muslim world.[61]

The Balfour Declaration 1917

Written on November 2, 1917, the Balfour Declaration appeared at once as the product of British wartime political expediency and emergent Jewish nationalism or Zionism. It came in the form of a brief letter from foreign secretary Lord Arthur Balfour to Lord Rothschild, president of Britain's Zionist Federation. The letter declared:

> His Majesty's Government view with favor the establishment in Palestine of national home for the Jewish people, and will use their best endeavor to facilitate the achievement of this object, it being clearly understood that nothing shall be done which may prejudice the civil and religious rights of the existing non-Jewish communities in Palestine, or the rights and political status enjoyed by Jews in any other country.[62]

This concept of a Jewish homeland, not a state, had received support from a number of British leaders, including Winston Churchill and Prime Minister Lloyd George. Chaim Weizmann, a prominent Jewish chemist who had developed synthetic acetone explosives for Britain's war effort, had influenced them. Hence, as the country's leading Zionist advocate with strong parliamentary connections, he won many to the Zionist cause, including Mark Sykes. Some supported the movement from earnest Biblical convictions, while others took a more pragmatic approach. They naively envisioned Palestine, with a Jewish population loyal to Britain, as a means of safeguarding the Suez Canal and, therefore, the empire. While some British officials sought to use Zionism to gain Palestine, the Zionists used Britain to gain first a homeland and then a state.

At the outbreak of the war, 80,000 Jews lived in Palestine, the result of two decades of immigration from Russia and Eastern Europe, while the Arab population totaled some 650,000.[63] This experience had proved relatively peaceful. But the new thrust was different; this was political Zionism, and it came courtesy of the British Empire. Moreover, the declaration never defined the rights of the Arab majority, as historian Arthur Goldschmidt Jr. states in *A Concise History of the Middle East*:

> The British government promised only to work for the creation of a Jewish national home *in* Palestine. Moreover, it pledged not to harm the civil and religious rights of Palestine's 'existing non-Jewish communities'— namely, the 93 percent of its inhabitants, Muslim and Christian, who spoke Arabic and dreaded being cut off from other Arabs as second-class citizens within a Jewish national home. Both Britain and the Zionist movement would have to find a way to assuage these people's fears and to guarantee their rights. They never did.[64]

Elizabeth Monroe's *Britain's Moment in the Middle East* provides a somber assessment of the document's impact on Britain. "To the Jews who went to Palestine, and to many who did not, it signified fulfillment and salvation, but it brought the British much ill-will, and complications that sapped their power. Measured by British interests alone, it was one of the greatest mistakes in our imperial history."[65]

Overall, the British government appeared incredibly naïve when it came to the Zionist agenda, and they would remain so for the next thirty years. It seems important to note that this concise and carefully worded document, meant for public consumption, never mentioned the non-Jewish inhabitants by name. The terms Arab or Palestinian are altogether absent from Balfour's letter to Rothschild, which might have meant nothing, or it might have meant much more, since a people without a name, without an identity, were presumably a people without power or general public recognition. In short, the term *non-Jewish communities*, left undefined, implied second-class status. If the declaration purposely aimed to denigrate this population as irrelevant, it did not work. The British government and the Zionists notwithstanding, the Palestinian Arabs knew who they were and where they lived and would make that perfectly clear in the years ahead. Regardless of intent, the declaration itself proved a bad start for the otherwise noble goal of Arabs and Jews living together in Palestine as equals.

Nonetheless, British assurances to Hussein and Feisal continued, and in March 1918, one month after Hussein's letter, that assurance came to

Jerusalem in the person of Chiam Weizmann. Weizmann's commission aimed to assist the Zionists and especially to assure the Arab population that they had no reason to fear. Historian Author Goldschmidt Jr. observes that "He dissuaded them from believing that Jews were to buy Moslem land and force them out of the area . . . and that a Jewish Government would be fatal to his plans . . . to provide a home to the Jews in the Holy Land where they could live their own natural life, sharing equal rights with the other inhabitants."[66]

That June, Weizmann visited the camp of Sherif Feisal at Gueira near Aqaba. "Weismann and Feisal established excellent personal relationship, and *Feisal expressed his opinion of the necessity of close co-operation between Jews and Arabs*, especially at that moment—and a cordial invitation to renew the meeting when Weismann returned from America" (author's italics).[67] The matter appeared settled, at least for the moment.

The great German offensive stalled in the summer of 1918 because of equipment and ration shortages, a mutiny, and the arrival of the Americans at the front. As the Allies slowly pushed the Germans into a dogged retreat on the Western Front, Allenby pursued the stubborn Turks from Palestine into Syria, and, at long last, the Arabs were poised to take Medina. "At that point Turkish Official Fakhri Pasha sent a farewell message and considered Medina doomed, while the purchasing agent for the Hejaz Expeditionary Force (Turkish) at Damascus received orders to close his accounts and make no further purchases."[68] Four centuries of Ottoman rule were about to end with the closure of an accountant's ledger.

As British and Arab forces converged on Damascus toward the end of September 1918, however, another blow hit the Arab cause. A second Arab force, led by Ibn Saud in Arabia, had taken the town of Khurma from Hussein. Since the majority of Hussein's forces remained with Feisal, fighting in the north, Hussein feared Mecca would fall to Saud as well. In an almost unbelievable scenario, two British administrations had come to blows. The British government through the Arab Bureau in Cairo had largely supported Hussein and Feisal's war against the Turks. The Government of India, however, still having influence in eastern and central Arabia, subsidized Ibn Saud and the more conservative Wahhabi Muslims in a separate war effort against the Turks. But that effort had gone terribly wrong, as Saud used his money to make war on Hussein as well as the Turks. The British and Indian governments remained chagrined and conflicted on the issue as their old rivalry had reignited, bringing their clients into collision. Attempts at mediation failed.[69] "At the present moment Bin Saud's claims are championed by Colonel Wilson and Mr. Philby (India), while those of King Husain have the support of Sir R. Wingate and Colonel Lawrence (Foreign Office, Cairo Bureau)."[70] Ultimately, this conflict, which lasted a decade, ended with Saud's conquest of the Hejaz and the creation of the kingdom of Saudi Arabia.[71] Later, as one British official noted, "We have to recognize that in Hussein we have, whether we could help it or not, backed a poor horse. . . . He is nothing but a pampered querulous nuisance."[72] So much for gratitude.

Nonetheless, with the Great War's end in sight, Allenby pressed ahead and defeated Ottoman forces at the Battle of Megiddo (Biblical Armageddon) on September 19, while Hussein, as Britain's staunch ally, loyally supported those efforts to the finish. His one brief moment of glory finally arrived on October 1, 1918, with the fall of Damascus. His son, Feisal, was allowed to take the fabled city so important to Arab history and any future Arab state. "Lawrence arranged for Feisal's Arab forces to make the triumphal entry and install their own governor."[73]

Toward mid-October, Mustafa Kamel, hero of Gallipoli, withdrew the last Turkish forces from Syria to Anatolia. Aleppo, the final stronghold, fell to Allenby on October 26. Five days later on October 30, 1918, the Ottomans signed the Mudros Armistice with the British and capitulated the following day. At long last, Britain and her Allies gained final victory in the Middle East, and that victory propelled the ultimate triumph as Churchill and Lloyd George had urged.

On November 11, 1918, an armistice on the Western Front announced the surrender of Germany and ended what had been the bloodiest conflict in human history. The war had killed 10,000,000 soldiers and 10,000,000 civilians and left 21,000,000 wounded. The Russian, German, Austrian, and Ottoman empires had been erased from the map along with their dynasties. Certainly, and fortunately for the Entente powers, Britain's long-contested hegemony in the Middle East had proved a deciding factor in winning the twentieth century's first great global conflict. British supplies through Persia kept Russia in the conflict until the 1916 Brussilov Offensive destroyed the Austrian Army. Moreover, the protracted Mesopotamian and Palestinian campaigns at last crushed the Ottoman threat. Finally, the Middle East at the Suez Canal served as conduit for an additional million imperial troops to bolster the Western Front until the allies together with US forces brought a final victory.

Somehow Britain had survived this war with its empire and dynasty intact, but would its expanded vision of the greater Middle East as the essential hub of imperial control survive the peace? Would the time-tested and all-important formula of informal influence and formal control of this vital region unravel under newer conditions and greater international scrutiny? Yet, a British-controlled Middle East had just proven its worth in winning the Great War. There could be no turning back. Britain had now become a captive to this foremost regional policy, which would soon bring another great triumph but in the end would destroy her as a great power.

CHAPTER ELEVEN

War's aftershock:
The watershed 1918–22

"Arabs recognize many conflicting interests are central in Palestine. *They admit the moral claims of the Zionists. They regard the Jews as Kinsmen whose just claims they will be glad to see satisfied.*" He concluded: "The interests of the Arab inhabitants may safely be left in the hands of the British Government."

AMIR FEISAL ON PALESTINE AND THE JEWS.
India Office note, December 27, 1918

Mesopotamia (Iraq), Palestine, and Trans-Jordan: The British mandate and informal influence

It should have been obvious to the victorious allies that suspicions and animosities resulting from the conflicted diplomatic wartime decisions would not suddenly end with the arrival of peace. It fact, they only intensified following the cessation of hostilities. Between the Armistice of November 11, 1918, and the Treaty of Versailles of June 28, 1919, a brief window of opportunity opened and allowed each would-be victor a claim to the spoils. It was now or never. As such, Versailles and its related treaties unlocked the floodgates to every conceivable national demand from Europe to the Middle East.

Punctuated by the Ottoman withdrawal from its Middle Eastern provinces, various national groups formerly under Ottoman control now seized the moment. Egyptians demanded independence and Arabs sought their own state, while Armenians and Kurds fought for national recognition. In addition, European Jews, nonindigenous to the region, pursued a homeland in Palestine. Undeterred by all these claims, Britain and France, always resolute, doggedly pursued their own spheres. One sticking point remained, however. The entry of President Woodrow Wilson and the United States into the war had proved a decisive factor in the ultimate allied victory. Thus, Wilson's views on peace and the vision of national self-determination contained in the Fourteen Points had to be taken seriously. When applied to the Middle East, like it or not, the British and French spheres as well as a Jewish homeland might have to be scrapped in favor of the recognition of indigenous national rights over all other claims. But Wilson's illness in late 1919 and untimely death soon after spared both the Anglo-French spheres and Jewish homeland from what otherwise might have been an early demise.

Although illness had forced Woodrow Wilson out of the picture by 1920, the League of Nations, as part of his dream, now emerged. In April of that year, members of the league met in San Remo and granted Britain and France special mandates to administer former German and Ottoman territories. In the Middle East, the French mandate included Lebanon and Syria, while the British received jurisdiction over Iraq, Trans-Jordan, and Palestine—the bulk of the former Ottoman Middle East. This could be understood as a compromise between the Sykes-Picot Agreement, the McMahon–Hussein correspondence, and Wilson's vision, since the mandates were to prepare the native population for ultimate self-rule. For Britain, the mandate system also confirmed areas once under informal influence (Ottoman guarantorship: Palestine, Jordan, and Iraq) and now restored through conquest of war.

Throughout November and December 1918 and before the mandates had been assigned, Sherif Feisal, established at Damascus, had asserted quasi-authority over Syria, Lebanon, Trans-Jordan, and Palestine. His brother Abdullah briefly claimed Mesopotamia, while his father, King Hussein, and younger brother Ali controlled the Hejaz. The Hashemite dream and British promise of an Arab state and a restored Sunni caliphate had become reality—or so everyone thought. A few wrinkles remained, however. The Saudis had chipped away at Hashemite control in Arabia, the French demanded Feisal withdraw from Lebanon, and the Zionists pressed their demands in Palestine. In view of these conditions, Feisal and T. E. Lawrence met in London to garner British assurances for his claims. On December 27, 1918, he and Lawrence convened with Indian Secretary Edwin Montagu, an anti-Zionist Jew, and several other British officials to settle these issues and clarify the British and Arab positions once and for all. Lawrence interpreted for Feisal throughout the discussions.[1]

First, Feisal explained the solidarity of the Arab movement and the essential unity of the Arab race. He then tackled the problem in Arabia between the Saudi-Wahhabi movement and Hashemite authorities in the Hejaz. He had no objection to Saudi theology, "but it is essentially a militant creed and being made to serve political ends. Intolerant of anybody outside of their own sect. Would exclude non-Wahhabis from pilgrim sites if they control the holy places—if in the Nejd OK—but not westward in settled areas—that was significance of Khurma incident."[2] Feisal proposed to expel them from Khurma, and "His Majesty's Government should have no fear because he (Feisal) does not intend to expand into the Nejd."[3]

Next, he addressed the problem of Syria. Speaking for Feisal, Lawrence stated that he "has always trusted the British—but in lieu of the Sykes-Picot Agreement which was not made known to him until long after its conclusion, had no idea during the long struggle with the Turks such an agreement existed—'or that Arab rights in Syria had been bargained away in advance.' Syria is the granary of the Hejaz. . . . And its possession absolutely essential to the Arabs."[4] He then asserted categorically that "The Arabs hate the French and compared them to 'well-leeches'. . . . Feels British obligation to honour the French Alliance was OK, but shouldn't be done at expense of the Arabs . . . and hinted at war between the Arabs and French in the future."[5]

Finally, Feisal explained his position on the Zionists in Palestine, revealing surprising tolerance. Feisal expressed deep obligation to the British government and said that "it would ill become the Arabs to make difficulties over a question of which they regard the British Government as the best judges. Arabs recognize many conflicting interests are central in Palestine. *They admit the moral claims of the Zionists. They regard the Jews as Kinsmen whose just claims they will be glad to see satisfied.*" He concluded that "the interests of the Arab inhabitants may safely be left in the hands of the British Government"[6] (author's italics). One British observer, apparently shaken by later Arab-Jewish conflicts in Palestine, returned to reexamine the document and commented in the margin, "Yes, excellent I think," in regards to his recollection of Feisal's astonishing comments.[7]

Much of Feisal's Arab dream, nonetheless, soon deteriorated. As noted, the Saudis, with Indian government support, inevitably took Arabia, including the Hejaz and Holy Sites. By 1924, they drove King Hussein into exile. In the end, the British government offered little resistance. Meanwhile, Feisal hoped for better in Syria and Palestine. On February 6, 1919, he attended the Paris Peace Conference. Feisal pled his cause for the independence of all the Arab territories to the proposed mandatory powers, who were to verify the wishes of the region's inhabitants. They never did. Although the British supported Hussein and Feisal in principle, the French balked, and the British backed down. At that point, President Wilson stepped in and in June 1919 sent the King-Crane Commission to Syria and Palestine, which discovered determined opposition to any separation of the two regions. The inhabitants revealed "a preference for an American mandate and failing that a British one, but under no circumstances would Syrians peaceably accept France as the mandatory power."[8] Moreover, the commission opposed Jewish immigration as detrimental to Arab self-determination and, despite

Weizmann's assurances, discovered that from the beginning the Zionists had planned to create a Jewish state and dispossess the Arabs. The commission's ominously prophetic report reads:

> We recommended, in the fifth place, serious modification of the extreme Zionist program for Palestine of unlimited immigration of Jews looking finally to making Palestine distinctly a Jewish State . . . If however, the strict terms of the Balfour Statement are adhered to—favoring "the establishment in Palestine of a national home for the Jewish people," "it being clearly understood that nothing shall be done which may prejudice the civil and religious rights of existing non-Jewish communities in Palestine"—it can hardly be doubted that the extreme Zionist Program must be greatly modified. For "a national home for the Jewish people" is not equivalent to making Palestine into a Jewish State: nor can the erection of such a Jewish State be accomplished without the gravest trespass upon the "civil and religious rights of existing non-Jewish communities in Palestine." The fact came out repeatedly in the Commission's conference with Jewish representatives, that the Zionists looked forward to a practically complete dispossession of the present non-Jewish inhabitants of Palestine, by various forms of purchase. . . . The Peace Conference should not shut its eyes to the fact that the anti-Zionist feeling in Palestine and Syria is intense and not lightly to be flouted.[9]

The commission never made it to Mesopotamia or Egypt, and because of Wilson's declining health, the King-Crane report was ignored, and then shelved.

While the commission was still operational, however, the British government apparently made one last effort to fulfill McMahon's promise to Hussein and recognize Feisal's de facto rule over Syria. "We had handed over to absolute Arab rule, represented by the Arab Government at Damascus, the head of which was the Emir Feisal, the portion of the vilayet of Syria in which we were free to act without consulting the French. . . . This point was soon to be raised in an acute form by the French occupation of Damascus."[10]

In March 1920, an elected assembly at Damascus proclaimed Feisal king of Syria, which still included Lebanon, Trans-Jordan, and Palestine.[11] One month later, the League of Nations declared in favor of the mandates. Quick to respond, the French seized Lebanon, and, though unauthorized, Feisal's forces attacked. They proved no match for the French, who countered with 90,000 troops. On July 25, 1920, they seized Damascus, throwing out Feisal and with him the dream of an Arab state—or so it seemed. Without a doubt, the British promise to create a great Arab state and restore the caliphate had been crushed by the Sykes–Picot Agreement for the immediate future. The ruthless enforcement of the mandate, however, provoked an Arab insurrection in British-held Mesopotamia (Iraq), where Feisal's brother

Abdullah, who briefly claimed kingship, threatened to aid Feisal and attack the French in Syria. To calm all concerned and resolve the dilemma, the British presently installed Feisal as king of Iraq and Abdullah as ruler of Trans-Jordan two years later. This solution proved satisfactory and held for the duration.

In Palestine, however, where the British mandate remained firm, there were no solutions. Chaim Weizmann's promises to the Arabs in Jerusalem and to Feisal at Aqaba in 1918 were soon broken. Equally, all assurances made by Feisal to Weizmann and the Zionists at Aqaba and the India Office in London proved, at best, ephemeral. Promises were one thing, reality another. Despite their words, Feisal, who was driven out by the French, and Weizmann, who had returned to London, were no longer in a position to control the outcome in Palestine. In September 1922, British authorities determined that the Palestine Mandate in regards to Zionist aspirations would not include Trans-Jordan and effectively separated their jurisdictions. While they installed Abdullah as emir in Trans-Jordan, this action did not offset growing Arab outrage over increased Jewish immigration and land

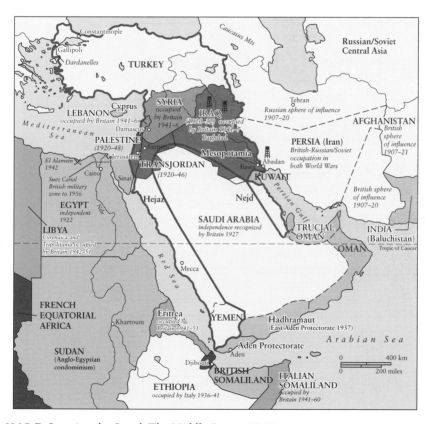

MAP 7 *Securing the Canal: The Middle East to 1945.*

purchases in Palestine, as the King-Crane Commission had warned. British attempts at mediation notwithstanding, anti-Zionist riots and reprisals erupted in 1922 and continued their bloody course until the British withdrew from the Palestine Mandate in 1948. Needless to say, the issues remain, as they had been in 1922, unresolved. Like the promise of a grand Arab state and caliphate, so Britain's vision of a unitary binational state of Arabs and Jews in Palestine would continue unfulfilled to the present.

In Mesopotamia, meanwhile, the interval between the armistice and Wilson's effective departure saw the British and Indian governments desperately scramble to preserve their sphere by whatever means. Correspondence between the Political Department of the India Office in London and Indian Government Representative Sir Percy Cox in April 1918 recount those efforts. Written on April 3, the government's note to Cox reveals that the original idea in 1915–16 was "to set up an Arab state under strong British tutelage and with King Hussein as the titular head. Hussein felt, however, that British interference in the new Arab state would be too strong and demanded much more freedom politically. His ideas were then shelved."[12] An India Office document states that the newer British position of 1918, however, placed more emphasis on the concept of liberated peoples and less on British administration: "Due to the spread of the doctrine of 'self-determination' under powerful advocacy of the President of the United States, British annexation looks out of the question—especially idea of a Protectorate—unless population demands it on their own accord."[13] In the final analysis, Britain would resort to the time-honored mechanism of informal control.

Clearly, the position of the British government was that if they could not control the area more directly, they would find a way to exert British influence indirectly. Cox's response on April 22 revealed a categorically different and more deceptive point of view. The Indian government's analysis decidedly supported the direct control of Mesopotamia and/or annexation as opposed to any form of informal influence. Cox recounts that his original idea, or that of the Indian government, had been to create an Arab state as a disguised protectorate, with the capital at Baghdad; and that Britain would take Basra and surrounding territory under direct control. He lamented that American demands for self-determination had changed everything. One final and exasperated thought remained: "Need to find an Arab façade for the Province of Iraq—under British guidance. . . . Foreign relations in British hands i.e. a protectorate—2nd solution, a native Titular ruler . . . find one from the family of the Sherif of Mecca."[14] Cox remained very cautious about this second alternative. He felt that Hussein should never have been called king of Arabia (which included Iraq) but confirmed only as the king of Hejaz, because he had no recognition in Iraq.[15] Cox's total solution to the Iraq dilemma proved very revealing: "Who should rule Iraq?—Nagib of Baghdad—much older family in region—respected by all, whereas Sherif Hussein and his family are almost unknown in Iraq. . . . His Administration (Nagib's)—friendly to the British. As far as running the country . . . but run by British officers—until Arab officials are trained to replace them."[16]

Why did the Indian government and Cox reject informal influence in Mesopotamia out of hand? Because neither Cox nor his Indian colleagues wanted to sanction an independent or autonomous Arab state in Iraq for fear of its impact on India's nationalists and their drive for independence. They still held out hope for direct British or Indian government control in southern Iraq and a puppet regime in the north. In the end, the Indian government's arcane views would not prevail. The newly created League of Nations gave Britain administrative control of Iraq through the mandate system, and, in view of Wilson's pronouncements, the British chose informal influence over direct control.

On the eve of the mandate, however, British officials in Iraq faced a serious disturbance from the Kurds, who demanded independence. The Kurds, as non-Arab Muslims, demanded an independent state in northern Mesopotamia, eastern Anatolia, and western Persia. The British military had occupied "Kurdistan" during the war and presently established a quasi government to preserve order and feed the populace.[17] "Following the war, movements to achieve Kurdish Autonomy under British protection and moves to achieve Kurdish Independence clashed. The Kurds of Mesopotamia fell under control of the British High Commissioner, Mesopotamia. However, other tribes fell within Turkish or Persian territory."[18] The situation proved impossible and demonstrated that Kurdistan, if even an independent state, could not include this territory.

The border issue was problem enough, but Kurds in the south raised the stakes. "Southern Kurds, however, resented British rule from Mesopotamia and killed several British officers."[19] The British now decided "to leave the Kurds to their own devices, since it was impossible to control the region militarily, or else it would become another Northwest Frontier problem on the North East border of Iraq."[20] Hence, the government opted to leave Kurdistan's population under whatever regimes evolved in Turkey, Persia, and Mesopotamia. An independent Kurdistan simply proved too impractical for further consideration. Britain's continued desire to control Mesopotamia rested on the oil-rich deposits throughout its eastern region. Moreover, by keeping the northern Kurdish areas attached to Iraq proper, the newly discovered oil fields near Mosul would remain under British control.

Operating on the premise "to the victors go the spoils," British oil brokers had engaged in price gouging; this caused a second and greater uprising of the general Iraqi population, which quickly escalated into a major revolt when the mandate was announced. An emergency session at the India Office determined "that the middle men Messrs. Strick, Scott and Company were taking too big a profit and should be removed from the equation and that the Anglo–Persian representatives should replace them."[21] Their decision had come too late. This issue of price gouging, along with the French ouster of Feisal from Syria in 1920, provoked the Iraqi revolt into a national cause. Some £40,000,000 and 2,000 casualties later, A. T. Wilson, head of Iraq's civil administration, urged the British government to quickly reappraise its policies. Hoping to assuage Arab anger, Wilson and the government agreed in August 1921 to install Feisal at Baghdad as king of Iraq.[22] With that, the riots slowly subsided, and Feisal emerged as titular head of an Arab state, as would his brother Abdullah in Trans-Jordan two years later.

In the end, the Hashimites had lost Arabia to the Saudis and Syria-Lebanon to the French and had resigned Palestine to British administration. The two kingdoms of Iraq and Trans-Jordan, staffed with British officials and rulers friendly to Britain, remained mandates and thus guaranteed British control through informal influence. Full independence came to Iraq eleven years later under Feisal, who, together with Abdullah in Jordan, at last could claim a truncated Arab state and a piecemeal Hashimite victory.[23] By using Feisal and Iraq's Sunni Arab minority to control the Shia Arab majority as well as the Kurds, however, the British set a precedent for problems in Iraq lasting to the present, as future leaders, including Saddam Hussein, would follow suit.

The question of independence, "reserved powers," and formal control in Egypt

During the war, as noted, Britain had declared Egypt, still smarting under formal control, a protectorate, and had utilized thousands of Egyptian soldiers and laborers to serve the British effort in Palestine, Syria, and Mesopotamia and on the Western Front. In reward for this service, most Egyptians anticipated full independence from Britain. By not recognizing Egypt's contributions to the war, however, the government deliberately lowered those expectations. Instead, British officials, including Winston Churchill and Sir Reginald Wingate, now advocated Egypt's formal annexation into the British Empire. In response, Said Zaghlul, vice president of the Egyptian legislature and a nationalist in the Urabi tradition, formed the Wafd (delegation) to proceed to London in 1918. He no doubt remembered those arrogantly tactless comments from Mark Sykes in 1915 and determined to pursue Egypt's independence despite them and at whatever cost. High Commissioner Wingate twice rejected Zaghlul's travel request, ordered his arrest and exiled him to Malta.[24] Major E. P. Newman, still stationed in Egypt, candidly observed, "Again a deaf ear was turned to the national aspirations of the people of Egypt. This refusal on the part of Great Britain even to consider the political position of a country which had given valuable help to the British Empire in time of need roused bitter feelings amongst the Egyptians."[25]

Those "bitter feelings" produced a violent revolution against the protectorate in 1919 and resulted in substantial British casualties and over 1,000 Egyptian deaths.[26] Under pressure, the British returned Zaghlul to Egypt, who, still undaunted, ventured to the Paris Peace Conference with other nationalists to present a case for Egypt's independence. Their appeals fell on deaf ears because Egypt's protectorate status exempted it from further examination by the

League of Nations or President Wilson's King-Crane Commission. Britain held all the cards, but in view of the continued violence, Lloyd George sent colonial secretary Lord Alfred Milner to Egypt to secure further recommendations on Egypt's status. While there, a Wafd-led boycott prompted Milner to drop the term *protectorate* and seek a compromise with the nationalists. Thereafter, he met Zaghlul in London and engaged in a series of discussions from June 9 to August 18, 1921, to no avail. In no mood for compromise, Zaghlul refused any agreement that allowed the British to continue in Egypt on any level. Equally frustrated and resolute, Milner devised a unilateral plan for a transfer of power, which contained a formula for certain political components "transferred to Egypt and those reserved for Britain."

Some doubt remains whether Zaghlul ever signed the Milner-Zaghlul Agreement, since he immediately denounced the memorandum upon his return to Egypt and encouraged further rioting. Egypt's newly appointed high commissioner, General Allenby, however, supported the plan. Incensed, Britain's next colonial secretary, Winston Churchill, criticized the scheme as a "needless give away," while Zaghlul condemned it as "a disguised Protectorate." In the end, Allenby had his way. He ignored Churchill, suppressed the riots, and exiled Zaghlul for the second time. Thereafter,

FIGURE 19 *Egyptians demand independence, 1922. Leemage. Getty Images.*

he pressured Lloyd George to declare unilaterally Egypt's independence on August 28, 1922, based on the agreement. Those powers reserved to the British government included "(1) the right to protect British imperial communications in Egypt, (2) oversight of Egypt's defense against foreign aggression, (3) the power to protect foreign interests and minorities in the country, and (4) control of the Sudan."[27]

Overall, the declaration provided Egypt with a qualified degree of independence, which might otherwise have been delayed for decades. Without Zaghlul's tenacity, however, it remains doubtful that even this much independence would have been achieved at the time. As Egypt proceeded into an uncertain future, it did so with a new constitution written in 1923, wherein Sultan Fuad became King Fuad, and a new legislature was instituted, dominated by the Wafd (now a political party). Zaghlul returned from exile to become Egypt's prime minister, a position he held until his death in 1927.

Having lost the protectorate, the British resorted to the uncertainties of their "reserved powers" and informal management of the king and Wafd in a strategy of divide and conquer. Yet, formal control technically continued as long as British troops and administrators remained in Egypt to secure Britain's "reserved powers." Owing to the manifest importance of the Suez Canal as well as the political and international stresses of the postwar era, the British could give no more, and the Egyptians could take no less. Hence, the British would remain in Egypt until another global war and more conflict forced their complete withdrawal in 1954.

Eastern Question and the Great Game revisited: Turkey, Persia, Afghanistan— the Soviet challenge

Britain's on-again, off-again relations with imperial Russia throughout the nineteenth century had been finally resolved by their joint effort to defeat the Triple Alliance in the First World War. The projected division of the Ottoman Empire under the Sykes-Picot Agreement reversed decades of British opposition to Russian encroachment on the Straits and Constantinople (Istanbul). Moreover, Britain had agreed with Russia to create mutual spheres of influence in Persia and avoid collisions in Afghanistan for the duration of the war. The Bolshevik Revolution and Russia's withdrawal from the conflict, however, ended this brief period of accommodation and terminated any Russian claims to the spoils of war.

With Russia out of the picture, Lloyd George had urged an American mandate over Constantinople, the Dardanelles, and Armenia, which of course, never materialized. As early as January 1919, Lord Curzon had even suggested the removal of Constantinople from Turkish control altogether. To Curzon's memorandum, Indian Secretary Montagu stated that "to dislocate

Constantinople from Turkey would be an unnecessary offense to Moslems under British control—especially Indian Moslems who fought and died for the British cause—only to now be slapped in the face. We're not taking Berlin from the Germans or Vienna from the Austrians and to do this to Turkey would be ridiculous. In addition, not one single Indian Moslem is being sent to the Councils in Europe for discussions of peace terms etc. The least we can do is not insult them further. Neither is it worth it to return the Church of Saint Sophia to the Christians."[28] Ultimate control of those former Ottoman territories of Armenia, Kurdistan, etc., which had comprised part of the "Eastern Question" and the "Great Game," would be withheld from the Russians (Soviets), refused by the United States, and, finally, retaken by Turkish military force. In 1923, Kemal Ataturk declared a Turkish Republic and reoccupied those disputed territories in eastern Anatolia. He then drove the Greeks from the western portions of Turkey that had been awarded them by the Treaty of Sèvres in 1920. Whatever divisions the Allies had in mind Ataturk quickly laid to rest by swift and decisive action. The Treaty of Lausanne, signed on July 24, 1923, confirmed those gains as part of the new Republic of Turkey.[29] Likewise, Persia, always a thorn to British policy makers, as noted, had been divided between Russian and British spheres during the war. After the Bolshevik revolution and Russia's withdrawal from the conflict, Britain unilaterally increased her sphere in Persia through informal influence and hoped to guide this otherwise independent country with British military and civil officials indefinitely. Lord Curzon, now Britain's foreign secretary, proposed an Anglo-Persian Agreement for that purpose in 1919. Both governments signed the protocol, but to everyone's surprise, it proved illegal. "A short time after execution of the agreement, it was discovered in London and Teheran that a provision in the Persian Constitution required that all treaties had to be ratified by the Majlis (as the legislature was called). The Majlis had not met since 1915 and had been ignored by both governments in arriving at the agreement."[30] Angered and insulted, the Majlis steadfastly refused to sign.

In 1921, a palace revolution in Persia saw Reza Khan (after 1925, Reza Shah Pahlavi) replace the old Qajar Dynasty, evict the British, and, instead, to the government's shock, endorse a similar agreement with the Soviets on February 26, 1921.[31] By the new Soviet-Persian treaty, Russia canceled Persian debts as well as extraterritorial privileges for Russian nationals. Moreover, if Persia became a base for action against Russia, then Russian troops could be sent into Persia. This time, the Majlis ratified the treaty.[32]

Clearly, the Persians felt they had more to fear from British imperialism, based on their long experience, than from Bolshevism, of which they knew little. But Britain's problems had only begun. Afghanistan signed a similar treaty with the Russians on the same day as Persia, while Turkey signed a mutual agreement with the new Soviet government a month later. The nightmare had returned all too soon: The Eastern Question and the Great Game now reemerged with a vengeance.

Afghanistan's relations with the British and Indian governments, never understood as particularly good, had proved tentative since the conclusion of the Second Afghan War and the Treaty of Gandamack, signed on May 26, 1879, which made it a British dependency.[33] This arrangement began poorly. "As a result of an attempt by Ayub Khan, (son of the Emir) to occupy Kandahar, there was a clash between his troops and the British force sent out to intercept him at Maiwand on the July 27th, 1880, which ended in a severe defeat for the British."[34] Although a second British force defeated him, "Her Majesty's Government [which since the fall of the Beaconsfield (Disraeli) administration had decided not to follow a 'forward policy'] gave orders for its evacuation, and Abdur Rahman (Emir) was invited to take possession of the province. By 1881 the evacuation of the entire country by British forces was complete."[35] Despite Russian intrigues, Prime Minister Gladstone determined to end hostilities permanently and reconfirmed the treaty. Emir Abdur Rahman and his successor, Habibullah, continued the British dependency and received £180,000 per year in the face of growing nationalist opposition throughout Afghanistan.[36] Dependency or not, no single British advisor could be found throughout the country over the next forty years because of widespread suspicions of British intent, real or imagined. In 1905, Indian Secretary Lord John Morley expressed his bewilderment over this arrangement in a note to the Government of India: "How we are bound to defend the Amir's country, yet are forbidden to take a single step for defense within its border, or to send a single officer to reconnoitre the best means for its defense; how we give the Amir an annual subsidy of 18 lakhs (£180,000), yet are not allowed to place a European agent at his capital."[37] Furthermore, this allowed the arms flow and general fanaticism of the country to remain unchecked.

Morley believed that despite these limitations and restrictions, the arrangement served a special purpose: "Evidently so singular a position is only tolerated or upheld for peculiarly strong reasons, arising from the belief in the minds of Afghan and British rulers equally that each of them requires and receives some valuable considerations from the other."[38] For the British, that meant no other foreign power, especially Russia, could meddle in Afghan affairs, and the emir would guarantee this bottom line regardless of those annoying anomalies. For Afghanistan's rulers, it meant a considerable subsidy and an unrestricted weapons flow, essentials for the maintenance of power; for Britain, this proved a cheap price, indeed, to secure India's border.

Above all, the arrangement worked surprisingly well despite the stresses brought on the country by the First World War, when a majority of Afghan nationalists hoped to side with the Germans and Ottomans in a jihad against British control in the region. Amir Habibullah expelled the German-Turkish mission in 1916 and "succeeded against much opposition in preserving his country's neutrality."[39] Ultimately, Habibullah's stance proved costly. In February 1919, he was murdered in his sleep during a hunting expedition, courtesy of his wife and son.[40]

Thereafter, relations with Britain again hit bottom. "Afghanistan rose in a national revolt against British control in summer of 1919. Though this 3rd Afghan War lasted only a month (May 3 to June 3) it resulted in the British relinquishing control over Afghan foreign affairs, and from this time on is known as the Period of Independence."[41] The ink had barely dried on the treaty ending this brief conflict when the new Soviet government, quick to respond, moved in where the British left off. The British, nonetheless, continued to lose influence to the Russians in Afghanistan as well as Persia.[42]

The Government of India tried in vain to rescue the historic relationship with a Treaty of Friendship with Afghanistan to neutralize it, at the very least. While its mission negotiated at Kabul, Afghan representative Mohammed Wali Khan arrived in London in August 1921, only to be rebuffed by Foreign Secretary Curzon. "The mission was received with some coldness by the Foreign Secretary, Lord Curzon. . . . This rebuff deeply offended the Afghan Government and added further to the difficulties of the British delegates to the Kabul Conference."[43]

This lack of support proved a costly mistake. In the end, the assurances of informal influence had failed because of Curzon's antagonism. The best the Indian government could salvage was a greatly weakened treaty, signed on November 22, 1921, which basically guaranteed nothing and was cynically viewed "as a Treaty of Neighborly Relations."[44] Thereafter, the Soviets assumed the subsidies and delivered arms to the Afghans "by a Russian offer to the Afghans of money, arms and material in return for an undertaking by Afghanistan to facilitate the dispatch of Russian arms to the British frontier tribes in India."[45]

The Soviet (Russian) entry or reentry into the arena of the historic Great Game was unanticipated and troublesome, but, more seriously, Britain's inability to check it foreshadowed a lessening of her power throughout the region, as the British themselves acknowledged. "By the summer of 1920 British relations with both Russia and Turkey had worsened, while in Persia, Egypt and Mesopotamia British influence was on the wane."[46] The situation in India had deteriorated as well. There, Muslim national insurgencies erupted, "whereby many thousands of discontented Muslims migrated across the frontier into Afghanistan, to the discomfiture of the Amir."[47] The situation with Afghanistan remained tenuous, and minus the subsidies, which the British could no longer afford, it proved illustrative of Britain's general economic decline. The world's greatest creditor nation had emerged from the First World War as the globe's largest debtor. Quick to detect weakness, the wolves were soon at the door.

With the exception of control over the Gulf sheikdoms, which remained British protectorates, and Aden, a colony, Britain's overall authority in the Middle East from 1919 to 1922, tested at every point, appeared to falter inch by inch. In 1919, Egypt's bloody revolution produced quasi-independence, while the Afghan War against Britain ended the dependency. The 1920 revolution in Iraq, which toppled direct British control in favor of an Arab regime and informal influence, was followed by a revolt in Persia and the termination of the British presence altogether. Moreover, the Saudi conquests ended whatever leverage Britain hoped to maintain in Arabia. The mandates in Iraq and Trans-Jordan were soon to be independent, while that of riot-torn Palestine could not be freed soon enough. By 1922, the British sphere in the Middle East, a product of three centuries of development, proved more illusion than reality. Both informal influence and formal control had been stretched to the breaking point. The British sphere had survived the peace, but just barely, as historian Bernard Porter states in *The Lion's Share*: "One conflagration could have been kept under control; so many at the same time was rather stretching the resources of the imperial fire service. 'Our small army is far too scattered', wrote the Chief of the General Staff in May 1920; 'in no single theatre are we strong enough'."[48]

Yet the British had determined to remain in the region. They would not back down. Control of the Middle East had provided them with a conduit for victory against the central powers. The wisdom of Palmerstone's almost century-old policy had found fulfillment. Britain would find a way to manage the Middle East. It had become the key, in every sense, to a triumphant empire.

CHAPTER TWELVE

Tenacity enshrined:
Holding on 1922–40

*1936 treaty opened some prospect of removing the
British slowly by stages. Anthony Eden, the British Foreign
Secretary, and all the other signatories appeared on an
Egyptian postage stamp to commemorate the treaty. Nahas,
the Wafd leader, was applauded in the streets.*

BRIAN LAPPING, *End of Empire*

Egypt: A contest of wills

Despite the obvious weakness of their postwar position, neither civil strife, Second World War nor the Cold War could sway Britain's imperial-minded warriors to lessen their grip on the region. Gritty, tough, and determined, successive British governments clung to their Middle Eastern sphere and contested almost every withdrawal for the next half century. While Britain's mandates over Iraq, Palestine, and Trans-Jordan assured some degree of influence, her continued presence at the Suez Canal was the most critical and the greatest challenge because of the loss of Egypt's protectorate status. Legalities aside, nothing had changed: Egypt remained crucial as the highway to India and to the economy and defense of the British Empire. The British could not and would not leave. The techniques of either formal control or informal influence would prove elastic enough to maintain a degree of British power in the Middle East as the vital artery of empire. In reality, Britain had no other option. Thanks to the efforts of Roe, Baldwin,

Palmerston, and, in more recent times, Churchill and Lloyd George, Britain, in essence, had become Middle East dependent. After three centuries, control of the Middle East had become an addiction, more so than that of India.

Despite assurances to the contrary, Egypt's new sovereignty appeared a legal fabrication despite the declaration of 1922, since the British refused to depart, and her proconsuls, the high commissioners, proved as meddling and controlling as the former governor-generals. Britain, on the other hand, saw no way to depart or diminish her hold over Egypt without endangering her strategic position. Consequently, to maintain control until the start of the Second World War, British representatives in Egypt managed a program of divide and conquer, pitting the Wafd party against the monarch. In turn, the population perceived and supported the Wafd or the monarchy as pronationalist if either moved to force a British ouster. As Arthur Goldschmidt Jr. put it, this was the period of "Egypt's ambiguous independence."[1] The undefined nature of such a relationship quickly spawned misunderstandings and political violence. When Britain's anti-imperialist Labour Party briefly came to power in 1924 and advocated Egypt's complete independence, Prime Minister Ramsay MacDonald shockingly reversed position when he met with Zaghlul and announced his decision to enforce Britain's reserved powers.[2] Enraged on hearing the news, terrorists from a recently formed secret society assassinated Sir Lee Stack, British commander (Sirdar) of the Egyptian army, and governor-general of the Sudan.[3]

That the incident transpired openly in the streets of Cairo stunned Zaghlul, the Wafd, and King Fuad. Clearly, a new element had entered the equation to challenge the British by force, and it proved merely the beginning. These terrorists came from one of several secret societies spawned in the 1919 revolution as an alternative to the normal political agenda. More such groups soon followed, including the Muslim Brothers, organized in 1928 as the first Islamic fundamentalist movement, who were determined to expel the British and establish Egypt as an Islamic state. Within the ranks of Egypt's military, an intensely nationalistic Free Officer Corps evolved during the Second World War to force a British ouster as well. In time, they would prove the greatest threat.

Britain's protracted and tenacious imperial presence, permitted through informal control as much as any single factor, produced this new breed of Islamic extremism and military nationalism in Egypt. As Britain's emasculation of Egypt's legitimate institutions continued, the population moved to support these newer, more confrontational options, which would not sell out to the British. Stack's murder foreshadowed this new reality, and British reprisals confirmed the inevitable.

Allenby promptly retaliated for Stack's murder. He ordered that the Nile flow into Egypt be restricted in favor of Sudanese agriculture and then reduced the ranks of Egyptian officers and regiments in the Sudan to zero. These punitive actions at once attacked Egypt's lifeblood and her legal claim to the Sudan. The Wafd and monarch stood powerless to prevent it. Historian

Elizabeth Monroe notes "Allenby had on his own responsibility demanded, after the murder, retribution so excessive that it looked like an intention to do Egypt permanent harm. . . . Zaghlul, for his part, resigned over his inability either to stop extremist outrages or to mitigate British reprisals."[4]

Allenby's anticipated departure in 1925, however, offered no improvement, as Egypt's new postwar high commissioner, Lord George Lloyd (1925–29), a staunch, old-school imperialist, "hoped for a strict application of the Declaration [of 1922] and restoration of British influence in Egypt to its former prestige."[5] Lloyd soon forced the British government into another collision with the Egyptians. Sparing no one, he set about to ambush Zaghlul, the Wafd, and the army as threats to British interests. For his part, Zaghlul, ever resolute despite his resignation, returned as premier by popular mandate in 1926. Resorting to gunboat diplomacy, Lloyd saw to it that he never took office. When Lloyd used the reserved powers to reduce the Egyptian army, the Wafd countered by demanding the abolition of the office of British sirdar of Egypt's military.[6] Lloyd angrily responded that such measures infringed on British rights and attacked the Wafd party's attempt to control the army.[7] According to British sources, the Wafd undermined the status quo and attempted to propagandize the newly enlarged Egyptian army with its own political extremism.[8]

In a threat reminiscent of 1882, he ordered two warships to Alexandria to intimidate all concerned. Humiliated, the Wafd backed down, as the Zaghlul affair and the army crisis proved who still controlled Egypt. Zaghlul died in 1927, a premier out of office but forever remembered as the father of Egyptian independence, while the army, reduced to 10,000 until 1936, would someday fulfill Zaghlul's mission as unfinished business.[9]

Since no Egyptian government ever could or would sign the declaration of 1922, which contained the reserved powers, Britain's presence in Egypt had persisted through devious diplomacy and, failing that, the threat of force. Ultimately, a greater menace compelled both parties to bridge the diplomatic impasse and save face. The brutal invasion of Ethiopia in 1935 by Italy's Fascist dictator, Benito Mussolini, pointed up a new reality. Egypt, as well as the British position there, had become vulnerable to a possible Italian threat from Ethiopia as well as from Libya. A year later, Germany's Nazi dictator, Adolf Hitler, occupied the Rhineland in violation of the Versailles Treaty. The situation soon acquired a character of greater menace when Italy moved closer to Germany in 1936 and signed the Axis Agreement. These ominous events prompted the British government to pursue a legal formula to remain in Egypt that would finally prove acceptable to the Egyptians.

Foreign Office Secretary Anthony Eden's Treaty with Egypt, engineered in 1936, appeared to erase those cumbersome ambiguities in regards to Egyptian sovereignty.[10] "The Anglo-Egyptian Treaty removed most of the reservations on Egypt's formal independence, except for the British military presence in the Canal and her colonial presence in the Sudan."[11] Britain's new point man in Egypt, High Commissioner Sir Miles Lampson (Lord Killearn), cleared the way for newly elected Wafd premier Mustafa al-Nahas to sign the agreement on August 26, 1936.[12] To reduce Egyptian fears of repeating the abuses of the First World War, Britain promised to defend Egypt in the event of future conflict, while Article 7 of the treaty held Egypt accountable for internal territorial defense and maintenance of public order. Both armies shared the canal's defense, and, as a concession, Egypt granted Britain use of all military facilities. In return, Egypt terminated special foreign privileges, including the hated capitulations under Article 17 and under separate agreement.[13] To the relief of Egypt's politicians, the treaty also reduced the office of British high commissioner to that of ambassador. Most significantly, the agreement secured a permanent, although gradual, British withdrawal in twenty years.

The treaty also redefined the role of Egypt's army that had up to this time been "regarded by some as little more than a parade ground body of quasi-police forces and cavalry squadrons."[14] Steady Egyptian pressure had at last forced a promise from Britain to upgrade Egypt's military and withdraw British personnel from its command.[15] The office of inspector-general (usually British) now passed to an Egyptian, meaning that the newly defined army had become an independent force. As an ally, Egypt accepted a British military mission for advice and received new armament and equipment equal to that used in the British army.[16] In view of Britain's long-held determination to limit and dominate the Egyptian army, this treaty proved a remarkable turnaround. Yet apprehensions remained. British parliamentary critics voiced doubts about weakened defenses at the canal.[17] In the Egyptian assembly, outspoken Senator Mohammed Haikal bemoaned the uselessness of an Egyptian army if British arms were severed, as indeed occurred in 1941–42.[18] Notwithstanding, the Egyptian army, under British dominance since 1882, was for the first time freed by the treaty as an autonomous force under native command. That at last they had achieved a tangible form of independence proved a hopeful sign for most Egyptians.

Whether or not the Anglo-Egyptian Treaty as a whole provided greater sovereignty for Egypt or more control for the British remains a subject of some historical debate.[19] "Each side interpreted the treaty in its own way: to the British it meant permanency; to the Egyptians it meant twenty years. Since the Wafd was a popular party that had to win elections, the treaty was presented as a triumph for Egyptian nationalism. . . . Nahas, the Wafd leader, was applauded in the streets."[20]

In the final analysis, the circumstances that produced this treaty were not propelled by the morality of the issue or Egyptian demands, since the British had been content to remain in Egypt regardless. Clearly, the outside pressure of an Italian threat alone forced the British to grant significant legal and binding concessions to the Egyptians, who were all too glad to accept them as the road to genuine freedom, minus any formula of formal or informal control. British attitudes regarding Egypt, however, remained as obdurate as ever, as the Second World War would demonstrate.

But it no longer mattered: The new agreement had irretrievably altered their legal position. Like it or not, the British would be forced to leave within twenty years. Even then, the British would find a way to return and provoke a catastrophic climax to an unwelcome presence.

Questions aside, in the context of 1936, the treaty appeared to solve long-standing dilemmas and offer guarantees sufficient for both parties to live with at that critical juncture. At the same time, Britain secured a treaty with the pro-British government of Iraq for use of airfields and military installations. These treaties came not a moment too soon, as anti-Zionist riots and British reprisals erupted in Palestine, considerably souring the mood in Egypt as well as the rest of the Arab Middle East.

As the threat of war increased from 1936 until 1939, British military authorities increasingly worried about the security of the Egyptian–Libyan border, where an Italian motorized attack against Egypt and the Suez Canal appeared most likely. The treaty of 1936 opened the way for Britain to modernize the Egyptian army's Frontier Force facing Libya. It still used outmoded light car patrols from the last war as well as camel-mounted forces for police work and countersmuggling operations.[21] Under War Office direction, British military missions sought to upgrade these forces as a first line of defense and as desert military intelligence to be used in time of war, requiring further training.[22] But the long and oft-tortured history of Anglo-Egyptian relations hindered clear sailing, as Egypt's leaders remained inordinately suspicious of British intentions, even if it compromised the country's defense. Although Egyptian military authorities permitted British military missions after 1936, they prevented British army operations in the western desert as a violation of Egypt's sovereignty. Nationalist General Muhammad Neguib succinctly stated their reasons. "I recommended that such permission be refused on the ground that it would constitute a violation of the treaty. . . . I was not insensible to the growing danger of war, but neither was I insensible to the desire of the British to reoccupy Egypt as their first opportunity."[23]

Moreover, British attempts to crush anti-Zionist riots in Palestine had produced a strong Arab nationalist backlash in Egypt. This was originally not an Egyptian problem, but as Egyptians began to identify with the larger Arab national cause, it became one. This had not been predicted, and it quickly altered the delicate military balance. Egypt's new and independent-minded premier, Ali Mahir Pasha, and his military chief of staff, General Aziz Ali al-Misri, a strident nationalist, immediately replaced all British Frontier Administration officers with Egyptians.[24] To the British commanders, this action completely compromised the Egyptian army as an effective force in the western desert where the Italians might invade.[25]

Although the British became increasingly worried about the reliability of the Egyptian army in time of war, the Italian invasion of Albania in April 1939 prodded a major readjustment of British thinking relative to the defense of Egypt and the Middle East. It now followed the course suggested earlier by Ambassador Lampson to Foreign Secretary Lord Halifax, involving "Remodeling the strategic and tactical doctrine of the Egyptian Army, besides reorganizing it on modern lines and converting it to a mechanized basis."[26] As a result, the War Office commissioned General Archibald Wavell as general officer and commander-in-chief for designated Middle East command. He had served with General Allenby and T. E. Lawrence in the First World War and, as an "old Middle East hand," seemed the best man to coordinate British efforts with Egypt, "acting to develop the Egyptian Forces . . . into efficient forces capable of cooperating . . . in the defense of Egypt."[27] Wavell's appointment indicated the determination of the British government, and especially the War Office, to develop and use the Egyptian army at the start of the war in 1939–40, despite doubts about its loyalty or that of the Egyptian government under its new monarch, King Farouk (1936–52).

In line with the new policy and as part of the treaty, a British-run Egyptian military academy established in 1936 had graduated its first cadets in 1938, including the young lieutenants Gamel Abdel Nasser and Anwar Sadat.[28] Moreover, the army improved its overall fighting capability and had increased from 11,814 to an expanded force of 42,000 by 1940.[29] Following the completion of Wavell's reorganization, he added a new and controversial component and placed experienced British advisors to oversee the Egyptian Frontier Force. According to the British view at least, the use of these advisors to overcome the inertia and inexperience of Egyptian officers sharpened the command of this force. The appointment of Lieutenant-Colonel Robinson of the 8th Hussars to the Frontier Force exemplified Wavell's tactic, according to a Foreign Office memo. "The senior officers of the Egyptian Army are so lacking in power of command and initiative that it will certainly be for consideration in war whether the British should take over command."[30]

Whatever the case, the upgraded defense force now included a cavalry corps, light tanks, numerous howitzer units, an anti-tank battery, and a unit of field engineers. As of 1939, Egyptian units shared responsibility with British regiments as an integrated force and guarded Egypt's western border from the Mediterranean south to the oasis at Siwa.[31] Wavell indicated that the much larger Italian force, which by early 1940 numbered 250,000, could not construe this troop placement as provocative.[32] On the eve of war, British and Egyptians, on the surface at least, appeared unified and ready to meet the challenge. This unity proved an illusion soon enough. Egypt's growing nationalism, now in the military ranks, as well as the heightened Palestinian crisis and the British reaction to both, would explode in the summer of 1940 with dire consequences.

Interwar Palestine 1918–39

Palestine had presented problems for the British since the end of the First World War and implementation of the mandate in 1920, when clashes erupted between the Zionist newcomers and Palestinian Arabs. Whatever governance or semblance of rule the Palestinian Arabs thought would be theirs as part of the short-lived Arab kingdom (Syria, Lebanon, Jordan, and Palestine) had suddenly vanished when the French took Syria and ousted King Feisal in 1920. Effectively cut off from political ties or guidance from Damascus, they grudgingly fell under the separate British Palestine Mandate. Their loose connection to Emir Abdullah of Trans-Jordan also disappeared when the British separated the jurisdictions of Trans-Jordan and Palestine in 1922.

Denied much political experience or leadership during four centuries of Ottoman rule, Palestinian Arabs simply proved unable to jumpstart an indigenous and complicated political process in response to the highly organized Zionists or unrealistic British expectations for self-government. Isolated and indignant over their fate, the majority of Muslim and Christian Arabs in Palestine flatly rejected the legitimacy of the British mandate or its authority to enforce the Balfour Declaration. Having lived there for centuries, they saw Palestine as their land, pure and simple, with or without recognition from the League of Nations, the mandate, or the British.

In contrast, the newly arrived Zionist settlers had based their claim to Palestine on Jewish history, inasmuch as their ancestors, the Israelites of the Old Testament, had settled the land and established a kingdom in Palestine (ancient Israel) at the time of King David, about 1000 BCE. After the territory became part of the Roman Empire and was renamed Judea, two serious revolts (67–70; 125–29 CE) brought about the destruction of Jerusalem and the dispersal of the Jewish population throughout the empire (diaspora). Although the Jewish state had disappeared, a small number of Jews remained in the land alongside their Arab neighbors up to the First World War. In the centuries between the diaspora and the modern age, Arab–Jewish relations throughout the Mediterranean and Middle East remained fairly positive and mutually beneficial, even after the rise of Islam.

The majority of Jews who came to Palestine in the nineteenth century, however, were culturally distinct. They had emigrated from Eastern Europe and Russia. Impacted by nationalism's romantic ideology, they brought with them a dream and a mission to return to the land and rebuild a homeland on the soil of their ancestors. These early Zionists of the first Aliyah (return), who settled in Palestine courtesy of the Ottoman Empire and modestly numbered about 20,000 in 1870, presented no immediate threat to the Arab population.[33]

Then came the second Aliyah from 1905 to 1914, somewhat inspired by the nationalistic writings of Jewish journalist Theodore Herzl proposing to create a state for Jewish survival somewhere, anywhere, including Palestine. The British had suggested Kenya (Uganda Protectorate), but the Zionists wanted Palestine because without Zion (Jerusalem), Zionism meant nothing. Because of Herzl's efforts, the World Zionist Organization and the Jewish National Fund were established to support the new endeavor, but, unlike the first settlers, the new emigrants were more nationalistic, culturally self-contained, and aloof from the Arabs. Historian Charles Smith notes, "Nevertheless, despite their small numbers, the Zionist drive to purchase land and the openness of their commitment to a separate Jewish entity in Palestine had already aroused Arab fears, which had become well-known to Zionist leaders in Palestine by 1914 but were ignored or downplayed by Zionist leaders in the West."[34]

During the Great War and immediately after, many British Christian organizations promoted the Zionist cause because they understood the Bible to support the claims of early Jewish history and the Jews' right of return to the Holy Land (Palestine) as a fulfillment of Biblical prophecy. They, as well as pro-Zionist British leaders Lloyd George and Churchill, either ignored or were ignorant of the fuller Zionist agenda and Arab reaction to it. Moreover, support of the Balfour Declaration, the Zionist movement, and thus, the third Aliyah (1919–23) had become the official policy of the British government, despite the fact it contradicted promises inherent in the Hussein–McMahan correspondence and ignored the dire warnings from the King-Crane Commission.[35] Quite apart from the Biblical imperative, British authorities envisioned Palestine, with a Jewish population loyal to Britain, as a means of protecting the Suez Canal and, therefore, the empire and the Palmerstonian equation for Middle East control. While some British officials sought to use Zionism to gain Palestine as an extended security for the Suez Canal, the Zionists used the British to gain a homeland and eventually a state.

Thus, the British, who had used the Arabs to defeat the Turks and preserve the empire, now utilized the Jews and the Zionist movement to secure Palestine, again for the sake of empire. The Arabs, especially those of Palestine, therefore, had suddenly become an expendable distraction, while the Zionists emerged as a viable necessity. In short, the situational ethics of British imperialism displayed no conscience; the security of the region, and thus the needs of empire, came first. Hence, at war's end, the third Aliyah and political Zionism hit the shores of Palestine, courtesy of and enforced by the authority of the British Empire. When the mandate began, 60,000–80,000 Jews lived in Palestine, the result of two decades of immigration from Russia and Eastern Europe, while the Arab population stood at 650,000.[36] Tensions were building, and the stage had been set for a collision.

The growing hostility became painfully clear in the decade following the implementation of the British mandate, when an uneasy truce was enforced on the Zionist settlers and Palestinian Arabs, punctuated by random acts of terror and growing violence. In the face of increased Jewish immigration and more disorder, reexamination of the Hussein–McMahan correspondence, the Sykes-Picot Agreement and the Balfour Declaration continued to perplex British leaders in regards to Palestinian rights.[37] And no wonder; from the start, these accords were at cross purposes, if not mutually exclusive. As a result, British authorities had been unable to satisfy the League of Nations' call for national self-determination or to fulfill the mandate's demand for eventual self-government for the indigenous, majority Arab population.

On the other hand, Palestine's growing Jewish community, forged in the caldron of European politics, persecution, and pogroms, quickly established ownership of self-governance to pursue its own national agenda. As long as the British government remained in a state of denial regarding the supreme purpose of the Zionists to turn a "Jewish Homeland" into a Jewish state, the ultimate fate of the Palestinian Arabs remained in limbo.[38] According to historian Brian Lapping, "The creation of a Jewish state in Palestine had always been the aim of most Zionists. They had denied it in public and tried to keep it out of their writings because in this the British did not support them."[39] This illusion allowed the British to believe they could still guarantee the rights of Palestine's Arab population.

Since no time limit was placed on this mandate, compared to Iraq or Syria, British authorities allowed the question of Arab self-rule and how to implement it to drift, undefined and unanswered. The appointment of Sir Herbert Samuel as high commissioner of Palestine in 1920, the embodiment of British and Zionist goals, proved a calculated blunder, inasmuch as the Arabs immediately perceived his bias and responded accordingly. As a Jew, a Zionist, and a Liberal, he seemed most prepared to fulfill the league mandate to secure a "Jewish Homeland" in Palestine.[40] But would he secure the rights of the Arabs, who, quite naturally, refused to trust him because of his pedigree and Zionist affiliations? They thought not, and throughout the 1920s, divided between important familial and political loyalties, Arab policy—if it can be called that—became one of reaction against whatever Samuel proposed or Jewish settlers did.[41]

Samuel's tenure (1920–25) set the tone of mistrust for the remainder of the British occupation. On principle alone, the Arabs rejected *a priori* whatever he advanced, while the Jews denounced him as a traitor for assuaging Arab grievances immediately following the 1921 anti-Zionist riots.[42] All of Samuel's subsequent attempts to build an Arab–Jewish Council to work with his office found quick rebuff from Arab leaders, who saw this council as a tacit endorsement of the mandate and the Balfour Declaration. Having few options, Samuel determined to use instead the preexisting Supreme Muslim Council, under the leadership of hard-liner Haj Amin al-Husseini, to fulfill the goal of Arab representation. This decision proved fateful, as al-Husseini, an outspoken enemy of Zionism and the British, soon assumed a position of power as the mufti (Sunni Muslim religious leader) of Jerusalem.[43]

Frustrated with Samuel and suspicious of al-Husseini, a separate Arab committee had formed, which rationalized the Arabs as the only legitimate Palestinian nation. They took their case directly to London in the summer of 1921 and implored the British to support an Arab national government and to retract the Balfour Declaration.[44] Instead, Colonial Secretary Churchill reaffirmed support for the Zionist cause, both in person and in a subsequent

1922 White Paper.[45] He repudiated the Arab case and urged the delegation to return to Samuel's proposed council. They could not do so and thus became trapped in their own ideological bottleneck. Samuel and Churchill's decision to ignore this delegation and instead to work with al-Husseini proved a mistake of historic proportions, and it demonstrated that despite three centuries in the region, the British had learned nothing of Arab Islam or regional politics. The delegation, angered and hapless, without a voice in their own land, watched as Jewish immigration, land purchases, and institutions multiplied, without an effective political means to prevent it. Thus, the Jews took ownership through the mandate system and won, while the Arabs claimed ownership apart from that system and lost.

> Between 1917 and 1931 the number of Jews in Palestine rose from about 60,000 to 175,000. After Hitler came to power in Germany, another quarter million Jews immigrated to Palestine, so that by 1939 they made up about 28 percent of the population. During this period, Jewish ownership of land more than doubled, from 150,000 to 384,000 acres.[46]

Notwithstanding their success, association with the imperialism of British power politics had now tainted whatever moral or historical rights the Zionists had envisioned for their claim to Palestine. Thus, Chaim Weizmann and Sherif Feisal's vision of Arab–Jewish goodwill expressed in March of 1918 and Feisal's affirmation in 1919 regarding the "moral claims of the Zionists" and the "Jews as kinsmen whose just claims they will be glad to see satisfied" had been irretrievably compromised.[47] Palestinian Arabs now perceived the Zionist settlers as agents of British imperialism—participants in another Western land grab and in their actions the Crusades reborn. But Arab opinion had divided on how to challenge it. At the time of Samuel's departure in 1925, most, especially al-Husseini's followers, still argued for continued confrontation, while others urged moderation with Samuel's successors in order to gain a voice in the direction of affairs.[48] Compromise finally won out in 1929 when the Arabs agreed to participate in a newly proposed legislative body, but the decision came too late.

A furious clash that had erupted between Muslims and Jews in Jerusalem's sacred space at the Wailing Wall in August 1929 shattered the peace and aborted plans for the projected legislature.[49] While some saw al-Husseini as the culprit, the hundreds of dead and wounded testified to the suspect nature of British policy as the underlying cause. The government, however, blamed the incident on an earlier reduction of its military force, a problem easily rectified.[50] But that was not the end of it. Confusion over the affair multiplied in 1930–31 when a White Paper issued by new Colonial Secretary Sidney Webb (Lord Passfield) blaming the Zionists was suddenly and atypically reversed under pressure from Zionist supporters in the British government. Ambiguity reigned as both Jews and Arabs felt betrayed. In substituting a "Black Letter" favoring the Jews for the original White Paper supporting the

Arabs, the British revealed a breach in their system and immediately called in additional military reinforcements from Malta and Egypt.[51]

Ultimately, international tension forced the British government to reverse policy in Palestine, as it had in Egypt. The problem began in Germany. After Hitler came to power in 1933, he began a ruthless and systematic persecution of the country's Jewish population. The Nuremberg Laws of 1935 deprived Jews of German citizenship, prompting thousands to emigrate. As an omen of things to come, many more fled Poland as well. With options limited, some 60,000 entered Palestine in 1935.

When Jewish numbers hit 400,000, or roughly one-third of the population, in 1936, British high commissioner Sir Arthur Wauchope suggested that this number was "beyond the absorptive capacity of the country." To mitigate Arab anxieties, Wauchope then offered to set up another Arab-Jewish legislative body with an Arab majority based on population figures, and, to everyone's surprise, the Arabs accepted, but the Jews refused. Suspecting they would lose influence, the Zionists and their supporters in parliament flatly rejected the idea.[52]

This rejection prompted the Arab rebellion of 1936, which lasted three blood-filled years and required 20,000 British troops to subdue it. Arab attacks on fellow Arabs who were seen as traitors, as well as on Jews and British soldiers, prompted equal retaliation. In all, some 5,000 died in an escalating series of assaults and reprisals.[53] Urged on by al-Husseini, mufti of Jerusalem, a general strike enlarged the rebellion, and, as in Egypt, a Muslim fundamentalist movement to oust the British and Zionists alike began under Sheik Izz al-Din al-Qassam.[54] In response, Britain sent a Royal Commission in 1937 under Lord Peel to make recommendations. Their solution: to partition Palestine. One-third in the northwest corner would be given to the Jews; the remaining two-thirds would be conferred to the Arabs, which could be connected to the Hashimite kingdom of Jordan.[55] The report not only divided Arabs and Jews but the British government itself. While the Colonial Office approved the recommendations, the Foreign Office feared a reaction from the rest of the Arab world and denounced it. Their spokesman George Rendel, an Arabist, warned Foreign Secretary Anthony Eden that "Ibn Saud could turn to Italy, driven in despair by British policy in Palestine. The same might happen in Iraq, and Transjordan could follow. Lampson had warned Rendel that Egypt would do the same."[56] In other words, for the good of British policy in the Middle East, Palestine should not be treated separately but in consideration of the wider Arab reaction. If war came with Germany and Italy, the Arab Middle East as well as Muslims in the empire must be kept in the British camp. Above all, as always, the pacification of regional sensitivities was made to serve the needs of empire. Such a rollercoaster policy could not long endure.

To satisfy government critics, the Colonial Office would put Peel's proposal to the test. If Arabs and Jews accepted it, then no harm, no foul. It would satisfy everyone as well as the needs of empire. The answer came soon enough, and, true to form, it was not what the British wanted to hear: The Jews said yes, but this time, the Arabs said no. The Jews accepted in order to gain a state with unlimited immigration, but they urged that the borders remain undefined so as not to preclude later expansion in Palestine.[57] To forestall Zionist claims, the Arabs rejected partition and claimed all of Palestine as an Arab state. Minus either desire or determination to enforce a partition on unwilling subjects, as this would mean more bloodshed, the British withdrew the offer.[58]

In the end, the Foreign Office had won the day. A government White Paper released on May 17, 1939, declared that Palestine would be an independent Arab-Jewish state in ten years. In the meantime, trade connections with Britain were to be maintained for the prosperity of all parties. To placate the Arabs, it restricted Jewish immigration to 75,000 for the next five years and limited, or in some cases prohibited, further land purchases.[59] Historian Elizabeth Monroe best summarized the lack of British resolve: "In 1931, they reversed a policy rather than enforce it; they did the same in 1937–8, when they accepted the Peel Commission's recommendation that they partition Palestine."[60] The problem of Palestine had grown completely out of hand.

To ensure that the Arab Middle East, and thus the vital supply of oil and troops through the canal, remain on the British side in the eventuality of war with Germany and Italy, Zionism now went on the back burner of British policy. British authorities correctly surmised that in a war against Hitler, the Jews would have to support them regardless. Down but not out, Jewish leader David Ben-Gurion reluctantly agreed but thoughtfully retorted: "We must assist the British in the war as if there were no White Paper and we must resist the White Paper as if there were no war."[61] Overall, the 1936 rebellion, the Peel Commission and the White Paper had both exposed and politicized the problem beyond Palestine, engaging the rest of the Arab world.[62] The Second World War would only postpone the wider and unavoidable conflict ahead.

Meanwhile, Britain prepared for the inevitable war and, as always, understood her Middle Eastern assets as absolutely essential for survival as well as victory. In this context, Britain had modernized the Egyptian army and settled the Palestinian crisis with a pro-Arab stance. Britain secured air bases within Iraq and Egypt to protect her Iraqi and Persian oil reserves, guard the canal route to India and safeguard the British Empire and economy. On the eve of the Second World War, informal influence and formal control still held in Egypt through Britain's greatly reduced "reserved powers" and in Palestine through the mandate. Though wracked with internal upheaval in both cases, this remarkably flexible system endured and so did its contribution to the preservation of the empire. In 1938, Prime Minister Neville Chamberlain stressed that

> Britain would go to war if the empire were attacked or if the territory of . . . Iraq or Egypt were violated . . . Iraq was important for oil; and

Egypt was also of strategic and economic value and under strong British informal influence. . . . All . . . were members of the Sterling Area and this connection with Britain was bolstered by loans.[63]

Britain's control of the Middle East would once more become that vital entity of deliverance and triumph as it had been in the Great War. Yet, this unchallenged policy unknowingly and inevitably bore the seeds of Britain's demise in the region and retreat in the world.

CHAPTER THIRTEEN

The Middle East in the Second World War 1939–45

This strange assembly of Arabs, Jews, Free French and British troops now took on a fiercely obdurate Vichy force in a five-week slugfest—and won. An armistice signed on July 14 [1941] recognized the Allied occupation of Syria and Lebanon under a Free French governor.

PETER YOUNG, *A Short History of World War II: 1939–45*

Second World War phase I: Europe and the Middle East 1939–42

Unlike the First World War, the origins of the Second World War began with conflicts in Asia and Africa then finally exploded in Europe and the Middle East. Spurred on by the ravages of the Great Depression, the hunt for resources and quest for empire, Japan conquered Manchuria (Manchuko) in 1931, despite League of Nations protests, then occupied three Chinese provinces in 1933. In 1937, Japan launched a full-scale invasion of China. Thus, under the banner of the Japan-East Asia Co-Prosperity Sphere, and as a clear challenge to British, American, and Dutch interests, war in Asia was on—four years before Pearl Harbor.

Equally driven to pursue resources and the dream of empire, or *Mare Nostrum*, Italian dictator Benito Mussolini attacked defenseless Ethiopia (Abyssinia) in 1935, threatening British interests in the Red Sea and Egypt.

The British and French decision to support the League of Nations' petroleum embargo on Italy drove Mussolini from the Western democracies and closer to Hitler. For its part, the Anglo-Iranian Oil Company refused to honor the embargo. In May 1936, Ethiopia's capital, Addis Ababa, fell to Italian forces. Two months later, the Spanish Civil War (1936–39) erupted, with Germany and Italy deciding to support General Franco and the Falange (Fascists) against the forces of the Loyalist Republicans. The die had been cast. In October 1936, Germany and Italy formed the Rome–Berlin Axis, shortly followed in November by Hitler's Anti-Comintern Pact with Japan.

Since these were such widespread conflicts, few viewed them as a whole or as leading to a catastrophic global conflict. Just as confusing to most observers at the time was Hitler's piecemeal yet peaceful reoccupation of territory stripped from Germany by the Versailles Treaty in 1919. Under the rubric of repudiating the injustice of Versailles, Hitler had retaken the Saar in 1935 and the Rhineland in 1936 and, in 1938, annexed Austria into union (Anschluss) with Germany.

More ominous, however, was Hitler's demand for and subsequent acquisition of the Sudetenland from Czechoslovakia in October of 1938, in accord with those very democracies sworn to defend the country's integrity. British Prime Minister Neville Chamberlain and French premier Edouard Daladier thus signed the Munich Agreement with Hitler in order to avoid a war. It proved much more than a justifiable reversal of Versailles, as the Sudetenland, although heavily German, had never been part of Germany. Churchill lambasted this "Appeasement Policy" or "Sellout" which, without representatives or allies at Munich, rendered the Czech government defenseless. Moreover, the Soviets, who had offered to assist, were never consulted.

Chamberlain's proclamation of "Peace in our time" evaporated six months later when the Germans occupied the remainder of the hapless state. At that point, the British government made it clear that further seizure of territory, most likely in Poland, would mean war. It came soon enough. When Germany stole the march on British and French efforts to gain a treaty with the Soviet Union and signed the Non-Aggression Pact with the Soviets on August 23, 1939, it opened the way for the German invasion of Poland in September.[1] Not wishing to be outdone, Mussolini had invaded and overpowered tiny Albania in April of that year. Few noticed except the British, who viewed Italy's Balkan adventure as a possible stepping-stone to the Middle East and the Suez Canal.

The Second World War began with Hitler's brutal Blitzkrieg of Poland on September 1, 1939. Poland fell within a month, yet six months after the defeat, little else had happened despite the British and French declarations of war against Germany on September 3. This strange period of the "Phony War" or "sitzkrieg," however, came to a ruthless conclusion with Hitler's invasion of Denmark and Norway in April 1940. A German assault on the Low Countries and France followed on May 10. On that day, Chamberlain stepped down, and Winston Churchill formed a new government determined to fight the Nazis, wherever and at whatever cost. He immediately sent a British expeditionary force to support the Belgians and French, which quickly became trapped at Dunkirk. On Churchill's order, a heroic naval and civilian flotilla evacuated some 300,000 troops before the port city fell on June 4. Paris collapsed on June 14, and on June 22, France capitulated. The battle for France was over; the battle of Britain was about to begin.

French surrender terms created a German puppet regime in Vichy, France, which controlled French colonies in North Africa and the mandate in Syria.[2] French naval and military forces throughout those regions, now loyal to Vichy, had to be dealt with. Since Mussolini had declared war against France and occupied a small southeast corner of the country at the time of the surrender, it meant that Italy clearly had entered the conflict and that her position in Libya, Ethiopia, and Albania would have to be handled as well.

While Hitler planned operation Sea Lion for the invasion of Britain, an aggressive Churchill struck first—in North Africa. On July 3, the Royal Navy (RN) destroyed much of the French fleet at Oran, Algeria, to prevent the Axis using it for the upcoming attack on Britain or further conflict in the Mediterranean.[3] The Battle of Britain began on July 10 with the first German air attacks. The blitz was on, but in the absence of adequate naval strength to support Sea Lion, the invasion was postponed and then canceled on October 12. The ruthless German air blitz continued, nonetheless, until 1942.

Churchill determined to fight back, but where? Standing alone, Britain had neither the manpower nor resources to challenge Axis control of the Continent. Instead, as in the conflict of 1914–18, Churchill evolved an imperial grand strategy that encompassed control of the Middle East to secure resources as well as critical transportation and communication systems, and above all, the springboard for offensives against the Axis in North and East Africa, the Balkans, and the Middle East. Britain's heavily contested and maligned hegemony in the Middle East had suddenly reemerged as in the First World War to offer another victory in this new and greater conflict. Once again, the Middle East became the catalyst for Britain's survival and only hope of success. "The vital issues were the route to India and oil. . . . India was likely, as in the First World War, to provide Britain's largest single military recruiting ground; so the way to India had to be kept open for ships through the Suez canal, for aircraft via Palestine and Iraq and for a variety of overland and undersea cables."[4] Moreover, to support this strategy, Churchill, always a Zionist supporter, reversed policy and subordinated Zionism to gain the Arabs for the war effort. He now prepared for a showdown where the British at least stood a chance of success. By this time in the minds of most, the Middle East was not merely an extension of British hegemony but an integral part of the British Empire and the essential element for ultimate victory.

While Britain fought for survival throughout the summer and fall of 1940, the Italians invaded British Somaliland in August and in September launched a full-scale invasion of Egypt. These two actions threatened British control of the Red Sea and the Suez Canal. Wavell had 36,000 British troops in Egypt and 27,000 more in Palestine, and with this small force had been commissioned to defend the entire Middle East.[5] To supplement the British force, use of the newly increased and modernized Egyptian army seemed more essential than ever. In the interval between Italy's June 4 declaration of war on Britain and the invasion of Egypt on September 13, however, everything related to the Anglo-Egyptian military effort that could go wrong did so.

On the eve of the Italian invasion, "the Egyptian Frontier Force patrolled the Libyan frontier," while British forces were thinly stretched from the canal to the western desert.[6] On August 14, Churchill, acting as his own war minister, urged Wavell to use Egyptian troops against a probable Italian invasion from Libya. "All trained or Regular units, whether fully equipped or not, must be used in the defense of Egypt against invasion. . . . The Egyptian Army must be made to play its part in support of the Delta front, thus leaving only riotous crowds to be dealt with in Egypt proper."[7]

Unfortunately for all concerned, the joint war effort so carefully planned by Wavell and the government would suffer irreparable damage at the hands of the very individual responsible for carrying it out, Ambassador Miles Lampson. Lampson compromised those institutions necessary to assure Anglo-Egyptian cooperation inherent in the 1936 treaty. The monarchy, the Wafd and the Egyptian army all fell victim to the ambassador's brutish tactics, forever decimating whatever remained of mutual accommodation during and after the war.

Lampson believed that King Farouk, as well as Premier Ali Mahir and Military Chief of Staff Aziz Ali al-Misri, harbored anti-British, pro-Axis attitudes.[8] True or not, suspicions in hand, Lampson argued belatedly with the Foreign and War Offices against bringing Egypt into this war and urged that her troops be removed from the firing line.[9] When an Italian probe crossed the Egyptian border on June 23, 1940, Lampson cowed Farouk to replace nationalist Premier Mahir with the more moderate Hussein Sirri.[10] As a young lieutenant at the time, Anwar Sadat observed: "Britain preferred a tame tyrant to a strong democracy, and the monarchy brought itself into disrepute by collaborating with the British."[11]

But Lampson was not finished. In July, while the Italians were massing on the border, he saw to the dismissal of Egypt's popular chief of staff, General al-Misri. As Egypt's most experienced and respected commander, al-Misri had developed theories and tactics of desert warfare that Lampson feared might be used against the British. He declared, "The aim of the army must be the liberation and reconstruction of Egypt on a sound basis—Have faith! Act!"[12] No doubt al-Misri's strident nationalism had generated enthusiastic loyalty from his young officers, but his abrupt dismissal triggered an even greater outrage throughout the army, which in fact politicized it. According to Sadat, at least, Lampson's clumsy action united numerous officers in solid opposition to British war aims and sparked the formation of a secret society known as the Free Officer Corps.[13] Moreover, it short-circuited all of Wavell's efforts as well as those of the Foreign and War Offices.

No one had seen the Egyptian opposition coming, and the timing could not have been worse. Just as the internal strife peaked, the Italians struck and struck hard with a full-scale invasion of Egypt on September 13, 1940. Within a week, they had penetrated eighty miles into Egypt; then nothing.[14] While British and Egyptian forces readied for an attack west of Alexandria, an unexpected lull had developed in the Italian offensive.[15] Short of mobile armor, the Italians had prepared to dig in before renewing their advance. The brief respite allowed Churchill time to review the situation. With the security of British forces at stake and fully mistrusting Egyptian troops in the wake of Lampson's actions, Churchill ordered the Egyptian army's neutralization and withdrawal from the front.[16] Sadat records the implications of that decision. "Nevertheless, we refused to hand over our arms to the British. We simply marched to the base. I told myself that better days would come. We had to hang on, see it out. For the moment we were defeated, but, soon, Egypt's day would dawn."[17]

Although many in Egypt's army had been anti-British, they were not necessarily pro-Axis, but these actions virtually guaranteed they would become pro-anyone who threw out the British. Wavell, as well as the Foreign and War Offices, angrily disputed Churchill's decision and pushed for an Egyptian declaration of war and the use of her troops in combat. According to Lampson, at least, Wavell, now exposed to the anger of Egyptian troops after Churchill's action, finally concluded that using them was not in Britain's best interest. Having complied with Churchill's order, Wavell assured Premier Hussein Sirri that he was satisfied that their army should not serve in Western Desert combat. "He (Wavell) did not want more than they at present were doing, namely, guarding the Canal, looking after railroad bridges, etc. . . . As far as the Western Desert was concerned, thought it preferable not to mix British and Egyptian troops there."[18]

Despite this setback, Churchill chose not to simply defend the Middle East but to aggressively use it to launch offensive forays against the Axis. In the end, this strategy would save the day and help win the war much sooner. Without the British control of the region, it was doubtful that the allied cause would have gained a victory anytime soon. For Britain, the Middle East was not a sideshow, but the main event. This was quickly confirmed when on December 9, 1940, Wavell launched a successful counteroffensive and encircled the enemy's fixed positions. Within two months, the Italians had abandoned Egypt and were pursued halfway across Libya. Because of the efforts of Wavell's field commander, General Richard O'Conner, the British took Libya's strategic port of Tobruk in January 1941. By February, O'Conner's force, now reinforced with Australians, captured El Agheila as well as 130,000 Italian prisoners.[19] This remarkable achievement led Foreign Secretary Anthony Eden to remark: "Never has so much been surrendered by so many to so few."[20]

At the same time, Wavell saw to an equally successful campaign in East Africa where British, South African, Indian, and Australian forces decimated the Italians in Somaliland and Eritrea. The operation culminated with a lightning push into Ethiopia and the surrender of its capital on April 6, 1941.[21] Thus far, Churchill's grand strategy had proved an unqualified success. The Red Sea, the Suez Canal, and much of North Africa had been secured, guaranteeing that essential manpower and material would pour into Egypt, the hub of imperial survival, and that Wavell could envelop the rest of Libya and eradicate the Italian threat for good. But it did not happen.

In February 1941, German General Erwin Rommel and the first elements of the Afrika Korps had landed in Libya and, together with Italian troops, launched a sustained counteroffensive in late March, reversing many of the British gains. From April to November, Rommel laid siege to Tobruk. Something had gone terribly wrong, but what? Just prior to Rommel's landing, the British had removed half their North African force to Greece and the Island of Crete to support the Greeks against the Italians. Alas,

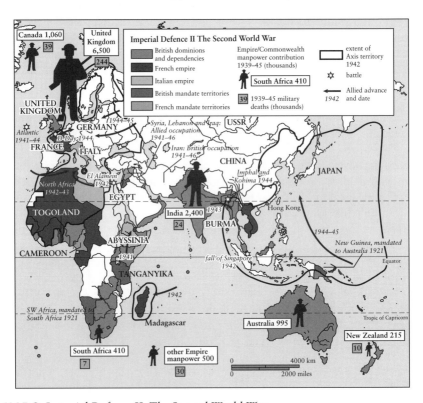

MAP 8 *Imperial Defense II: The Second World War.*

Mussolini had struck again. From his position in Albania, he had invaded Greece in October 1940, but the attack backfired when the Greeks went on the offensive and, joined by British forces in February 1941, drove the Italians back to Albania. The Greek success also prompted partisans in neighboring Yugoslavia to overthrow a pro-Nazi regime.

In Berlin, meanwhile, Hitler had planned for an invasion of the Soviet Union in May 1941, but he was now forced to rescue his Italian ally in North Africa and the Balkans in order to secure his southern flank before attacking the Soviet Union. Alas, the British effort to secure the Balkans at the expense of the North African campaign proved costly, as the Germans soon enveloped the Balkans, while Rommel steamrolled through greatly weakened British forces in Libya.

The Nazi military machine dealt with Yugoslavia, Greece, and the British in short order, forcing a Greek and Yugoslav surrender by the end of April. British forces evacuated Greece on May 2 and on June 1 withdrew from Crete, having lost their military bases, airfields, port facilities, and a third of their army to superior German weaponry and blitzkrieg tactics. Britain's aggressive and seemingly disastrous foray from Egypt to the Balkans paid at least one substantial dividend. This interlude cost the Germans much more, for it postponed the planned invasion of Russia (Operation Barbarossa) until June 22, 1941, which, some historians have argued, may ultimately have cost Hitler the war.

Notwithstanding, Britain's tenacious but tenuous grip on the Middle East appeared more at risk than ever. The Germans now stood poised to launch air attacks from Greece and Crete, while Rommel, having bypassed Tobruk, pushed the British to the border and readied for an assault on Egypt. Moreover, unsettling news had reached Cairo that a pro-Nazi regime had taken over Iraq, supported by Vichy Syria, and that disaffected elements of the Egyptian army were prepared to derail British efforts against Rommel. Lampson as well as Wavell and the other British commanders gathered in Cairo on April 14, 1941, to deal with the growing menace in Iraq, Syria and Egypt.[22]

The revolution in Iraq came as a shock, since King Feisal's pro-British government had continued after the mandate's termination in 1931. Although strained relations emerged under Feisal's heir, King Ghazi, his death in 1939 (possibly at British hands) allowed the new leader, Abdullah (regent for Feisal II), and Premier Nuri al-Said to reaffirm the 1930 treaty, securing British military personnel and Royal Air Force (RAF) installations. It was not to last.

As it happened, British policies in Palestine had finally come to haunt Iraq. Recently exiled Haj Amin al-Husseini (mufti of Jerusalem) had arrived in Baghdad and, together with disaffected Iraqi army officers, sparked a nationalist, anti-British revolt in April 1941. Colonel Salah al-Din al Sabbagh, who played a leading role in the anti-British campaign, exemplified the Arab nationalist views of many officers when he wrote, "I do not believe in the democracy of the English nor in the Naziism of the Germans nor in the Bolshevism of the Russians. I am an Arab Muslim. I do not want anything as a substitute in the way of pretensions and philosophies."[23]

Supported by the military, Iraq's new leader, Rashid Ali al-Gaylani, a determined nationalist, had forced Abdullah and Premier Nuri al-Said into exile.[24] His subsequent refusal to honor the 1930 treaty immediately threatened vital British oil supplies, communications, airfields, and military preparedness. Al-Gaylani's posture, presumed to be pro-Axis by the British, induced Hitler's promise of military aid through Vichy Syria as well as the decision to use Syrian bases to bombard British installations in Iraq. This prompted Wavell's novel but decisive military response to deal with Iraq and Syria in a single strategy.[25]

Another offense was in the offing. Since the British had their hands full with Rommel and had suffered substantial losses in the Greek campaign, Wavell could only collect a limited force to do the job, consisting of a small British contingent from Palestine and Free French elements from Syria. Importantly, it also included support from the still loyal Hashimite king of Trans-Jordan, Abdullah (Hashimite relative of Iraq's royal family), and his well-trained Arab Legion, led by British officer Sir John Glubb (Glubb Pasha). Together, this odd but determined little army, escorted by the tough and very savvy Arab Legion, pushed into Iraq, relieved the British air bases, took Baghdad, and restored the monarchy on May 31, 1941. In the aftermath, al-Husseini fled to Berlin.[26]

Thus victorious, this small but resolute contingent now headed west to Syria, while more British elements from Palestine, including the outlawed Haganah, a small Jewish force under young commander Moshe Dayan, pressed to Damascus.[27] This strange assembly of Arabs, Jews, Free French, and British troops now took on a fiercely obdurate Vichy force in a five-week slugfest— and won. An armistice signed on July 14 recognized the Allied occupation of Syria and Lebanon under a Free French governor.[28] Thus in four months, from April to July 1941, Wavell had orchestrated the return of a pro-British government to Iraq and creation of a pro-Allied administration in Syria-Lebanon. In conjunction with this campaign, British and Indian detachments together with Soviet forces also occupied Iran (Persia) on August 25 in order to supply the Soviet Union, now under German attack, as well as to protect the oil fields. These arrangements would last for the duration of the war.

In Cairo, meanwhile, in line with the April 14 discussions about Iraq and Syria, Lampson, Wavell, and the other British commanders again debated the question of Egypt's neutrality. They at last concluded that bringing Egypt into the war would serve no purpose except to precipitate Afrika Korp's air attacks against Alexandria, Cairo, and the Suez Canal. Since American president Franklin Roosevelt had declared the Red Sea a non-war zone through which the British hoped to receive substantial military aid, Egypt's neutrality and that of the Red Sea remained an absolute necessity.[29] While drafting this position to his opponents in the Foreign Office, Lampson reflected, "I have a suspicion they may not entirely approve there of our line in that they are pressing for Egypt to come into the war . . . all and all and on balance we are right . . . and all 3 service Chiefs were perfectly clear in their minds that at present they want nothing more."[30]

In the end, Lampson had won the day and the issue passed, or so everyone thought, until Rommel pushed within fifty miles of Alexandria. The situation had become so desperate that "in Cairo the British burned embassy documents and planned to move into Palestine."[31] At that point, young King Farouk, who detested Lampson, made plans of his own. No doubt impressed with the rapidity of Rommel's advance in the winter of 1941–42 and probable occupation of Egypt, Farouk sought to reinstate nationalist al-Mahir as premier, who, in collaboration with Rommel, might secure a permanent British removal. Most Egyptians, now cheering for Rommel in the streets of Cairo, had only become pro-Axis to the degree that Rommel might finally liberate them from the British. Both the king and the cheering crowds were soon disabused of their hopes when Lampson led his own counterattack, not against Rommel but Farouk.

On February 4, 1942, elements of the Egyptian army who guarded Farouk at Cairo's Abdin Palace stood stunned, helpless, and without orders, and they watched their king, surrounded by British tanks and troops, succumb to Lampson's threat to depose him—unless he formed a pro-British government under Wafd leader Mustafa al-Nahas. Terrified and humiliated, Farouk signed.[32]

While Lampson no doubt viewed this government shift as essential for Britain's survival and a "job well done," many Egyptian officers saw this incident as critical to the later British expulsion. General Neguib recounted his profound disgust at not being allowed to defend the king, while Nasser viewed this British action "as the most critical affront to Egypt—and gave new stimulus to the revolutionary movement."[33] In the immediate aftermath, Sadat recalls that "the hostility of the Egyptian Army resulted in the mobilization of considerable British forces, which Britain could more usefully have employed elsewhere."[34]

Elements of the Egyptian army thereafter attempted to sabotage British units retreating from Rommel's offensive. "This group managed to collect maps of British installations, military roads, and other strategic points with a view to organizing raids on supply and communications lines."[35] For these treasonable activities, many young officers, including Sadat, went to prison for the war's duration.[36] In short, Lampson had compromised the monarchy and the Wafd to the point where most Egyptians viewed them as vestigial remnants of a dysfunctional regime, while the young officers, seen as true heroes, would emerge from the war as the hope of Egypt's future.

Despite British attempts to keep up appearances, Egypt's neutrality proved a cynical myth. Massive deployment of British forces made her a target whether she wanted to be or not. While Egypt's army, as a nonbelligerent, could not officially fight, many of her soldiers unofficially died in the country's defense.[37] As Sadat retorted, "How could Egypt remain neutral, when British troops occupied the whole country and controlled the bases, communications, shipping routes, ports and natural resources of the country?"[38] At home, parliament demanded to know how Egypt could remain neutral while under attack: "Egyptian territory has been invaded without resistance and the task of repelling the enemy was undertaken at heavy cost of British lives without armed resistance from Egypt."[39] In defense of the government's baffling policy, Foreign Secretary Eden could only respond, "Egypt has faithfully disclosed her obligations under the Anglo-Egyptian Treaty of Alliance."[40] General Neguib remembered the Egyptian version in a somewhat different light. "They expected Egyptians to behave as loyal allies while being treated as conquered subjects. . . . All they knew was that Egypt was occupied by the British Army, as always, and that its soldiers treated them like dirt."[41]

Thus, in grim determination to survive the war's darkest hours, Lampson, Britain's man on the spot, had sallied forth like an imperial proconsul from a bygone era. He had forcefully curtailed the government's forward policy in Egypt into one of emasculating the country—not by the slaughter of war, but by the ruse of neutrality in the midst of war. It proved a costly mistake, as historian Elizabeth Monroe thoughtfully observed: "All these arbitrary British acts may have been necessities of war, but they were by local standards never-to-be-forgotten indignities, and all were entered on a bill of reckoning for presentation after the war."[42] At the end of the day, when forced to choose between winning the war and the expediency of inflicting abuses on the Middle East's native population, Britain obviously chose the latter. Importantly, when this was discovered, Britain's American, Soviet, and Free French allies remained oblivious and never objected. The view prevailed that this war had to be won over a ruthless Nazi enemy who, if victorious, would have ultimately inflicted far greater indignities than anything the British ever did. In the end, the British won the war, but it cost them the Middle East.

All seemed lost when Rommel's forces finally took Tobruk on June 21, 1942. After two weeks, however, his drive stalled in the face of determined British opposition near a remote outpost just west of Alexandria. Rommel would never get beyond that point. Events took a dramatic turn on October 23, when the British launched a staggering counteroffensive from that now famous outpost, El Alamein. The tide of war had changed and there was no turning back.

The Second World War phase II: Global conflict 1942–45

It had become obvious to Churchill from the beginning of the war that, while he might harass the Axis on the margins of Continental Europe and from the

Middle East, he could never hope to utterly defeat them without substantial help. His one hope—to bring isolationist America into the conflict—seemed impossible. On September 3, 1940, however, President Roosevelt signed an agreement to lease British bases in the western hemisphere for future defense but nothing more; that is, until Germany, Italy, and Japan declared the Tripartite Pact four weeks later on September 27. In response, Roosevelt agreed to full-blown material aid for Britain through the Lend-Lease Act of March 27, 1941.[43] Despite Roosevelt's gesture, Churchill still had to conduct this war alone—until Hitler provided the unexpected. At long last, Churchill's successful Middle East war strategy revealed itself. Britain had held until the big guns arrived, and arrive they did, as both the Soviet Union and the United States had entered the war by the end of 1941.

On June 22, 1941, Germany launched Operation Barbarossa, a full-scale invasion of the Soviet Union. Within two months, on August 14–15, Churchill and Roosevelt signed the Atlantic Charter, agreeing jointly to aid the Soviets and conduct a future meeting in Moscow.[44] The result, as noted earlier, was that British and Soviet troops occupied Iran (Persia) on August 25 as the main artery to supply the Soviets and to prevent German penetration of the oil fields.[45] Four months later, on December 7, 1941, Japan's attack on Pearl Harbor forced America into the war.

On January 1, 1942, those states now fighting the Axis met in Washington, D.C. to create the United Nations as a unified front to defeat the enemy. Thus, in the few months between June and December 1941, the Axis had managed to bring the combined assets of the Soviet Union, the United States, and the British Empire—70 percent of the world's resources—against them. Moreover, the new Allies agreed to coordinate their efforts in a series of wartime conferences, while the Axis's failure to do so proved disastrous.

Axis's triumphs throughout the globe were brought to a sudden and irreversible standstill during the summer and fall of 1942. Six months after Pearl Harbor, Japan's unrelenting drive into Southeast Asia and the Pacific against the Americans and British was blunted at the Battle of Midway on June 4, 1942. Thereafter, there would be no more sweeping Japanese victories. Meanwhile, from November 1942 to January 1943, the German advance in the Soviet Union suffered a major reversal at the battle of Stalingrad, whereupon the Soviets took the offensive and never looked back. Likewise in Egypt, Britain's new commander, General Bernard Montgomery, opened a devastating and sustained offensive against Rommel at El Alamein on October 23, 1942, which Churchill deemed "the end of the beginning." The Egyptian offensive, combined with American Operation Torch in French Morocco and Algeria, crushed the Axis threat in North Africa by May 1943. The tide of war had turned against the Axis on all fronts, never to be regained.

British efforts in Iraq and Syria, as well as her venture with the Soviets in the joint occupation of Iran in the summer of 1941, had ended the Axis threat from those locales. Her combined efforts with American forces the following year had all but eliminated the Axis peril in Egypt and North Africa as well. As a result, the entire region became a safe haven for the important Allied wartime conferences at Casablanca, Cairo, and Tehran to decide the direction of the war.

First, in January 1943 at Casablanca, Morocco, Churchill, and Roosevelt agreed, in communication with Soviet Premier Joseph Stalin, that "unconditional surrender" would be applied equally to Germany, Italy, and Japan at the war's conclusion.[46] After a brief but important foreign ministers' meeting in Moscow to reaffirm the goals of the United Nations, the center of activity again returned to the Middle East. Second, at the Cairo conference on November 26–28, 1943, Churchill and Roosevelt met with Chinese leader Chaing Kai-shek to plan war operations against the Japanese (Figure 20). It became abundantly clear at this meeting, however, that the American goals in this war were not necessarily in line with British purposes. American General Joseph "Vinegar Joe" Stilwell's representative at Cairo stated that while American and British forces joined in the South East Asia Command to defeat Japan, American cooperation was limited: "Why should American boys die to recreate the colonial empires of the British and their Dutch and French satellites?"[47]—a clear warning that American postwar policy would not support British imperialism anywhere, including the Middle East.

FIGURE 20 *Roosevelt, Churchill, and Chang Kai Chek, Cairo, 1943. Photo 12. Getty Images.*

Meanwhile, Stalin had pressured British and American leaders for a cross-channel invasion or "Second Front" to relieve the hard-pressed Soviets. Instead, at Churchill's insistence, British and American forces launched a successful invasion of Sicily (Operation Husky) on July 10, 1943, and on September 3 would continue with a landing in southern Italy, forcing an Italian surrender five days later. The fact that twenty-five German divisions in Italy continued to fight, however, made this one of the most difficult campaigns so far and fulfilled in Churchill's mind, at least, his promise to Stalin for a "second front."

Finally, at the conference at Tehran, Iran, held from November 28 to December 1, 1943, Churchill's views prevailed no longer. This most critical of wartime gatherings saw the Big Three—Stalin, Roosevelt and a reluctant Churchill—eventually agree, at American insistence, to a cross-channel invasion of France, Operation Overlord, set for May 1944. In addition, the Allies gave great praise to the Iranian government for its cooperation as a conduit for massive wartime assistance to the Soviet Union.[48] In the end, the historic Muslim centers of North Africa and the Middle East had provided sanctuary for many momentous allied decisions that ultimately led to the Axis defeat. In the case of Tehran and Cairo, at least, the peaceful conferences belied the fact that they had been achieved through forced British occupation as well as the political manipulation of both regimes.

Internal politics: Iran, Egypt, and Palestine 1942–45

As noted, Germany's invasion of the Soviet Union in the summer of 1941 prompted the British to respond by supplying the Soviets through the most secure route possible. Since U-boats and a hostile climate would limit the use of either Baltic Sea or Arctic passage, the British turned to the Persian Gulf and Iran as the most likely conduit for the flow of British and American aid to the Russians. One problem remained: Reza Shah Pahlavi, Iran's ruler since 1925. As a resolute nationalist, he had no fondness for the British and had done everything possible to minimize their influence. In his rise to power, he had toppled the pro-British Qajar Dynasty in 1921 and trashed a British-sponsored security treaty in favor of one with the Soviets, which lasted until 1927, when he outlawed the Communist Party.[49]

As such, neither the British nor the Soviets liked or trusted him. The feeling was mutual. Reza Shah then targeted the British-dominated Anglo-Persian Oil Company, canceled its contract in return for one more favorable to Iranian interests and, in 1935, renamed it the Anglo-Iranian Company to coincide with the country's new name and growing nationalist spirit.[50]

Although Reza Shah was considered the father of modern Iran, his growing association with German and Italian businessmen throughout the 1930s, as well as his increased repression, provoked British suspicions and in 1941 provided a pretext for a British engineered coup. Historian Ali Ansari thoughtfully observes, "Indeed, it would appear that Reza Shah frowned on attempts to start a 'Nazi' party in Iran. It may be fair to conclude that allegations of German sympathies, while plausible, were largely a mechanism of justification for the Allied policy of occupation, following Hitler's drive towards Moscow. . . ."[51]

Thus, in the summer of 1941, a joint Soviet-British occupation of Iran commenced, much as it had in 1917. In anticipation of his ouster along with the choice of his successor, Britain's new BBC Iranian service propagandized the shah's misdeeds. Having set the stage, British forces quickly overcame the Iranian army, forced the shah's abdication and hustled him to the port of Bandar Abbas (British Residency) and then to exile in South Africa, where he died after three years. Amazingly, the event provoked little opposition. Again Ansari states, "Such was the unpopularity of the Shah that little effort was actually needed from either front."[52] His young and pliable son, Mohammad Reza Shah Pahlavi (1941–79), now took power under British tutelage.[53] Iran's new government, praised by the British at the Tehran Conference in 1943, had also hatched the unanticipated. "A small group of politicians, of whom the most prominent was Dr. Mohammed Mussadeq (Mosaddeq), enjoyed the unexpected freedom to speak out against the Russians and the British alike."[54] Like Reza Shah, he too would raise the banner of anti-British, Iranian nationalism in the years ahead and suffer a fate not unlike the shah's.[55] Notwithstanding, the government of Mohammad Reza Shah survived the war by sticking to internal affairs and, as a pro-British ally, became a sponsored member of the United Nations. After the war, his pro-Western and anti-Soviet stance remained the hallmark of his reign until the Islamic Revolution of 1979 prompted his ouster.

In Egypt, after the defeat and surrender of Rommel's forces in May 1943, most Egyptians had resigned themselves to a British victory and the unhappy prospect of continued occupation. There was, indeed, little to celebrate. Although British and imperial forces received enthusiastic praise in parliament, the government, still captive to Lampson's policy, refused to acknowledge that the Egyptians had also fought and incurred military casualties in defense of the canal and Alexandria.[56] A year later, the government admitted the omission to parliament as an embarrassing oversight, indicating a change in position.

With an eye to the future of Anglo-Egyptian relations, Lampson's policies had been called into question. The British government performed a sudden about-face and offered support to Egypt's status as a warring power, setting her military record in a positive light in parliament and at the Crimean (Yalta) Conference, February 4–11, 1945.[57] In line with this new policy, on

February 24, Egypt's latest premier, Ahmad Mahir, declared war on the Axis to avoid the hypocrisy of being a neutral nation at war and to gain status as a cobelligerent in the United Nations. Siding with the British cost him his life. He was assassinated the following day, most likely a victim of the Muslim Brothers.[58]

The abrupt British policy change had come too late to rectify the indignities done to Egypt throughout the war. Anyone aligning with the British, for whatever cause, now had reason to fear. Historian Peter Mansfield notes, "Without doubt it was the first of a series of political murders which were primarily the work of the Brotherhood and continued until the Revolution of 1952. Egyptian political life became violent as it had after World War I but the difference that this time the victims were mainly prominent Egyptians."[59] Ultimately, a continued British presence after the war had less to fear from the king, political parties or the Muslim Brothers than it did from the secret society of resolute officers within Egypt's army—the Free Officer Corps. Formed in the caldron of Britain's abusive wartime practices, many of its members, mostly young officers, went to prison for espionage and treason born in the anger of the army's emasculation. As a further humiliation, many more were staffed at remote desk jobs until the end of the war in an attempt to keep them away from strategic fighting areas.[60] Their lack of experience during the war as well as the king's purchase of defective weapons directly contributed to their failure in the Palestinian campaign in 1948–49. Their outrage at this last indignity would provoke a "Free Officers" revolution in 1952 to oust the monarchy and force a complete British withdrawal from Egypt in 1956.

In Palestine, meanwhile, the situation remained confused and tense during the war. While 12,000 Arabs had joined British forces, the mufti of Jerusalem, Britain's sworn enemy, had escaped to Baghdad and then to Germany, recruiting Arabs to fight for Hitler.[61] Overall, his efforts during the war did the Arabs no good after it, as the victorious Allies would remember this affront. At the same time, some 27,000 Jews had joined the British armed forces determined to defeat Hitler and liberate the death camps.[62] A number of them formed a separate Jewish Brigade Group and for its insignia adopted the Star of David as a powerful political statement. The British government frowned on this development and "continued to reject Zionist demands for the formation of a Jewish army, flying the Zionist flag, to fight alongside the Allies."[63]

British policy had resolved to uphold the 1939 White Paper to resist Jewish immigration to Palestine. This was done to prevent another Arab rebellion or wider disaffection of Arab and Muslim states from the British cause during and after the war. This British policy only insured more recruits to the Haganah, the secret Jewish army in Palestine, which, as noted, had helped the British defeat the Vichy government in Syria. Since its inception in 1921, the Haganah, which had been clandestinely armed by British army units, acted as a defense force to protect Jewish settlers against sporadic

Arab attacks and covertly funneled small numbers of Jewish refugees into Palestine.

By 1944–45, however, the stakes rose dramatically when the world began to realize the enormity of Hitler's Holocaust: the systematic annihilation of 6,000,000 Jews. In response to this greatest of manmade historical tragedies, the Haganah now determined to ignore British law altogether, whatever the cost, and smuggle thousands of Jews into Palestine. In this effort, it was aided by two secret, extremist, and decidedly anti-British groups, the Stern Gang and the Irgun, who targeted British personnel and installations. The majority of their members had escaped from Eastern Europe, especially Poland, and had witnessed the Holocaust at its worst. Moreover, Irgun leader Menachim Begin blamed the British for not rescuing the Jews and, therefore, had no compunction about killing them. The Haganah did not share their violent political agenda. When an Irgun bomb killed six British military police in March 1944 and the Stern Gang murdered the British minister of Middle East affairs, Lord Moyne, the following November in Cairo, the Haganah and the Jewish Agency in Palestine hunted them down as criminals. As a good friend of Moyne, Churchill's emotional speech before the House of Commons had a chilling effect on Zionist leaders. "If our dreams for Zionism are to end in the smoke of assassins' pistols and our labours for its future to produce only a new set of gangsters worthy of Nazi Germany, many like myself will have to reconsider the position we have maintained so consistently in the past."[64]

If Britain's prewar problems in Palestine appeared insoluble, those emerging at the war's conclusion would prove totally insurmountable. Faced with the moral imperative of providing justice and a safe haven for Jewish Holocaust survivors against the need to preserve imperial assets in the Middle East, Britain chose the latter. Sir Kinahan Cornwallis, Britain's representative in Iraq, as well as Sir Miles Lampson in Egypt, expressed what became official British policy. "Whittling down of the 1939 White Paper, and even more, the establishment of a Jewish state, would mean that Britain would lose its influence in the Middle East and the maintenance of oil and other interests would be endangered. . . . Palestine should be retained as a vital link in Britain's defense system."[65] Britain's reaction to Moyne's murder only served to reinforce that position. Immigration restrictions would remain, and there could be no partition.

In 1944, the British still had a viable empire, and despite the Zionist sympathies of many in the government, traditional imperialists, including Churchill, could in no way envision the future without it. To allow immigration or partition would propel the unthinkable destruction of the British position in this all-important region and open the door to an American or Soviet domination of the postwar Middle East. Churchill's Foreign Secretary, Anthony Eden, said it best: "If we lose Arab goodwill, the Americans and the Russians will be on hand to profit from our mistakes."[66] While British imperialists in 1917 had patronized Zionism with a view to strengthening the empire, they had never intended that support be used instead to subvert the empire as appeared to be the case in 1944. In short, the British would not now or in the future sacrifice her role in the region or the needs of empire for the sake of the Zionists in Palestine.

At the same time, a public-relations war had erupted on the Palestinian question, wherein both Jew and Arab took their fight to the court of world opinion—to Britain's allies and the United Nations. The Jews, with more connections in the West, struck first and took their fight to the United States, home to one of the world's largest Jewish communities, to solicit pressure to change British policy. During the war's darkest days, before British, American, and Soviet forces had turned the tide of battle, the Zionists gathered at the Biltmore Hotel in New York in May 1942 and unanimously adopted a policy of unrestricted immigration and the creation of Palestine as a Jewish commonwealth "integrated in the structure of the new democratic world."[67] Although they gained a sympathetic ear, the jury was still out in regards to wider American public opinion and that of President Roosevelt.

Two years later, while the war raged in Europe and the Pacific and with the inevitability of an Allied victory inching onto the horizon, Secretary of state Cordell Hull warned American chief of staff General George Marshall in February 1944 that an upcoming congressional resolution to support a Jewish state in Palestine could propel the Arabs to "play hell" with American oil interests.[68] The resolution was subsequently scrapped, and Roosevelt, ambiguous in the face of Zionist pressure, took a year to respond. In private conversations with Saudi Arabian King Ibn Saud held on February 14, 1945, Roosevelt assured the king that "he would do nothing to assist the Jews against the Arabs and would make no move hostile to the Arab people."[69] Moreover, in reference to the Zionist Biltmore conference of 1942, Saud "mentioned the proposal to send an Arab mission to America and England to expound the case of the Arabs and Palestine." Roosevelt agreed to this as "a very good idea."[70] He also promised Saud to support, along with the British, the complete independence of Syria and Lebanon from France, which ultimately forced the reluctant French to relinquish their mandate at the war's conclusion.[71] Roosevelt died on April 12, 1945, two months after the meeting, and as the public-relations war intensified, Harry S. Truman, a virtual unknown, became America's next president.

Although Arab deliberations on nationalism had preceded the war, Zionist actions and the war itself had provoked increased discussions of Arab unity and political activism. As a result, a month after the Roosevelt–Saud meeting, Arab representatives convened at Cairo in March 1945 to establish the Arab League: an expression of pan-Arab national solidarity. The seven founding members—Egypt, Trans-Jordan, Iraq, Saudi Arabia, Syria, Lebanon, and Yemen—had gathered to promote further means of cooperation, to affiliate with the United Nations and, above all, to present a united front on the explosive question of Palestine. Just as an upcoming Zionist conference in August of that year would demand Palestine as a Jewish state, so the League of Nations preemptively declared that Palestine was already an Arab state. "She has come to be independent in herself, not subordinate to any other state . . . the Covenant of the League of Nations in 1919 made provision for a regime based upon recognition of her independence."[72]

The Arab conference at Cairo had raised the stakes. It was now up to the Jews to make the next move—and move they did. Shortly thereafter, the World Zionist Conference met in London in August 1945, following the final defeat of the Axis. With the full revelation of Nazi atrocities charging the atmosphere, Zionist leader and elder statesman Chaim Weizmann gave the opening address. "The great and powerful European Jewry of ten years ago is no more. We have instead a broken remnant. . . . The words of Herzl, 'that the Jewish State is a world need,' have never been more true than they are today."[73]

The conference then produced a scathing condemnation of Britain's Palestine policy. "But for the White Paper hundreds of thousands who perished in Europe could have been saved in time by being admitted to Palestine."[74]

Outraged, British officials decried this as an unfair, self-serving, and one-dimensional attack on their Palestine policy, which by implication blamed the British government for affairs in Nazi Germany over which it had no control.[75]

An important fact, almost lost amidst the acrimonious Zionist–British debate, would ultimately come to haunt the postwar world: Both Arab and Jew had mutually excluded one another in their declarations and definitions of a Palestinian state. When the British would be forced to withdraw in 1948 and leave the United Nations to handle a proposed partition, as should have been anticipated, the result was, a blood-filled civil war. As the war of words over Palestine intensified, the greatest war in human history concluded.

Following Italy's collapse in 1943, American and British divisions slowly pressed stubborn German forces up the Italian peninsula, while the Russians doggedly pushed the Germans back into the Ukraine. On June 6, 1944, the massive landing of British and American forces in Normandy provided the necessary second front to squeeze the Nazis between them and the advancing Soviets to the point of unconditional surrender one year later on May 8, 1945. Meanwhile, the vice inevitably tightened around Japanese forces in China, Southeast Asia, and the Pacific. While Japan hastened preparations to defend the home islands, on June 26 in San Francisco, the Allies declared the United Nations charter and then met at Potsdam (Berlin) for a final wartime conference from July 17 to August 2. Four days after the conference, on August 6, America dropped the first atomic bomb on Hiroshima; two days later, the Soviets declared war on Japan. The end came suddenly when a second atomic bomb, released on August 9 on Nagasaki, forced Japan's unconditional surrender at Tokyo Bay aboard the American battleship *Missouri* on September 2, 1945.

The Second World War, the deadliest war in human history, had ended. It produced at least 17,000,000 military and 20,000,000 civilian deaths and millions more displaced persons, who, as homeless refugees, proved unable or unwilling to return to their native lands.[76] The conflict had propelled Germany and Japan's total destruction, the emergence of the Atomic Age and, with it, the Cold War between the new superpowers—the United States and the Soviet Union—as well as the British and French retreat from great power status.

Moreover, it accelerated the end of Britain as an imperial power and, with it, her control of the Middle East. Financially strapped and under American pressure, postwar Britain would be forced into humiliating retreats from India, Palestine, Egypt, and Aden; suffered loss of influence in Iraq and Iran; and was obliged to withdraw from the Gulf protectorates. Britain's imperial-minded warriors, however, had not anticipated this result, and their lack of a preplanned withdrawal strategy and hasty departure would leave much of the postwar Middle East irretrievably compromised to a dangerously uncertain future.

Yet, the vital role the British-controlled Middle East had provided in defeating the Axis proved undeniable. British campaigns from Aden and the Sudan decimated the Italians in Ethiopia. Wavell's expeditions from Palestine to Iraq and Vichy Syria stymied another Nazi threat. From Egypt, British, Anzac, and Indian forces routed the Italians in North Africa, while their failed Balkan incursion, according to some, delayed Hitler's Soviet invasion long enough to cost him the war. Moreover, Britain and the United States again supplied the Russians through Persia (Iran). At the same time, Montgomery's thrust from El Alamein together with the Americans from Operation Torch finally strangled Rommel and the Afrika Korps. Again, the British-controlled Suez Canal channeled troops to the North African and European theaters as well as reinforcements to beleaguered British forces in the Far East. Britain's informal control of the Middle East allowed her forces to remain in the region long enough to keep the Axis forces at bay until the entry of the Soviet Union and the United States brought total victory. Could it be said that British control of the Middle East directly saved both the Western democracies and Asia from the worst forms of totalitarian oppression in human history? The answer must be a resounding yes.

But this came at a great price. Britain's informal control over the Middle East, which had so long guarded the communication and transportation arteries of the British Empire, protected the territorial integrity of the region from foreign expansion or conquest and brought ultimate victory in two global conflicts, had at last depleted British finances to the point of destroying the very empire it had sustained. Moreover, Britain's wartime methods had eroded whatever remained in the Middle East of trust for the British. It would remain for the next generation of British leaders to finally call it quits, and they would not do so without a fight.

CHAPTER FOURTEEN

End of the road: Exit from empire 1945–71

The problems were different in each country . . . but the consistent way in which the British handled the transfer of imperial authority in the Middle East worse than anywhere else is easily explained. The Middle East was the area of the grand strategic delusion.

BRIAN LAPPING, *End of Empire*

Britain's decline and hasty retreat from Palestine 1945–48

Britain's two centuries of dominance both in world politics and the Middle East faced its greatest test at the end of the Second World War. Squeezed between the superpowers in the rising Cold War, financially hobbled by enormous wartime debts and, further still, by postwar commitments in Europe, Asia, and the Middle East, Britain simply succumbed to the reality that somehow the age of empire, as it had been understood, was over. Britain's heroic efforts in the Middle East, which had helped to produce final victory in two world wars, had busted the treasury beyond repair. Imperial liabilities now outweighed whatever assets the empire provided. Britain's Labour government and new prime minister, Clement Attlee, who had replaced Churchill on the eve of the Potsdam Conference in July 1945, appeared with a clear mandate to "scuttle the empire." There was no way around it; fiscal responsibility and restraint demanded it. "The bankruptcy brought on by the 1939–45 war—a war the British Government knew was beyond its means—was the principal reason why the British Empire ended so much more quickly than anyone expected."[1] To some degree, the empire also was forced into an earlier than expected retirement because of American pressure. Historian Bernard Porter points this up. "'One thing we are sure we are not fighting for', said *Life* magazine in 1942, 'is to hold the British Empire together'. From some accounts it appeared that the Americans were 'making the liquidation of the British Empire one of their war aims'."[2]

It had become obvious during the war that in every major theater of operation, except the Middle East, the British could only succeed with American assistance and that after the war, Britain as an imperial power appeared doomed without it. But the American role proved ambiguous, and the immediacy of the Cold War made it so. While it became clear that America would not support the continuance of Britain's colonial empire, America would help sustain Britain's postwar European commitment against Soviet expansionism and the growing Communist challenge in Eastern Europe, Greece, Turkey, and Iran. For its part, Britain's Labour government now prioritized its limited resources to defend national security in locales where American aid was assured and, without it, to retreat regardless of the consequences.

From 1946–49 Britain redoubled its commitment to her zone in western Germany and, together with the American zone, created the Bizone (forerunner of the German Federal Republic) to keep the Soviets at bay and preserve British security closer to home.[3] While this joint operation would cost the British taxpayers a hefty £20,000,000 a year, it proved far less expensive than going it alone.[4] The Labour government considered this money well spent; it would guarantee a major American presence in Europe for the duration. But the Bizone created a new and unanticipated dilemma. The question of zonal fusion became inexorably tied to Britain's most intractable problem, Palestine, since thousands of Jewish refugees flooding into America's zone in Germany pursued that destination in opposition to British policy. Here, British and American expectations collided. This factor, among others, would force the British into an unexpected and painful choice.

At precisely the same time and in view of her fiscal restraints and European commitments, Britain began the distressing process of rapid decolonization in India, Ceylon, and Burma, where her national security proved negligible and no American aid was possible. The hasty withdrawal demonstrated that until the recent past, British authorities never seriously contemplated an end to the empire, which clearly precluded a well-thought-out, orderly retreat and, in the case of India, left disaster in its wake and numerous problems that remain unresolved to this day.

The Labour government, however, envisioned a new take on empire to replace Britain's former colonial presence—a free association of equals still loyal to Britain, a commonwealth based on shared values. This relationship proved attractive to much of the empire, including India, to the amazement of some.[5] This association also guaranteed a continuation of British influence in place of formal empire, an idea generally acknowledged and accepted—except in the Middle East, where there were no takers. Brian Lapping observes, "The exceptions to this pattern were all in the Middle East: Palestine, Iran, Egypt, Aden and Cyprus. The British in the Middle East, it was said, never saw the writing on the wall until they hit their heads against it. . . . The Middle East was the area of the grand strategic delusion."[6]

India, whose security before the Second World War provided the original reason for a British presence in the Middle East, again fell under intense nationalist pressure from the Congress Party and the Muslim League to force the British out. In response, after two centuries of British rule, the unthinkable moment arrived—Britain terminated the Raj. Britain's last viceroy, Lord Louis Mountbatten, promptly partitioned India between rival Hindu and Muslim cantonments. With the borders hastily drawn separating Hindu India from Muslim Pakistan, an official transfer of power occurred on August 15, 1947, followed by immediate independence and a sectarian bloodbath. Nevertheless, both India and Pakistan joined the British Commonwealth. Although the pattern of violence accompanied a similar withdrawal in Palestine, it would be minus the formalities of partition, transfer of power or commonwealth status. Surprisingly, Britain would offer much greater resistance to retain her Middle East position than to hold India. While Britain let Palestine go in 1948, this was only because her other Middle East assets still remained in Egypt, Aden, Iraq, and the Baghdad Pact.

In Palestine, unlike India, no withdrawal, planned or unplanned, had been envisioned for the immediate future or at least until the projected end of the mandate in 1949. The British would not choose to leave sooner; it was forced upon them. Here they hoped to maintain sufficient leverage to provide a continual flow of petroleum to fuel the British economy. Oil, regional security, and the global struggle against Communism replaced India as the reason for staying in the Middle East. Maintenance of Arab goodwill remained high on the to-do list in reference to Palestine inasmuch as Prime Minister Attlee upheld the 1939 White Paper, restricting Jewish immigration as steadfastly as Churchill before him. Attlee had hoped for American support for whatever policy he devised for Palestine in order to preserve their mutual interest in keeping the Soviets out of the Middle East. Despite American interest, things would go terribly wrong, very fast. The Americans demonstrated absolutely no understanding or appreciation for how vital a role the British-dominated Middle East had played in the outcome of the two titanic global conflicts. This became obvious soon enough, first in Palestine, then in Egypt. Postwar Anglo-American cooperation in the region never developed, and as a result, the region's Cold War transition has proven uneven and problem-laden to the present.

President Harry Truman might support the British in keeping the Russians out of the region, but he would not do so to preserve British influence there so long as it depended on restricting Jewish immigration into Palestine to garner Arab favor. Truman's position had been based on the fact that well over 250,000 Jewish refugees now inundated America's occupation zone in Germany, and to relieve that pressure, Truman pressed the British to accept 100,000 into Palestine. The Labour government's desire to unite its zone with the American zone in Germany and to relieve the British treasury rested on solving the refugee problem in a manner acceptable to the Americans.

It fell to British foreign secretary Ernest Bevin to find a solution to the zonal problem as well as the intractable problem of Palestine and to secure American assistance in both instances. Bevin, consistently resolute against further admission of Jewish refugees, had hoped to win the Americans to his point of view by a diplomacy of consensus. Confident of success, he proposed on November 4, 1945, the creation of an Anglo-American Committee of Inquiry on the question of admitting Jews from the American zone in Germany into Palestine.[7] Bevin felt assured the committee would support his view that such a move would displace thousands of indigenous Arabs and create another humanitarian problem and a likely bloodbath. Truman agreed to the proposal, but the twelve-member committee, half British and half American, produced a report very unfavorable to Bevin's position. He would not live it down. Historian William Roger Louis thoughtfully notes, "His sense of assurance, some would say arrogance, helps to explain his incautious statement, when he announced the appointment of the Anglo-American Committee . . . 'I will stake my political future on solving the problem'."[8]

Issued on May 1, 1946, the committee's official report recommended the immediate admission of 100,000 Jews to Palestine, to which Truman said yes; but Bevin, despite a promise to support the committee, said no. Bevin's position appeared to be based on Attlee's decision to withdraw British forces from Egypt with a presumed relocation of most to Palestine.[9] Arab goodwill remained, therefore, more vital than ever. As the two governments moved at loggerheads, Attlee saw a way out. With the bigger picture in mind, including that of the shared German zones, Attlee agreed to the proposal if the Americans would provide some of the costs and military forces to support the 80,000 British troops already in Palestine. But Truman's military advisors urged a "no go." Ironically, the American view proved not unlike the British position. Why send an estimated 100,000 American soldiers to protect Jewish refugees, get caught in a civil war, alienate the Arabs, and thus endanger America's own oil interests in the region? In time, the American position would change but not in the direction the British had hoped.

Although many Jews would have preferred to settle in the United States or Western Europe despite immigration restrictions, the Zionists demanded their immediate relocation to Palestine, using, as the Americans suspected, the refugee issue for their own agenda to gain a Jewish state.[10] Because neither the British nor the Americans would immediately compromise, the situation drifted long enough for extremists among the Zionists to force the issue as they turned on their former patrons and took matters into their own hands. The Irgun, the Stern Gang, and now the Haganah increasingly resorted to violence against the British in a vicious series of attacks and reprisals. British installations and personnel became the targets of savage assaults culminating in the most ruthless incident of all, the Irgun's destruction of the King David Hotel in Jerusalem on July 22, 1946. The blast killed ninety-one people, including forty-one Arabs, twenty-nine British, seventeen Jews, and five others.[11] Enraged, the British forbade renewed Jewish immigration; they would not yield to terror.

Nor could the Zionists retreat. As the radicals gained the initiative, Weizmann and the moderates increasingly lost influence.[12] Since the extremists refused to work with the British in Palestine, they now sought to remove and replace them altogether through further acts of violence. Understandably, the atrocities of the Holocaust had unified many in their resolve to gain an independent state for national survival, but the fact that it would be at the expense of their greatly weakened British host clearly demonstrated the changed nature of the relationship. Britain had become the enemy.

When Arabs and Jews rejected another British plan (Morrison-Grady), and Truman would commit to nothing offensive to Jews or Arabs throughout most of 1946, British morale sank further. Truman's Yom Kippur speech of October 4, 1946, which appeared to totally undermine British policy, did the rest. He leaned toward partition, which allowed immigration, and stood against the idea of a unitary state, which did not.[13] Having no stomach for further bloodshed, the Labour government rejected General Montgomery's plan to execute British military will on Palestine forcefully, while Churchill's call to abandon Palestine made more sense to an electorate hardened against both Zionists and Arabs alike.

Under public pressure and utterly frustrated, the British turned the case of Palestine over to the United Nations in February 1947 and, cognizant of Arab and American reaction, did so minus any recommendation for or against partition. One thing was certain; since 1917 and the Balfour Declaration, the British had been fairly consistent in advocating Palestine as a unitary, binational state. If partition occurred, the British decided to let the United Nations take the responsibility and the blame.

Formed in April 1947, the United Nations Special Committee on Palestine (UNSCOP) endorsed partition, which, true to form, the Jews accepted and the Arabs rejected. And no wonder: Of Palestine's 10,000 square miles, 1,270,000 Arabs were to be allotted 43 percent of the worst land, while 608,000 Jews were to receive 57 percent of mostly fertile country.[14] Interestingly, this proposal was far better than one devised by the Jewish Agency in August 1946, which gave the Arabs even less.[15] The final UN plan, which was presumed to be the result of much back-room Zionist pressure, provided a formula tailor-made for disaster.[16] Even if the Arabs had agreed to partition, they could never accept this one-sided formula, which only added insult to injury. But the Arabs, including the Arab League, who always believed that the case for Palestine as an Arab state to be self-evident, presented their point in no uncertain terms. "By legitimizing the Balfour Declaration and the mandate, in essence stated that the claims of the Jews, the majority of whom had been in Palestine less than thirty years, were equal to those of the Arabs, many of whose ancestors had lived there for hundreds of years."[17] The Arab decision to give nothing and the Zionist position to take everything possible could only lead to armed conflict. Had the Americans and British resolved their earlier differences and jointly enforced a more equitable solution in Palestine, things might have gone differently, minus bloodshed. In the end, the British, without additional resources, could do little else, while the Americans, who had the means, would do little more. Thus, one of the lingering and still unresolved tragedies and conflicts of the modern era was about to unfold.

For their part, the British accepted UNSCOP's proposal to end the mandate, but the partition plan proved another matter. Although colonial secretary Arthur Creech Jones had advocated some form of partition consistent with prewar Colonial Office initiatives, he now sided with Bevin and refused to support the proposed partition as patently unfair. As a result, the Labour government again chose to remain neutral on the question.[18] According to some historians, this decision evolved so as not to further alienate the Arabs and jeopardize British oil interests or the future of their Suez Canal bases in talks with the Egyptians.[19] Yet a no vote on partition would have more firmly served that purpose. The choice of neutrality appears more clearly to have been made to alleviate friction with the Americans in concurrent Anglo-American negotiations to join their zones in Germany, wherein the Americans would shoulder two-thirds of the financial burden.[20]

Since the Soviet Union also supported partition as a means of gaining influence in what might become a Jewish state in Palestine, the Americans as well as the United Nations had urged the British to remain at least until the end of their mandate in 1949.[21] No doubt the British preferred an orderly withdrawal and dignified transfer of power commensurate with their international obligations, but, alas, the Irgun struck again in July 1947 and forever altered Palestine's political landscape.

In retaliation for Britain's execution of several terrorists, the Irgun kidnapped, mutilated, and hung two British soldiers and then booby-trapped their bodies.[22] Despite American and international outrage against the horror of this insane act, the greater outrage of the British public forced the government, now in the process of withdrawal from India (August 1947), to follow suit in Palestine—the mandate be damned. On September 20, 1947, the government made its decision for a final evacuation of Palestine set for May 15, 1948.[23]

Meanwhile, in retaliation for the Irgun's actions, Bevin prevented the ship *Exodus* and its cargo of 4,500 Jewish refugees from landing in Palestine;

they were to be returned instead to refugee camps in Germany. The British now looked little better than the Nazis.[24] While the Irgun's British victims had had international sympathy, the Jews who had suffered the atrocities of the Holocaust had more. After this incident, little support remained for the continuance of the British in Palestine. As a result of Bevin's callous handling of the *Exodus*, the Zionist cause won the day in the court of world opinion, while that of the Arabs became lost in the furor. Consequently, on November 29, 1947, the United Nations voted 33–13 in favor of partition.[25] Britain, as anticipated, voted to abstain.[26]

At this point, despite the concerns of the Americans and United Nations, who offered little help, the exasperated British threw in the towel. The Labour government, having committed £50,000,000 along with 80,000 troops and 20,000 police since the war's end, all to no avail, now resolved to maintain their commitment to the May deadline only.[27] Moreover, being shot at from both sides, the government chose to execute their pullout in such a way as to prevent further British military and civilian casualties. The British decided to leave it to the United Nations to enforce the partition after their departure and, in the interval, to distance themselves as much as possible from sporadic Arab-Jewish clashes, which killed hundreds. In view of that decision, the Irgun's ruthless massacre of 250 defenseless old men, women, and children in the Arab village of Deir Yassin on April 9— an event Jewish neighbors condemned—as well as a brutal Arab attack killing 77 innocent Jewish doctors and nurses on the road to Jerusalem on April 13 proved a low point in the saga of the British retreat.[28] Angered and frustrated, British officials decided against the traditional transfer of power and, instead, in one of the most exasperating and humiliating retreats in Britain's imperial history, simply evacuated Palestine on May 15, 1948, abandoning the Jews and Arabs to their own devices. Elizabeth Monroe concisely notes, "It consigned to chaos a territory that it had taken on as 'a sacred trust for civilization'."[29]

On the eve of the British departure, the Jews in Palestine and their leader, David Ben-Gurion, who had always proved more organized, declared the new Jewish state of Israel on May 14.[30] Their readiness became more apparent when the Haganah, as well as the outlawed Stern Gang and the Irgun, having circumvented an American-British arms embargo, secretly obtained Russian-approved Czechoslovakian weapons for self-defense against the Arabs.[31] They soon went on the offensive, however, and not only secured their partitioned area but occupied those districts deserted by 300,000 mostly unarmed Arabs, whom Jewish propaganda as well as Arab radio broadcasts had terrorized into fleeing their land in the wake of the events at Deir Yassin. Whether the Israelis had planned or foreseen the acquisition of this additional territory remains the subject of intense historical debate.[32] It seems more likely that in view of the upcoming war, the Israelis seized this area as an expanded buffer and security zone for self-defense. Since the arms embargo impacted the Arabs more than the Jews, the remaining Palestinian Arabs, divided by internal factions, offered uneven resistance. Those loyal to Haj Amin al-Husseini, the mufti of Jerusalem, whom the Arab League supported, steadily lost ground to the Israelis, many of whom were experienced war veterans.[33] Palestinians loyal to Jordan's King Abdullah and his well-trained and well-equipped Arab Legion, however, stood their ground. Abdullah, more sympathetic to the Jews and wishing to control the Arab-partitioned area, had secretly agreed not to join this fight.[34] At the last minute, he succumbed to Arab League pressure and brought his battle-tested legion into the fray as the only Arab army effective against the Israelis.[35]

Outside of Palestine, the Arab Liberation Army (ALA), composed of detachments from Egypt, Iraq, Lebanon, Syria, and now Jordan, prepared for war. Surprisingly few Palestinians joined these ranks, suspecting their Arab neighbors of harboring territorial designs on Palestine. Significantly, a majority of Palestinian Arabs had recently come to favor the United Nations partition and "indicated a willingness to live in peace alongside a Jewish state."[36] Their decision, if it ever mattered, had come too late as the mufti's ever-present call for revenge, the Arab League's clamor for war and the ongoing Israeli land grab muffled their voice. They proved the true losers, as the Palestinian cause, the supposed justification for this conflict, collapsed when most fled, and took refuge behind Jordanian lines, only to discover their new situation had become frustratingly permanent.

Division among the states of the Arab League in terms of strategy and tactics resulted in uncoordinated attacks on Israeli territory beginning in mid-May. The "David versus Goliath" analogy, the successful product of Israeli propagandists, was hardly true on any level. Excepting the Jordan Legion, neither in size, quality, training or weaponry did the disparate Arab detachments prove a match for the unified and determined Israelis, who soundly defeated them from May 15 to June 11 and again between July 6 and 19, 1948.[37] A United Nations truce ended the immediate conflict in July 1949, but since no peace treaty was signed, a state of war continued to exist.

In the final analysis, Britain's premature departure, Israel's immediate proclamation of statehood, the Arab League's declaration of war, and the flight of the Palestinian Arabs all provided the Israelis with a unique chance to acquire over 70 percent of Palestine.[38] As the opportunity of a lifetime, they would never restore the designated Arab lands, UN demands or the Stern Gang's assassination of UN representative Count Folke Bernadotte to the contrary.[39] They might have allowed some displaced Arabs to return but not without a major concession from the Arab states: a peace treaty and recognition of Israel. Regardless of the offer's sincerity, no individual Arab state could or would agree to this demand without incurring the wrath of the Arab League. Thus, the wellbeing of the Palestinians was ignored as they became pawns entangled in the larger Arab-Israeli power struggle. So it would remain. Although 120,000 Arabs stayed in Israel, nearly 500,000 crowded into Jordanian and Egyptian refugee camps in the West Bank and Gaza, while another 300,000 secured refuge within the surrounding Arab states.[40]

Problems created by the Arab "Diaspora" of 1949, exacerbated by subsequent Arab–Israeli wars in 1956, 1967, and 1973, only served to enlarge this human tragedy.[41] As the fodder for Arab nationalism, Israeli occupation policy, and more recently, Islamic extremism, the Palestinian plight continues to perpetuate the landscape with unending acts of terror and revenge. Although one can blame Arab intransigence, Zionist expansionism or American politics for what happened in Palestine, at the end of the day, British imperial policy from 1917 to 1948 must bear the responsibility for naively setting the stage that produced this overall, and as yet unresolved, problem.

In the end, no amount of manipulating the formula of informal influence or formal control could secure Palestine for British interests. Neither political pressure nor force of arms had ever proved satisfactory. Alas, Attlee settled the issue of Palestine by washing his hands of it altogether. By remaining neutral on partition, he lessened the friction with Truman enough to finalize the Anglo-American zonal agreement in Germany and for the Americans to send 100,000 refugees from their zone to the new state of Israel under the UN plan.[42] After deserting Palestine, the British again were forced to shift their defense of the Middle East to Egypt and the Suez Canal zone, where, as might be expected, they would not be welcome. Welcome or not, Atlee would only leave Palestine because, indeed, he had other options, and Palestine could be jettisoned without losing the Middle East.

Egypt: Retreat and another humiliation 1946–56

After sixty-three years of occupation since 1882, nothing had really changed in terms of the Egyptian mood to remove the ever-present British. If anything, the Second World War had only exacerbated anti-British sentiments. "Egypt for the Egyptians" emerged again not only as the clarion call for Egypt's traditional institutions, the Wafd, and the monarchy, but also for the newer and more aggressive secret societies: the Muslim Brothers and the Free Officers. Nothing had changed for the British either, inasmuch as the Suez Canal remained the major artery of trade and security for the empire and commonwealth, and, according to the 1936 treaty, the British were not legally bound to leave until 1956. At the end of the Second World War, Egypt's revived nationalism and the British resolve to guard the canal appeared again on a collision course, when, to the surprise of most, the British performed an about-face.

The Labour government announced a plan to relocate the bulk of its military force to Libya and Palestine and to guard the canal from those locations in order to relieve tension with Egypt and to treat her as an equal rather than a subservient state.[43] Since the British had recently supported the removal of the French from Syria and Lebanon, Foreign Minister Bevin's promise to withdraw all British forces from Egypt by 1949 appeared a genuinely auspicious sign.[44] Attlee's official announcement to parliament on May 7, 1946, came as a shock to Britain's Conservatives, especially Churchill, who called this "a very grave statement, one of the most momentous I have ever heard in this House."[45] It no doubt stunned many Egyptian nationalists as well, who, after hearing this decision, could never settle for anything less.

In May 1946, however, no one foresaw a British disaster in Palestine or resistance from Libya, which, over the next two years, would force a major readjustment of British thinking relative to a withdrawal from Egypt and the canal. Neither did anyone envision that Britain's unanticipated return to an Egyptian defense strategy would be impeded by conflicts over Egypt's claim to the Sudan and the outbreak of the first Arab-Israeli war. Overall, Britain's attempts to maintain its position in Palestine or Egypt rested on its continued assumption of dominance in the Middle East. The fact, however, that Britain was forced to choose between the two countries revealed the weakness of that presumption following the Second World War. As events unfolded in Egypt from 1946 to 1956, it appears neither the Labour government nor the Conservatives comprehended the depth of that weakness, or that in the end, the British would have no more success in Egypt than it had in Palestine or that, indeed, another humiliation was in the offing. Britain had no intention of leaving the Middle East and would find every way conceivable to retain that three-and-a-half-century presence either through well-meaning diplomacy known as the "right of return" or the imperialism of brute force.

The Labour government had looked to the idea of equality with Egypt as the linchpin of a new and more progressive policy in the Middle East, especially in view of Egypt's prominence in the Arab League, which Britain also supported. The government had hoped that its more liberal attitude toward Egypt would better solidify its position in the Arab world and promote mutual respect and loyalty in place of imperial management. Bevin "optimistically suggested, Anglo-Arab friendship would spread from Egypt through the Muslim world into India."[46] High-minded as this idea sounded, however, no British government of whatever political stripe ever proved completely free of the imperial mystique. This attitude became perfectly clear, as Roger Louis concludes, from Bevin's remark, "'I will be no party to leaving a vacuum'. Bevin thus demonstrated that he had his own sense of Imperial responsibility, both as a socialist and as a protector of Britain's strategic position in the eastern Mediterranean."[47]

Bevin was about to reveal a new take on informal influence. Since the British had committed to a withdrawal of all her forces by 1949, which meant the termination of the treaty of 1936, they moved to replace it with another treaty reflective of the Labour government's equal-partner philosophy. As the British envisioned the new treaty, it would require the Egyptians to call on Britain, their mutual defense partner, for aid in time of war and allow British troops to reenter the country. In short, even the Labour government refused to leave Egypt completely without being granted a legal mechanism of return. As the British Empire's strategic artery, the Suez Canal could not be simply abandoned without a guarantee of defending it in the future, if required. Britain's Labour government might scuttle the empire, but could never bring itself to scuttle the Middle East. It had become too deeply engrained into the mindset and philosophy of empire. It bore the heritage of Roe, Baldwin, Palmerston, Gladstone, Lloyd George, and Churchill; of Napoleon, the Crimea, and two world wars. The British would find a way to stay.

To this end, throughout the summer and fall of 1946, Bevin met with Egypt's new premier, Ismail Sidki, to hammer out a new agreement. The question remained as to why the Egyptians would agree to another treaty that could grant a British return, since such an accord would repeat the mistakes of 1922 and 1936. Obviously, the attraction for Sidki was the immediate removal of 70,000 British troops from Cairo and Alexandria set for 1947 and the remaining 10,000 from the canal by 1949. If no new formula satisfactory to the Egyptians could be found to allow a British return, then the old treaty could continue de jure as well as de facto until 1956, permitting British forces to remain. Since Sidki and the Egyptian nationalists wanted them out, and Bevin desired a more equitable treaty in place while removing British forces, the negotiations should have proceeded quickly to a satisfactory conclusion, but they did not.[48] Sidki reasoned that if Bevin wanted Egypt to recognize a British prerogative of reentry under a new treaty, and wanted it enough, they would have to give something in return: acknowledgment of Egypt's historical and legal sovereignty over the Sudan—an issue of the highest importance for Egyptian pride. The claim had been based on Egyptian ruler Muhammed (Mehmet) Ali's conquest of the Sudan under Ottoman authority as well as the extension of that authority under Egypt's Khedive Ismail in the 1860s. Moreover, the Anglo-Egyptian reconquest of the Sudan in 1899 had been based on that claim, and, more recently, (in theory at least) Ottoman sovereignty had passed to the Egyptian crown. In short, Farouk was king of Egypt and the Sudan.[49] Sidki's position was so stated, and he wanted it affirmed in the new treaty, which might have been a moot point had not the British, in reality, ruled the Sudan as their private preserve since 1899 and had promised the Sudanese independence when they left. In fact, General Montgomery had looked to secure the Sudan as another base of operations after the withdrawal from Egypt.[50] Thus, the best Bevin could do for Sidki in October 1946 was to "logically acknowledge that a 'union' existed between the Sudan and Egypt in the form of a common crown if at the same time he could secure the political guarantees of Sudanese self-determination."[51]

It seemed both parties had achieved what they wanted—an acknowledgment of the other's position—but, as usual, they each interpreted the
protocol in their own way. To Sidki, it meant Egyptian sovereignty over
the Sudan and, for Bevin, continued British administration of and eventual
self-rule for the Sudan. Thereafter, both stated their positions in public,
whereupon British Conservatives and Egyptian nationalists, outraged at the
claims of the other side, branded the negotiations a sellout, to the point that
Sidki was forced to resign and neither government ever signed the agreement
despite continued discussions.[52]

More trouble loomed ahead. While Britain still hoped for an agreement,
Attlee, acting in good faith, had pulled British forces out of Alexandria and
Cairo in early 1947. Unfortunately, since the British would be forced to
withdraw from Palestine and were refused entry into Libya, these 70,000
troops could be placed nowhere except the Canal zone. Once there, they
proved a festering sore. "There, instead of the ten thousand stipulated in
the 1936 Treaty, Britain retained almost eighty thousand men. Egyptian
nationalists felt that Britain, as usual, had completely disregarded them."[53]
In clear violation of the 1936 treaty and without a new accord, the British
were stuck.

Thereafter, Sidki's successor, Mahmud Nokrashi Pasha, took the issue of
the Sudan and Britain's occupation of the Canal zone to the UN in August
1947 but lost ground. The UN proved more sympathetic to the Sudanese,
who had made it clear they would never accept Egyptian rule in view of
Britain's promise of independence.[54] For their part, the Americans had
urged the British to return the Sudan to Egyptian authority to appease
Egypt and thus gain the new treaty allowing a British right of return in case
of war. American concern in this affair had been peaked by a Communist
insurgency in Greece (1946–50), necessitating the continuation of a British
military presence in the Eastern Mediterranean, preferably Egypt. Ironically,
the Americans had remembered and learned all too late the value of the
British position in the Middle East, which had just helped to save the free
world in the Second World War and could do so again in the Cold War.
Britain, however, refused to yield on the Sudan, stating that it would spark
a civil war there and destroy whatever remained of Arab goodwill in the
region. So the situation at the canal deteriorated, while emotions in Egypt
intensified. Egypt's role in the upcoming war in Palestine, however, would
dramatically alter the Egyptian political equation and ultimately compel a
British withdrawal—for good.

While Anglo–Egyptian recriminations raged over the issue of British
troops in the canal, on December 27, 1947, the UN had voted to partition
Palestine. In response, the Palestinian Arabs' self-styled leader, Haj Amin
al-Husseini, now in Cairo, had aligned himself with the Muslim Brothers
and together called for a jihad in Palestine. Moreover, they forced the issue
with the Egyptian government, as titular head of the Arab League, to declare
war on the Jews in Palestine as well. While popular opinion in Egypt joined

the demand, Farouk, who knew his country was ill prepared, vacillated until the British withdrew from Palestine and the Jews proclaimed a state in May 1948. As Egypt's politicians and the members of the Arab League, except Jordan, clamored for war, Egyptian military leaders knew they were not ready for a conflict. Plagued with problems of communication, transportation, and logistical support and, above all, supplied with antiquated and defective weapons, the army could not hope to maintain a sustained offensive. Moreover, having suffered emasculation at the hands of the British during the Second World War, the Egyptian army remained inexperienced and its morale low. Even British military observers had to agree with this assessment and in 1947 warned that "It [Egyptian army] is no more than a hollow skeleton, unfit for any warfare, lacking all the necessary weapons of a modern army. If the army were sent to war, it would sustain a heavy defeat, if not a massacre."[55]

Farouk, however, began to realize the political capital to be gained by entering the Palestinian conflict—a means of restoring his popularity in the face of mounting criticism of his corrupt regime.[56] Such a move would at the same time check the ambitions of his rival, King Abdullah, who aspired to seize Arab-partitioned Palestine for Jordan. Just as a glorious Egyptian victory could undeniably bolster his throne, an inglorious defeat would most certainly bring it down. The end came soon enough.

Egypt's humiliating failure in the 1948 Palestine War occasioned the removal of Farouk by 1952 and left the British under virtual siege at the Suez Canal until their 1956 withdrawal. Following Egypt's defeat against the Israelis, the king, rather than the military, proved culpable for the loss in Palestine owing to his alleged decision to use cheap and defective weapons.[57] True or not, the Free Officers used this and other accusations to organize the Revolutionary Command Council (RCC) to plan Farouk's ouster. Egypt's military equally blamed this defeat on Britain's humiliating reduction of the Egyptian army during the Second World War. As a result and before the king's fall, outraged Egyptians besieged the British at the canal while setting fire to numerous symbols of the British presence in Cairo, including Shepheard's hotel. The "Black Saturday" events of January 26, 1952, and the continued inability of Farouk or the ruling party to force the British from the canal propelled the downfall of the king and the Wafd in July.[58] Farouk, the last ruler in the line of Muhammed Ali, sailed into exile while the Free Officers, operating through the RCC, gained control of Egypt at the expense of the traditional political parties.[59] Churchill, who had returned to power in 1951, along with Foreign Secretary Anthony Eden, could only watch as Egypt slipped from any hope of future British influence. From Churchill's point of view, all this had proven bad enough, but a series of miscues from 1954 to 1956 led to another catastrophic humiliation of the British government in the process.

Ironically, Britain's relations with the new Egyptian government took a very positive turn at the outset. By the Anglo-Egyptian Agreement signed on February 12, 1953, General Muhammed Neguib, Egypt's titular head and symbolic leader of the RCC, with Foreign Secretary Eden, settled the long-standing crisis over the Sudan.[60] This agreement came as a surprise, but since Neguib was half-Sudanese, he as well as other Egyptians reasoned that the self-determination clause in the agreement would result in an ultimate Sudanese decision to unite with Egypt in three years. It did not. When Colonel Gamal Abdul Nasser, the real leader of the RCC, replaced Neguib as Egypt's head a year later, the Sudan opted instead in 1956 for independence.[61]

Eden's stance in these negotiations grated on Churchill, who wanted neither the Sudan's independence nor its union with Egypt. Eden had hoped, nonetheless, that good relations with Egypt on this point might produce a favorable outcome on the important question of British troops at the Suez Canal as well as the implementation of a new scheme to enhance or resurrect informal influence in the region, the Baghdad Pact. His plan was simple. British troops could be immediately removed if Egypt, along with Iraq, Iran, and Turkey, joined the British-sponsored pact as a bulwark against Soviet penetration into the Middle East. Egypt, seen as the linchpin of this grand strategy, would have to agree to a British return if threatened by invasion—an old story, of course. Nasser, who saw the pact as simply the resurrection of British imperialism, tactfully refused to join but instead agreed to a gradual British withdrawal by 1956 as well as their right to return if the region was threatened. Nasser saw the gradual withdrawal and right of return of British troops as necessary concessions, while Eden, who talked down to Nasser throughout the discussions, understood his refusal to join the Baghdad Pact as a reason to mistrust him. Eden's suspicion of Nasser would only intensify.[62] Nevertheless, British undersecretary Anthony Nutting and Colonel Nasser signed the document, known as the Heads of Agreement, on October 18, 1954. It mandated that Britain leave the Canal zone within twenty months, that the base be maintained by civilians only and that it be reactivated "in the event of an attack on any Middle Eastern Arab country or Turkey."[63] Importantly, the agreement upheld the 1888 Suez Canal Convention allowing freedom of navigation.

Churchill and Eden got far less than they wanted, and the agreement was touted as "not a sellout, but a giveaway."[64] "Even the independence of India and Pakistan in 1947 was a less bitter pill for diehard imperialists to swallow than the 1954 agreement to leave Suez."[65] Nasser, however, got more than he wanted from critics in Egypt, including an attempted assassination by his greatest rivals, the Muslim Brothers, just a week after signing the agreement.[66]

Nasser's subsequent purge of the Muslim Brothers as well as other political opponents, among other things, would ultimately lead to Egypt's virtual dictatorship under a one-party system. While it could be said that Egypt chose this system over genuine parliamentary democracy, it must be understood that Britain's intransigence on troop withdrawal and the right of return prompted this clash between Nasser and his critics, driving the subsequent course of events, including the direction of Egypt's political future. When the last British detachments exited Egypt in March 1956, the Free Officers, the RCC, and Nasser may not have created a perfect political system, but they had at long last accomplished something of great moment in the tradition of Urabi and Zaghul: Egypt's complete independence.

No one suspected that seven months after Britain's departure, a subsequent invasion to eliminate Nasser would instead bring down the British government. The affair, known as the Suez Crisis, which quickly elevated Nasser to hero status, would ultimately destroy the Baghdad Pact as well as the remnants of British and French power in the region and, above all, would propel the fall and humiliation of the new British prime minister, Anthony Eden.

Nasser had always understood the Baghdad Pact and those Arab regimes connected to it as nothing more than instruments and lackeys of British imperialism. Indeed, the Baghdad Pact represented one of the last bastions of Britain's informal empire in the Middle East. Nasser's new tool, Cairo Radio, or the "Voice of the Arabs," directly aimed to increase Arab nationalism in the Middle East and create opposition to the Pact, the British and the new state of Israel. When Nasser joined the Bandung Conference of nonaligned nations in 1955, he clearly positioned himself apart from the Anglo-American Cold War doctrine as well. In defiance of Britain and the United States, he purchased considerable weaponry from the Soviet Union to defend against and confront Israel.

Ironically, it was his domestic agenda and not his flirtation with the Soviets that finally led to a crisis with Britain and France. Nasser's land reforms and projects to rebuild portions of Cairo for greater public use were soon to be followed by the greatest scheme of all, the Aswan High Dam. In Nasser's view, the new dam would curtail the Nile's destructive floods, double crop production, and create vast hydroelectric power for Egypt's growing population. For this project, he secured loan guarantees from the world's financial institutions as well as from the United States and Britain. In a surprise move, however, the Eisenhower administration and US Secretary of State John Foster Dulles on July 18 reneged on the promised loan. "Withdrawing the High Dam offer was the worst diplomatic blunder Dulles ever committed."[67] Nasser responded quickly. On the fourth anniversary of the revolution, July 26, 1956, he nationalized the Suez Canal in a rousing speech before cheering thousands in Alexandria. Proceeds from the canal would pay for the dam.

The announcement on Cairo Radio electrified the Arab world and stunned the West, especially Anthony Eden, who had by now developed a very personal and obsessive dislike of Nasser. No doubt his attitude had been prompted by an incident just four years earlier, when another Muslim leader attempted to seize something the British held dear. In 1952, Iran's duly elected premier, Mohammed Mosaddeq, had nationalized the Anglo-Iranian Oil Company (AIOC). As part of a plot to remove him, Britain and America accused him of being a Communist as well as a Soviet sympathizer. Their secret agents (MI-6 and CIA) engineered a coup, resulting in his ousting in August 1953. They then restored the exiled pro-Western shah. This move represented a Cold War regime change for the sake of oil.[68] The Iranians never forgot and returned the favor, first expelling the AIOC in 1958, then exiling the shah in favor of an Islamic Republic in 1979, with repercussions to the present.

Eliminating Mosaddeq was one thing, but replacing Nasser was another. Although Eden's hatred of Nasser far outdistanced his feelings about Mosaddeq, ridding Egypt of Nasser would prove much more difficult. Moreover, if any such scheme backfired, the consequences could prove immediate and devastating. Eden, however, viewed Nasser as another Hitler and yielding to him as the "appeasement policy" reborn. He had convinced himself that Nasser had been behind King Hussein's recent dismissal of General Glubb as head of the Jordanian military, which meant the end of British influence in Jordan.[69] When France and Israel hatched a plot to overthrow Nasser, Eden willingly joined the conspiracy.[70]

France had maintained the controlling shares in the Suez Canal Company, while Britain held 44 percent. Although some financial issues were at stake and both parties believed the Egyptians incapable of running the canal, diplomacy could have prevailed had not both determined on a war to remove Nasser. Their reasons were clear enough, albeit not entirely valid. Eden saw Nasser's policies as a threat to Britain's strategic oil route as well as the source of destabilization of her Middle Eastern allies, Iraq and Jordan, whereas the French held him responsible for an Arab nationalist revolt in Algeria. For its part, Israel had been dealing with Nasser-supported *fidaiyin* guerrilla raids through Gaza and an Egyptian blockade of the Gulf of Aqaba. Regardless, justification for a British and French invasion of Egypt remained insufficient, and the Americans, although antagonistic to Nasser, refused to support military action. A pretext proved necessary, and the French and Israeli plan provided it.[71]

In retaliation for the guerrilla raids and the blockade, Israel was to invade Egypt through the Sinai and push to the Suez Canal. In order to separate the combatants, following an ultimatum, British and French paratroopers were to land in the Canal zone and force each side to retreat ten miles on either side of the disputed waterway, as per the 1954 Anglo-Egyptian agreement to protect the canal. The Israelis struck on October 29 but remained far from the canal when British warplanes bombed Egyptian airfields near Cairo and an Anglo-French force invaded the canal on November 5, allegedly to separate the two forces, which were nowhere near each other. Egypt and Israel had already agreed to a UN-sponsored ceasefire when British and French forces landed, exposing the plan and leaving it in shambles.[72]

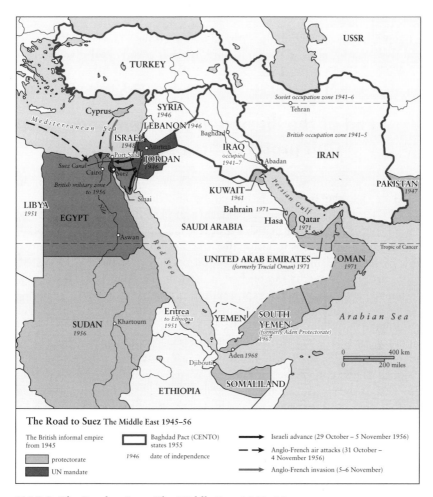

MAP 9 *The Road to Suez: The Middle East 1945–56.*

It was 1882 over again, but where Urabi had failed, Nasser would triumph. This time, the transparent nature of Britain's action thwarted its success and brought down Eden in abject humiliation. The United States and the Soviet Union, in a rare act of singularity, condemned it. "Two months after the debacle Anthony Eden, sick and ruined, resigned. On December 20, 1956, he told the House of Commons, 'There was not foreknowledge that Israel would attack Egypt'—an outright lie."[73] Fallout from this most blatant of imperialist adventures not only doomed the French in Algeria but destroyed the Baghdad Pact and spelled the end of the British Empire in the Middle East.[74] In the end, to everyone's surprise, the Soviets built the Aswan High Dam and gained a firm foothold in Egypt, while Nasser emerged from the ashes as a hero to the Arab world. His new breed of Arab nationalism or *Nasserism* and Cairo Radio would hound the British at every turn until their forced retreat from the region a decade later. Yet after the Palestine and Egyptian fiascos, Britain determined to somehow retain its Middle East position, as that imperial philosophy and mindset could never give thought to retreat.

End of the illusion: Iraq, Aden, and Gulf protectorates 1958–71

Inspired by Nasser's success and within two years of the Suez Crisis, on July 13, 1958, the pro-British monarchy in Iraq was overthrown and longtime Prime Minister Nuri al-Said was gunned down in the streets of Baghdad.[75] Nuri, an ardent British supporter and cosponsor of the Baghdad Pact, fell victim to an Arab nationalist uprising in Iraq not unlike that in Egypt. In similar fashion, the Iraqi revolution had overthrown the British collaborationist monarchy established under King Feisal in 1921. Iraq's new government, a military dictatorship, would give way in 1968 to a unique brand of Iraqi nationalism in the form of the Sunni-dominated Baath Party. According to historian William Polk, this "disregard for the workings of democracy," a legacy of "British-Iraq," ultimately would spawn the rise of Saddam Hussein.[76] Clearly, the dream of Arab unity under British tutelage envisioned at the end of the First World War was not that expressed after 1958. The Arab world no longer wanted or needed the British and would make that perfectly clear once more and for the last time in Aden.

Britain was unprepared for this final showdown. Recent events in Palestine, Egypt, and Iraq should have provided the British with adequate alarm that shifting their strategic efforts to another location in the Middle East, even godforsaken Aden, could simply bring on another disaster. Aden's location, on the southwest corner of the Arabian Peninsula, guarding the entrance to the Red Sea, made it the most remote outpost in the British Empire. First occupied during the war with Napoleon, then wrested from the claim of Egyptian ruler Mehmet Ali by a British military force in 1839, it became the primary coal station for steam traffic to India and beyond, especially after the completion of the Suez Canal in 1869. Subsidies paid to local sultans and sheiks guaranteed Aden and adjacent regimes through informal influence as British protectorates. Aden's strategic value during the First World War resulted in its being placed under formal control and declared a Crown Colony in 1937, the only one in the Middle East. It seemed only logical in view of its continued wartime role, and following Britain's departure from Egypt, that Aden would emerge as the new strategic and military center to protect British interests in the region, especially the oil trade. Following its expulsion from Iran in 1958, the Anglo-Iranian Oil Company had relocated to Aden, refineries and all. By 1958, Aden had awakened to become the busiest and most prosperous port in the region and the hub of British strategic and maritime efforts. And the British planned to keep it that way, with limited self-government under British authority. Furthermore, they stated as much to moderate Arab representatives who had demanded more political control. Colonial Office undersecretary Lord Lloyd informed the group at Aden, "But I should like you to understand that for the foreseeable future it would not be reasonable or sensible, or indeed in the interests of the Colony's inhabitants, for them to aspire to any aim beyond that of a considerable degree of internal self-government."[77]

In other words, the British might provide something between formal control and informal influence. Understandably, Lloyd's speech backfired. Repeated disasters of the past decade had taught the British absolutely nothing. Within three years, Arab nationalism in the form of Aden's trade unions and "Nasserism" would arrive at the colony's doorstep to challenge those assumptions and bring down this last bastion of British imperialism in the Middle East. In 1963, several rival nationalist groups sprang up in fierce and bloody competition to confront the British. Thereafter, the conflict worsened and casualties mounted. In 1966, the socialist-backed National Liberation Front (NLF) and the Nasser-sponsored Front for the Liberation of Occupied South Yemen (FLOSY) had emerged the major players in a protracted guerilla war with each other and against the now overwhelmed British, who had finally decided in desperation to evacuate Aden. Of greatest concern for the besieged British force was to get out alive, as one officer stated: "Time is short if we are to avoid a major disaster, lets get cracking."[78] It was Palestine all over again, with one important exception. On November 30, 1967, Harold Wilson's Labour government managed to effect a transfer of power to the political victor, the NLF, not in the dangerous environs of Aden but at Geneva, Switzerland. After 128 years, the British Crown Colony of Aden fell into the Soviet camp, as the People's Democratic Republic of Yemen and as hosts to the Soviet navy. "The departure of the British from Aden was certainly the worst shambles in the End of Empire, the successor regime the most completely opposed to all Britain had stood for."[79] In 1990, however, it became the Republic of Yemen along with the demise of the Soviet Union.

Meanwhile, the British already had begun the process of leaving the Persian Gulf. They departed Kuwait in 1961, except for a brief return to beat off an Iraqi invasion. The Iraqis never gave up the claim that Kuwait had been an artificial construct of the British during the Ottoman period and that it remained legally part of Iraq. Saddam Hussein's invasion of Kuwait in 1990 served to punctuate that belief. Following the Aden nightmare, the British hastened to turn over the remainder of its Persian Gulf protectorates to independence in 1971, having neither the will nor the finances to continue the imperial illusion.

A quarter century following Britain's victory in the Second World War, due in part to her control of the Middle East, a protracted reaction to her wartime abuses continued to haunt the British effort at every turn. Formal control and informal influence, stretched to the limits, finally faltered under the weight of Palestine's chaos, Nasser's Egypt, the Baghdad Pact's demise (Iraq, Iran, and Turkey), the calamity of Aden, and departure from the protectorates. At the end of the day, Britain had withdrawn from one Middle East base to another until not one remained. Notably, the final exit occurred, of course, when no empire remained to protect.

In looking back at Britain's significant legacy in the Middle East, it can be seen that what had originally begun as a search for trade in the "Indies" resulted in the newly created English East India Company laying its roots in India and Persia by the early seventeenth century. From this simple start, company influence spread into the Middle East through trade with the Mughal, Safavid, and Ottoman Empires, creating an East–West network not seen in the region since the great days of the Arab-Abbasid Empire (750–1000 CE). It brought together three continents—Europe, Africa, and Asia—forming those arteries that would later connect the far reaches of the British Empire. It survived wars and conflicts with the Portuguese, Dutch and French and emerged in the nineteenth century as the unassailable and dominant power in the region. It managed most of this through informal influence, not military control or colonization, and kept the more predatory European powers at bay, including the French, Germans, and Russians.

Certain well-known negatives finally drove the British from the region. These included the 72-year British occupation of Egypt (1882–1954), which effectively destroyed Egypt's fledgling democracy and brought on later wartime abuses. It also encompassed the failure to fulfill the promise of a great Arab state and a restored caliphate due to the Sykes-Picot Agreement; and finally, it failed to maintain Palestine as a unitary binational state or as part of a larger Arab state because of the Balfour Declaration. Most of the feudal dynasties and military dictatorships that have emerged as Middle Eastern nation-states in the modern era have done so as a result of these specific British actions. While some have been overthrown by the "Arab Spring," others have succumbed to latter-day extremists' attempts to restore the Arab state caliphate in their own image. In Palestine, far from becoming a unitary state, Arabs and Jews have sought to exclude each other from the beginning and now Israel collides with the occupied West Bank and an isolated Gaza in unending conflict.

Yet a more positive British legacy had been generated and guaranteed by extraordinary traders and politicians who manifested a vision for the region. Sir Thomas Roe, George Baldwin, Lord Palmerston, David Lloyd George, and Winston Churchill extended efforts that saved and preserved the geopolitical integrity of the area and destroyed piracy and the slave trade. In a fitting climax, Britain's integration of the region into the wider global system provided an avenue of triumph for the democratic West and the free world over the most heinous of totalitarian oppressors in human history. After 352 years (1619–1971), the British Empire in the Middle East had ended. Its legacy remains.

CONCLUSION

Britain's presence in the Middle East began as an outgrowth of trade from India, which spread into Persia (Iran), the Gulf, Afghanistan, and the Ottoman Empire during the seventeenth and eighteenth centuries. From the first, however, this trade had a built-in political edge to it, created because Sir Thomas Roe represented the English crown as well as the trade company and demanded equal status in *fermans* (contracts) with the Mughal and Persian courts. This turned to a position of political ascendancy after victories over the French in the eighteenth century. Tradesman George Baldwin proved most responsible for seeing the value of this region, especially Egypt, for security and communications purposes during the War of American Independence. Thereafter, a British sphere developed in this special region to become a protective and vital link connecting the far-flung reaches of the British Empire. In time, the use of informal control evolved as the most practical way to secure this vast area. Thus, British representatives, working with native elites or "sub-imperialists" (sultans, pashas, and tribal sheiks) provided an economical and generally unobtrusive process to guide portions of the Middle East to satisfy British concerns. Although successful if measured by British interests alone, the process also had its downside, since policy was directed above all by British imperial benefit rather than any selfless concerns for the region or its people. In short, the strategy had evolved to manage the region not for its own sake but as an essetial linchpin guarding the route to Britain's "Crown Jewel," India, and to protect of the rest of the British Empire in South Asia and the Pacific. As a result, the area suffered a degree of political retardation due to British support of these native elites or puppet regimes, since British pressure often kept them in power in the face of growing popular discontent.

On the plus side, the most successful of these endeavors involved the preservation of the Middle East's largest political entity, the Ottoman Empire. It was to prove both the linchpin and jugular vein of the British Empire, and Britain defended it as the heart of nineteenth-century British foreign policy in the face of French intrigues, Napoleon's invasion and Russian expansion. In the aftermath, Lord Palmerston, foreign secretary and later prime minister, formed the first government policy to officially control the region. This policy propelled the rise of the "Eastern Question," which brought on the Crimean War against Russia and later conflict with France over the Suez Canal. Occasionally, such informal management failed, as in Aden and Egypt in 1840, whereupon Palmerston settled the question by implementing more formal control at the point of a gun. Aden became a British colony, while a rebellious Egypt under Muhammed Ali was firmly restored to Ottoman control through British guarantee (the treaty of 1840) and thereafter managed by informal influence over Ali's dynasty. Palmerston's political philosophy guided every prime minister and all decisions covering the Middle East thereafter, including that of Liberal Prime Minister William Gladstone, who, in 1882, invaded Egypt at a time when Britain's informal guidance appeared successful to most observers; Britain was to occupy the country for seventy-two years. This particular action in Egypt appears an exception to the formula of imperial control devised by historians Ronald Robinson and John Gallagher, "Informal where possible, formal when necessary." Britain's occupation of Egypt appeared contrived and unnecessary to observers at the time. The invasion secured Egypt to the Ottoman Empire as a British veiled protectorate, which safeguarded British ties to the empire. Ironically, the very effort to save Egypt to the Ottoman Empire was in fact to drive the Ottomans from British hegemony into the arms of Germany in the years ahead. At the same time, Britain had established the Gulf protectorates and brought an end to piracy and the slave trade in the Persian Gulf and the Red Sea. Britain managed these protectorates, like the Ottoman Empire, through informal control and proved successful at keeping other Europeans out. As a result, the dynasties of Kuwait, Bahrain, and the United Arab Emirates remain today.

This story also has addressed one of the lesser-known problems confronting the British government's imperial presence in the Middle East: the periodic confrontations with the government of British India over regional jurisdiction. British trade from India had early on spread into the greater Middle East, which in time resulted in confusion over the Government of India versus the London government's authority in the Middle East and proved a constant source of embarrassment. British policy over Egyptian affairs in the eighteenth and nineteenth centuries evidenced this collision, as did the issue of representation at the Persian court, the 1840 Afghanistan invasion, the Mesopotamian Campaign in the First World War, and, finally, the Hashemites–Saudi feud over control of the Arabian Peninsula. The Indian government's support of a Saudi victory compromised an earlier British government agreement calling for the creation of an Arab state under the Hashemites after the war.

The greatest problems stemming from the British presence came as a result of the First World War. The British government produced mutually exclusive treaties through various government agencies to control the destiny of the Middle East after the war. The 1915 McMahon–Hussein correspondence called for a large Arab state and a reborn caliphate to cover much of the Middle East. This pact conflicted with the Sykes-Picot Agreement of 1916, which divided most of the same region between British and French spheres. The accord also collided with the 1917 Balfour Declaration's support for a Jewish settlement in Palestine. Although the McMahon–Hussein and Balfour agreements had humanitarian goals, their agendas collided and produced the most contradictory aspects of British imperial policy, generating perpetual and bloody conflicts to this day. The promise of a large Arab state and caliphate were left unresolved and unfulfilled until its recently attempted revival by latter-day extremists. Equally, the dream of Palestine as a binational, unitary state remains illusive and conflict-ridden.

The more constructive facets of British policy contributed to the area's stability through the eradication of the slave trade and piracy as well as the development of a transportation–communications infrastructure and economic integration. Above all, Britain protected the area's political integrity from the eighteenth to the twentieth century with its defense against more predatory French and Russian colonialism, German hegemony, and the Nazi menace. The British effort, whether through "formal" control or "informal" influence, preserved the greater Middle East as a geopolitical entity, which has survived to the present. Despite growing financial hardship, Britain protected the region's geographical integrity through the First and Second World War and afterward. Her control of the Middle East provided an avenue for certain Allied victory in those titanic conflicts, a long-forgotten and unappreciated fact. It could be said that British control of the Middle East directly saved both the Western democracies and Asia from the worst forms of totalitarian oppression in human history. But that tenacious hold had its well-remembered downside of financial ruin and an alienated population. Notwithstanding, as long as Britain had an empire, it remained firmly fixed in the Middle East with military and naval bases in Palestine, Egypt, and Aden, until it was forced to withdraw in 1948, 1954, and 1967 respectively, when at last, there remained no popular trust and no empire to guard.

This work has sought to provide a better understanding of the mechanics of British imperialism by evaluating the impact of treaties, protectorates, guardianships or outright occupation of a particular locale. While these schemes proved beneficial for the British, they undercut the need to accommodate the expectations of the common inhabitants, and, therefore, substituted control through elites in place of the needs or desires of the subject population. In some cases, such methods and the attitudes that kept them in place provoked resentment, strident nationalism, feudal dynasties, and one-party rule. Moreover, Britain's prolonged stay in Egypt sparked the rise of Islamic extremism, which has grown and developed in various forms throughout the Middle East in the ensuing decades. It must be understood, however, that only with rare exception did the British attempt to promote democracy in the region. It was not in their interests to do so, nor did they ever say it was.

Most importantly, the vital role the British sphere played in the Middle East helped to secure and maintain the fabric of the larger British Empire, one of the most successful geopolitical institutions in history. Britain achieved this, for the most part, without direct control of the region, but through informal management for over 350 years with minimal military effort. When force proved necessary, it was utilized sparingly in Aden and Egypt and only to a greater degree in two world wars to prevent a more heinous military and political power from dominating the region. Indeed, Britain's Middle Eastern assets provided the free world with the necessary survival time as well as an offensive springboard to gain a final victory over the Axis—a momentous legacy, indeed, for which it has received little credit. Using the Middle East without restraint, however, came at an enormous cost; Britain lost the region and with it great power status. Yet without the British role, which integrated the region into the larger British imperial system, it remains questionable whether the various countries that are now a part of the Middle East would have so readily adjusted to modern geopolitical systems, global values, and institutions to the degree that they have. Overall, the British legacy seems more positive if measured by what could have been the alternative. In the end, it is hoped this study has provided some understanding of the role and heritage of Britain's long moment in the Middle East.

NOTES

Chapter 1

1 F. C. Danvers, *Report on the India Office Records Relating to Persia and the Persian Gulf* (London: Eyre and Spottswoodie, 1975), 13.

2 Ibid., 14.

3 Ibid., 13–14.

4 J. C. Hurewitz, *Diplomacy in the Near and Middle East* (Princeton: D. Van Nostrand Company, 1956), Vol. I, 6–7.

5 Danvers, *Report on the India Office Records Relating to Persia and the Persian Gulf*, 15–16.

6 Hurewitz, *Diplomacy in the Near and Middle East*, 9–15.

7 A. C. Wood, *A History of the Levant Company* (Oxford: Oxford University Press, 1955), 7–14; Hurewitz, *Diplomacy in the Near and Middle East*, 1–4.

8 Hurewitz, *Diplomacy in the Near and Middle East*, 1–5.

9 John Shaw, *Charter Relating to East India Company* (Madras: 1887), 6; also see Martin Moir, *A General Guide to the India Office Records* (London: The British Library, 1988), 1–4.

10 Holden Furber, *Rival Empires of Trade in the Orient 1600-1800* (Minneapolis: University of Minnesota Press, 1978), 38–44.

11 H. Dodwell, *The Cambridge History of India*, Vol. 5 (Cambridge: University Press, 1929), 81.

12 J. G. Lorimer, *Gazetteer of the Persian Gulf and Oman and Central Arabia*, Vol. I, part I (Calcutta: Government Printing, India, 1915), 12.

13 Ibid., 12–13.

14 Moir, *A General Guide to the India Office Records*, 5.

15 W. Foster (ed.), *The Embassy of Sir Thomas Roe to India, 1615-19: As Narrated in his Journal and Correspondence* (London: Oxford University Press, 1926); Dodwell, *The Cambridge History of India*, Vol. 5, 80.

16 Lorimer, *Gazetteer of the Persian Gulf and Oman and Central Arabia*, Vol. I, part l, 22; Furber, *Rival Empires of Trade in the Orient 1600-1800*, 40–42.

17 Danvers, *Report on the India Office Records Ewlating to Persia and the Persian Gulf*, 23–26; Moir, *A General Guide to the India Office Records*, 4–6.

18 Hurewitz, *Diplomacy in the Near and Middle East,* 18–20; see also A. A. Amin, *British Interests in the Persian Gulf* (Leiden: E. J. Brill, 1967), 4.

19   Lorimer, *Gazetteer of the Persian Gulf and Oman and Central Arabia*, Vol. I, part l, 13, details the exploits and misadventures of the shah's ambassador to Spain, Englishman Robert Shirley, who Sir Thomas Roe greatly mistrusted; also see Amin, *British Interests in the Persian Gulf*, 4.

20   Lorimer, *Gazetteer of the Persian Gulf and Oman and Central Arabia*, Vol. I, part I, 16.

21   Ibid., 19.

22   Dodwell, *The Cambridge History of India*, Vol. 5, 81.

23   Lorimer, *Gazetteer of the Persian Gulf and Oman and Central Arabia*, Vol. I, part l, 22.

24   Furber, *Rival Empires of Trade in the Orient 1600-1800*, 46.

25   Lorimer, *Gazetteer of the Persian Gulf and Oman and Central Arabia*, Vol. I, part I, 26; Danvers, *Report on the India Office Records Ewlating to Persia and the Persian Gulf*, 18–19.

26   Dodwell, *The Cambridge History of India*, Vol. 5, 82; Lorimer, *Gazetteer of the Persian Gulf and Oman and Central Arabia*, Vol. I, part I, 27.

27   Danvers, *Report on the India Office Records Ewlating to Persia and the Persian Gulf*, 19.

28   Hurewitz, *Diplomacy in the Near and Middle East*, 18.

29   India Office Records R/15/1, 1–9.

30   Dodwell, *The Cambridge History of India*, Vol. 5, 80.

31   Furber, *Rival Empires of Trade in the Orient 1600-1800*, 42.

32   Lorimer, *Gazetteer of the Persian Gulf and Oman and Central Arabia*, Vol. I, part I, 21.

33   Furber, *Rival Empires of Trade in the Orient 1600-1800*, 65–66, provides evaluation of stresses on East India Company stock after 1622; Amin, *British Interests in the Persian Gulf*, 7; see also K. N. Chaudhuri, *The English East India Company, The Study of an Early Joint Stock Company 1600-1640* (London: Cass, 1965) for the most exhaustive account of the company's early economic history.

34   Hurewitz, *Diplomacy in the Near and Middle East*, 18–20.

35   Amin, *British Interests in the Persian Gulf*, 7.

36   Lorimer, *Gazetteer of the Persian Gulf and Oman and Central Arabia*, Vol. I, part I, 40; Amin, *British Interests in the Persian Gulf*, 7–8; Danvers, *Report on the India Office Records Ewlating to Persia and the Persian Gulf*, 22–23.

37   Danvers, *Report on the India Office Records Ewlating to Persia and the Persian Gulf*, 25, 29.

38   India Office Records G/17/1, 1–2 for connection of Gulf trade to Mocha and Socotra to avoid the Dutch; see also Danvers, *Report on the India Office Records Relating to Persia and the Persian Gulf*, 22 on Mocha trade and factory at Basra.

39   Danvers, *Report on the India Office Records Ewlating to Persia and the Persian Gulf*, 23; see also Amin, *British Interests in the Persian Gulf*, 8–9.

40   Ibid., 23.

41 Lorimer, *Gazetteer of the Persian Gulf and Oman and Central Arabia*, Vol. I, part I, 42.

42 Amin, *British Interests in the Persian Gulf*, 10.

43 Ibid.; Danvers, *Report on the India Office Records Ewlating to Persia and the Persian Gulf*, 25.

44 Amin, *British Interests in the Persian Gulf*, 11; Moir, *A General Guide to the India Office Records*, 4–5.

45 Lorimer, *Gazetteer of the Persian Gulf and Oman and Central Arabia*, Vol. I, part I, 61.

46 Amin, *British Interests in the Persian Gulf*, 13.

47 A. T. Wilson, *The Persian Gulf: An Historical Sketch from the Earliest Times to the Beginning of the Twentieth Century* (Oxford: Clarendon Press, 1928), 172–73, 192–96; Lorimer, *Gazetteer of the Persian Gulf and Oman and Central Arabia*, Vol. I, part I, 62.

48 Lorimer, *Gazetteer of the Persian Gulf and Oman and Central Arabia*, Vol. I, part I, 76.

49 Ibid., 81–82; Danvers, *Report on the India Office Records Relating to Persia and the Persian Gulf*, 30–33; Amin, *British Interests in the Persian Gulf*, 14–15.

50 Amin, *British Interests in the Persian Gulf*, 96–97.

51 Ibid., 134–41; see also K. N. Chaudhuri, *The Trading World of Asia and the East India Company 1660-1760* (Cambridge: Cambridge University Press, 1978), 174–89, which provides full discussion on question of silver bullion trade in Asia.

52 J. B. D. Kelly, *Britain and the Persian Gulf 1795-1880* (Oxford: Oxford University Press, 1968), 51–52; Amin, *British Interests in the Persian Gulf*, 20–21, 57–63.

53 Amin, *British Interests in the Persian Gulf*, 75–79.

54 Ibid., 9: Lorimer, *Gazetteer of the Persian Gulf and Oman and Central Arabia*, Vol. I, part I, 62.

55 L. Lockhart, *Nadir Shah. A Critical Study Based Mainly on Contemporary Sources* (London: Luzac and Company, 1938), 221; Amin, *British Interests in the Persian Gulf*, 16.

56 Lorimer, *Gazetteer of the Persian Gulf and Oman and Central Arabia*, Vol. I, part I, 86; Amin, *British Interests in the Persian Gulf*, 17.

57 Amin, *British Interests in the Persian Gulf*, 14–16; also see Lorimer, *Gazetteer of the Persian Gulf and Oman and Central Arabia*, Vol. I, part I, 82–83.

58 Danvers, *Report on the India Office Records Relating to Persia and the Persian Gulf*, 34.

59 Ibid., 36; also see Kelly, *Britain and the Persian Gulf 1795-1880*, chap. 1.

60 Lorimer, *Gazetteer of the Persian Gulf and Oman and Central Arabia*, Vol. I, part I, 95; Amin, *British Interests in the Persian Gulf*, 21–22.

61 John Marlowe, *Perfidious Albion* (London: Elek Books, 1971), chapter 1; see also H. L. Hoskins, *British Routes to India* (New York: Longmans, Green and Company, 1928); H. Furber, "The Overland Route to India in the Seventeenth and Eighteenth Centuries," *Journal of Indian History*, vol. XXIX (1951); Amin, *British Interests in the Persian Gulf*, 22, chap. 3.

62 Danvers, *Report on the India Office Records Ewlating to Persia and the Persian Gulf*, 37.

63 Amin, *British Interests in the Persian Gulf*, 26–27.

64 Ibid., 27, 30–31.

65 Danvers, *Report on the India Office Records Relating to Persia and the Persian Gulf*, 37–38; Amin, *British Interests in the Persian Gulf*, 45; Wilson, 175–77.

66 India Office Records R/15/1, 1; C. U. Aitchison, *Collection of Treaties, Engagements, and Sanads Relating to India and Neighboring Countries A* (Calcutta: Government of India, 1933), Vol. XIII, 41–43; Lorimer, *Gazetteer of the Persian Gulf and Oman and Central Arabia*, Vol. I, part I, 138–39; Danvers, *Report on the India Office Records Relating to Persia and the Persian Gulf*, 40; Amin, *British Interests in the Persian Gulf*, 49; Wilson, 177–79.

67 Amin, *British Interests in the Persian Gulf*, 23.

Chapter 2

1   India Office Records (IOR) R/15/1, 1; Moir, *A General Guide to the India Office Records*, 15; Lorimer, *Gazetteer of the Persian Gulf and Oman and Central Arabia*, Vol. I, part I, 81; P. Spear, *A History of India* (New York: Penguin Books, 1981), Vol. 2, 85–86.

2   Marlowe, *Perfidious Albion*, 22, provides discussion on continuing private trade by East India Officials; Spear, *A History of India*, 86.

3   Kelly, *Britain and the Persian Gulf 1795–1880*, 53–54; Amin, *British Interests in the Persian Gulf*, 80–84, also 73 footnote 1 offers additional background on the origin and location of Kab tribe and pirate activities against Ottomans and Persians.

4   Amin, *British Interests in the Persian Gulf*, 82–84.

5   IOR/Factory Records, Vol. 13, Letter to Ambassador Wrench at Constantinople, April 6, 1764, cited in Amin, *British Interests in the Persian Gulf*, 81.

6   Amin, *British Interests in the Persian Gulf*, 83–84.

7   Aitchison, *A Collection of Treaties, Engagements, and Sanads Relating to India and Neighboring Countries*, vol. XIII, 42–44; IOR/R/15/1, 1; Kelly, *Britain and the Persian Gulf 1795–1880*, 51; Amin, *British Interests in the Persian Gulf*, 75; Lorimer, *Gazetteer of the Persian Gulf and Oman and Central Arabia*, Vol. I, part I, 138–39.

8   IOR/Dispatches to Bombay, Vol. II. Letter to Bombay, March 22, 1765, cited in Amin, *British Interests in the Persian Gulf*, 75.

9   Lorimer, *Gazetteer of the Persian Gulf and Oman and Central Arabia*, Vol. I, part I, 139; Amin, *British Interests in the Persian Gulf*, 73–79; Kelly, *Britain and the Persian Gulf 1795–1880*, 52–53.

10 Kelly, *Britain and the Persian Gulf 1795–1880*, 52; Amin, *British Interests in the Persian Gulf*, 72–73.

11 Danvers, *Report on the India Office Records Relating to Persia and the Persian Gulf*, 42–43; Lorimer, *Gazetteer of the Persian Gulf and Oman and Central Arabia*, Vol. I, part I, 139–40.

12 Lorimer, *Gazetteer of the Persian Gulf and Oman and Central Arabia*, Vol. I, part I, 139–42; Amin, *British Interests in the Persian Gulf*, 76.

13 IOR/F.R., Vol. 16. Letter to the Agency, March 3, 1765, cited in Amin, *British Interests in the Persian Gulf*, 77, footnote 4.

14 Wilson, *The Persian Gulf: An Historical Sketch from the Earliest Times to the Beginning of the Twentieth Century*, 182; Amin, *British Interests in the Persian Gulf*, 77–78.

15 Danvers, *Report on the India Office Records Relating to Persia and the Persian Gulf*, 41–42; Amin, *British Interests in the Persian Gulf*, 78.

16 IOR/R/15/1, 1; Kelly, *Britain and the Persian Gulf 1795–1880*, 52–53; Lorimer, *Gazetteer of the Persian Gulf and Oman and Central Arabia*, Vol. I, part I, 139–40.

17 Amin, *British Interests in the Persian Gulf*, 85.

18 Danvers, *Report on the India Office Records Relating to Persia and the Persian Gulf*, 41, names the four ships—*Defiance*, *Salamander*, *Bomb*, and *Wolf*—and states that the *Defiance* blew up shortly after beginning the operation.

19 IOR/Bombay Public Consultation (BPC), Vol. 29, letter to the agent, March 1, 1766, cited in Amin, *British Interests in the Persian Gulf*, 87.

20 Ibid., 88–89.

21 Kelly, *Britain and the Persian Gulf 1795–1880*, 53, sees this incursion as the primary reason for deterioration of relations between the Bushire resident and the Persian ruler, leading to the closure of the factory in 1769.

22 Amin, *British Interests in the Persian Gulf*, 92–93: British determination was demonstrated by sending five additional warships to the blockade, forcing Kab to back down.

23 Lorimer, *Gazetteer of the Persian Gulf and Oman and Central Arabia*, Vol. I, part I, 143, points up Bombay government's disagreement with London council over closure of Bushire; see also Kelly, *Britain and the Persian Gulf 1795–1880*, 53.

24 Kelly, *Britain and the Persian Gulf 1795–1880*, 53.

25 Lorimer, *Gazetteer of the Persian Gulf and Oman and Central Arabia*, Vol. I, part I, 145; Wilson, *The Persian Gulf: An Historical Sketch from the Earliest Times to the Beginning of the Twentieth Century*, 183–84.

26 Amin, *British Interests in the Persian Gulf*, 134–38, 141, provides excellent discussion on depletion of silver specie from Persia for British woolen goods up to the mid-1700s.

27 IOR/R/15/1, 1; P/341/45, Bombay public proceedings, July 24, 1778; also see discussion on mail routes in Kelly, *Britain and the Persian Gulf 1795–1880*, 53; Marlowe, *Perfidious Albion*, chap. 1; Danvers, *Report on the India Office Records Relating to Persia and the Persian Gulf*, 43, Amin, *British Interests in the Persian Gulf*, 116.

28 IOR/R/15/1, 1; Amin, *British Interests in the Persian Gulf*, 138. East India Company trade with China depended on silver since the Chinese government would accept little else in the way of barter or commodities.

29 Danvers, *Report on the India Office Records Relating to Persia and the Persian Gulf*, 43; Kelly, *Britain and the Persian Gulf 1795–1880*, 53.

30 IOR/Factory Records/G/17, introduction, 7–9.

31 IOR/G/17/1, Part 1, 1–2, March 23, 1644; see also Furber, *Rival Empires of Trade in the Orient 1600–1800*, 69.

32 IOR/G/17, introduction, 7–9.

33 IOR/G/17/1, Part 1, 5–6.

34 IOR/G/17/1; G/17/2; G/17/3; G/17/4 provides full discussion on a century of Mocha trade from company factory records; see also Furber, *Rival Empires of Trade in the Orient 1600–1800*, 254.

35 IOR/G/17/1, 526–33: Letter from chief factor Robert Cowan, 1726; also see Furber, *Rival Empires of Trade in the Orient 1600–1800*, 254–55. Cowan not only controlled the English trader's dealings but also those of other Europeans.

36 IOR/G/17, introduction, 7–9.

37 Ibid.: No specific date is recorded for this event, but it appears to have been about the mid-eighteenth century, when the company was beginning to flex its political and military muscle.

38 IOR/G/17/1, Part 1, 2–3 specifies the nature of the ferman as an incentive that also allowed the British to buy and sell freely and without tariff. Here the British spelling of "Beetlefuckee" occurs. See also K. N. Chaudhuri, *The Trading World of Asia*, 17–18.

39 IOR/G/17, introduction, 7–9.

40 Ibid.

41 Ibid.

42 IOR/G/17/5, prelude, 75–80.

43 Marlowe, *Perfidious Albion*, chap. 1.

44 IOR/G/17/5, prelude, 77; G/17, series 5–7; see also C. A. Bayly, *Imperial Meridian: The British Empire and the World, 1780–1830* (London: Longman, 1989), 51; H. L. Hoskins, *British Routes to India* (London: British Routes to India, 1928).

45 IOR/G/17/5, 1.

46 IOR/G/17/5, 2–3: Extract from Bengal public consultations, November 18, 1773. The project was organized by merchants Captain Thornhill, Robert Halford, and David Killican with use of schooner *Cuddalore* for the purpose of "taking a survey from Bussora to Suez, that navigation being hitherto unknown."

47 IOR/G/17/5, 4: Letter of March 15, 1774.

48 IOR/G/17/5, 4–5, and prelude, 77.

49 IOR/G/17/5, prelude, 77–78.

50 IOR/G/17/5, 21–40: Extract from Bengal public consultations, November 4, 1776. Minute prepared by Sir Philip Francis on objections to the Red Sea route.

51 P. Spear, *A History of India*, 89–90, 94. Francis was an avowed enemy of Hastings and worked on the Council of Four in Calcutta, which oversaw the work of the governor-general.

52 IOR/G/17/5, 43–44: Extract from Ainslie's general letter to Bengal, July 4, 1776; also see G/17/5, prelude, 78, on Ainslie's diplomatic concerns, and appendix to IOR/G/17/1-5, i, for biographical details on Ainslie.

53 IOR/G/17/5, 21–40, November 4, 1776, Extract from Bengal public consultations: Minute prepared by Mr. Francis about benefits, liabilities, and objections to Bengal trade to Red Sea.

54 Spear, *A History of India*, 89.

55 IOR/G/15/5, 43–45; G/17/5, prelude, 78.

56 Marlowe, *Perfidious Albion*, 20, 22.

57 IOR/G/17/5, July 4, 1777, extract from Ainslie's general letter to Bengal.

58 Ibid., April 23, 1778, extract from general letter from Bengal.

59 Ibid., May 25, 1775, letter from committee of correspondence of the E. I. Co., appointment of Baldwin as agent for Levant Co. in Cairo, and to handle packages for E. I. Co. bound for London. Also see G/17/5, Prelude, 75.

60 Ibid., September 6, 1776, letter addressed to Baldwin as consul for His Majesty the King of Great Britain. See also Marlowe, *Perfidious Albion*, 23. Although Baldwin had been British consul to Cyprus in 1768, this letter is too late to refer to that. Ambassador Murray's untimely death in 1776 left the issue unclear.

61 Foreign Office, state papers, Turkey 53, January 22, 1777, and FO/SP Turkey 54, January 21, 1778, cited in Marlowe, *Perfidious Albion*, 24–25, 28.

62 IOR/G/17/5, 197–99, December 17, 1778, letter from Sir Robert Ainslie to Foreign Secretary Lord Weymouth. Report on English ship that went from India to Suez in order to trade before the ban was in place, and fresh negotiations for trade with Egypt's Beys despite Porte's orders.

63 FO/SP, Turkey, 54, June 20, 1778, cited in Marlowe, *Perfidious Albion*, 30. In response to Ainslie's request, Baldwin stated he had sent a letter regarding French hostilities to Bombay on May 7, 1778, and another one to Bengal and Madras on May 14.

64 IOR/G/17/5, 65–86, May 25, 1775 to April 15, 1778, series of letters regarding Baldwin's successful efforts at handling trade and mail through Egypt.

65 Ibid.

66 Ibid., 77–79, September 19, 1777, E. I. Co. He was 18,000 Turkish dollars in arrears to Baldwin by his own account.

67 Ibid., 89–122, March 23, 1779 to February 19, 1784, series of letters regarding payment and salary as well as difficulties with Ambassador Ainslie.

68 IOR/G/17/6, 409–38, series of French trade agreements with Morat Bey.

69 IOR/G/17/5, October 4, 1779, Ainslie to Foreign Secretary Lord Weymouth, targets favored French treatment by Porte.

70 Ibid., 252–53, September 24, 1779, Ainslie to the Porte, decrying seizure of British ships; and G/17/5, 256–57, September 31, 1779, Porte to the pasha of Egypt ordering release of British ships with passengers and merchandise.

71 IOR/G/17/5-7, prelude, 78–79.

72 IOR/G/17/5, 53, *Dundas Papers* and "No. 11" "Report: Speculations on the situation and resources of Egypt, 1773–1785"; regarding England's national honour, and 57, "If France possessed Egypt she would control world trade, while England would hold India at the mercy of France."

73 Ibid., 52, *Dundas Papers*, "Egypt vital in communication to India and for previous defeats of the French in India due to rapid communications."

74 IOR/G/17/5, 447–48, November 25, 1785, Ambassador Ainslie to new foreign secretary, the Marquis of Carmarthen. Warns of French encouragement to Beys to seek independence.

75 Ibid., 127–28, Letter of 1785 from George Johnstone (a director of the East India Co.) to Lord Henry Dundas recommending George Baldwin as consul in Egypt. Feels company and government could save £25,000 a year on packets usually sent around the Cape.

76 IOR/G/17/5, 52–53, *Dundas Papers*, undated, 1785. For further comments on Dundas' patronage see C. A. *Bayly, Imperial Meridian: The British Empire and the World 1780–1830* (London: Longman, 1989), 83–84, 100.

77 IOR/G/17/5, 394–95, January 27, 1785, on Baldwin forwarding packets and dispatches through Egypt.

78 Ibid., 127–28, Johnstone to Dundas, undated 1785.

79 Ibid., 457–58, May 19, 1786, announces Baldwin's appointment as consul-general to Egypt and willingness to forward packets to and from India. See also 469–81, "Whitehall," May 19, 1786, for proposal for sending dispatches to India by way of Egypt; and 467–68, May 25, 1786, Baldwin to E. I. Co. court of directors on estimated costs for communication route through Egypt.

80 IOR/G/17/5, *Dundas Papers*, Vol. 10, 382, January 22, 1785, paper on Turkish trade and Egypt; also 383–84, January 22, 1785, examines claims on diminishing Levant Co. trade, and calls for free trade to restore markets with Turkey and Egypt; also 388–90, January 26, 1785, relative to the Suez route and the country trade with India. See also 394–95, January 27, 1785, wherein Baldwin tied these questions to that of the communication and mail route to India as part of his upcoming appointment.

81 IOR/G/17/5, 415–19, February 7, 1785; see also discussion in Marlowe, *Perfidious Albion*, 37–40.

82 Ibid., 409–10, August 22, 1785.

83 Ibid., 436–38, November 10, 1785.

84 Public Record Office/Foreign Office, (PRO/FO) 78/6, May 19, 1785; also G/17/5, 453–54, same date.

85 PRO/FO 78/6, November 25, 1785; and G/17/5, 447–48, same date.

86 IOR/G/17/6, 473–75, undated, 1786, Baldwin as British consul signs trade treaty with Morat and Ibrahim Bey.

87 IOR/G/17/5, prelude, 79; Lorimer, *Gazetteer of the Persian Gulf and Oman and Central Arabia*, Vol. I, part I, 149–50; Wilson, *The Persian Gulf: An Historical Sketch from the Earliest Times to the Beginning of the Twentieth Century,* 189–91.

88 Ibid.

89 IOR/G/17/6, 255–56, April 1, 1792, for correspondence on the issue.

90 PRO/FO 24/1, February 8, 1793, Grenville to Baldwin: terse note terminating the Egyptian consulate, which may have been restored again by Dundas; see G/17/6, 260, April 28, 1794, Baldwin to Dundas, thanking him for intervention. Whether or not the consulate was closed permanently or not remains a question.

91 IOR/G/17/6, 268–69, October 9, 1799, Baldwin discusses prior loss of his consulship, which may have been temporary, and that his property had fallen into French hands; see G/17/6, 306, March 23, 1798, letter reveals he left Egypt due to illness in March, and that he left the consulate in the charge of Carlo de Rossetti.

Chapter 3

1 C. Brinton, *A Decade of Revolution 1789–1799* (New York: Harper Torchbooks, 1963), 212–18.

2 Ibid., 224–26.

3 O. Connelly, *The Epoch of Napoleon* (New York: Holt, Rinehart and Winston, 1972), 11–12; see also F. Markham, *Napoleon* (New York: A Mentor Book, 1963), 25–26; also Brinton, *A Decade of Revolution 1789–1799*, 223.

4 Connelly, *The Epoch of Napoleon*, 19–20; also Brinton, *A Decade of Revolution 1789–1799*, 224–26.

5 Markham, *Napoleon*, 57–58; Brinton, *A Decade of Revolution 1789–1799*, 227. During the Reign of Terror, radical revolutionaries had exiled or executed the nobles responsible for French naval command.

6 Markham, *Napoleon*, 56–57; Brinton, *A Decade of Revolution 1789-1799*, 227–28.

7 India Office Records/G/17/5, Prelude, 79 traces a number of French agents working throughout the region including Persia, Muscat, Jedda, and Egypt; see also Lorimer, *Gazetteer of the Persian Gulf and Oman and Central Arabia*, Vol. I, part I, 149–50; and Wilson, *The Persian Gulf: An Historical Sketch from the Earliest Times to the Beginning of the Twentieth Century*, 189–91 for similar discussion; see Markham, *Napoleon*, 57; and Marlowe, *Perfidious Albion*, 51–54 for relevant activities of the French consul in Cairo, Charles Magellon.

8 IOR/G/17/5, Prelude, 79; Lorimer, *Gazetteer of the Persian Gulf and Oman and Central Arabia*, Vol. I, part I, 149–50; Wilson, *The Persian Gulf: An Historical Sketch from the Earliest Times to the Beginning of the Twentieth Century*, 189–91 for observations on French activities in the region by British agents.

9 Brinton, *A Decade of Revolution 1789–1799*, 228; see also F. Charles-Roux, *Autour d'une route: L'Angleterre, l'isthme de Suez et l'Egypte au XVIIIème siècle* (Paris: Plon-Nourrit, 1922), 376; and Charles-Roux, *Les origines de l'expedition d' Egypte* (Paris: Plon-Nourrit, 1910), for full background leading to Napoleon's invasion.

10 Markham, *Napoleon*, 59.

11 S. Ghorbal, *The Beginnings of the Eastern Question and the Rise of Mohamed Ali* (London: 1928), 31; Charles-Roux, *L'Angleterre*, 362–63; Connelly, *The Epoch of Napoleon*, 21; Brinton, *A Decade of Revolution 1789–1799*, 228; Markham, *Napoleon*, 58–59; Marlowe, *Perfidious Albion*, 52–54.

12 Marlowe, *Perfidious Albion*, 54–55; Markham, *Napoleon*, 60.

13 Markham, *Napoleon*, 60–61; Marlowe, *Perfidious Albion*, 55–56.

14 Brinton, *A Decade of Revolution 1789–1799*, 229; Markham, *Napoleon*, 61.

15 Ibid., 229; Marlowe, *Perfidious Albion*, 56–57.

16 Markham, *Napoleon*, 61.

17 Ibid., 61–62.

18 G. Blaxland, *Objective Egypt* (London: Frederick Miller, 1966), 24; see also I. Abu-Lughod, *Arab Rediscovery of Europe* (Princeton: Princeton University Press, 1963), 11–27; and Al-Jabarti Abd-al Rahman, *Journal d'un notable du Caire durant l'expedition française, 1780–1801*, trans. Joseph Couq (Paris: Editions Albin Michel, 1979).

19 Markham, *Napoleon*, 63.

20 Public Record Office/Foreign Office (PRO/FO) 78/20, September 9, 1798, letter from British representative at Constantinople, Spencer Smith, to Foreign Secretary Lord Grenville; also Markham, *Napoleon*, 63; and Marlowe, *Perfidious Albion*, 58.

21 Brinton, *A Decade of Revolution 1789–1799*, 230–31.

22 Markham, *Napoleon*, 66; Connelly, *The Epoch of Napoleon*, 22; Marlowe, *Perfidious Albion*, 63.

23 IOR/G/17/7, 28–30, November 16, 1798, British lease island of Perim as military base; G/17/7, 74–88, December 15, 1799, permanent base moved to Aden. Also see G/17/5, Prelude, 79 for complete discussion.

24 Aitchison, *Collection of Treaties, Engagements, and Sanads Relating to India and Neighboring Countries*, Vol. XI, 269, 287, details the first British treaty with Muscat in 1798 to prevent a French foothold.

25 Brinton, *A Decade of Revolution 1789–1799*, 231; Markham, *Napoleon*, 69–70, 83, 89.

26 Connelly, *The Epoch of Napoleon*, 22.

27 Ibid., 25–29.

28 G. Bruun, *Europe and the French Imperium 1799-1814* (New York: Harper Torchbooks, 1963), 43–44; Markham, *Napoleon*, 89–90.

29 Marlowe, *Perfidious Albioun*, 65–74, provides a detailed narrative of British efforts to contain the French in Egypt after Napoleon's departure.

30 IOR/G/17/7, 14–24, May 16, 1798, A. Dalrymple to the admiralty. Offers lengthy discussion on feasibility of cutting a canal from Mediterranean to the Red Sea and one from Alexandria to the Nile to facilitate communications. See also J. C. B. Richmond, *Egypt, 1798–1952: Her Advance toward a Modern Identity* (New York: Columbia University Press, 1977), 91; and C. Hallberg, *The Suez Canal—Its History and Diplomatic Importance* (New York:

Columbia University Press, 1931), 61–67, for evaluation of Napoleon's intent to construct a canal at the Suez Isthmus.

31 Aitchison, *A Collection of Treaties, Engagements, and Sanads Relating to India and Neighboring Countries*, Vol. XI, 287, provides full text of the 1798 Treaty with Muscat. Also see Wilson, *The Persian Gulf: An Historical Sketch from the Earliest Times to the Beginning of the Twentieth Century*, 190, which describes activities of French agents at Muscat who spied on British shipping from India to the Persian Gulf.

32 IOR/G/17/7, 28–30, November 16, 1798, Perim leased as British naval base. G/17/7, 31–73, February 26, 1800, negotiations for British withdrawal from Perim finalized. Island too harsh for survival.

33 Aitchison, *Collection of Treaties, Engagements, and Sanads Relating to India and Neighboring Countries*, Vol. XI, 2.

34 IOR/G/17/7, December 17, 1799, Bombay Political Consultations, Letter: Offer of friendship to Ahmad bin Abdul Khinim from the British, and specifies "Commercial and Religious Pact between the Company and the Sultan of Aden." See Aitchison, *Collection of Treaties, Engagements, and Sanads Relating to India and Neighboring Countries*, Vol. XI, 1–2, 53–55 for treaty details. Also G/17/7, 74–96, December 15, 1799 to February 4, 1800, negotiations for relocation of naval command and garrison to Aden.

35 IOR/G/17/7, 98, December 4, 1800, Letter to the governor-general in council, Bengal, details Popham's diplomatic assignment; G/17/7, 97, "Mission of Sir Home Popham to the States of Arabia," Popham sent to the Sheriff of Mecca and others in the Red Sea to secure ties to the British and circumvent the French.

36 IOR/G/17/7, 99, June 26, 1801, Popham to the Secret Committee; also see G/17/7, 100, August 11, 1801, extract of political letter from Bombay to acquaint Popham with details about trade decline between India and the Red Sea since French arrival.

37 IOR/G17/7, 130–37, May 11, 1801, Popham to Marquis Wellesley, governor-general of Bengal, detailing meeting with Sheriff; G/17/7, 114–29, July 10, 1801, opposition from Sheriff noted; G/17/7, 141–44, June 26, 1801, Popham to Lord Elgin at Constantinople, reports nature of his mission and behavior of the Sheriff of Mecca. "Sheriff is an usurper." G/17/7, 145–48, June 10, 1801, Ali Khan (relative of former Sheriff) to Major General Baird, commander of British troops in the Red Sea, seeks to undo current sheriff; G/17/7, 149–50, Ali Khan describes plight of former sheriff and looks for British help to regain the throne; 152–54, undated, Baird to Popham, requests Popham investigate situation; 155–57, July 7, 1801, Ali Khan's life in danger, seeks asylum with Popham aboard ship *Warren Hastings*.

38 IOR/G/17/5–7, Prelude, 80, specifies Popham's assignment to convey troops from India, Cape of Good Hope, and Mediterranean to Egypt.

39 IOR/G/17/7, 296–99, May 22, 1801, secret memoranda ordering Indian force be sent to help expel the French from Egypt.

40 Ibid., 300–03, February 7, 1801, "Secret," letter from Colonel Arthur Wellesley to Jonathan Duncan, governor of Bombay, on mobilization of Indian forces to leave Ceylon; 308–13, February 14, 1801, Wellesley to Duncan, orders troops at Bombay to depart for Mocha to join with troops from Ceylon bound for Egypt.

41 Ibid., 346–49, March 13, 1801, Ali Khan sent to Arabia to purchase horses and camels for the army.

42 Marlowe, *Perfidious Albion*, 76–83, provides account of the British Expeditionary Force in Egypt from March to September 1801.

43 PRO/FO 78/33, June 12, 1801, letter to British ambassador at Constantinople, Lord Elgin. Discusses possible division of power and territory between Ottomans and Mameluk Beys.

44 IOR/G/17/7, 108, June 30, 1802, Popham requested to expedite removal and transport of Indian regiments. G/17/7, 109–10, August 2, 1802, Popham (at Mocha) to secret committee, India House, London, reported the job done and that India's governor-general, Lord Wellesley, had approved the operation.

45 Connelly, *The Epoch of Napoleon*, 60; Markham, *Napoleon*, 104–09; and IOR/G/17/7, 431–32, July 15, 1803, intelligence reports reach Egypt regarding declaration of war between Britain and France.

46 Blaxland, *Objective Egypt*, 20; for further descriptions of Egypt at the time see D. Crecelius, *Al-Damurdashi's Chronicle of Egypt, 1688–1755*, trans. A. al-Wahhab Bakr (New York: E. J. Brill, 1991), 1–13; also D. Crecelius (ed.), *Eighteenth Century Egypt: The Arab Manuscript Sources* (Claremont, CA: Regina Books, 1990) for analysis of histories written in eighteenth-century Egypt; and Ahmed Cezzar, *Ottoman Egypt in the Eighteenth Century*, trans. S. J. Shaw (Cambridge, MA: Harvard University Press, 1962).

47 Abu-Lughod, *Arab Rediscovery of Europe*, 11–27. Examines numerous Egyptian historians' contemporary responses to Napoleonic and French influence in the eighteenth and nineteenth centuries; also Abd-al Rahman al-Jabarti, who sees French military power as more impressive to Egyptians than obscure ideology; see also Tom Little, *Modern Egypt* (New York: Praeger, 1967), 10, which describes breakdown of Ottoman authority in Egypt.

48 A. L. Al-Sayyid Marsot, *Egypt in the Reign of Muhammed Ali* (Cambridge: Cambridge University Press, 1984), chapter 4, provides most recent and solid scholarship on this figure and his relation to Egyptian nativism; see also S. J. Shaw, *Between Old and New* (Cambridge, MA: Harvard University Press, 1971), on Egypt during the reign of reforming Ottoman Sultan Selim III.

49 S. J. Shaw and E. Shaw, *History of the Ottoman Empire and Modern Turkey* (Cambridge: Cambridge University Press, 1977), Vol. 2, 10.

50 Connelly, *The Epoch of Napoleon*, 60; see also Marlowe, *Perfidious Albion*, 101, who sees French activities in Egypt as commercial rather than political.

51 Marlowe, *Perfidious Albion*, 98.

52 IOR/G/17/7, 426–27, May 19, 1803, East India Company appoints Briggs, who at same time is Levant Company agent, and serving as vice-consul.

53 Marlowe, *Perfidious Albion*, 98.

54 Ibid., 101–02.

55 IOR/G/17/7, 444–45, February 8, 1805, Samuel Briggs to A. Vondiziano, British agent in Cyprus.

56 Connelly, *The Epoch of Napoleon*, 61.

57 Marlowe, *Perfidious Albion*, 112; also Connelly, *The Epoch of Napoleon*, 62–64.

58 A. L. Macfie, *The Eastern Question 1774–1923* (New York: Longman, 1989), 12; Connelly, *The Epoch of Napoleon*, 138–39.

59 Ibid., 12.

60 P. Mackesy, *The War in the Mediterranean, 1803–1810* (New York: Longman, 1957), for full discussion on British decision to invade Egypt.

61 J. Marlowe, *A History of Modern Egypt and Anglo-Egyptian Relations, 1800–1956* (Hamden, CT: Archon Books, 1956), 30–60; see also Marlowe, *Perfidious Albion*, 115–16.

62 Macfie, *The Eastern Question 1774–1923*, 12–13.

63 Al-Sayyid Marsot, *Egypt in the Reign of Muhammed Ali*, chapter 4.

64 Ibid.

65 IOR/G/17/7, 474–75, May 2, 1807, Ernest Missett to Isaac Morier (council-general of the Levant Company), relates Fraser's disasters at Rosetta, and failure of Arab and Mameluk help to materialize.

66 Al-Sayyid-Marsot, *Egypt in the Reign of Muhammed Ali*, chapter 4; see also Marlowe, *Perfidious Albion*, 119–22.

67 Brunn, 123–29.

68 October 11, 1808, Sir Robert Adair (British diplomat) to Reis Effendi (Ottoman foreign minister) regarding Tilsit agreement, cited in R. Adair, *The Negotiations for the Peace of the Dardanelles* (London: Longman, 1845), Vol. I, 37.

69 Marlowe, *Modern Egypt*, 30–60; Marlowe, *Perfidious Albion*, 120.

70 Kelly, *Britain and the Persian Gulf 1795–1880*, 60.

71 Ibid., 60–61.

72 Ibid., 61.

73 Aitchison, *Collection of Treaties, Engagements, and Sanads Relating to India and Neighboring Countries*, Vol. XI, 269.

74 Ibid., 288.

75 IOR/R/15/4, 127; Aitchison, *Collection of Treaties, Engagements, and Sanads Relating to India and Neighboring Countries*, Vol. XI, 239–40.

76 Aitchison, *Collection of Treaties, Engagements, and Sanads Relating to India and Neighboring Countries* Vol. XI, 239–40.

77 IOR/R/15/1, 2.

78 IOR/G/17/7, 401–04, February 12, 1802, Lord Elgin to the secret committee of the East India Company.

79 Aitchison, *Collection of Treaties, Engagements, and Sanads Relating to India and Neighboring Countries* Vol. XI, 3, 53–54.

80 Ibid., 56–179.

81 IOR/L/P&S/9/1 (India Office Agency Records, Political and Secret Department), January 11, 1840, Captain Haines to the secret committee. "Aden and the vicinity is quiet." This followed by the entry of British troops.

82 IOR/G/17/7, 104–06, February 27, 1802. Secret letter from Bengal authorizing Popham's mission to the Red Sea Sheikdoms with details of trade and protection.

83 Ibid., 105–06.

84 Ibid., 106.

85 IOR/17/5-7, Prelude, 79–80.

86 Aitchison, *A Collection of Treaties, Engagements, and Sanads Relating to India and Neighboring Countries*, Vol. XIII, *The Treaties Relating to Persia and Afghanistan* (Calcutta: Government of India, 1933), 45–48, January 1801, Treaty of Friendship and Alliance concluded with the shah of Persia.

87 Ibid., 49–52, Ferman from Fateh Ali Shah for certain commercial privileges granted to the English; and 53, additional article relating to the above treaty, January 1801.

88 IOR/G/17/5-7, 79–80; Aitchison, *Collection of Treaties, Engagements, and Sanads Relating to India and Neighboring Countries*, Vol. XIII, *Treaties Relating to Persia and Afghanistan*, 6–7.

89 Aitchison, *Collection of Treaties, Engagements, and Sanads Relating to India and Neighboring Countries*, Vol. XIII, 6.

90 Ibid., 7; see also 53–55, for preliminary treaty concluded with Fateh Ali Shah for the prevention of a passage to European armies through his dominions toward India, signed March 12, 1809.

91 Ibid., 7.

92 IOR/R/15/1, 1.

93 Aitchison, *Collection of Treaties, Engagements, and Sanads Relating to India and Neighboring Countries*, Vol. XIII, 7, and 55–63 for definitive treaty concluded with Fateh Ali Shah annulling the alliances formerly contracted with European states, March 14, 1812; and adjustment of the terms of the definitive treaty, November 25, 1814.

94 IOR/R/15/1, 1.

95 Ibid.

96 Aitchison, *Collection of Treaties, Engagements, and Sanads Relating to India and Neighboring Countries*, Vol. XIII, 9.

97 Ibid., 8, Treaty of Gulistan between Russia and Persia, October 1813; see also Appendix No. V.

Chapter 4

1 R. Hyam, *Britain's Imperial Century, 1815–1914: A Study of Empire and Expansion* (London: Macmillan, Second Edition, 1995), 13–15.

2 Ibid., 16.

3 P. J. Cain and A. G. Hopkins, *British Imperialism: Innovation and Expansion 1688–1914* (London: Longman, 1993), Vol. I, 77–78.

4 Hyam, *Britain's Imperial Century, 1815–1914*, 17–18.

5 Kelly, *Britain and the Persian Gulf 1795–1880*, chap. 3.

6 Spear, *A History of India*, Vol. 2, 94.

7 T. O. Lloyd, *The British Empire 1553–1995* (New York: Oxford University Press, Second Edition, 1996), 109–11; Spear, *A History of India*, 95.

8 Bayly, *Imperial Meridian: The British Empire and the World, 1780–1830*, Introduction and chap. 4.

9 Spear, *A History of India*, 95; Lloyd, *The British Empire 1553–1995*, 109–10.

10 Spear, *A History of India*, 102–05, Lloyd, *The British Empire 1553–1995*, 130–33.

11 IOR/R/15/4, 127; also Aitchison, *A Collection of Treaties, Engagements, and Sanads Relating to India and Neighboring Countries*, Vol. XI, 269, 287–88, 239–40 for specific treaties with Muscat, Oman, and Trucial Coast; see also Wilson, *The Persian Gulf: An Historical Sketch from the Earliest Times to the Beginning of the Twentieth Century*, 199–209 on treaties and piracy.

12 Kelly, *Britain and the Persian Gulf 1795–1880*, 108.

13 Ibid., 123.

14 Ibid., 135.

15 Ibid., 151–52.

16 Al-Sayyid Marsot, *Egypt in the Reign of Muhammed Ali*, 200–02; Kelly, *Britain and the Persian Gulf 1795-1880*, 135–37.

17 Kelly, *Britain and the Persian Gulf 1795–1880*, 148.

18 Aitchison, *A Collection of Treaties, Engagements, and Sanads Relating to India and Neighboring Countries*, Vol. XI, 240–49, for "General Treaty of Peace with the Arab Tribes"; 248–49, signed by ibn Saqr of the Qasimi and five other sheikhs of the Pirate Coast with the British, January 20, 1820; see Kelly, *Britain and the Persian Gulf 1795–1880*, 154–56, for detailed evaluation of the treaty.

19 Ibid., 240–41; also Kelly, *Britain and the Persian Gulf 1795–1880*, 155.

20 Ibid., 240–49.

21 Ibid., 233–34, extension of General Treaty to Bahrain in 1820.

22 IOR/Bombay Secret Proceedings, vol. 43, February 15, 1819, cited in Kelly, *Britain and the Persian Gulf 1795–1880*, 156.

23 Lorimer, *Gazetteer of the Persian Gulf and Oman and Central Arabia*, Vol. I, 673–74; also Kelly, *Britain and the Persian Gulf 1795–1880*, 158.

24 Kelly, *Britain and the Persian Gulf 1795–1880*, 159.

25 Aitchison, *Collection of Treaties, Engagements, and Sanads Relating to India and Neighboring Countries*, Vol. XI, 233–34.

26 Kelly, *Britain and the Persian Gulf 1795–1880*, 163–65.

27 Ibid., 165.

28 IOR/Bombay Secret Proceedings, vol. 46, April 5, 1820, cited in Kelly, *Britain and the Persian Gulf 1795–1880*, 166.

29 B. Lewis, *Race and Slavery in the Middle East* (New York: Oxford University Press, 1992), chap. 10; also see discussion in Kelly, *Britain and the Persian Gulf 1795–1880*, 412–16.

30 Kelly, *Britain and the Persian Gulf 1795–1880*, 420.

31 Ibid., 422.

32 Ibid., 423

33 IOR/R/15/1, 2.

34 Kelly, *Britain and the Persian Gulf 1795–1880*, 442–43.

35 IOR/Political Despatches to Bombay, vol. 6, Court of Directors to the Gov. in Council, September 21, 1842.

36 Aitchison, *A Collection of Treaties, Engagements, and Sanads Relating to India and Neighboring Countries*, XI, 249.

37 Ibid., 250–51.

38 Ibid., 251–52.

39 Ibid., 252–53.

40 B. R. Pridham (ed.), *The Arab Gulf and the West* (New York: St. Martin's Press, 1985), 4.

41 J. Marlowe, *A History of Modern Egypt and Anglo-Egyptian Relations, 1800–1956* (Hamden, CT: Archon Books, 1965), 30–60; see also J. B. C. Richmond, *Egypt, 1789–1952: Her Advance Towards a Modern Identity* (New York: Columbia University Press, 1977), 35–40.

42 M. W. Daly (ed.), *The Cambridge History of Egypt, Vol. 2, Modern Egypt* (Cambridge: Cambridge University Press, 1998), chapter 6; M. Hanioglu, *A Brief History of The Late Ottoman Empire* (Princeton: Princeton University Press, 2008), 65–67; S. Shaw and E. Shaw, *History of the Ottoman Empire and Modern Turkey* (Cambridge: Cambridge University Press, 1977), vol. 2, 10.

43 IOR/G/17/10, Letters from Company Agents in Cairo to the company, October 23, 1825, Agent P. Campbell to company, writes to forward material given him by Mehmet Ali demonstrating Egypt's modernization—cotton, cotton seed, and two machines for seed removal. Also included three-page description and diagram of cotton machine able to deseed 61 lb. of cotton per day; see Al-Sayyid Marsot, *Egypt in the Reign of Muhammed Ali*, chaps. 4, 6, 7, 8; also Shaw, *History of the Ottoman Empire and Modern Turkey*, 11 for further analysis of modernization.

44 T. Little, *Modern Egypt* (New York: Praeger, 1967), 10.

45 Al-Sayyid Marsot, *Egypt in the Reign of Muhammed Ali*, 200–02.

46 Ibid., 205–06.

47 Ibid., 214–17.

48 H. Dodwell, *The Founder of Modern Egypt: A Study of Muhammad Ali* (Cambridge: Cambridge University Press, 1931), 134–269 offers an older Eurocentric analysis of Ali's model for empire. See also F. H. Lawson, *The Social Origins of Egyptian Expansionism during the Muhammad Ali Period* (New York: Columbia University Press, 1992), 144–47; also P. K. Hitti, *History of the Arabs from the Earliest Times to the Present* (New York: St. Martin's Press, 1967), 724–25.

49 I. Abu-Lughod, *Arab Rediscovery of Europe; A Study in Cultural Encounters* (Princeton: Princeton University Press, 1963), 20–21; also A. Abd-al Rahman, *Journal d'un notable du Caire durant l'expedition francaise, 1780–1801* (Paris: Editions Albin Michel, 1979), 72–77, 161–62, 170–78.

50 Al-Sayyid Marsot, *Egypt in the Reign of Muhammed Ali*, 196–97.

51 J. Hurewitz, *Diplomacy in the Near and Middle East: A Documentary Record, 1555–1914* (Princeton: D. Van Nostrand, 1956), vol. 1, 109–10, provides complete development and assessment of documents concerning British trade agreements with Sultans Mahmud II and Abdulmecid and fermans relative to Egypt and curtailment of Mehmet Ali, 1834–41; also see Al-Sayyid Marsot, *Egypt in the Reign of Muhammed Ali*, 232–45.

52 *Parliamentary Papers*, August 16, 1838 (vol. 50, 1839), 291–95, examines the British position on trade and of granting hereditary rights to Mehmet Ali's successors in Egypt; also see Little, *Modern Egypt*, 30–60.

53 IOR/G/17/10, June 28, 1835, Agent in Cairo, P. Campbell to company in London, reports progress of the Euphrates Expedition; also see Marlowe, *Albion*, 216–18, and Al-Sayyid Marsot, *Egypt in the Reign of Muhammed Ali*, 240–42 for expedition's historical perspective relative to Mehmet Ali.

54 B. Lewis, *The Emergence of Modern Turkey* (London: Oxford University Press, 1968), 106–11, for explanation and development of reform (Tanzimat) under British pressure in the wake of Ottoman military defeat by Ali; see also Hurewitz, "The Hatti Serif of Gulhane," November 3, 1839, found in *Diplomacy in the Near and Middle East*, 113–16.

55 IOR/G/17/10, Letters from agents in Cairo to the East India Company, London 1834–38. June 28, 1835, Agent P. Campbell to company on progress of Euphrates Expedition now supplied with camels and bullocks due to efforts of Ali's son, Ibrahim Pasha; October 24, 1835, Campbell to the company, expedition moving successfully due to Ibrahim, who has ordered all supplies en route and has written to his father, Ali, to report safisfaction.

56 IOR/G/17/11, Letters to company from agent in Egypt 1838–40. December 1838, series of letters from Governor-General Auckland to Ali Pasha, (forwarded by Campbell to the company) thanking him for all his invaluable services rendered to the British nation and India, including repair of steamship *Bernice* and expressing thanks by sending two elephants under Commander Graham to the pasha as a gift; April 20, 1839, Campbell to the company, "Mehamet Ali Pasha received two elephants as gifts from the Gov. Gen. of India (Auckland) for his favorable disposition to the British." A day earlier, April 19, Campbell describes how both elephants were mounted with 5.5-inch howitzers.

57 IOR/G/17/8, Company to agents in Egypt 1837–46. June 9, 1837, company to E. I. Co. deputy packet agent in Egypt T. Waghorn, who had created a practicable overland transit system with substantive coaling stations at Alexandria and Suez; IOR/G/17/11, July 12, 1838, supports idea that two steamships per month from England to Alexandria would enhance connection for mail to India and back; August 4, 1838, Campbell to company, requests steamship also be stationed at Mocha for run to Suez, which would take only eight days as compared to twenty-six days by sail; May 16, 1838, Campbell to company, Mr. Henry Sevick takes position as new packet agent at Suez. Speaks Arabic and will deal with Arabs on the coal run; November 8, 1838, company's favorable response to Campbell about regular steamship runs from London to Alexandria and Suez to Calcutta and Madras; November 8, 1838,

notice of Peninsular Steamship Company starting regular runs throughout the Mediterranean to Alexandria with cross-land connections to Suez; November 24, 1839, Campbell to company (secret committee), indicating that British steamers will now run from Suez to Bombay.

58 IOR/G/17/11, November 8, 1838, Peninsular Steamship Company (P&O) begins regular runs in Mediterranean to Alexandria and from India to Suez and back. See also notice of November 24, 1839. IOR/L/P&S/9/1, letters from Captain Lyons (Cairo) to secret committee of the company in London, July 6, 1840, P&O applies to Ali for ferman to establish two steam boats on the Nile and two track boats on the canal (from Nile to Red Sea) to convey the mail through Egypt.

59 Ibid., Simla (headquarters of British government in India), April 16, 1838, Governor-General Auckland to Mehmet Ali, praising him for all his help to the British and keeping Egypt open for transit. Calls him "enlightened"; April 14, 1839, Ali to Auckland, thanking him for the presents and all the attention and includes a reaffirmation of friendship between himself and the British government; G/17/8, February 4, 1841, James C. Melvill, Sec. E. I. Co. to Ali Pasha, letter affirming that during the crises years of confrontation between Ali and the British government, Ali kept the mail routes open and secure and received praise from the East India Company Board of Directors, thanking Ali for expediting the mails through Egypt with protection and escorts.

60 IOR/G/17/11, May 2, 1838, Campbell to the company, "Mehmet Ali appears to assume that he has a right to Aden—the British only need it as a coaling station. The British could have certain rights there." Campbell supports this since the British have gotten so much in Egypt from Ali and it would be in both parties' interests to support the idea. June 13, 1838, Campbell writes company to encourage the British to delay occupation of Aden or establishment of residency there and to allow coaling station at Aden to be protected by Ali. (This would presumably maintain Ali's goodwill and still protect British interests at Aden without undue expense of occupation.)

61 Ibid., June 13, 1838, Enclosure 733 Political Department, steps to be taken if British occupy Aden; November 24, 1838, reports "Ali very much regrets having given up Aden to us and wishes to possess it himself." Also see Marlowe, *Albion*, 222–23, who states that troops from the Bombay Presidency had occupied Aden in January 1838.

62 Lewis, *Modern Turkey*, 106–11; Hurewitz, *Diplomacy in the Near and Middle East*, 113–16.

63 *Hansard's Parliamentary Debates* (London: Cornelius Buck, 1842), series 3, vol. 60, 618–19, presents Palmerston's speech on free-trade imperialism given at the House of Commons, February 16, 1842.

64 Marlowe, *Albion*, 223.

65 IOR/G/17/11, Campbell to Company, May 11, 1838; also June 13, 1838.

66 Ibid., November 13, 1838, Commander J. B. Haines (Aden) to Campbell (Cairo) writes that the British had not yet taken Aden. Seven hundred bedouins loyal to Hamid Al Houssain, son of the old sultan, have invested the city, keeping the British out. November 23, Commander W. Soine to Campbell,

British moving in more troops and ships with artillery against Adenites, who have commenced hostilities. IOR/L/P&S/9/1 (political and secret department) abstracts of secret letters from political agents and commentary; January 11, 1840? (1839), from Captain Haines to company, "Aden and vicinity is quiet. Old Sultan has abdicated in favor of his son." British have presumably occupied the city; G/17/11, June 27, 1839, Campbell to company, recommends that since the British have taken Aden, the residency post be shifted from Mocha to Aden.

67 IOR/L/P&S/9/1, series of letters from February 1840 to December 1844 denote the state of Aden under siege through 1841 and continued tension until 1844. Last anticipated attack from Mocha in 1845, never materialized.

68 IOR/G/17/11, June 10, 1839, Campbell to forward dispatches to company's secret committee in London from Baghdad and Bushire relative to Ali and the Baghdad Pashalik issue. See also Marlowe, *Albion*, 222.

69 *Parliamentary Papers*, June 28, 1839 (vol. 29, 1841), 117–19, outlines the specifics on the Treaty of London, whereby Britain became the guarantor of Mehmet Ali's line in Egypt; also see S. Pamuk, *The Ottoman Empire and European Capitalism. 1820–1913* (Cambridge: Cambridge University Press, 1987), 1–21, for full discussion on British free trade and the treaties of 1838–41 in the Ottoman Empire.

70 L/P&S/9/1, August 26, 1840, report that pasha refused any further negotiations with representatives of the four European Powers; see also Marlowe, *Albion*, 258–65, which offers lively discussion on French support of Ali and his reluctance to sign the document; also Al-Sayyid Marsot, *Egypt in the Reign of Muhammed Ali*, 245–46.

71 IOR/R/19/3, Letters to the agency in Egypt, August 11, 1840, J. Lloyd Hodges to T. M. Larking esq. Consul in Egypt; August 14, committee meeting of British merchants and subjects in Egypt suggesting they were taken off guard but still on good terms with Ali. Of 47,000 tons of purchased cotton valued at £140,000, only half already shipped. Also merchants and subjects owned 25,000 acres including homes in Egypt. "How urgent is the situation and can we have British protection?"

72 Ibid., August 15, 1840, Hodges (Foreign Office) to the Merchants. Said he could give them nothing definite and had received no special instructions from Her Majesty's Government regarding the commercial interests of British subjects in this country.

73 Ibid., August 15, 1840, Merchants to Hodges.

74 Ibid., January 7, 1840, governor of Bengal to secretary of the Tea Committee (Egypt), letter regarding delicate botanical shipment of rare tropical plants to Egypt's pasha, with detailed instructions about care and trans-shipment on the vessel *Columbo*. January 10, 1840, governor of Bengal to Campbell, letter regarding care of the tropical shipment to Ali Pasha.

75 IOR/L/P&S/9/1, July 6, 1840, P&O successfully negotiating with Ali for ferman for Nile route and canal run between Nile and Red Sea for mail trans-shipment.

76 PRO/FO 78/472, October 5, 1840, Palmerston to admiralty, backs British naval call to rally Syrian subjects to support the allied effort against Ali's

forces; also L/P&S/9/1, December 22, 1840, report on retreat of Ibrahim
Pasha from Syria; also see C. Napier, *The War in Syria* (London: John W.
Parker, Harrison and Company, 1842), vol. 1, 139, 270–71; also Marlowe,
Albion, chap. 10.

77 IOR/G/17, abstracts of letters to and from Egypt to the company, dated from
October 18, 1840, to December 17, 1840, relative to evacuation from Egypt
and resettlement in Malta.

78 Ibid., December 17, 1840, Malta, "Mehemet Ali continued to afford every
assistance for the passage of the mails through Egypt." December 21, company
agent (Johnson) to the company, suggests a letter of thanks be sent to Mehemet
Ali to acknowledge his protection in escorting the mail from Cairo to Suez and
for his ready aid and courtesy on several occasions. December 28, Johnson
to company, "Mails still protected by Mehemet Ali while desert still unsafe."
G/17/8, February 4, 1841, letter from board of directors of E. I. Co. to Ali
Pasha, thanking him for expediting the mails through Egypt and protective
escorts. James C. Melvill, Secy.

79 IOR/R/19/3, October 22, 1840, Johnson (packet agent) to Bombay Presidency,
Ali completely blockaded in Egypt and Syria, and accounts from Syria very
unfavorable to Ali. "Not knowing what these acts of aggression will have on
Ali," Johnson departs to Malta.

80 Al-Sayyid Marsot, *Egypt in the Reign of Muhammed Ali*, 246–47.

81 IOR/L/P&S/9/1, Captain Lyons to secret committee, June 18, 1841, ferman
from the Porte for the Government of Egypt; June 19, meeting between
Ottoman, British, and Egyptian representatives respecting the settlement of
Egypt—freedom of trade, departure of troops and letters from Commander
Napier; June 19, 1841, departure of Egyptian troops from Syria; June 26,
arrival of Ibrahim Bey at Constantinople from Cairo with transmission of
£50,000 tribute and presents.

82 Little, *Modern Egypt*, 34; Al-Sayyid Marsot, *Egypt in the Reign of Muhammed
Ali*, 246–48.

83 Marlowe, *Modern Egypt*, 44–47; and Hitti, *History of the Arabs from the
Earliest Times to the Present*, 726 for details on treaty; see parliamentary
papers, June 28, 1839 (vol. 29, 1841), 117–18 for statement on the pashalik.

84 C. Finkel, *Osman's Dream, The Story of the Ottoman Empire 1300–1923*
(New York: Basic Books, 2007), 445–46; Lord Eversley and V. Chirol, *The
Turkish Empire from 1288 to 1914* (New York: Howard Fertig, 1969),
284–92; Daly, *The Cambridge History of Egypt*, Vol. 2, 173–76.

85 Daly, *Cambridge History of Egypt*, Vol. 2, 175–76; Marlowe, *Albion*, 290.

86 L/P&S/9/1, series of secret letters from political agents to the company dated
July 30 to September 6, 1841, detail a number of suspicious incidents labeled
as French intrigues in Cairo, Baghdad, Muscat, and Tehran to offset British
influence. This included a projected joint Franco-Portuguese attack on Muscat,
as well as an attempt to breakup the British Euphrates Expedition in concert
with the Russians; see also Marlowe, *Albion*, 258–65; and Al-Sayyid Marsot,
Egypt in the Reign of Muhammed Ali, 245–46.

Chapter 5

1 J. H. Waller, *Beyond the Khyber Pass, The Road to British Disaster in the First Afghan War* (Austin: University of Texas Press, 1990), 126.

2 L/P&S/18/19, A. W. Moore, *Relations with Afghanistan since 1838*, August 31, 1878, Political and Secret Department.

3 L/P&S/18/A/221, *A Survey of Anglo-Afghan Relations*, Part I. 1747–1919., I.

4 Ibid.

5 P. Hopkirk, *The Great Game: The Struggle for Empire in Central Asia* (New York: Kodansha International, 1994), 190.

6 Palmerston to Hobhouse, August 25, 1838, Broughton papers 46915, FOS 105, 106 cited in Waller, *Beyond the Khyber Pass*, 1268. Ibid., 128.

7 Waller, *Beyond the Khyber Pass*, 126.

8 Ibid., 128.

9 L/P&S/18/19, A. W. Moore, *Relations with Afghanistan since 1838*.

10 L/P&S/18/A/221, 2.

11 Ram, Subedar Sita, *From Sepoy to Subedar*—A memoir of the Afghan Expedition from viewpoint of a non-commissioned Sepoy, cited in Waller, *Beyond the Khyber Pass*, 138–39.

12 B. Farwell, *Queen Victoria's Little Wars* (New York: W. W. Norton and Co., 1985), 9.

13 Ibid.

14 Hopkirk, *The Great Game*, 270.

15 Farwell, *Queen Victoria's Little Wars*, 9.

16 L/P&S/18/A/221, 3; Waller, *Beyond the Khyber Pass*, 40; Hopkirk, *The Great Game*, 272.

17 Waller, *Beyond the Khyber Pass*, 282.

18 Ibid., 282.

19 Ibid., 280, L/P&S/18/A/221, 2–3; Waller, *Beyond the Khyber Pass*, 275–78; Hopkirk, *The Great Game*, 276–77.

20 Hopkirk, *The Great Game*, 276–77.

21 L/P&S/18/A/221, 3.

Chapter 6

1 A. L. Macfie, *The Eastern Question 1774–1923* (New York: Longman, 1994), document 1, the Treaty of Hunkiar-Iskelesi, 92; R. Bartlett, *A History of Russia* (London, UK: Palgrave MacMillan, 2006), 40.

2 Bartlett, *A History of Russia*, 40.

3 N. V. Riasanovsky and M. D. Steinberg, *A History of Russia* (New York: Oxford University Press, Eighth Edition, 2011), 333.

4 D. Mackenzie and M. W. Curran, *A History of Russia, the Soviet Union and Beyond* (Belmont, CA: Wadsworth, Inc., 2002), 375.

5 Riasanovsky and Steinberg, *A History of Russia*, 332.

6 O. Figes, *The Crimean War: A History* (New York: Metropolitan Books, 2010), xxii.

7 Riasanovsky and Steinberg, *A History of Russia*, 334.

8 Ibid., 333.

9 Ibid.

10 Ibid.

11 N. V. Riasanovsky, *A History of Russia* (New York: Oxford University Press, 1993), 338.

12 Ibid.

13 IOR/R/15/1/704, 36, June 14, 1862, draft of secret treaty between Persia and Russia—C. Alison Agent at Tehran to Rt. Hon Earl Russell.

14 Bartlett, *A History of Russia*, 55.

15 Ibid., 55–56.

16 Ibid., 56.

17 Riasavovsky and Steinberg, *A History of Russia*, 335. See also parliamentary papers, 1856, lxi, 21–27 for full British text of the treaty.

18 Ibid., 335.

19 B. Farwell, *Queen Victoria's Little Wars* (New York: W. W. Norton and Co., 1985), 69.

20 Ibid., 69–70.

21 Ibid., 70.

22 Figes, *The Crimean War*, xxii.

23 P. Spear, *A History of India*, vol. II (New York: Penguin Books, Reprint, 1983), 139–44.

24 Ibid., 141.

25 Ibid., 141–42.

26 Farwell, *Queen Victoria's Little Wars*, 122.

27 Ibid., 125.

28 Ibid., 126.

Chapter 7

1 *Parliamentary Papers*, June 28, 1839 (vol. 29, 1841), 117–19, outlines specifics on Treaty of London and nature of the guarantee; also see S. Pamuk, *The Ottoman Empire and European Capitalism, 1820-1913* (Cambridge: Cambridge University Press, 1987), 1–21, for full discussion on British treaties from 1838 to 1841.

2 J. Marlowe, *Anglo-Egyptian Relations: 1800–1953* (New York: Cresset Press, 1954), 44–47; see also Finkel, *Osman's Dream*, 446.

3 Finkel, *Osman's Dream*, 446; Lord Eversly and V. Chirol, *The Turkish Empire from 1288–1914* (New York: Howard Fertig, 1969), 284–92.

4 A. Goldschmidt, Jr., *Modern Egypt: the Formation of a Nation State* (Boulder: Westview Press, 2004), 21.

5 Al-Sayyid-Marsot, *Egypt and Cromer: A Study in Anglo-Egyptian Relations*, 249.

6 Ibid., 247.

7 Daly, *The Cambridge History of Egypt*, Vol. 2, *Modern Egypt*, 165–79, for full discussion of Ali's reign after Palmerston's intervention; G. Baer, "Continuity and Change in Egyptian Rural Society, 1805-1882," *L'Égypte au XIXe Siècle*, 231–45; see also Marlowe, *Anglo-Egyptian*, 54.

8 Marlowe, *Anglo-Egyptian*, 54–55.

9 J. R. I. Cole, *Colonialism and Revolution in the Middle East: Social and Cultural Origins of Egypt's Urabi Revolt* (Princeton: Princeton University Press, 1993), 56–57, for analysis of population figures. British figures collected in the nineteenth century are lower by 15 percent. See *British Documents on Foreign Affairs*, Part I, Series B, The Near and Middle East, 1856–1914, Doc. 155, chap. 2, 127–35, and chap. 4, 165–66.

10 Ibid., 85–90; see also G. Blaxland, *Objective Egypt* (London: Fredrick Muller, 1966), 51; also T. Little, *Modern Egypt* (New York: Praeger, 1967), 35.

11 Little, *Modern Egypt*, 35.

12 Goldschmidt, *Modern Egypt: The Formation of a Nation State*, 22.

13 C. Harris, *Nationalism and Revolution in Egypt: The Role of the Muslim Brotherhood* (London: Mouton and Co., 1964), 21, 24; see also C. Issawi, *An Economic History of the Middle East and North Africa* (New York: Columbia University Press, 1982), 62–71; A. Scholch, "The Formation of a Peripheral State: Egypt, 1854–1882," *L'Egypt au XIXe Siècle* (Paris: Colloques Internationaux du Centre national de la Rechereche Scientifique, 1982), no. 594, 175–85.

14 Harris, *Nationalism and Revolution in Egypt*, 24.

15 Goldschmidt, *Modern Egypt: The Formation of a Nation State*, 21–22.

16 Al-Sayyid-Marsot, *Egypt and Cromer: A Study in Anglo-Egyptian Relations*, 251–52.

17 R. J. Cain and A. G. Hopkins, *British Imperialism: Innovation and Expansion 1688–1914* (New York: Longman, 1993), 363.

18 J. Gelvin, *The Modern Middle East, A History* (New York: Oxford University Press, 2011), 91–93; Goldschmidt, *Modern Egypt: the Formation of a Nation State*, 23.

19 Al-Sayyid-Marsot, *Egypt and Cromer: A Study in Anglo-Egyptian Relations*, 248.

20 Nubar Pasha, Ali's advisor and later Egypt's Finance Minister in *Memoirs*, cited in Al-Sayyid-Marsot, *Modern Egypt: the Formation of a Nation State*, 255.

21 Ibid.

22 *Hansard's Parliamentary Debates*, series 3, vol. 150, 1386–89, presents full text of Gladstone's June 1, 1858, address before Commons.

23 F.O. 78/804. Murray to Palmerston, August 6, 1849, cited in Al-Sayyid-Marsot, *Egypt and Cromer: A Study in Anglo-Egyptian Relations*, 256.

24 Marlowe, *Anglo-Egyptian*, 56.

25 Daly, *Cambridge History of Egypt*, Vol. 2, *Modern Egypt*, 187-88; Little, *Modern Egypt*, 34.

26 H. Rivlin, "The State and Land Tenure in Egypt, 1805-1882," *L'Égypte au XIXe Siècle*, no. 594, 247-61, offers well-documented discussion on loss of fallahin land; see also Daly, *Cambridge History of Egypt*, Vol. 2, *Modern Egypt*, 182-83.

27 IOR/G/17/9/2—February 1, 1847, 2,000 tons coal for Alexandria; G/17/9/3—February 1, 1847, 250 tons coal for Aden; G/17/9/4—February 18, 1847, 530 tons coal for Alexandria for Lord Palmerston; G/17/9/5—March 18, 1847, more coal for Alexandria and Aden. G/17/9/10, 1854–56, spike in coal shipments and tonnage stored. October 10, 1855, Company alarmed by size of stockpiles. G/17/9/6,7,9, August 10–26, 1847 to July 24, 1856, dramatic increase in passengers and mail to and through Egypt.

28 G/17/9/10, April 7, 1848, Capt. Lyons, co. agent in Alexandria, requests six months leave because of overwork and exhaustion. His successor, Mr. Johnson, requests second health and fatigue leave, April 26, 1856. Second leave canceled due to emergency in India (Sepoy Mutiny) November 4, 1857. Increased coal stockpiles at Aden 4,455 tons alone for June and July as per letter of September 10, 1857.

29 G/17/9/10, July 24, 1856, British agents in Alexandria awaiting completion of Suez-Alexandria line and on action from Said Pasha to finish the project.

30 G/17/9/10, February 11, 1860, "All letters from Co. to various agents between 5 Nov. 1857 to 31 Aug. 1858 have been destroyed by order of Sir Charles."

31 Marlowe, *Perfidious Albion*, 11–296, covers eighty years of Anglo-French rivalry in Egypt to 1841, with excellent documentation.

32 J. Marlowe, *World Ditch: The Making of the Suez Canal* (New York: Macmillan, 1964), 2–3, presents documentation covering French efforts to build a canal from Louis XIV to Napoleon; see also C. Hallberg, *The Suez Canal—Its History and Diplomatic Importance* (New York: Columbia University Press, 1931), 39, 43; also Harris, *Nationalism and Revolution in Egypt*, 18.

33 R. Tignor, *Modernization and British Colonial Rule in Egypt, 1882–1914* (Princeton: Princeton University Press, 1966), 12–13. This is the best and most detailed account of British development up to and following their occupation of Egypt.

34 D. Farnie, *East and West of Suez: The Suez Canal in History* (Oxford: Clarendon Press, 1969), 5–31, presents the most thorough scholarship on Suez Canal and its impact on Egypt to date. See also Hallberg, *The Suez Canal—Its History and Diplomatic Importance*, 98.

35 P.R.O./F.O. 78/408 "Transit through Egypt, 1841–1848," also Farnie East and West of Suez, 10–31, for an insightful examination of Franco-British rivalry from 1830 to 1859.

36 Hallberg, *The Suez Canal—Its History and Diplomatic Importance*, 118.

37 Daly, *The Cambridge History of Egypt*, Vol. 2, *Modern Egypt*, 189, for the impact of the Suez Canal on Egypt's indeptedness; Little, *Modern Egypt*, 34–35.

38 P.R.O./F.O./78, 887, 1156, 1340, 1421, 1489, 1560, on firman and concession issue; see also A. T. Wilson, *The Suez Canal: Its Past, Present, and future* (Oxford: University Press, 1933), chap. 2; details British opposition to the Sultan's grant of firman from 1854 to 1863; also Hallberg, *The Suez Canal—Its History and Diplomatic Importance*, 103, 122; see Little, *Modern Egypt*, 38.

39 Hallberg, *The Suez Canal—Its History and Diplomatic Importance*, 134.

40 M. Zayid, *Egypt's Struggle for Independence* (Beirut: Khayat's Publishers, 1965), 8; Lord Kinross, *Between Two Seas: The Creation of the Suez Canal* (New York: William Morrow, 1969), 170.

41 Hallberg, *The Suez Canal—Its History and Diplomatic Importance*, 188.

42 *Parliamentary Debates*, series 3, vol. 150, 1386–89. full text of Gladstone's speech, June 1, 1858, address to Commons as well as opposition speeches.

43 Hallberg, *The Suez Canal—Its History and Diplomatic Importance*, 181–83.

44 Ibid., 214.

45 Zayid, *Egypt's Struggle for Independence*, 9.

46 P. Crabites, *Americans in the Egyptian Army* (London: George Routledge and Sons, 1931), 222–48, compares Ismail's ambition with Mehmet Ali's earlier imperial aspirations with a focus on the use of US Civil War veterans as staff officers for a modern Egyptian army to conquer Abyssinia and the Sudan.

47 Ibid., chaps., 17, 18.

48 The London *Times*, cited in P. Mansfield, *The British in Egypt* (New York: Holt, Rinehart, and Winston, 1971), 40.

49 Goldschmidt, *Modern Egypt: the Formation of a Nation State*, 28.

50 Parliamentary Papers, vol. 78, 1879, 265–67, "Ottoman Ferman Consolidating the Special Privileges Conferred on the Khedive of Egypt," June 8, 1873; also see Hurewitz, *Diplomacy in the Near and Middle East*, 174–77.

51 Farnie, *East and West of Suez*, 131, provides comprehensive analysis of Ismail's "Greater Egypt" controlling much of Central and East Africa, and British fears of an independent Egypt.

52 E. Hobsbawn, *Industry and Empire* (New York: Penguin Books, 1979), 130.

53 R. Robinson, J. Gallagher, and A. Denny, *Africa and the Victorians* (London: Macmillan, 2nd Edition, 1981), 82–84; Mansfield, *British in Egypt*, 4.

54 P. Gifford and W. Louis, *France and Britain in Africa* (New Haven: Yale University Press, 1971), 82–87.

55 Goldschmidt, *Modern Egypt: the Formation of a Nation State*, 31, calculates debt in Egyptian pounds. Marlowe, *Anglo-Egyptian*, 93–95, uses English pounds as does *British Documents on Foreign Affairs*, Part I, Series B, The Near East, vol. 9, "The Ottoman Empire and North Africa: Intervention in Egypt and the Sudan, 1876–1885," Doc. 155 (New York: University Publications of America, 1984), chap. 3, 144–46, estimates debt growth at £97.5 million English pounds in 1881; see also D. Landes, *Bankers and Pashas: International Finance and Economic Imperialism in Egypt* (Cambridge, MA: Harvard University Press, 1958) for further debt analysis.

56 Marlowe, *Anglo-Egyptian*, 94–95.

57 P. Mansfield and N. Pelham, *A History of the Middle East* (New York: Penguin Books, 2013), 99; Mansfield, *British in Egypt*, 11.

58 Marlowe, *Anglo-Egyptian*, 94–95.

59 A. L. Al-Sayyid-Marsot, *Egypt and Cromer: A Study in Anglo-Egyptian Relations* (New York: Praeger, 1968), 5, 6.

60 A. Ward and P. Gooch, *The Cambridge History of British Foreign Policy, 1793-1919* (New York: Macmillan, 1923), vol. III, 5.

61 Al-Sayyid-Marsot, *Egypt and Cromer*, 4.

62 Ibid., 3.

63 F.O./2997, October 16, 1879, Salisbury to Malet.

64 V. O'Rourke, "The Juristic Status of Egypt and the Sudan," *Johns Hopkins University Studies in History and Political Science*, 53, no. 1 (1935), 30–31.

Chapter 8

1 H. Temperly and L. Penson, *The Foundations of British Foreign Policy from Pitt to Salisbury or Documents, Old and New* (Cambridge: Cambridge University Press, 1938), 416.

2 F.O./2997, October 16, 1879, Salisbury to Malet.

3 P. Stansky, *Gladstone: A Progress in Politics* (London: W. W. Norton, 1979), 123.

4 A. P. Saab, *The Reluctant Icon: Gladstone, Bulgaria, and the Working Classes, 1856–1878* (Cambridge, MA: Harvard University Press, 1991), 6, 7, 193–201.

5 R. T. Shannon, *Gladstone and the Bulgarian Agitation*, 1876 (Hamden, CT: Archon Books, 1975), vi, 266–81; see also T. A. Jenkins, *Gladstone, Whiggery and the Liberal Party, 1874–1886* (Oxford: Clarendon Press, 1988), 26, 56–57, 60–63.

6 J. L. Garvin, *The Life of Joseph Chamberlain* (London: Macmillan, 1932), 442–43.

7 J. Landau, *Parliament and Parties in Egypt* (Tel Aviv: Israel Oriental Society, 1953), 85.

8 M. Y. Zayid, *Egypt's Struggle for Independence* (Beirut: Khayat's Publishing Co., 1965), 19.

9 D. Wallace, *Egypt and the Egyptian Question* (New York: Russell and Russell, 1967), 104–07.

10 E. W. Polson-Newman, *Great Britain in Egypt* (London: Cassell and Co., 1923), 57; see also *The Orabi Revolution* (Cairo: Arab Republic of Egypt, Ministry of Information, State Information Service, 1984), 20–21.

11 Al-Sayyid-Marsot, *Egypt and Cromer*, 11; also see M. Rowlatt, *Founders of Modern Egypt* (Bombey: Asia Publishing House, 1962), 5.

12 Landau, *Parliament and Parties in Egypt*, 31–32.

13 Rowlatt, M., *Founders of Modern Egypt*, 56.

14 W. S. Blunt, *A Secret History of the English Occupation of Egypt* (New York: Alfred A. Knopf. 1922), 116.

15 Lord Cromer, *Modern Egypt* (London: Macmillan, 1908), vol. 1, 212; also Al-Sayyid-Marsot, *Egypt and Cromer*, 13.

16 Temperly and Penson, *The Foundations of British Foreign Policy from Pitt to Salisbury or Documents, Old and New*, 416.

17 Ibid.

18 Garvin, *The Life of Joseph Chamberlain*, 443.

19 M. Fletcher, "The Suez Canal in World Shipping, 1869-1914," *Journal of Economic History*, vol. 18 (1958), 564.

20 *British Documents on Foreign Affairs,* Part 1, Series B, "The Near and Middle East," vol. 9, Doc. 53 (no, 389A), 64, "Granville to Dufferin," July 11, 1882.

21 A. L. Burt, *Evolution of the British Empire to Commonwealth from the American Revolution* (Boston: D. C. Heath Co., 1956), 156–57; see also Saab, *The Reluctant Icon: Gladstone, Bulgaria, and the Working Classes*, 192–201.

22 *British Documents*, 64, "Granville to Dufferin," July 11, 1882.

23 H. C. G. Matthew, *The Gladstone Diaries with Cabinet Minutes and Prime Ministerial Correspondence* (Oxford: Clarendon Press, 1990), vol. X, January 1881 to June 1883, lxxi–lxxii.

24 Ibid.

25 S. Gwynn and G. M. Tuckwell, *The Life of the Right Hon. Sir Charles Dilke* (New York: Macmillan Co, 1917), vol. 1, 450–51.

26 Ibid., 451.

27 P.R.O. 30/29/124, F.O. 78/3365, August 30, 1881, Gladstone to Granville: Supports Pauncefote's view relative to Ottoman water rights as legally applied to Egypt.

28 Gwynn and Tuckwell, *The Life of the Right Hon. Sir Charles Dilke*, 451.

29 Temperly and Penson, *The Foundations of British Foreign Policy from Pitt to Salisbury or Documents, Old and New*, 416; also Gwynn and Tuckwell, *The Life of the Right Hon. Sir Charles Dilke*, 452–53.

30 E. Hertslet and E. C. Hertslet (eds.), *British Foreign and State Papers* (London: William Ridgway, 1890), vol. 74, 376.

31 Ibid., vol. 73, 1130–31.

32 P.R.O. 30/29/160, MS 44174, cited in A. Ramm, *Political Correspondence of Mr. Gladstone and Lord Granville, 1876–1893* (Oxford: Clarendon Press, 1962), vol. 1, 328, Doc. 60, January 12, 1882, "Granville to Gladstone." Also see Matthew, *The Gladstone Diaries with Cabinet Minutes and Prime Ministerial Correspondence*, lxix, "The Egyptians could work out their destiny only within a tightly defined and controlled framework, externally supervised and consequently, by implication, externally policed."

33 Landau, *Parliament and Parties in Egypt*, 32–33.

34 P.R.O. 30/29/125, January 16, Gladstone to Granville.

35 Ibid., January 17, Gladstone to Granville.

36 Ibid.

37 A. Scholch, *Egypt for the Egyptians! The Socio-Political Crisis in Egypt, 1878–1882* (London: Ithica Press, 1981), 210–11.

38 *British Documents*, vol. 9, "The Ottoman Empire in North Africa: Intervention in Egypt and the Sudan, 1876–1885," Doc. 155, "Egypt's Army and Navy", 235–57.

39 H. Field, *On the Desert: With a Brief Overview of Recent Events in Egypt* (New York: Charles Scribner's Sons, 1883), 15–19.

40 P. Mansfield, *The British in Egypt* (New York: Holt, Rinehart, and Winston, 1971), 35.

41 F.O. 78/3435, Encl. No. 1, Malet no. 93, Malet to Granville, Cairo, February 25, 1882; also see Landau, *Parliament and Parties in Egypt*, 31–32, 34, 37–38.

42 Blunt, *A Secret History of the English Occupation of Egypt*, 144; also P.R.O. 30/29/125, June 27, Gladstone to Granville, bemoans sultan's award as tantamount to diplomatic recognition.

43 Garvin, *The Life of Joseph Chamberlain*, 447–48.

44 Ibid., 447; Scholch, *Egypt for the Egyptians*, 210–11.

45 D. C. Douglas, *English Historical Documents* (New York: Oxford University Press, 1977), vol. 12, no. 2, 366.

46 Ibid., 365–67.

47 Ibid., 367.

48 Polson-Newman, *Great Britain in Egypt*, 96; also Landau, *Parliament and Parties in Egypt*, 38.

49 A. Scholch, "'Men on the Spot' and the English Occupation of Egypt in 1882." *The Historical Journal*, vol. 19, no. 3 (1976), 782.

50 Blunt, *A Secret History of the English Occupation of Egypt*, 187–88.

51 *State Papers*, vol. 74, 421–22, "Malet to Granville"; also Gwynn and Tuckwell, *The Life of the Right Hon. Sir Charles Dilke*, 458.

52 *Hansard's Parliamentary Debates*, vol. 269, 1781, 1937, June 1; also P.R.O. 30/29//125, June 2, Gladstone to Granville.

53 *State Papers*, vol. 74, 438, June 11, 1882, "Vice-Consul Calvert to Earl Granville," reported riot and troops that came to restore order. European casualties mentioned, but no figures of Egyptians killed. June 12, "About 50 Europeans were killed, and only 3 Arabs . . ."

54 Ibid., 440, June 12, "Earl Granville to Viscount Lyons," makes no mention of Egyptians killed in urgent dispatch to Paris.

55 *Parliamentary Papers*, vol. 82, "Correspondence respecting the Conference at Constantinople on Egyptian Affairs," Encl. no. 265, "Consul Cookson to E. Malet," June 8, 1882; Baron de Kusel, *The Gladstone Diaries with Cabinet Minutes and Prime Ministerial Correspondence* (London: John Lane, 1915), 172–73; E. Farman (US consul-general in Cairo), *Egypt and its Betrayal: An Account of the Country during the Periods of Ismail and Tewfik Pashas, and of How England Acquired a New Empire* (New York: Grafton Press, 1885); Scholch, "Men on the Spot," 780.

56 S. de Kusel (Baron), *An Englishman's Recollections of Egypt, 1863–1887* (London: John Lane, 1915), 172–73.

57 Farman, *Egypt and its Betrayal: An Account of the Country during the Periods of Ismail and Tewfik Pashas, and of How England Acquired a New Empire*, 308–10.

58 Gwynn and Tuckwell, *The Life of the Right Hon. Sir Charles Dilke*, 462; Garvin, *The Life of Joseph Chamberlain*, 446–47.

59 Farman, *Egypt and its Betrayal: An Account of the Country during the Periods of Ismail and Tewfik Pashas, and of How England Acquired a New Empire*, 305, 311.

60 *State Papers*, 469–71.

61 Ibid., 477; Gwynn and Tuckwell, *The Life of the Right Hon. Sir Charles Dilke*, 465; Matthew, *The Gladstone Diaries with Cabinet Minutes and Prime Ministerial Correspondence*, 291, cabinet of July 3, 1882.

62 C. Stone, "Introductory Letter," *The Century Magazine*, vol. 23, New Series, vol. 6 (1884), 288–89.

63 P. Knapland, *Gladstone's Foreign Policy* (New York: Harper and Brothers, 1939), 183.

64 Daly, *The Cambridge History of Egypt*, vol. 2, *Modern Egypt*, 231–37; Ramm, *Political Correspondence of Mr. Gladstone and Lord Granville*, 385, Doc. 739, footnote 1, for Seymour's orders of July 3; *State Papers*, vol. 74, 477, July 3, "Granville to Mr. Cartwright," cites telegram of July 3, authorizing Seymour to stop Urabi's fortification efforts by force.

65 Knapland, *Gladstone's Foreign Policy*, 183.

66 Matthew, *The Gladstone Diaries with Cabinet Minutes and Prime Ministerial Correspondence*, 292–93.

67 P.R.O. 30/29/126, Gladstone to Granville, July 9, 1882.

68 Scholch, *Egypt for the Egyptians*, 257.

69 W. L. Clowes, *The Royal Navy: A History from the Earliest times to the Death of Queen Victoria*, (London: Sampson Low, Marston and Co., 1937), vol. 7, 328.

70 Ibid., 327, 330.

71 Clowes, *The Royal Navy: A History from the Earliest Times to the Death of Queen Victoria*, vol. 7, 338; for Egyptian figures see Stone, "Introductory Letter," 289–91.

72 E. E. Bradford, *Life of Admiral of the Fleet Sir Arthur Knyvet Wilson* (New York: E. P. Dutton, 1923), 67.

73 Clowes, *The Royal Navy: A History from the Earliest Times to the Death of Queen Victoria*, vol. 7, 334.

74 Stone, "Incidents at Alexandria," *The Century*, 27, New Series, vol. 6 (May to October 1884), 289–91, eyewitness account of hundreds of dead and wounded civilians in the city; A. Forbes, "An American Criticism of the Egyptian Campaign," *The Nineteenth Century*, vol. 16 (1884), 228–37; F. Stone, "Diary of an American Girl in Cairo, During the War of 1882," *The Century*, vol. 28,

New Series, vol. 6 (May to October 1884); see also Matthew, 297, cabinet of July 13, 1882, telegram sent to avoid further destruction after Seymour bombarded Alexandria second time on July 12; see also R. T. Harrison, *Gladstone's Imperialism in Egypt* (Westport, CT: Greenwood Press, 1995), for clear photographs from Lady Anna Brassey Album 331, vol. 31, taken at the time of bombardment of Alexandria by Italian photographers L. Fiorillo and P. Sebah showing extensive destruction by British artillery. Huntington Library Archives.

75 P. C. Scott, *Fifty Years in the Royal Navy* (London: John Murray, 1919) presents graphic, factual and concise picture of destruction by Seymour's fleet.

76 G. Arthur, *The Letters of Lord and Lady Wolseley, 1870–1911*(New York: Doubleday, Page and Co.), 77.

77 *State Papers*, vol. 74, 516–17, 520–22.

78 Ibid., 573.

79 J. Maurice, *Military History of the Campaign of 1882 in Egypt* (London: J. B. Howard and Son, 1883, Reprint, 1973), chap. 4, classic military history of Wolseley's campaign shows little or no enemy forces at the Suez Canal. Also see C. Field, *Britain's Sea Soldiers: A History of the Royal Marines* (Liverpool: Lyceum Press, 1924), vol. 2, 169–70, confirms no enemy resistance in the area of the canal.

80 Blunt, *A Secret History of the English Occupation of Egypt*, 300–01.

81 C. Goodrich, "Report of the British Naval and Military Operations in Egypt, 1882," *House Miscellaneous Documents*, No. 29 (Washington: Government Printing Office, Office of Naval Intelligence, 1885), War Series no. 3, 127–28, 148, 151, 153, presents account of an American military observer. Very reliable. See also Arthur, *The Letters of Lord and Lady Wolseley, 1870-1911*, 74, 78–79; E. Holt, "Garnet Wolseley: A Soldier of the Empire", *History Today*, vol. 8, no. 7 (1958), 712; Field, *Britain's Sea Soldiers: A History of the Royal Marines*, 173–74; Blunt, *A Secret History of the English Occupation of Egypt*, 318–19; Scholch, *Egypt for the Egyptians!*, 292–93; Maurice, *Military History of the Campaign of 1882 in Egypt*, 80–81.

82 A. M. Broadley, *How We Defended Urabi and His Friends* (London: Chapman and Hall, 1884; Reprint, Cairo: Arab Research Publishing Center, 1981), 43–55, 290–309, offers complete account of Urabi's trial, inadequacies of government case, and decision to exile him to Ceylon; see also Blunt, *A Secret History of the English Occupation of Egypt*, 351–54; Gwynn and Tuckwell, *The Life of the Right Hon. Sir Charles Dilke*, 550.

83 P.R.O. 30/29/126, Gladstone to Granville, September 16, details Gladstone's immediate goals for Egypt, as does September 19, on question of the canal. Also see Ramm, *Political Correspondence of Mr. Gladstone and Lord Granville*, vol. 1, 425–26; Knapland, *Gladstone's Foreign Policy*, 280–86. See Matthew, *The Gladstone Diaries with Cabinet Minutes and Prime Ministerial Correspondence*, lxxii, on bondholders' "established rights" after occupation as subject to the British government's "guardianship which it was moving to guard directly."

84 A. J. P. Taylor, *The Struggle for Mastery in Europe, 1848–1919* (Oxford: Clarendon Press, 1954), 289.

Chapter 9

1 Daly, *The Cambridge History of Egypt*, Vol. 2, *Modern Egypt*, 239–40; Knapland, Gladstone's *Foreign Policy*, 190–94.

2 P.R.O. 30/29/126, Gladstone to Granville, September 16, 1882, for Gladstone's immediate goals for Egypt. September 19, Granville to Gladstone, on issues regarding the canal; see P. Mansfield and N. Pelham, *A History of the Middle East* (New York: Penguin Books, Fourth Edition, 2014), on extent of occupation.

3 P.R.O. 30/29/126, Gladstone to Granville, September 16.

4 Garvin, *The Life of Joseph Chamberlain,* 456.

5 Ibid., 453.

6 E. Fitzmaurice, *The Life of Granville George Loveson Gower* (London: Longmans, Green, and Co. 1905), vol. 2, 307.

7 *Hansard's Parliamentary Debates*, vol. 274, 41–42.

8 D. Wallace, *Egypt and the Egyptian Question* (New York: Russell and Russell, 1967), 379.

9 A. J. P. Taylor, *The Struggle for Mastery in Europe, 1848–1919* (Oxford: Clarendon Press, 1954), 289; see also J. Gelvin, *The Modern Middle East, A History*, 91–95, which provides concise information on impact of Britain's occupation.

10 *Hansard's Parliamentary Debates*, vol. 272, 1526, 1584, 1598–1603; B. Holland, *The Life of Spencer Compton, Eighth Duke of Devonshire* {Lord Hartington} (London: Longman, Green, and Co., 1911), vol. 1.

11 Goodrich, "Report of the British Naval and Military Operations in Egypt, 1882," 158.

12 Blunt, *A Secret History of the English Occupation of Egypt*, 325.

13 *British Documents on Foreign Affairs, Part 1, Series B, The Near and Middle East, 1856–1914*, vol. 9, Doc. 50, 62, Dufferin to Granville, 8.00 p.m. July 10, 1882.

14 Al-Sayyid Marsot, *Cromer*, 26, on *jihad* or "Holy War"; also Scholch, *Egypt for the Egyptians*, 177–215, 273–303, on support by Assembly and Majlis al-'Urfi (War Council) relative to call for jihad; also see Goodrich, "Report of the British Naval and Military Operations in Egypt, 1882," 157, regarding Sudanese regiments at Tel el-Kabir.

15 Al-Sayyid Marsot, *Egypt and Cromer*, 39.

16 R. Robinson, J. Gallagher, and A. Denny, *Africa and the Victorians: The Official Mind of Imperialism* (London: Macmillan Education Ltd, 1988), 132–33.

17 Al-Sayyid Marsot, *Egypt and Cromer*, 39–40.

18 Ibid., 41.

19 Goldschmidt, *Modern Egypt: The Formation of a Nation State*, 43; see Gelvin, *Modern Egypt*, 92–95, for insightful comments on occupation.

20 Fitzmaurice, *The Life of Granville George Loveson Gower*, vol. 2, 273.

21 Ibid., 274–76; also Gwynn and Tuckwell, *The Life of the Right Hon. Sir Charles Dilke*, 477; and Garvin, *The Life of Joseph Chamberlain*, 450.

22 Al-Sayyid Marsot, *Egypt and Cromer*, 130, 132–33; Robinson, Gallagher, and Denny, *Africa and the Victorians: The Official Mind of Imperialism*, 358.

23 B. Bond, *Victorian Military Campaigns* (London: Hutchison and Co. Ltd., 1967), 286.

24 Ibid.

25 B. Farwell, *Queen Victoria's Little Wars* (New York: W. W. Norton and Co., 1985), 335; also Bond, *Victorian Military Campaigns*, 287.

26 Bond, *Victorian Military Campaigns*, 297.

27 Ibid., 299.

28 F.O. 78/5050, Salisbury to Cromer, no. 109, secret, August 2, 1898, cited in Robinson, Gallagher, and Denny, *Africa and the Victorians: The Official Mind of Imperialism*, 368.

29 Robinson, Gallagher, and Denny, *Africa and the Victorians: The Official Mind of Imperialism*, 370.

30 Ibid., 370–71.

31 Telegram of Monson to Salisbury, September 18, 1898, cited in Robinson, Gallagher and Denny, *Africa and the Victorians: The Official Mind of Imperialism*, 370.

32 Bartlett, *A History of Russia*, 89.

33 Telegram of Monson to Salisbury, November 3, 1898, cited in Robinson, Gallagher, and Denny, *Africa and the Victorians*, 374.

34 Al-Sayyid Marsot, *Egypt and Cromer*, 133; also Robinson, Gallagher and Denny, *Africa and the Victorians: The Official Mind of Imperialism*, 374.

35 Ibid., 134.

36 Zayid, *Egypt's Struggle for Independence*, 58.

37 M. Refaat Bey, *The Awakening of Modern Egypt* (Lahore: Premier Book House, 1976), 234.

38 Al-Sayyid Marsot, *Egypt and Cromer*, 134–45, also chaps. VII, VIII.

39 Goldschmidt, *Modern Egypt: The Formation of a Nation State*, 49.

40 Daly, *The Cambridge History of Egypt*, Vol. 2, 243–44; Goldschmidt, *Modern Egypt*, 50–52.

41 P. Mellini, *Sir Eldon Gorst: The Overshadowed Proconsul* (Stanford: The Hoover Institution, 1977) for details on Gorst in Egypt; see Mansfield and Pelham, *A History of the Middle East*, 123–25, for a brief account of Gorst's tenure in Egypt.

42 IOR/L/P&S/18 Memoranda B, B 127, Kowait, Confidential, 1898.

43 Bartlett, *A History of Russia*, 99.

44 L/P&S/18 Memoranda B, B 127.

45 Ibid., January 23, 1899.

46 Ibid.; see also B. C. Busch, *Britain and the Persian Gulf 1894–1914* (Berkeley: University of California Press, 1967), chaps. VII and IX, for the most complete discussion on Baghdad RR, Kuwait, and British diplomacy. Excellent documentation for period 1898–1913.

47 Ibid.

48 Ibid.; Mubarak's annual subsidy was Rs. 15,000.

49 Aitchison, *A Collection of Treaties, Engagements, and Sanads Relating to India and Neighboring Countries* Vol. XI.

50 L/P&S/18, B 151.

51 Ibid., Lord Landsdowne's Minute, March 21, 1902.

52 L/P&S/18, B 133a, R. V. Harcourt, Foreign Office, December 11, 1905.

53 Ibid.

54 Ibid.

55 Ibid.

56 L/P&S/18, B 285, from the *Quarterly Review*, October 1917 for private circulation.

57 Ibid.

58 L/P&S/18, B 153.

59 L/P&S/18, B 160.

60 L/P&S/18, B 153.

61 L/P&S/18, B 160.

62 L/P&S/18, B 197, Baghdad Railway and the Persian Gulf—British Negotiations with Hakki Pasha, May 3, 1913, Secret—Louis Mallet and Arthur Hirtzel (Secretary of the Political and Secret Department), India Office.

63 Ibid.

64 Cain and Hopkins, *British Imperialism: Innovation and Expansion 1688–1914*, 410.

65 L/P&S/18, B 285, from the *Quarterly Review*; October 1917.

Chapter 10

1 M. J. Lyons, *World War I: A Short History* (Upper Saddle River, NJ: Prentice Hall, 2000), 56.

2 L. C. Brown, *International Politics and the Middle East: Old Rules, Dangerous Game* (Princeton: Princeton University Press, 1984), 112.

3 D. Fromkin, *A Peace to End All Peace* (New York: Avon Books, 1989), 155–62; A. J. P. Taylor, *A History of the First World War* (New York: Berkley Medallion, 1966), 59–66; Lyons, *World War I: A Short History*, 117–26.

4 C. Finkel, *Osman's Dream, The Story of the Ottoman Empire 1300–1923* (New York: Basic Books, 2005), 533, 536–37, offers a good summary of the war's impact on the Ottoman Empire; J. O'Rourke, "The Juristic Status

of Egypt and the Sudan," *Johns Hopkins University Studies in History and Political Science*, series 53, no. 1 (1935), 28–55.

5 State Papers, vol. CIX, 1915, 429–33.

6 Ibid., 434.

7 P. Elgood, *Egypt and the Army* (London: Oxford University Press, 1924), 157.

8 Lyons, *World War I: A Short History*, 116–17.

9 Ibid., 116.

10 Elgood, *Egypt and the Army*, 128.

11 Ibid, 86–87.

12 E. Newman, *Great Britain in Egypt* (London: Cassell and Co. Ltd.), 213.

13 Ibid.

14 Elgood, *Egypt and the Army*, 87, 316.

15 Ibid., 87.

16 Ibid., 303–35.

17 Newman, *Great Britain in Egypt*, 207–08.

18 Lyons, *World War I: A Short History*, 258.

19 L/P&S/18 B221, Germany and the Middle East to the Cabinet, December 27, 1915.

20 L/P&S/18, B 217.

21 L/P&S/18, B 217 Section I—Military Situation in Mesopotamia, November 15, 1915.

22 T. Wilson, *The Myriad Faces of War: Britain and the Great War 1914–1918* (Cambridge, UK: Polity Press, 1986), 278.

23 Ibid., 380.

24 Lyons, *World War I: A Short History*, 260.

25 Wilson, *The Myriad Faces of War*, 380.

26 Ibid.

27 L/P&S/12, 3349, Letter July 14, 1915 Hussein to McMahon H. M. High Commissioner at Cairo.

28 Ibid., McMahon to Sherif Hussein, October 24, 1915.

29 Ibid., Summary of Extracts of McMahon–Hussein Correspondence.

30 Ibid., July 11, 1930, Foreign Office, 184 pages and maps, 95–96.

31 Ibid., Foreign Office, January 23, 1940.

32 R. Ovendale, *The Middle East Since 1914* (London: Longman, 1992), 9.

33 L/P&S/18, B 217, Policy in the Middle East, Sections I, II from Lt. Colonel Sir Mark Sykes to Major C. E. Caldwell, Director of Military Operations, Confidential—from S. S. Khyber, Red Sea November 15, 1915.

34 Ibid., Section III, Lines to take Against the Enemy, Under Line 1.

35 L/P&S/18, B 218, No. 14 Secret, Shepherds Hotel, Cairo, July 14, 1915.

36 Ibid.

37 Ibid., No. 19, Aden, August 10, 1915.

38 Ibid.

39 Ibid.

40 L/P&S/18, B 217, Section III.

41 L/P&S/18, B 281, Note by Political Department, India Office on Points for Discussion with Sir Percy Cox relative to views of 1915–1916, April 3, 1918.

42 L/P&S/18, B 217, Section III, November 15, 1915.

43 Fromkin, *A Peace to End All Peace,* chap. 24.

44 Ovendale, *The Middle East Since 1914,* 9.

45 W. G. Ratliff, "Sykes–Picot Agreement of 1916," in J. S. Olson (ed.), *Historical Dictionary of the British Empire* (Westport, CT: Greenwood Press, 1996), 1077–78.

46 Fromkin, *A Peace to End All Peace*, 192.

47 Ibid.

48 L/P&S/18, B 233, Secret, The War with Turkey, memorandum, Political Department, India Office, May 25, 1916; also Appendix II document written by Mark Sykes, June 20, 1916.

49 L/P&S/18, B 287, Eastern Committee, Summary of the Hejaz Revolt up through 1917, General Staff, War Office, August 31, 1918, 1–2.

50 Ibid., 2.

51 Ibid., 2–3; see also D. Murphy, *The Arab Revolt 1916–18, Lawrence sets Arabia Ablaze* (Oxford: Osprey Publishing, 2008), 46–54, which offers a vivid description of Arab revolt against the Turks and role of T. E. Lawrence.

52 L/P&S/18, B 287, 4.

53 Ibid., 5.

54 Ibid., 4–5.

55 Ibid., 5.

56 Lyons, *World War I: A Short History,* 269.

57 L/P&S/18, B 268, Employment of Japanese Troops in Mesopotamia, Secretary of State for India, Secret, December 18, 1917.

58 L/P&S/18, B 241, Germany, Turkey, England, and Arabia, Confidential, October 31, 1916.

59 P. Mansfield and N. Pelham, *A History of the Middle East* (New York: Penguin Books, 2013), 166–68, for evaluation of oil fields and effort of the Anglo-Persian Oil Company to exploit Persian and Mesopotamian deposits.

60 L/P&S/18, B 287, The Arab Revolt, August 31, 1918, 5.

61 Ibid., 5-7.62. Gelvin, *The Modern Middle East,* 217–22, on the background of the Balfour Declaration and aftermath, 230, for Balfour Document.

62 Mansfield and Pelham, *A History of the Middle East,* 181.

63 Ibid., 181–82.

64 A. Goldschmidt Jr. and L. Davidson, *A Concise History of the Middle East* (Boulder: Westview Press, 2012), 238.

65 E. Monroe, *Britain's Moment in the Middle East 1914–1956* (London: Methuen Paperbacks, 1965), 43.

66 L/P&S/18, B 287 Appendix G, Zionist Movement.

67 Ibid.

68 L/P&S/18, B 287, 1918, 9.

69 L/P&S/18, B 288 Appendix, Secretary of State for India, telegram, August 15, 1918.

70 L/P&S/18, B 288, Relations with Bin Saud/Note by Political Office, Secret, India Office September 22, 1918; and B 308, Arabia-the Nejd-Hejaz Feud, Secret Note by Political Department India, January 7, 1919.

71 L/P&S/10, 1127, Political and Secret Department File, India Office, Situation in Arabia 1925–1928, The Nejd-Hejaz War.

72 L/P&S/18, B 353, Arabia—Question of Future Policy, Subsidies to the Chiefs, Confidential, Political Department India Office, October 19 and 20, 1920.

73 Mansfield and Pelham, *A History of the Middle East*, 180.

Chapter 11

1   L/P&S/18/, B 309. Interview with Sherif Feisal and T. E. Lawrence and Secretary of State for India—conducted at the India Office, December 27, 1918.

2   Ibid., Feisal on Arabia and the Saudi creed.

3   Ibid., expected Saudi removal from Khurma.

4   Ibid., Feisal's view of Syria and Sykes–Picot.

5   Ibid., view of the French and Syria.

6   Ibid., Feisal on Palestine and cooperation with the Jews.

7   Ibid., penciled comment by Sir H. Grant in margin of L/P&S/18, B 309, Palestine, December 27, 1918, left some years later. No date.

8   Ovendale, *The Middle East since 1914*, 11.

9   I. J. Bickerton and C. L. Klausner, *A Concise History of the Arab-Israeli Conflict* (Englewood Cliffs, NJ: Prentice Hall, Second Edition, 1995), 61–62.

10 L/P&S/12, 3349, Annexure, Foreign Office, July 11, 1930.

11 Ovendale, *The Middle East since 1914*, 11.

12 L/P&S/18, B 281, Future of Mesopotamia—Note by Political Department, India Office on Points for Discussion with Sir Percy Cox, April 3, 1918.

13 Ibid.

14 L/P&S/18, B 284, Eastern Committee: The Future of Mesopotamia, Note by Sir Percy Cox, April 22, 1918.

15 Ibid.

16 Ibid.

17 L/P&S/18, B 332, Mesopotamia, British Relations with Kurdistan, Political Department India Office, August 27, 1919.

18 Ibid.

19   Ibid.

20   Ibid.

21   L/P&S/18, B 322 Mesopotamia: Oil Policy, Secret, Interdepartmental Conference at India Office, April 10, 1919.

22   A. Goldschmidt Jr., *A Concise History of the Middle East* (Boulder: Westview Press, 19880), 187–89.

23   Mansfield and Pelham, *A History of the Middle East*, 207–12.

24   Zayid, *Egypt's Struggle for Independence*, 82–83.

25   Newman, *Great Britain in Egypt*, 217.

26   Fromkin, *A Peace to end All Peace*, 417–20; Goldschmidt, *Modern Egypt*, 56–58, and *Middle East*, 175–79.

27   Daly, *The Cambridge History of Egypt*, Vol. 2, *Modern Egypt*, 250; Mansfield and Pelham, *A History of the Middle East*, 201–02; Goldschmidt, *Middle East*, 220.

28   L/P&S/18, B 306 F, The Future of Constantinople, Secret, Secretary of State for India, E. S. Montagu, January 8, 1919.

29   E. Goldstein, *The First World War Peace Settlements 1919–1925* (London: Longman, 2002), 63; see M. S. Hanioglu, *A Brief History of the Late Ottoman Empire* (Princeton: Princeton University Press, 2008), 193, on Kamel Ataturk and defending Anatolia against the Treaty of Sèvres and Greek incursion.

30   Fromkin, *A Peace to end All Peace*, 457.

31   Ibid., 457–61.

32   Ovendale, *The Middle East since 1914*, 12.

33   L/P&S/18, A 221 Confidential Memo, A Summary of Anglo-Afghan Relations, Part I, 1840–1918.

34   Ibid., 7.

35   Ibid., 7.

36   Ibid., 8.

37   Ibid., 8, 9.

38   Ibid., 9.

39   Ibid.

40   Ibid.

41   L/P&S/18, A 206, August 8, 1919.

42   L/P&S/18, A 221 Confidential Memo, A Summary of Anglo-Afghan Relations, Part II, 1919–1947.

43   Ibid., 11.

44   Ibid., 12.

45   Ibid., 11.

46   Ibid.

47   Ibid.

48   B. Porter, *The Lion's Share, A Short History of British Imperialism 1850–1983* (New York: Longman, Second Edition, 1989), 252.

Chapter 12

1 Goldschmidt Jr., *Modern Egypt*, 55–65; see also Daly, *The Cambridge History of Egypt*, 239–51, for full account of Egypt's "ambiguous independence" under British administration.

2 B. Lapping, *End of Empire* (New York: St. Martin's Press, 1985), 239.

3 Monroe, *Britain's Moment in the Middle East 1914–1956*, 75, also Lapping, *End of Empire*, 239, and Goldschmidt Jr., *Modern Egypt*, 61.

4 Monroe, *Britain's Moment in the Middle East 1914–1956*, 75–76.

5 Zayid, *Egypt's Struggle for Independence*, 124.

6 G. Lloyd, *Egypt Since Cromer*, vol. II (London: Macmillan and Co., Ltd., 1933), 200, Zayid, *Egypt's Struggle for Independence*, 125–26.

7 Lloyd, *Egypt Since Cromer*, 200.

8 M. Rifaat Bey, *The Awakening of Modern Egypt* (Lahore: Premier Book House, 1976), 224; Lloyd, *Egypt Since Cromer*, 218–20; Zayid, *Egypt's Struggle for Independence*, 125–26.

9 Lapping, *End of Empire*, 239–40.

10 Zayid, *Egypt's Struggle for Independence*, 125–26.

11 B. Porter, *The Lion's Share, A Short History of British Imperialism 1850–1983* (New York: Longman, Second Edition, 1989), 296.

12 T. Evans (ed.), *The Killearn Diaries 1934–46* (London: Sidgwick and Jackson, 1972), 2–3.

13 Zayid, *Egypt's Struggle for Independence*, 197–237.

14 J. Gordon, *The Other Desert War: British Social Forces in North Africa 1940–1943* (New York: Greenwood Press, 1987), 36.

15 Ibid., 86; Zayid, *Egypt's Struggle for Independence*, 173.

16 *Parliamentary Debates* (London: Cornelius Buck Publishers, 1938), vol. 318, cls. 1800–01.

17 Ibid., vol. 317, cl. 678.

18 Zayid, *Egypt's Struggle for Independence*, 183.

19 Lapping, *End of Empire*, 240; and Goldschmidt Jr., *Modern Egypt*, 67–69.

20 Lapping, *End of Empire*, 240.

21 M. Neguib, *Egypt's Destiny* (London: Victor Gollancz Ltd., 1955), 71–72; J. Connell. *Wavell: Scholar and Soldier* (London: Collin, 1954), 215.

22 War Office 32/4159, The Defense of Egypt, Appendix "A," Egyptian Military Intelligence, March 21, 1937, I, cited in Gordon, *The Other Desert War: British Social Forces in North Africa 1940–1943*, 37–38.

23 Neguib, *Egypt's Destiny*, 73–75.

24 A. Sadat, *Revolt on the Nile* (London: Allan Wingate, 1957), 31–32.

25 War Office 32/4167 and 32/4167, British Military Mission to Egypt—Reorganization of the Egyptian Army: Soan 1936–1938, 3–4, cited in Gordon, *The Other Desert War: British Social Forces in North Africa 1940–1943*, 37.

26 F.O. 407/222 Defense, Sir Miles Lampson to Viscount Halifax—Report on the Progress of the Egyptian Army in 1937, March 3, 1938.

27 War Office 3W10125, Army Council instructions to General Officer Commanding-In-Chief in the Middle East, July 1939, cited in Gordon, *The Other Desert War: British Social Forces in North Africa 1940–1943*, 37.

28 A. Nutting, *Nasser* (London: Constable, 1972), 19.

29 M. Abd al-Wahhab Bakr, *al-Wujud al-Baritani fi al-Jarish al-Misri, 1937-1947* (Cairo, 1982), 26; Bey, 234.

30 F.O. 371/2337 Quarterly Report No. 11 on the Egyptian Army, October 31, 1939.

31 Abd al-Wahhab Bakr, *al-Wujud al-Baritani fi al-Jarish al-Misri*, 132–33.

32 *Parliamentary Debates*, vol. 319, cls. 1800–01; vol. 342, cls. 1487–88; Connell, *Wavell: Scholar and Soldier*, 235; Nutting, 13.

33 Goldschmidt Jr. *Middle East*, 235; C. D. Smith, *Palestine and the Arab-Israeli Conflict* (New York: St. Martin's, Fourth Edition, 2001), 41.

34 I. J. Bickerton and C. L. Klausner, *A Concise History of the Arab-Israeli Conflict* (Englewood Cliffs, NJ: Prentice Hall, Second Edition, 1995), 61–62.

35 Mansfield and Pelham, *Middle East*, 181–87.

36 L/P&S/12, McMahon to Sherif Hussein, October 24, 1915, Summary of Extracts of McMahon-Hussein Correspondence, July 11, 1930, Foreign Office, 184 pages and maps, 95–96, Foreign Office, January 23, 1940.

37 Bickerton and Klausner, *A Concise History of the Arab-Israeli Conflict*, 61–62; Lapping, *End of Empire*, 114; Monroe, *Britain's Moment in the Middle East 1914–1956*, 44–45.

38 Lapping, *End of Empire*, 114.

39 Ibid., 112.

40 Smith, *Palestine and the Arab-Israeli Conflict*, 112–16.

41 Ibid., 113.

42 Lapping, *End of Empire*, 111.

43 Smith, *Palestine and the Arab-Israeli Conflict*, 113–14.

44 Churchill White Paper, 1922, cited in Bickerton and Klausner, *A Concise History of the Arab-Israeli Conflict*, 64–65.

45 N. Rich, *Great Power Diplomacy Since 1914* (New York: McGraw-Hill, 2003), 95.

46 L/P&S/18, B 287 Appendix G, Zionist Movement; L/P&S/18/, B 309 Interview with Sherif Feisal and T. E. Lawrence and Secretary of State for India— conducted at the India Office, December 27, 1918.

47 Smith, *Palestine and the Arab-Israeli Conflict*, 115.

48 Ibid., 129–30; see also Goldschmidt Jr., *Middle East*, 240–41.

49 Lapping, *End of Empire*, 111; Monroe, *Britain's Moment in the Middle East 1914–1956*, 81.

50 Monroe, *Britain's Moment in the Middle East 1914–1956*, 81.

51 Lapping, *End of Empire*, 112; Smith, *Palestine and the Arab-Israeli Conflict*, 137–33.

52 Lapping, *End of Empire*, 113.

53 Smith, *Palestine and the Arab-Israeli Conflict*, 137; Goldschmidt Jr., *Middle East*, 243; R. Ovendale, *The Origins of the Arab-Israeli Wars* (New York: Longman, Third Edition, 1999), 73–74.

54 Peel Commission/Palestine Royal Commission Report, 1937, Cited in Bickerton and Klausner, *A Concise History of the Arab-Israeli Conflict*, 65–66.

55 Ovendale, *The Origins of the Arab-Israeli Wars*, 75.

56 Smith, *Palestine and the Arab-Israeli Conflict*, 142.

57 Mansfield and Pelham, *Middle East*, on Peel Commission and partition proposal of 1937, 233.

58 The 1939 White Paper on Palestine, cited in Bickerton and Klausner, *A Concise History of the Arab-Israeli Conflict*, 66–67; see Ovendale, *The Origins of the Arab-Israeli Wars*, 78.

59 Monroe, *Britain's Moment in the Middle East 1914–1956*, 81.

60 Lapping, *End of Empire*, 114, Smith, *Palestine and the Arab-Israeli Conflict*, 147, Goldschmidt Jr., *Middle East*, 244.

61 A. J. Abdullah Thabit, *A Short History of Iraq* (New York: Longman, 2003), 142–43, on pogroms against ancient Jewish community in Iraq; Ovendale, *The Origins of the Arab-Israeli Wars*, 78–79, impact on wider Arab world; also Smith, *Palestine and the Arab-Israeli Conflict*, 210n 72, for the historiography.

62 P. J. Cain and A. G. Hopkins, *British Imperialism: Crisis and Deconstruction* (New York: Longman, 1993), 103.

63 Ibid.

Chapter 13

1 H. Jacobson and A. L. Smith Jr., *World War II Policy and Strategy, Selected Documents with Commentary* (Santa Barbara: Clio Books, 1979), 24–26, Russo–German Non-Aggression Treaty with Secret Protocol, August 23, 1939.

2 Ibid., 73–76, German–French Armistice Treaty, June 22, 1940.

3 Ibid., 76–81, Churchill's Speech on Destruction of French Fleet, July 4, 1940.

4 Lapping, *End of Empire*, 113.

5 P. Young, *A Short History of World War II: 1939–1945* (New York: Thomas Y. Crowell, 1966), 81.

6 Connell, *Wavell: Scholar and Soldier*, 235.

7 Ibid., 267.

8 L. Hirszowicz, *The Third Reich and the Arab East* (London: Routledge and Kegan Paul, 1966), 66.

9   Evans, *The Killearn Diaries 1934–46*, 161.

10 Hirszowicz, *The Third Reich and the Arab East*, 75–76.

11 A. Sadat, *Revolt on the Nile* (London: Allan Wingate, 1957), 16.

12 Ibid., 34.

13 Ibid., 19–25.

14 Hirszowicz, *The Third Reich and the Arab East*, 75.

15 Young, *A Short History of World War II: 1939--1945*. 81–83; also Michael J. Lyons, *World War II: A Short History* (Englewood Cliffs: Prentice Hall, Second Edition, 1994), 107–08.

16 W. Churchill, *The Second World War: The Grand Alliance* (Boston: Houghton and Mifflin Co., 1950), vol. III, 95; Mansfield, *Egypt*, 274.

17 Sadat, *Revolt on the Nile*, 24–25.

18 Evans, *The Killearn Diaries 1934–46*, 160.

19 Lyons, *World War II: A Short History*, 198–99; Young, *A Short History of World War II: 1939–1945*, 82–83.

20 Lyons, *World War II: A Short History*, 198.

21 Young, *A Short History of World War II: 1939–1945*, 87–90.

22 Evans, *The Killearn Diaries 1934–1946*, 161–62.

23 T. A. J. Abdullah, *A Short History of Iraq* (London: Longman, 2003), 141.

24 Ibid., 141–42.

25 Lyons, *World War II: A Short History*, 113; Young, *A Short History of World War II: 1939–1945*, 108.

26 Young, *A Short History of World War II: 1939–1945*, 107–08; Lyons, *World War II: A Short History*, 113; Lapping, *End of Empire*, 140.

27 Lapping, *End of Empire*, 117.

28 Young, *A Short History of World War II: 1939–1945*, 108, Lapping, *End of Empire*, 117.

29 Evans, *The Killearn Diaries 1934–1946*, 161–62.

30 Ibid., 161.

31 Goldschmidt Jr., *Modern Egypt*, 73; see also Daly, *The Cambridge History of Egypt*, Vol. 2, 298–300.

32 Lapping, *End of Empire*, 242–44, Goldschmidt Jr., *Modern Egypt*, 73–74.

33 M. Neguib, *Egypt's Destiny* (London: Victor Gollancz Ltd., 1955), 87; A. Nutting, *Nasser* (London: Constable, 1972), 19; Sadat, *Revolt on the Nile*, 44.

34 Sadat, *Revolt on the Nile*, 44.

35 P. Vatikiotis, *The Egyptian Army in Politics: Pattern for New Nations* (Bloomington: Indiana University Press, 1961), 52.

36 Ibid., 57.

37 *Parliamentary Debates*, vol. 409.

38 Sadat, *Revolt on the Nile*, 21.

39 *Parliamentary Debates*, vol. 409, 28 March 1945.

40 Ibid.

41 Neguib, *Egypt's Destiny*, 85.

42 Monroe, *Britain's Moment in the Middle East*, 90–91.

43 Jacobsen and Smith, Jr., *World War II, Policy and Strategy*, 89, 96, 138.

44 Ibid., 155–57, Joint-promise of Anglo-American aid to USSR, August 15, 1941.

45 Young, *A Short History of World War II: 1939–1945*, 107–08; Lapping, *End of Empire*, 200–03.

46 Jacobsen and Smith, Jr., *World War II Policy and Strategy*, Casablanca Meeting, "Unconditional Surrender" Statement, January 23, 1943.

47 Ibid., 288–89, Memorandum, Cairo, November 1943.

48 Ibid., 282–84, Teheran Conference, December 1, 1943.

49 Fromkin, *A Peace to End All Peace*, 457–61.

50 Ovendale, *Middle East*, 12; Rich, 95–96.

51 Ali M. Ansari, *Modern Iran Since 1921* (London: Longman, 2003), 72.

52 Ibid., 72.

53 Lapping, *End of Empire*, 203–04; Goldschmidt, Jr., *Middle East*, 204–06.

54 Lapping, *End of Empire*, 203.

55 Daly, *Middle East*, 294–96; see also Goldschmidt, Jr., *Middle East*, 206.

56 *Parliamentary Debates*, vol. 385, cls. 32, 36.

57 Jacobsen and Smith, Jr., 412–18, Crimean Conference at Yalta.

58 *Parliamentary Debates*, vol. 408, cl. 1287; Mansfield and Pelham, *Middle East*, 255.

59 Mansfield and Pelham, *Middle East*, 255.

60 Vatikiotis, 57.

61 Lapping, *End of Empire*, 120.

62 Lapping, *End of Empire*, 119; Mansfield and Pelham, *Middle East*, 261.

63 Mansfield and Pelham, *Middle East*, 261–62.

64 Ovendale, *Arab–Israeli*, 88.

65 Ibid.

66 Lapping, *End of Empire*, 119.

67 Mansfield and Pelham, *Middle East*, 262.

68 Ovendale, *Arab–Israeli*, 86.

69 Jacobsen and Smith, Jr., *World War II Policy and Strategy*, 390, Doc. 199. Memorandum of Conversation between King of Saudi Arabia and President Roosevelt, February 14, 1945.

70 Ibid.

71 Ibid., 390–91.

72 Ibid., 395–96, Doc. 198, Arab League Pact, Cairo, March 22, 1945.

73 Ibid., 383, Doc. 196, speech by Weizmann, August 1945.

74 Ibid., 383, Doc. 197, Political Declaration of World Zionist Conference, London, August 1945.

75 Ibid., 385.

76 Lyons, *World War II: A Short History,* 320–21.

Chapter 14

1 Lapping, *End of Empire*, 9.

2 B. Porter, *The Lion's Share, A Short History of British Imperialism 1850–1983* (New York: Longman, Second Edition, 1989), 308.

3 Ibid.

4 W. Hubatch, *The German Question* (New York: Herder Book Center, 1967), 25.

5 M. A. Fitzsimmons, *The Foreign Policy of the British Labor Government 1945–1951* (Notre Dame: Notre Dame University Press, 1953), 45–48; F. S. Northridge, *British Foreign Policy* (New York: Frederick A. Praeger Pub., 1962), 82; and F. S. V. Donnison, *Civil Affairs and Military Government Central Organization and Plannings* (London: Her Majesty's Stationery Office, 1966), 105–07.

6 W. R. Louis, *The British Empire in the Middle East* (Oxford: Clarendon Press, 1984), viii.

7 Lapping, *End of Empire*, 10.

8 Bickerton and Klausner, *A Concise History of the Arab-Israeli Conflict*, 79.

9 W. R. Louis and R. W. Stookey (eds.), *The End of the Palestine Mandate* (Austin: University of Texas Press, 1986), 8; Louis, *The British Empire in the Middle East*, 238.

10 Bickerton and Klausner, *A Concise History of the Arab-Israeli Conflict*, 82.

11 Lapping, *End of Empire,* 125–27; Bickerton and Klausner, *A Concise History of the Arab-Israeli Conflict*, 78; Louis and Stookey, *The End of the Palestine Mandate*, 10.

12 C. D. Smith, *Palestine and the Arab-Israeli Conflict* (New York: St. Martin's, Fourth Edition, 2001), 189.

13 Ibid.

14 Louis and Stookey, *The End of the Palestine Mandate*, 11–12, on Truman's Yom Kippur speech October 4, 1946.

15 M. Gilbert, *The Arab-Israeli Conflict: Its History in Maps* (Tel Aviv: Steimatzky Ltd., 4th Edition, 1984), 36; Bickerton and Klausner, *A Concise History of the Arab-Israeli Conflict*, 84.

16 Gilbert, *The Arab-Israeli Conflict: Its History in Maps,* 35.

17 Ovendale, *The Origins of the Arab-Israeli Wars*, 114–19. Bickerton and Klausner, *A Concise History of the Arab-Israeli Conflict*, 85, also Doc. 3–4, 95; also Smith, *Palestine and the Arab-Israeli Conflict*, 189.

18   Bickerton and Klausner, *A Concise History of the Arab-Israeli Conflict*, Doc. 5.3 on Palestinian Arab Reaction, 215–16.

19   Louis, *British Empire in the Middle East*, 472–73.

20   Bickerton and Klausner, *A Concise History of the Arab-Israeli Conflict*, 85.

21   Lucias D. Clay, *Decision In Germany* (New York: Doubleday and Co. Inc., 1950), 178.

22   Ovendale, *Arab-Israeli Wars*, 117.

23   Lapping, *End of Empire*, 129–30.

24   Louis and Stookey, *The End of the Palestine Mandate*, 20–21.

25   Lapping, *End of Empire*, 130–34.

26   Bickerton and Klausner, *A Concise History of the Arab-Israeli Conflict*, 86–87; Gilbert, *The Arab-Israeli Conflict: Its History in Maps*, 36.

27   Lapping, *End of Empire*, 138; Ovendale, *Arab-Israeli Wars*, 117–18.

28   Bickerton and Klausner, *A Concise History of the Arab-Israeli Conflict*, 85.

29   Louis and Stookey, *The End of the Palestine Mandate*, 25; Smith, *Palestine and the Arab-Israeli Conflict*, 199; Lapping, *End of Empire*, 142; Ovendale, *Arab-Israeli Wars*, 135. Some place the victims at Deir Yassin at half the 250 given, but that propaganda raised the figures to entice the Arabs to flee the area.

30   Monroe, *Britain's Moment in the Middle East*, 168.

31   Smith, *Palestine and the Arab-Israeli Conflict*, 219–22, Doc. 5.5; also Bickerton and Klausner, *A Concise History of the Arab-Israeli Conflict*, 113–15, Doc. 4–1, Declaration of the Establishment of the State of Israel.

32   Louis, *British Empire in the Middle East*, 555.

33   Smith, *Palestine and the Arab-Israeli Conflict*, 199; Louis and Stookey, *The End of the Palestine Mandate*, 24; Ovendale, *Arab-Israeli Wars*, 135, 138–39; Bickerton and Klausner, *A Concise History of the Arab-Israeli Conflict*, 103; Gilbert, *The Arab-Israeli Conflict: Its History in Maps*, 46–47.

34   Louis, *British Empire in the Middle East*, 555–56.

35   Louis and Stookey, *The End of the Palestine Mandate*, 24–25; Bickerton and Klausner, *A Concise History of the Arab-Israeli Conflict*, 89.

36   Louis, *British Empire in the Middle East*, 545; Smith, *Palestine and the Arab-Israeli Conflict*, 201.

37   Bickerton and Klausner, *A Concise History of the Arab-Israeli Conflict*, 89.

38   Smith, *Palestine and the Arab-Israeli Conflict*, 203.

39   Gilbert, *The Arab-Israeli Conflict: Its History in Maps*, 46.

40   Louis, *British Empire in the Middle East*, 540–50; Ovendale, *Arab-Israeli Wars*, 136–37; Bickerton and Klausner, *A Concise History of the Arab-Israeli Conflict*, 101.

41   Smith, *Palestine and the Arab-Israeli Conflict* 202–03; Bickerton and Klausner, *A Concise History of the Arab-Israeli Conflict*, 106; Gilbert, *The Arab-Israeli Conflict: Its History in Maps*, 47.

42   Lapping, *End of Empire*, 144–48.

43 US and UK Military Governors, *The European Recovery Program* (Adjutant General, OMGUS); Louis, *British Empire in the Middle East*, 238.

44 Lapping, *End of Empire*, 245.

45 Louis, *British Empire in the Middle East*, 238.

46 Ibid., 241.

47 Ibid.

48 Mansfield, *Egypt*, 287–88; Goldschmidt Jr., *Modern Egypt*, 77; Louis, *British Empire in the Middle East*, 248–49.

49 Louis, *British Empire in the Middle East*, 248–49.

50 Mansfield, *Egypt*, 287.

51 Louis, *British Empire in the Middle East*, 248.

52 Lapping, *End of Empire*, 245.

53 Ibid.

54 Mansfield, *Egypt*, 288–89.

55 P.R.O./F.O. 141, 8581-132 "Half Yearly Report on the Egyptian Army." Prepared by the Chief of the British Military Mission to the Egyptian Army, June 1947.

56 Abd al-Wahhab Bakr "The Faulty Arms Myth and the Palestine War of 1948," *Arms Manufacture in Modern Egypt: History and Myth*, Occasional Papers Series, No. 17, Udo Heyn, ed. (Los Angeles: California State University), 26.

57 Ibid., 27–31.

58 Lapping, *End of Empire*, 250–53.

59 Mansfield, *Egypt*, 290–302.

60 Ibid., 304.

61 Lapping, *End of Empire*, 254–56; Goldschmidt Jr., *Modern Egypt*, 88–92; Mansfield, *Egypt*, 304–05.

62 Lapping, *End of Empire*, 257–59.

63 Mansfield, *Egypt*, 308–09.

64 Ibid., 309.

65 Goldschmidt Jr., *Modern Egypt*, 100.

66 Mansfield, *Egypt*, 310.

67 Goldschmidt Jr., *Modern Egypt*, 107.

68 Ansari, *Modern Iran*, 112–24; Mansfield and Pelham, *Middle East*, 281–82.

69 D. Neff, *Warriors at Suez* (Brattleboro, VT: Amana Books, 1988), 178–80.

70 Lapping, *End of Empire*, 262–73.

71 Goldschmidt, Jr., *Modern Egypt*, 107–10; Mansfield and Pelham, *Middle East*, 28–88; Neff, *Warriors at Suez*, 330–48; Lapping, *End of Empire*, 270–77.

72 Lapping, *End of Empire*, 270–77.

73 Ibid., 277.

74 Mansfield and Pelham, *Middle East*, 290–91.

75 William R. Polk, *Understanding Iraq* (New York, NY: Harper, 2005), 107–10.

76 Ibid., 118.

77 Lapping, *End of Empire*, 283.

78 IOR/20/C 1952 TSR/432, Top Secret, Government of Aden—Anti Terrorist/ Sedition Measures, 1966.

79 Lapping, *End of Empire*, 310.

BIBLIOGRAPHY

Primary sources

National archives

British Library, India Office Records.
British Foreign Office/Public Records Office.
British Foreign and State Papers.
Parliamentary Debates (London: Cornelius Buck Publishers, 1938).
Parliamentary Papers.

Secondary sources

Abd-al Rahman, Al-Jabarti, *Journal d'un notable du Caire durant l'expedition française, 1780–1801*, trans. Joseph Couq (Paris: Editions Albin Michel, 1979).

Abd al-Wahhab, Bakr, "The Faulty Arms Myth and the Palestine War of 1948", *Arms Manufacture in Modern Egypt: History and Myth*, Occasional Papers Series, no. 17, Udo Heyn (ed.) (Los Angeles: California State University, 1977).

Abd al-Wahhab Bakr, M., *al-Wujud al-Baritani fi al-Jarish al-Misri, 1937–1947* (Cairo, 1982).

Abdullah, T. A. J., *A Short History of Iraq* (London: Longman, 2003).

Abu-Lughod, I., *Arab Rediscovery of Europe; A Study in Cultural Encounters* (Princeton: Princeton University Press, 1963).

Adair, R., *The Negotiations for the Peace of the Dardanelles* (London: Longman, 1845).

Aitchison, C. U., *A Collection of Treaties, Engagements, and Sanads Relating to India and Neighboring Countries*, vol. XIII, *The Treaties Relating to Persia and Afghanistan* (Calcutta: Government of India, 1933).

A. J. Abdullah, Thabit. *A Short History of Iraq* (New York: Longman, 2003).

Al-Sayyid Marsot, A. L., *Egypt and Cromer: A Study in Anglo-Egyptian Relations* (New York: Praeger, 1968).

Al-Sayyid Marsot, A. L., *Egypt in the Reign of Muhammed Ali* (Cambridge: Cambridge University Press, 1984).

Amin, A. A., *British Interests in the Persian Gulf* (Leiden: E. J. Brill, 1967).

Ansari, Ali M., *Modern Iran Since 1921* (London: Longman, 2003).

Arthur, G., *The Letters of Lord and Lady Wolseley, 1870–1911* (New York: Doubleday, Page and Co.).

Baer, G., "Continuity and Change in Egyptian Rural Society, 1805–1882," *L'Égypte au XIXe Siècle.*

Bartlett, R., *A History of Russia* (London: Palgrave Macmillan, 2006).

Bayly, C. A., *Imperial Meridian: The British Empire and the World, 1780–1830* (London: Longman, 1989).

Bickerton, I. J. and Klausner, C. L., *A Concise History of the Arab-Israeli Conflict* (Englewood Cliffs, NJ: Prentice Hall, Second Edition, 1995).

Blaxland, G., *Objective Egypt* (London: Frederick Miller, 1966).

Blunt, W. S., *A Secret History of the English Occupation of Egypt* (New York: Alfred A. Knopf, 1922).

Bond, B., *Victorian Military Campaigns* (London: Hutchison and Co. Ltd., 1967).

Busch, B. C., *Britain and the Persian Gulf 1894–1914* (Berkeley: University of California Press, 1967).

Bradford, E. E., *Life of Admiral of the Fleet Sir Arthur Knyvet Wilson* (New York: E. P. Dutton, 1923).

Braun, G., *Europe and the French Imperium 1799–1814* (New York: Harper Torchbooks, 1963).

Brinton, C., *A Decade of Revolution 1789–1799* (New York: Harper Torchbooks, 1963).

British Documents on Foreign Affairs, Part I, Series B, The Near and Middle East, "The Ottoman Empire and North Africa: Intervention in Egypt and the Sudan, 1876–1885," Doc. 155 (New York: University Publications of America, 1984).

British Documents on Foreign Affairs, Part 1, Series B, "The Near and Middle East," Doc. 53 (no. 389A) "Granville to Dufferin, 11 July 1882" (New York: University Publications of America, 1984).

Broadley, A. M., *How We Defended Urabi and His Friends* (London: Chapman and Hall, 1884; Reprint, Cairo: Arab Research Publishing Center, 1981).

Brown, L. C., *International Politics and the Middle East: Old Rules, Dangerous Game* (Princeton: Princeton University Press, 1984).

Burt, A. L., *Evolution of the British Empire to Commonwealth from the American Revolution* (Boston: D. C. Heath Co., 1956).

Cain, P. J. and Hopkins, A. G., *British Imperialism: Innovation and Expansion 1688–1914* (London: Longman, 1993).

Cezzar, A., *Ottoman Egypt in the Eighteenth Century*, trans. S. J. Shaw (Cambridge, MA: Harvard University Press, 1962).

Charles-Roux, F., *Autour d'une route: L'Angleterre, l'isthme de Suez et l'Égypte au XVIIIme siècle* (Paris: 1922).

Charles-Roux, F., *Les origines de l'expedition d' Égypte* (Paris: Plon-Nourrit, 1910).

Chaudhuri, K. N., *The English East India Company, The Study of an Early Joint Stock Company 1600–1640* (London: Cass, 1965).

Chaudhuri, K. N., *The Trading World of Asia and the East India Company 1660–1760* (Cambridge: Cambridge University Press, 1978).

Churchill, W., *The Second World War: The Grand Alliance* (Boston: Houghton and Mifflin Co., 1950).

Clay, L. D., *Decision In Germany* (New York: Doubleday and Co. Inc., 1950).

Clowes, Sir W. L., *The Royal Navy: A History from the Earliest Times to the Death of Queen Victoria* (London: Sampson Low, Marston and Co., 1937).

Cole, J. R. I., *Colonialism and Revolution in the Middle East: Social and Cultural Origins of Egypt's Urabi Revolt* (Princeton: Princeton University Press, 1993).

Connell, J., *Wavell: Scholar and Soldier* (London: Collin, 1954).

Connelly, O., *The Epoch of Napoleon* (New York: Holt, Rinehart and Winston, 1972).

Crabites, P., *Americans in the Egyptian Army* (London: George Routledge and Sons, 1931).

Crecelius, D., *Al-Damurdashi's Chronicle of Egypt, 1688–1755*, trans. A. al-Wahhab Bakr (New York: E. J. Brill, 1991).

Crecelius, D., *Eighteenth Century Egypt: The Arab Manuscript Sources* (Claremont, CA: Regina Books, 1990).

Cromer, Lord, *Modern Egypt* (London: Macmillan, 1908).

Daly, M. W. (ed.), *The Cambridge History of Egypt*, vol. 2, *Modern Egypt* (Cambridge: Cambridge University Press, 2008).

Danvers, F. C., *Report on the India Office Records Relating to Persia and the Persian Gulf* (London: Eyre and Spottswoodie, 1975).

de Kusel, S. (Baron), *An Englishman's Recollections of Egypt, 1863–1887* (London: John Lane, 1915).

Dodwell, H., *The Cambridge History of India*, vol. 5 (Cambridge: University Press, 1929).

Dodwell, H., *The Founder of Modern Egypt: A Study of Muhammad Ali* (Cambridge: Cambridge University Press, 1931).

Donnison, F. S. V., *Civil Affairs and Military Government Central Organization and Plannings* (London: Her Majesty's Stationary Office, 1966).

Douglas, D. C., *English Historical Documents* (New York: Oxford University Press, 1977).

Elgood, P., *Egypt and the Army* (London: Oxford University Press, 1924).

Evans, T. (ed.), *The Killearn Diaries 1934–1946* (London: Sidgwick and Jackson, 1972).

Eversley, L. and Chirol, V., *The Turkish Empire from 1288 to 1914* (New York: Howard Fertig, 1969).

Farman, E. (US Consul-General in Cairo), *Egypt and its Betrayal: An Account of the Country during the Periods of Ismail and Tewfik Pashas, and of How England Acquired a New Empire* (New York: Grafton Press, 1885).

Farnie, D., *East and West of Suez: The Suez Canal in History* (Oxford: Clarendon Press, 1969).

Farwell, B., *Queen Victoria's Little Wars* (New York: W. W. Norton and Co., 1985).

Field, C., *Britain's Sea Soldiers: A History of the Royal Marines* (Liverpool: Lyceum Press, 1924).

Field, H., *On the Desert: With a Brief Overview of Recent Events in Egypt* (New York: Charles Scribner's Sons, 1883).

Figes, O., *The Crimean War, A History* (New York: Metropolitan Books, 2010).

Finkel, C., *Osman's Dream, The Story of the Ottoman Empire 1300–1923* (New York: Basic Books, 2008).

Fitzmaurice, E., *The Life of Granville George Loveson Gower* (London: Longmans, Green, and Co., 1905).

Fitzsimmons, M. A., *The Foreign Policy of the British Labor Government 1945–1951* (Notre Dame: Notre Dame University Press, 1953).

Fletcher, M., "The Suez Canal in World Shipping, 1869–1914," *Journal of Economic History*, vol. 18 (1958).

Forbes, A., "An American Criticism of the Egyptian Campaign," *The Nineteenth Century*, vol. 16 (1884).

Foster, W. (ed.), *The Embassy of Sir Thomas Roe to India, 1615–1619: As Narrated in his Journal and Correspondence* (London: Oxford University Press, 1926).

Fromkin, D., *A Peace to End All Peace* (New York: Avon Books, 1989).

Furber, H., "The Overland Route to India in the Seventeenth and Eighteenth Centuries," *Journal of Indian History*, vol. xxix (1951).

Furber, H., *Rival Empires of Trade in the Orient 1600–1800* (Minneapolis: University of Minnesota Press, 1978).

Garvin, J., *The Life of Joseph Chamberlain* (London: Macmillan, 1932).

Gelvin, J., *The Modern Middle East, A History* (New York: Oxford University Press, 2011).

Ghorbal, S., *The Beginnings of the Eastern Question and the Rise of Mohamed Ali* (London: 1928).

Gifford, P. and Louis, W., *France and Britain in Africa* (New Haven: Yale University Press, 1971).

Gilbert, M., *The Arab-Israeli Conflict: Its History in Maps* (Tel Aviv: Steimatzky Ltd., Fourth Edition, 1984).

Goldschmidt Jr. A., *A Concise History of the Middle East* (Boulder: Westview Press, 1988).

Goldschmidt Jr. A., *Modern Egypt: the Formation of a Nation State* (Boulder: Westview Press, 2004).

Goldschmidt Jr. A. and Davidson, L., *A Concise History of the Middle East* (Boulder: Westview Press, 2012.).

Goldstein, E., *The First World War Peace Settlements 1919–1925* (London: Longman, 2002).

Goodrich, C., "Report of the British Naval and Military Operations in Egypt, 1882," *House Miscellaneous Documents*, no. 29 (Washington: Government Printing Office, Office of Naval Intelligence, 1885).

Gordon, J., *The Other Desert War: British Social Forces in North Africa 1940–1943* (New York: Greenwood Press, 1987).

Gwynn, S. and Tuckwell, G. M., *The Life of the Right Hon. Sir Charles Dilke* (New York: Macmillan Co., 1917).

Hallberg, C., *The Suez Canal—Its History and Diplomatic Importance* (New York: Columbia University Press, 1931).

Hanioglu, M., *A Brief History of the Late Ottoman Empire* (Princeton: Princeton University Press, 2008).

Harris, B., *Nationalism and Revolution in Egypt: The Role of the Muslim Brotherhood* (London: Mouton and Co., 1964).

Harrison, R. T., *Gladstone's Imperialism in Egypt* (Westport: Greenwood Press, 1995).

Hertslet, E. and Hertslet, E. C. (eds), *British Foreign and State Papers* (London: William Ridgway, 1890).

Hirszowicz, L., *The Third Reich and the Arab East* (London: Routledge and Kegan Paul, 1966).

Hitti, P. K., *History of the Arabs from the Earliest Times to the Present* (New York: St. Martin's Press, 1967).

Hobsbawn, E., *Industry and Empire* (New York: Penguin Books, 1979).

Holland, B., *The Life of Spencer Compton, Eighth Duke of Devonshire* (Lord Hartington) (London: Longman, Green, and Co., 1911).

Holt, E., "Garnet Wolseley: A Soldier of the Empire," *History Today*, vol. 8, no. 7 (1958).

Hopkirk, P., *The Great Game: The Struggle for Empire in Central Asia* (New York: Kodansha International, 1994).

Hoskins, H. L., *British Routes to India* (New York: Longmans, Green and Company, 1928).

Hubatch, W., *The German Question* (New York: Herder Book Center, 1967).

Hurewitz, J., *Diplomacy in the Near and Middle East: A Documentary Record, 1555–1914* (Princeton: D. Van Nostrand Company, 1956).

Hyam, R., *Britain's Imperial Century, 1815–1914: A Study of Empire and Expansion* (London: Macmillan, Second Edition, 1995).

Issawi, C., *An Economic History of the Middle East and North Africa* (New York: Columbia University Press, 1982).

Jacobson, H. and Smith Jr., A. L., *World War II Policy and Strategy, Selected Documents with Commentary* (Santa Barbara: Clio Books, 1979).

Jenkins, T. A., *Gladstone, Whiggery and the Liberal Party, 1874–1886* (Oxford: Clarendon Press, 1988).

Kelly, J. B., *Britain and the Persian Gulf 1795–1880* (Oxford: Oxford University Press, 1968).

Kinross, Lord, *Between Two Seas: The Creation of the Suez Canal* (New York: William Morrow, 1969).

Knapland, P., *Gladstone's Foreign Policy* (New York: Harper and Brothers, 1939).

Landau, J., *Parliament and Parties in Egypt* (Tel Aviv: Israel Oriental Society, 1953).

Landes, D., *Bankers and Pashas: International Finance and Economic Imperialism in Egypt* (Cambridge, MA: Harvard University Press, 1958).

Lapping, B., *End of Empire* (New York: St. Martin's Press, 1985).

Lawson, F. H., *The Social Origins of Egyptian Expansionism during the Muhammad Ali Period* (New York: Columbia University Press, 1992).

Lewis, B., *The Emergence of Modern Turkey* (London: Oxford University Press, 1968).

Lewis, B., *Race and Slavery in the Middle East* (New York: Oxford University Press, 1992).

Little, T., *Modern Egypt* (New York: Praeger, 1967).

Lloyd, G., *Egypt Since Cromer*, vol. II (London: Macmillan and Co., Ltd., 1933).

Lloyd, T. O., *The British Empire 1553–1995* (New York: Oxford University Press, Second Edition, l996).

Lockhart, L., *Nadir Shah. A Critical Study Based Mainly on Contemporary Sources* (London: Luzac and Company, 1938).

Lorimer, J. G., *Gazetteer of the Persian Gulf and Oman and Central Arabia*, vol. I, part I (Calcutta: Government Printing, India, 1915).

Louis, W. R., *The British Empire in the Middle East* (Oxford: Clarendon Press, 1984).

Louis, W. R. and Stookey, R. W. (eds.), *The End of the Palestine Mandate* (Austin: University of Texas Press, 1986).

Lyons, M. J., *World War I: A Short History* (Englewood Cliffs, NJ: Prentice Hall, 2000).

Lyons, M. J., *World War II: A Short History* (Englewood Cliffs, NJ: Prentice Hall, Second Edition, 1994).

Macfie, A. L., *The Eastern Question 1774–1923* (New York: Longman, 1989).

Macfie, A. L., *The Eastern Question 1774–1923* (New York: Longman, 1994).

Mackenzie, D. and Curran, M. W., *A History of Russia, the Soviet Union and Beyond* (Belmont, CA: Wadsworth, Inc., 1993).

Mackesy, P., *The War in the Mediterranean, 1803–1810* (New York: Longman, 1957).

Mansfield, P., *The British in Egypt* (New York: Holt, Rinehart, and Winston, 1971).

Mansfield, P., *A History of the Middle East* (New York: Penguin Books, 1991).

Mansfield, P. and Pelham, N., *A History of the Middle East* (New York: Penguin Books, 2013).

Markham, F., *Napoleon* (New York: A Mentor Book, 1963).

Marlowe, J., *A History of Modern Egypt and Anglo-Egyptian Relations, 1800–1956* (Hamden, CT: Archon Books, 1956).

Marlowe, J., *Anglo-Egyptian Relations: 1800–1953* (New York: Cresset Press, 1954).

Marlowe, J., *World Ditch: The Making of the Suez Canal* (New York: Macmillan, 1964).

Marlowe, J., *Perfidious Albion* (London: Elek Books, 1971).

Matthew, H. C. G., *The Gladstone Diaries with Cabinet Minutes and Prime Ministerial Correspondence* (Oxford: Clarendon Press, 1990), January 1881 to June 1883.

Maurice, J., *Military History of the Campaign of 1882 in Egypt* (London: J. B. Howard and Son, 1883, Reprint, 1973).

Mellini, P., *Sir Eldon Gorst: The Overshadowed Proconsul* (Stanford: The Hoover Institution, 1977).

Moir, M., *A General Guide to the India Office Records* (London: The British Library, 1988).

Monroe, E., *Britain's Moment in the Middle East 1914–1956* (London: Methuen Paperbacks, 1965).

Murphy, D., *The Arab Revolt 1916–1918, Lawrence sets Arabia ablaze* (Oxford: Osprey Publishing, 2008).

Napier, C., *The War in Syria* (London: John W. Parker, Harrison and Company, 1842).

Neff, D., *Warriors at Suez* (Brattleboro, VT: Amana Books, 1988).

Neguib, M., *Egypt's Destiny* (London: Victor Gollancz Ltd., 1955).

Newman, E., *Great Britain in Egypt* (London: Cassell and Co. Ltd.).

Northridge, F. S., *British Foreign Policy* (New York: Frederick A. Praeger Pub., 1962).

Nutting, A., *Nasser* (London: Constable, 1972).

O'Rourke, V., "The Juristic Status of Egypt and the Sudan," *Johns Hopkins University Studies in History and Political Science,* series 53, no. 1, 30–31 (1935).

Ovendale, R., *The Middle East since 1914* (London: Longman, 1992).

Ovendale, R., *The Origins of the Arab-Israeli Wars* (New York: Longman, Third Edition, 1999).

Pamuk, S., *The Ottoman Empire and European Capitalism, 1820–1913* (Cambridge: Cambridge University Press, 1987).

Polson-Newman, E. W., *Great Britain in Egypt* (London: Cassell and Co., 1923).

Polk, William R., *Understanding Iraq* (New York: Harper, 2005).

Porter, B., *The Lion's Share, A Short History of British Imperialism 1850–1983* (New York: Longman, Second Edition, 1989).

Pridham, A. R. (ed.), *The Arab Gulf and the West* (New York: St. Martin's Press, 1985).

Ramm, A., *Political Correspondence of Mr. Gladstone and Lord Granville, 1876–1893* (Oxford: Clarendon Press, 1962).

Ratliff, W. G., "Sykes-Picot Agreement of 1916," in J. S. Olson (ed.), *Historical Dictionary of the British Empire*, 1077–78 (Westport, CT: Greenwood Press, 1996.).

Refaat Bey, M., *The Awakening of Modern Egypt* (Lahore: Premier Book House, 1976).

Riasanovsky, N., *A History of Russia* (New York: Oxford University Press, 1993).

Riasanovsky, N. and Steinberg, M., *A History of Russia* (New York: Oxford University Press, 2011).

Rich, N., *Great Power Diplomacy Since 1914* (New York: McGraw-Hill, 2003).

Richmond, J. C. B., *Egypt, 1798–1952: Her Advance toward a Modern Identity* (New York: Columbia University Press, 1977).

Robinson, R., Gallagher, J. and Denny, A., *Africa and the Victorians* (London: Macmillan, Second Edition, 1981).

Robinson, R., Gallagher, J. and Denny, A., *Africa and the Victorians: The Official Mind of Imperialism* (London: Macmillan Education Ltd, 1988).

Saab, A. P., *The Reluctant Icon: Gladstone, Bulgaria, and the Working Classes, 1856–1878* (Cambridge, MA: Harvard University Press, 1991).

Sadat, A., *Revolt on the Nile* (London: Allan Wingate, 1957).

Scholch, A., *Egypt for the Egyptians! The Socio-Political Crisis in Egypt, 1878–1882* (London: Ithaca Press, 1981).

Scholch, A., "'Men on the Spot' and the English Occupation of Egypt in 1882," *The Historical Journal*, vol. 19, no. 3 (1976).

Scholch, A., "The Formation of a Peripheral State: Egypt, 1854–1882," *L'Égypte au XIXe Siècle* (Paris: Colloques Internationaux du Centre national de la Rechereche Scientifique, 1982).

Scott, P. C., *Fifty Years in the Royal Navy* (London: John Murray, 1919).

Shannon, R. T., *Gladstone and the Bulgarian Agitation, 1876* (Hamden, CT: Archon Books, 1975).

Shaw, J., *Charter Relating to East India Company* (Madras: 1887).

Shaw, S. J., *Between Old and New* (Cambridge, MA: Harvard University Press, 1971).

Shaw, S. J. and Shaw, E., *History of the Ottoman Empire and Modern Turkey* (Cambridge: Cambridge University Press, 1977).

Smith, C. D., *Palestine and the Arab-Israeli Conflict* (New York: St. Martin's, Fourth Edition, 2001).

Spear, P., *A History of India*, vol. 2 (New York: Penguin Books, 1981).

Spear, P., *A History of India*, vol. II (New York: Penguin Books, Reprint, 1983).

Stansky, P., *Gladstone: A Progress in Politics* (London: W. W. Norton, 1979).

Stone, F., "Diary of an American Girl in Cairo, During the War of 1882," *The Century*, vol. 28, New Series, vol. 6 (May to October 1884).

Stone, F., "Incidents at Alexandria," *The Century*, vol. 27, New Series, vol. 6 (May to October 1884).

Stone, C., "Introductory Letter," *The Century Magazine*, vol. 23, New Series, vol. 6 (May to October 1884).

Taylor, A. J. P., *A History of the First World War* (New York: Berkley Medallion, 1966).

Taylor, A. J. P., *The Struggle for Mastery in Europe, 1848–1919* (Oxford: Clarendon Press, 1954).

Temperly, H. and Penson, L., *The Foundations of British Foreign Policy from Pitt to Salisbury or Documents, Old and New* (Cambridge: Cambridge University Press, 1938).

The Annual Register; A Public Review of Events at Home and Abroad (London: Riorigtons Publishers, 1883).

The Orabi Revolution (Cairo: Arab Republic of Egypt, Ministry of Information, State Information Service, 1984).

Tignor, R., *Modernization and British Colonial Rule in Egypt, 1882–1914* (Princeton: Princeton University Press, 1966).

US and UK Military Governors, *The European Recovery Program* (Adjutant General, OMGUS, June 1949).

Vatikiotis, P., *The Egyptian Army in Politics: Pattern for New Nations* (Bloomington: Indiana University Press, 1961).

Wallace, D., *Egypt and the Egyptian Question* (New York: Russell and Russell, 1967).

Waller, J. H., *Beyond the Khyber Pass, The Road to British Disaster in the First Afghan War* (Austin: University of Texas Press, 1990).

Ward, A. and Gooch, P., *The Cambridge History of British Foreign Policy 1793–1919* (New York: Macmillan, 1923).

Wilson, T., *The Myriad Faces of War: Britain and the Great War 1914-1918* (Cambridge, UK: Polity Press, 1986).

Wilson, A. T., *The Persian Gulf: An Historical Sketch from the Earliest Times to the Beginning of the Twentieth Century* (Oxford: Clarendon Press, 1928).

Wilson, A. T., *The Suez Canal: Its Past, Present, and Future* (Oxford: Oxford University Press, 1933).

Wood, A. C., *A History of the Levant Company* (Oxford: Oxford University Press, 1955).

Young, P., *A Short History of World War II: 1939–1945* (New York: Thomas Y. Crowell, 1966).

Zayid, M., *Egypt's Struggle for Independence* (Beirut: Khayat's Publishers, 1965).

INDEX

Page numbers in *italics* refer to figures and page numbers in **bold** refer to maps.

Abbas I of Egypt   75, 77–8, 79
Abbas I, Shah of Persia   4, 5–6
Abbas II, Khedive of Egypt   115, 116
Abbas II, Shah of Persia   8
al-Abdali, Ahmad I, Sultan
        of Lahej   36
Abdin Palace Incident (1942)   177
Abdulla I, King of Jordan   135, 142,
        144–5, 148, 161, 176
Abdullah of Hejaz, Regent of
        Iraq   175, 176
Abdulmecid I, Sultan of Ottoman
        Empire   49, 79
Abdur Rahman Khan, Amir
        of Afghanistan   152
Abercromby, Sir Ralph   30
Adair, Robert (British diplomat)   34
Aden   36, 117, 230 n.60
    British occupation of   50–1,
        153, 230 n.66
    British withdrawal from   207
    Crown colony   206–7
    Front for the Liberation of Occupied
        South Yemen   207
    National Liberation Front   207
al-Afghani, Jamal al-Din (Muslim
        reformer)   87
Afghanistan
    Anglo-Afghan Treaty of 1921   153
    Battle of Maiwand (1880)   152
    British dependency   152
    British threat perception of   37
    First Afghan War (1838–42)   55–61
    invasion of Persia   9–10
    Soviet Union and   153
    Third Afghan War (1919)   153

Africa. *See also* Egypt
    colonization of   112
    First World War and   **125**
agents/agency. *See* East India Company
        agents/agency
agriculture, in Egypt   73
Ainslie, Sir Robert (British ambassador
        to Ottoman Empire)   20–1, 23
AIOC. *See* Anglo-Iranian Oil Company
ALA. *See* Arab Liberation Army
Albania   170, 175
Alexander I, Czar of Russia   31, 34, 38
Alexandria
    British bombardment and
        invasion of   98–101, 106
    British navy at   95, 96, 98
    British troops withdrawal (1947)
        from   200
    clashes at   96–7
Alexandria Convention (1841)   52–3
Ali Mahir Pasha, Prime Minister of
        Egypt   159, 172
Ali Shah, Mulla (admiral of the
        Persian fleet)   12
Alison, Charles (British agent in
        Tehran)   65–6
Allenby, Edmund   127, 130, 134–5,
        139, 149–50, 156–7, 160
Anatolian Railway Company   118
Anglo-Afghan Treaty of 1921   153
Anglo-American Committee of Inquiry
        (1946)   192
Anglo-Egyptian Agreement
        (1953)   201–2
Anglo-Egyptian Treaty of 1936   157–9,
        178, 199

Anglo-Egyptian War (1882)   98–101
Anglo-German Convention (1914)   118
Anglo-Iranian Oil Company
        (AIOC)   127, 170, 181–2
    nationalization of   203–4
Anglo-Iraqi Treaty (1930)   175, 176
Anglo-Iraqi War (1941)   175–6
Anglo-Persian Agreement (1919)   151
Anglo-Persian Oil Company. *See*
        Anglo-Iranian Oil Company
Anti-Comintern Pact (1936)   170
ANZAC. *See* Australian and
        New Zealand Army Corps
Arab Bureau (Cairo)   135, 139
Arab Bureau (Damascus)   136
Arab-Jewish Council   163, 164
Arab League   185–6, 194, 196, 198
Arab Legion   176
Arab Liberation Army (ALA)   196
Arab revolt (1916–18)   131–2, 135–6,
        139–40
Arab revolt in Palestine (1936–39)   165
Arab state
    promises for   130, 131, 133–4,
        142, 144, 146, 147
Armenia   150, 151
army, British
    ANZAC   124, 126, 137
    Indian troops   106, 124, 126, 127–8,
        129, 132, 136, 176
army, Egyptian
    Abdin Palace Incident (1942)
        and   177
    autonomy and native command   158
    downsizing   72, 73–4, 87
    enlargement and training   81, 160
    First World War and   126–7
    Free Officer Corps   156, 172–3,
        183, 197, 201
    Labor Corps   127
    modernization of   158, 159, 160
    Second World War and   172, 177–8
    Sinai and Palestinian Campaign
        (1917–18)   126
    Urabi revolt and   87, 91–2
Army of the Indus   59
Asquith, Herbert Henry, Earl
        of, Prime Minister of
        United Kingdom   124

Aswan High Dam (Egypt)   203, 205
Ataturk, Mustafa Kemal, President of
        Turkey   124, 140, 151
Atlantic Charter (1941)   179
Attlee, Clement, Prime Minister of
        United Kingdom   189–90, 191,
        192, 198
Auckland, George Eden, Governor-
        General of India
    First Afghan War (1838–42)
        and   56, 58–60
    Mehmet Ali and   50, 229 n.56,
        230 n.59
    Russian threat perception and   55, 56
Australian and New Zealand Army
        Corps (ANZAC)   124, 126, 137
Austria
    assassination of Archduke Franz
        Ferdinand   122
    Crimean War and   64
    Egyptian-Ottoman War
        (1839–41)   52
    German annexation of   170
    Napoleon and   26
    post-First World War   140
    War of the Second Coalition
        (1798–1801) and   28
    War of the Third Coalition
        (1805–07) and   33
Ayub Khan, Mohammad, Amir of
        Afghanistan   152

Baath Party (Iraq)   206
Baghdad   65, 66, 129, 136
Baghdad Pact (1955)   202, 203,
        205, 206
Bahrain
    Britain and   117, 118
    Persia's claims to   44–5
Baldwin, George (British merchant and
        diplomat)   20–4, 78
Balfour, Arthur James Balfour, Earl
        of, Prime Minister of United
        Kingdom   137
Balfour Declaration (1917)   130,
        137–40, 144, 161, 162
Balkans
    nationalism in   122
    Second World War in   174–5

Bandar Abbas   6, 7, 8, 9, 11, 12, 182
Baring, Sir Evelyn, Controller-General
    of Egypt   87, 107, 114, 116
al-Barudi, Mahmoud Sami,
    Prime Minister of Egypt   92, 95
Basra   8, 10, 19
    First World War and   127
    Karim Khan's invasion of   16, 35
    Pashalik   14
    strategic importance to
        British   11–12
Battle of Britain (1940)   171
Battle of El Alamein (1942)   179
Battle of El Obeid   107–9
Battle of Jutland (1916)   129
Battle of Kassassin (1882)   99
Battle of Maiwand (1880)   152
Battle of Megiddo (1918)   140
Battle of Omburman   112–14
Battle of Stalingrad (1942–43)   179
Battle of Tannenburg (1914)   123
Battle of Tel el-Kabir (1882)   *100*
    Sudanese Muslims and   106
Battle of the Nile (1798)   26, 27
Battle of the Pyramids (1798)   26, 27
Battle of the Somme (1916)   127
Battle of Verdun (1916)   127
BBC Iranian Service   182
Begin, Menachim (Leader of
    Irgun)   184
Belgium
    African colonies of   112
    Schlieffen Plan and   122
Bengal Government   18, 231 n.71.
        See also Government of (British)
        India
    Egyptian trade and communications
        and   19–20
    Persia and   37
Berlin–Baghdad Railway   116–18, 120
Berlin Congress (1878)   86
Bernadotte, Folke (Swedish
    diplomat)   196
Best, Thomas, Captain   4
Bevin, Ernest, Foreign Secretary   192,
    194–5, 198–200
Bismarck, Otto von, Chancellor of
    Germany   83, 86, 111
Blunt, Wilfrid S. (poet)   88

Bombay Marine   14, 17, 45
    Arab piracy threat and   42, 43
Bombay Presidency   5, 10, 11, 12, 15,
    16, 18, 37. *See also* Government
    of (British) India
Bosnian Annexation Crisis (1909)   122
Briggs, Samuel (British agent in
    Alexandria)   32
Britain. *See also* East India Company;
        Foreign Office (Britain)
    Afghan threat perception   37
    African colonies   112
    Arab piracy and   41–2, 43–4
    Arab slave trade and   42, 45–7
    Atlantic Charter (1941)   179
    Cairo Conference (1943)   180–1
    Casablanca Conference (1943)   180
    "Eastern Question" (*see* Gladstone,
        William; Palmerston, Henry
        John Temple)
    First World War and   122, 123–30,
        210–11
    General Maritime Treaty of
        1820   43–5
    German threat perception   116–18
    gunboat diplomacy of   **119**, 157
    imperial power and political
        dominance   38–9, 42, 105–6
    decline of   187, 189–91
    Japanese administrators for Middle
        East proposal   136
    Lend-Lease Act (1941)   179
    Munich Agreement (1938)   170
    Operation Sea Lion and   171
    Orders in Council   38
    political dominance
        (1815–42)   60–1
    protectorates and dependencies in
        Persian Gulf   35–6, 49–50,
        116–18, 120, 153
    Red Sea passage control   29–30
    Russian threat perception   55–6, 65,
        86, 116–17
    steamship network   **76**, 77, 229 n.57
    Tehran Conference (1943)   181
    War of the Second Coalition
        (1798–1802) and   28–9, 31
    War of the Third Coalition
        (1803–07) and   31–3

British Commonwealth   190–1
British consuls
    in Alexandria   97
    in Basra   14
    in Cairo   20, 22, 23–4, 33, 52
    in Egypt   83, 88
    in Ottoman Empire   2
British Zionist Federation   137
Bruce, James (traveler and
        explorer)   19
Brussilov Offensive (1916)   129, 140
Brydon, William (surgeon)   59
Bulgaria   122
    Bulgarian Massacres (1876)   86
Burnes, Sir Alexander (traveler and
        explorer)   56, 58, 59
Bushire   6, 12, 14, 37, 46

Cabot, Sebastian (Venetian explorer)   1
Cairo   20, 22, 23–4, 33, 111
    Arab Bureau in   135, 139
    British troops withdrawal (1947)
        from   200
Cairo Conference (1943)   180–1
Cairo Radio   203, 205–6
Campbell, P. (British agent in
        Cairo)   37, 51, 228 n.43,
        229 n.55, 229 n.57, 230 n.60,
        230 n.66, 231 n.71
Canning, Charles Canning, Earl,
        Governor-General of India   78
capitulatory system in Egypt   77
    termination of   158
Casablanca Conference (1943)   180
Catholics   64
Chamberlain, Joseph, Trade
        Secretary   86, 94, 103–4
Chamberlain, Neville, Prime Minister of
        United Kingdom   166–7, 170–1
Chiang, Kai-shek, President of the
        Republic of China   180
China   169
Churchill, Sir Winston, Prime Minister
        of United Kingdom   149
    in Egypt   113–14
    Egypt and   148, 198, 201
    First World War and   123, 124
    Second World War and   171, 172,
        173–4, 178–9, 180, 181

Zionist cause and   137, 162, 163–4,
        171, 184
Clive, Robert, Governor of the
        Presidency of Fort William   13
coffee trade   17–18, 51
Collingwood, Charles, Admiral   33
Colvin, Auckland, Controller-General
        of Egypt   87, 88, 95
commercial relations
    Anglo-Ottoman   50
    Anglo-Persian, seventeenth and
        eighteenth century   9–11
    Dutch-Persian   7–8
Committee of Union and
        Progress   132, 133
communications and trade, through
        Egypt   18–24, 50, 231 n.71,
        232 n.78
Concert of Europe   53
Congress of Vienna (1815), anti-slave
        trade provisions   42, 44
Constantinople Conference (1882)   98,
        110–11
constitutionalism, in Egypt   88, 104–5
Continental System   38, 49
Cookson, Charles Alfred (British
        Consul at Alexandria)   97
Cornwallis, Sir Kinahan (British
        Ambassador to Iraq)   184
Courteen Association   8
Cox, Sir Percy   146
Crimean War (1853–56)   64–8
Cromer, Lord. See Baring, Sir
        Evelyn, Controller-General
        of Egypt
Cromwell, Oliver, Lord Protector   8
Curzon, George Nathaniel, Marquis
        of, Viceroy of India   136, 150,
        151, 153
Czechoslovakia   170

al-Dahab, Mohammed Abou (Mamluk
        ruler and regent of Ottoman
        Egypt)   19
Daladier, Edouard, Prime Minister of
        France   170
Dalrymple, Alexander
        (hydrogapher)   29, 222 n.30
Damascus   139, 140, 142, 144

Dardanelles 150
Dayan, Moshe, Commander of
    Haganah 176
de Blignieres, M. 82
Deir Yassin massacre (1948) 195
De Lesseps, Ferdinand (French
    diplomat) 78, 79, 94, 100
Dervish Pasha (Egypt's Ottoman
    representative) 106
Devonshire, Spencer Compton
    Cavendish, Duke of 91, 105–6
Dilke, Sir Charles, Foreign
    Undersecretary 91, 92
Dinshaway incident (1906) 116
Disraeli, Benjamin, Prime Minister
    of United Kingdom 82, 83,
    84, 85–6
Dost Mohammed, Amir of
    Afghanistan 56, 60
Dufferin and Ava, Frederick Temple
    Blackwood, Marquis of (British
    Ambassador to Ottoman
    Empire) 106
Dulles, John Foster, US Secretary of
    State 203
Dundas, Lord Henry, Privy
    Councilor 21, 22, 23
Dutch East India Company (VOC) 3,
    7–8, 9

East India Company. See also
    Government of (British) India
    Anglo-Persian expedition (1622) 6
    coffee trade 17–18
    competition from other English
        companies 8–9
    dissolution of 69
    Dutch threat 7–8, 9
    establishment of 2, 3
    expansion into Egypt 18–24
    Mehmet Ali and 50–1, 229 n.55,
        230 n.59, 230 n.60, 231 n.71,
        232 n.78
    Mughal Empire fermans and 4–5,
        6–7
    Muscat and 29–30, 35, 42–3
    Oman and 35, 42–3
    Ottoman Empire and 14, 15–16
        1618 ferman 17

Persia and
    during eighteenth century 9–12,
        14–15
    during Karim Khan's reign 12,
        15, 16
    fermans 5, 6–7, 14–15
    impact of Shah Abbas I's death 7
    Persian Gulf and 16–17, 45–6
    expansion into 29–30, 35
    piracy threat 14, 15–16, 42–3
    Trucial Coast 34–5
    private trade issue 13
    reforms 42
    Regulating Act of 1773 and 18
East India Company agents/agency.
    See also Roe, Sir Thomas
    in Alexandria 32
    in Basra 14, 15
    in Egypt 77–8
    in Gulf 14
    in Mocha 18
    in Muscat 29–30
    in Persia 10, 12
Eden, Anthony, Foreign Secretary 157,
    165, 174, 178, 184, 201, 202,
    203, 204, 205
Edward VI, King of England 1
Egypt. See also Arab League;
    Mehmet Ali, Governor of Egypt
    Abdin Palace Incident (1942) 177
    agriculture 73
    Alexandria Convention (1841) 52–3
    Anglo-Egyptian Treaty of
        1936 157–9, 178, 200
    Anglo-French joint financial
        control of 82
    Anglo-French joint support
        of khedive 92
    Anglo-French rivalries in 78–9
    army of 72, 73–4, 87, 126–7, 156,
        158, 160, 172–3, 177–8, 183
    Aswan High Dam 203, 205
    British continued occupation (1922–
        39) of 156–60
    British invasion (1801) of 30–1
    British invasion (1807) of 33–4
    British occupation (1882–1914)
        of 98–101, 103–12, 115–16
    British protectorate 124, 130, 148–9

British withdrawal from 197–203
budget crisis 92–3
call for British withdrawal
    from 103–5
capitulatory system 77, 158
civil war 31, 32
claim to Sudan 198, 199–200, 202
constitution (1923) 150
constitutionalism 104–5
  birth of 88
cotton industry 73
declaration of war against Axis
    powers 183
dismissal of Ismail Pasha 83, 84, 86
Dinshaway incident (1906) 116
East India Company and 18–24
European population in 75, 77
First World War and 124, 126–7
French canal building
    schemes 78, 79–80
French commercial interests
    in 21, 22–3
French invasion (1798–1802)
    of 25–31
German defeat (1942) 179
German invasion (1941–42)
    of 177
independence campaign
    (1919–22) 148–50 (see also
    Egypt, nationalist movement)
internal politics (1942–45) of 182–3
Italian invasion (1940) of 172–4
London Convention (1840)
    and 71–4, 86, 101
modernization and expansion under
    Ismail Pasha 81–2
modernization under Mehmet Ali 48
Muslim resistance in 106
nationalist movement 115–16
nationalist movement/Urabi
    revolt 87–8, 91–8
Palestinian crisis and 159, 200–1
railroads 77–8
Revolution of 1919 148–9
Revolution of 1952 201
route to the East and **108**
Second Egyptian-Ottoman War
    (1839–41) 52–3
Second World War and 172–4, 176–8
self-government 81–2
steamship connections to 77,
    229 n.57
strategic importance to Britain
    19–20, 29, 33, 49–50
  post-First World War 155–6
Taba affair (1906) 116
terrorism in 156
Westernized Egyptians 74
Egyptian Military Academy 160
Elfi Bey 33–4
Elgin, Thomas Bruce, Earl of (British
    Ambassador to Ottoman
    Empire) 30, 36
Elgood, P. G., Colonel 127
Elphinstone, Mountstuart, Governor of
    Bombay 44
Entente Cordiale (1904) 115
Ethiopia 157, 169–70
Exodus 1947 (ship) 194–5

Fakhri Pasha, Governor of
    Medina 135, 139
Fane, Sir Henry (commander in chief of
    all Indian forces) 58
Faroukh I, King of Egypt and the
    Sudan 160, 172, 177, 199, 201
Fashoda incident (1898) *113*, 114–16
Feisal I, King of Iraq 135, 139, 140,
    142–3, 144, 147, 148, 161, 164,
    175
fermans. *See* trade agreements
First Anglo-Afghan War
    (1838–42) 55–61
First Battle of the Marne (1914) 123
First World War (1914–18)
  Eastern Front 129
  end of 140
  imperial defense **125**
  in Middle East 124–30
  prelude and progress of 121–4
  in Western Front 129, 139, 140
Five Power Straits Convention
    (1841) 63–4
FLOSY. *See* Front for the Liberation of
    Occupied South Yemen
Foreign Office (Britain)
  Arab sheikhdoms and 36
  Arab slave trade elimination 46

"Committee to consider the affairs of
    Egypt" 91
Egypt and 21, 22, 23, 31, 32, 50,
    52, 172, 173
First World War and 124
Government of (British) India
    and 41–2
Middle East and 132, 133
objections to Suez Canal
    construction 80
Palestine issue and 131, 165, 166
Urabi revolt and 91, 97
France
African colonies of 112
Allied invasion (1944) of 181, 186
capture of Tunis 88, 89, 91
Continental System 38
Crimean War (1853–56) and 67
dual entente with Russia 112
Egypt
    Anglo-French financial
        control of 82
    Anglo-French support for
        khedive 92
    canal building schemes 78–80
    commercial interests in 21, 22–3
    defeat in 30–1
    invasion (1798–1802) of 25–9
    opposition to British occupation
        of 111
Entente Cordiale (1904) 115
Fashoda incident 113, 114–16
First World War and 123
German occupation of 170–1
interests and influences in Jedda 30
interests in Persia 36–7
mandates in Middle East 142, 144
Munich Agreement (1938) 170
Second World War and 170–1, 181,
    186
Suez Crisis (1956) 204
Sykes-Picot Agreement (1916) 123
Triple Entente (1907) 115
War of the Second Coalition
    (1798–1802) 28–9, 31
War of the Third Coalition
    (1803–07) 31–3
Francis, Sir Philip (Bengal council
    member) 19–20

Franz Ferdinand, Archduke of
    Austria 122
Frazer, A. Mackenzie, General 33–4
Free Officers movement (Egypt) 156,
    172–3, 183, 197, 201
Front for the Liberation of Occupied
    South Yemen (FLOSY) 207
Fuad I, King of Egypt 150, 156

Gallipoli Campaign (1915–16)
    123–4
Gambetta, Leon, Prime Minister of
    France 92
al-Gaylani, Rashid Ali, Prime Minister
    of Iraq 176
Gaza 134
General Maritime Treaty (1820)
    43–5
George V, King of
    United Kingdom 122
German-Soviet Non-Aggression Pact
    (1939) 170
Germany
African colonies of 112
Allied zone occupation of 190
    Jewish refugee problem 192
Anglo-German Convention
    (1914) 118
Anti-Comintern Pact (1936) 170
Battle of Jutland (1916) 129
Battle of Tannenburg (1914) 123
Berlin–Baghdad Railway 116–18,
    120
defeat (1945) of 186
Egypt and 83, 86, 111
First World War and 122, 123,
    128, 129
invasion of Britain 171
invasion of Egypt 177
invasion of Iraq 175
invasion of Soviet Union 175, 179
Mesopotamia and 128
Nuremberg Laws (1935) 165
Rome-Berlin Axis (1936) 157, 170
Schlieffen Plan 122
Second World War and 170–1, 175,
    177, 179, 186
territorial expansion (1935–39)
    of 170–1

Treaty of Brest-Litovsk (1918)
and   137
Tripartite Pact (1940)   179
Triple Alliance (1882)   111, 112
Ghazi I, King of Iraq   175
Gladstone, William, Prime Minister of
United Kingdom
Afghanistan and   152
Eastern policy of   85, 86, 88–9, 92,
93, 94, 95–101, 103
Khartoum siege and   109
on nationalism   84
Ottoman Empire and   111
personal investments in Egypt   89
views on Suez Canal   75, 79–80
Glubb, Sir John, Commander of Arab
Legion   176, 204
Gordon, Charles, General   81, 106,
109, 112
Gorst, Sir Eldon, Consul-General in
Egypt   116
government of (British) India
Afghanistan and   153
Arab piracy and   41, 43
Arab slave trade and   45, 46
British government and   210
envoy to Persia   37–8
Mehmet Ali relations and   50–1
Mesopotamia and   127–9, 132,
146–7
Middle East and   124, 136
Pitt's India Bill (1784) and   42
support for Ibn Saud   139, 143
Granville, Granville George
Leveson-Gower, Earl,
Foreign Secretary   88, 92, 93,
95, 98, 103, 104, 106
Greater East Asia Co-prosperity
Sphere   169
Greece
Greek Revolt (1821)   48–9
Second World War in   174–5
Grenville, William Wyndham Grenville,
Baron, Foreign Secretary   23
Grey, Sir Edward, Foreign
Secretary   122–2
gunboat diplomacy   119, 157
Gurion, David Ben, Prime Minister of
Israel   166, 195

Habibullah Khan, Amir of
Afghanistan   152
Haganah (Jewish force)   176, 183–4,
193, 195
Haikal, Mohammed, Senator   158
Haines, J. B., Commander   230 n.66
Halifax, Edward Frederick Wood,
Earl of, Foreign Secretary   160
Hamilton, Ian, Field
Commander   124
Hartington, Lord. See Devonshire,
Spencer Compton Cavendish,
Duke of
Hastings, Francis Rawdon,
Marquis of   43
Hastings, Warren, Governor-General of
Bengal   18, 19
Havelock, Henry   59
Hawkins, William, Commander   4
Hejaz   132, 134, 139, 143
Hertslet, Sir Edward   91
Herzl, Theodore   161–2
Hicks, William, General   105, 107
Hindenburg, Paul von, President of
Germany   123
Hitler, Adolf, Fuhrer of Germany   157,
164, 175
expansionist aims   170–1
persecution of Jews   165, 183, 184
Hobhouse, Sir John, President of Board
of Control for India   58
Hodges, J. Lloyd   231 n.71, 231 n.72
Hursev Pasha (governor of Egypt)   32
Hussein bin Ali, Sheriff of Mecca
and King of Hejaz   130–2, 135,
137, 138, 139–40, 143, 146
al-Husseini, Amin, Grand Mufti of
Jerusalem   163, 164, 165, 175,
176, 196, 200
Hussein, Saddam, President of
Iraq   207

Ibn Saud, Abdulaziz, King of Saudi
Arabia   139, 165, 185
Ibrahim Pasha of Egypt   48, 49, 50,
52, 75, 229 n.55
India. See also government of (British)
India
Bengal Lancers   106

Britain's military recruiting
    ground 171
decolonization in 190
East India Company and
    eighteenth century 13–14
    during Mughal reign 4–7
    Sepoy Mutiny (1857) 68–9
European intrusions 3–7
independence 191
Indian troops in British army 106,
    124, 126, 127–8, 129, 132, 136,
    176
Indian National Congress 110, 191
India Office 91, 136, 146, 147
Iran. See also Persia
    1953 coup d'état 203–4
    internal politics (1942–45) of 181–2
    Second World War and 179, 181
    Soviet-British occupation of 182
    United Nations membership 182
Iraq. See also Mesopotamia
    1958 coup d'état 206
    Anglo-Iraqi Treaty (1930) 175, 176
    claim to Kuwait 207
    Iraqi Revolt (1920) 147–8
    Second World War in 175–6, 179
Irgun (Zionist paramilitary
    organization) 184, 193
    Deir Yassin massacre (1948) 195
    Sergeants affair (1947) 194
Islamic Union 106
Ismail Pasha, Khedive of Egypt and
    Sudan 80, 81–4, 86, 199
Israel. See also Jews; Palestine; Zionism
    new state of 195–6
    Palestinian Arabs in 195–7
    Sinai campaign (1956) 204–5
Italy
    Allied invasion of 181
    invasion of Egypt (1940) 172–4
    invasion of Ethiopia (1935) 157,
        169–70
    invasion of Greece (1940) 174–5
    Rome-Berlin Axis (1936) 157, 170
    Tripartite Pact (1940) 179

Jahangir, Mughal Emperor 4
Jamal I (commander-in-chief of
    Medina) 135

James I, King of England 4, 5
Japan
    Anti-Comintern Pact (1936) 170
    attack on Pearl Harbor 179
    expansion of 169, 179
    surrender (1945) of 186
    Tripartite Pact (1940) 179
Jedda 30
Jerusalem 134–5, 161
    King David Hotel bombing
        (1946) 193
    Palestine riots (1929) 164–5
Jewish Brigade Group 183
Jewish National Fund 161–2
Jews. See also Israel; Zionism
    in American occupation zone of
        Germany 192
    Diaspora 161
    Exodus 1947 (ship) 194–5
    first Aliyah 161
    Hitler's persecution of 165,
        183, 184
    Nuremberg Laws (1935) and 165
    population in Palestine 137, 162
    second Aliyah 161–2
    Second World War and 183
    third Aliyah 162, 164, 165
    violence against British 193
Jones, Arthur Creech, Secretary of
    State for the Colonies 194
Jones, Sir Hartford 37
Johnson, Mr. (British agent in
    Tehran) 65–6, 232 n.78,
    232 n.79, 236 n.28

al-Kabir, Ali Bey (Mameluk ruler of
    Ottoman Egypt) 19
Kab (tribe) piracy 14
Kamil, Mustafa (Egyptian nationalist
    activist) 115, 116
Karim Khan, Shah of Persia 12,
    14–15, 16, 35
Kaye, John, General 58, 59
Keir, William Grant, Major-
    General 43, 44, 45
Khartoum 109–10, 114
King-Crane Commission 143–4, 149
King David Hotel bombing
    (1946) 193

Kitchener, Horatio Herbert, Governor-General of Egypt 113–14, 130
Knox, S. B., Major, British Political Agent 117
Kurds and Kurdistan 147
Kusel, Samuel Selig, Baron (customs controller at Alexandria) 97
Kut 129, 136
Kuwait 116–18, 120, 207

Lampson, Sir Miles, Ambassador to Egypt 157–8, 159–60, 165, 172–3, 175, 176–7, 178, 182, 184
Landsowne, Henry Petty-Fitzmaurice, Marquis of, Viceroy of India 117, 118
Larking, T. M., British Consul in Cairo 52, 231 n.71
Lawrence (of Arabia), T. E., Colonel 132, 135, 139, 140, 142, 143, 160
League of Nations 142, 147, 149, 161, 169, 170. See also United Nations
Lebanon 142, 144
  independence 185
  Second World War in 176
Lend-Lease Act (1941) 179
Levant Company 1, 10, 14, 20
  establishment of 2
  trade jurisdiction 19
Libya 198
  Second World War in 171, 172, 173, 174–5
Lloyd, George Ambrose Lloyd, Baron, High Commissioner of Egypt 157
Lloyd George, David, Prime Minister of United Kingdom 127, 128, 130, 137, 149, 150, 162
London Convention (Treaty) (1840) 51–2, 53, 89
  impact on Egypt 71–4, 86, 101
London Straits Convention (1841). See Five Power Straits Convention (1841)
Ludendroff, Eric, General 123

MacDonald, Ramsay, Prime Minister of United Kingdom 156
McMahon–Hussein correspondence (1915) 130–1
McMahon, Sir Henry, High Commissioner of Egypt 130–1, 133, 144
Macnaghten, Sir William 59
Mahdi, Muhammad Ahmed (religious leader) 105, 106–8, 110
Mahir, Ahmad, Prime Minister of Egypt 183
Mahmud II, Sultan of Ottoman Empire 49, 50
Makram, Umar (religious leader) 34
Malcolm, Sir John 37
Malet, Edward, Consul-General in Egypt 83, 88, 89, 93, 94, 95
Maltese Greeks, in Egypt 96–7
Mameluks 22–3, 30–1, 32, 33–4, 50
Manchuria 169
Mansur, Abdullah bin (ruler of Mocha) 17–18
Marchand, J. B., Captain 114, 115
Mary I, Queen of England and Ireland 1
Maude, F. S., General 130, 136
Maxwell, General John 126
Mecca 131, 132, 139
Medina 132, 135
Mehmet Ali, Governor of Egypt 31, 32, 33–4, 41, 42, 43, 74–5, 199, 228 n.43
  fear and distrust of canal schemes 75
  Government of (British) India and Company officials support of 50–1, 229 n.55, 230 n.59, 230 n.60, 231 n.71, 232 n.78
  military campaigns 48–9
  modernization of Egypt 48
  subjugation of 47–53, 74
Mesopotamia. See also Iraq
  British mandate 142, 147
  First World War in 127–9, 130, 136–7
  Iraqi Revolt (1920) 147–8
  Kurds in 147
  post-First World War 146–7

Middle East. *See also* Egypt;
    Mesopotamia; Palestine; Persia;
    Persian Gulf
to 1945 **145**
Allied spheres in 130, 134, 142
Arab revolt (1916–18) 131–2,
    135–6, 139–40
Balfour Declaration (1917)
    and 137–40, 144
British diplomatic and political
    agreements and 130, 210–11
British legacy 207–9, 211–12
British mandates in 142, 145–6,
    148, 154, 155, 160–1
British policy and authority, post-
    World War I 153–6
British policy, inter-war
    years 166–7
British policy, Second World War
    years 171, 173
British proposal for Japanese
    administrators in 136
First World War in 124–30
French mandates in 142, 161
McMahon–Hussein correspondence
    (1915) and 130–1
Second World War in 170–80, 187
Sykes-Picot Agreement (1916)
    and 123, 132–4
Milner, Alfred Milner, Viscount,
    Colonial Secretary 149
Milner-Zaghlul Agreement 149
Minto, Gilbert Elliot, Earl of 37
Mir Mahanna, Governor of Bandar
    Rig 15
Missett, Ernest, Major 32, 34
al-Misri, Aziz Ali, General, Chief of
    Staff of Egypt 159
dismissal of 172–3
Mocha (Yemen)
    coffee trade 17–18, 51
    strategic importance 18
Mohammad Reza Pahlavi, Shah of
    Iran 182, 204
Monson, Sir Edmund (British
    Ambassador to Paris) 114
Montagu, Edwin, Secretary of State for
    India 142, 150–1

Montgomery of Alamein, Bernard
    Montgomery, Viscount 179,
    193, 199
Moresby Treaty (1822) 45
Morley, John, Viscount, Secretary State
    for India 118, 152
Mossadeq, Mohammed, Prime Minister
    of Iran 182, 203–4
Mountbatten of Burma, Louis
    Mountbatten, Earl, Viceroy
    of India 191
Moyne, Walter Guinness, Baron, Secretary
    of State for the Colonies 184
Mudros Armistice (1918) 140
Mughal Empire
    East India Company and 4–7
    European commercial relations
        and 3–4
Munich Agreement (1938) 170
Murray, Archibald, General 126,
    127, 130
Murray, Charles, Consul-General in
    Egypt 73, 75
Murray, John (British Ambassador to
    Ottoman Empire) 20
Muscat
    Britain and 117
    slave trade and 45
    treaties with East India
        Company 29–30, 35, 42–3
Muscovy Company
    establishment of 1
    trade expansion 2
Muslim Brotherhood 156, 183,
    197, 202
Muslim resistance, in Egypt 106
Mussolini, Benito, Prime Minister of
    Italy 157, 169–70, 171

Nadir Shah, Shah of Persia 10–11
al-Nahas, Mustafa, Prime Minister of
    Egypt 158, 177
Napier, Charles, Admiral 52
Napoleon III 64, 65
Napoleon Bonaparte
    downfall of 38
    Egyptian expedition (1798–1802)
        and 26–9

overtures to Persia 36–7
War of the Third Coalition
    (1802–07) 31–3, 34
Nasser, Gamel Abdel, President of
    Egypt 160, 202–3
  Suez Crisis and 204–5
Nasserism 205–6, 207
nationalist movement
  in Balkans 122
  in Egypt 87–8, 91–8, 115–16
  Kurds in Mesopotamia 147
  Ottoman Empire and 141–2
National Liberation Front (NLF)
    (Aden) 207
Neguib, Muhammad, President of
    Egypt 159, 177, 178, 201–2
Nelson, Horatio 26, 32–3
Nepean, Evan, Governor of
    Bombay 43, 44
Newman, E. P., Major 127, 148
Nicholas I, Czar of
    Russia 55–6, 64, 67
Nicholas II, Czar of Russia 122
Nixon, Sir John, General 128–9, 130
NLF. See National Liberation Front
Nokrashi Pasha, Mahmud,
    Prime Minister of
    Egypt 200
Northbrook, Thomas George Baring,
    Earl of, First Lord of the
    Admiralty 95, 98, 100
Nubar Pasha, Prime Minister of
    Egypt 82–3
Nuremberg Laws (1935) 165

O'Conner, General Richard 173–4
Oman, and East India Company 35,
    42–3
Operation Barbarossa
    (Germany) 175, 179
Operation Husky (Allies) 181
Operation Overlord (Allies) 181, 186
Operation Sea Lion (Germany) 171
Operation Torch (Allies) 179
Orthodox Christians 64
Ottoman Empire
  Alexandria Convention
    (1841) 52–3
  Allied spheres in 130, 134, 142

Anglo-Ottoman Convention
    (1913) 118
Anglo-Ottoman trade agreement
    (1618) 17
Anglo-Russian understanding
    on 63–4, 150
Arab revolt (1916–18) and 131–2,
    135–6, 139–40
Baghdad Pashalik and 14
Battle of Megiddo (1918) 140
British commercial privileges
    in 50, 72
British declaration of war
    on 123, 126
declaration of Urabi as Pasha 94
declaration of war on
    France 28–9
downfall of 135–6, 139, 140
"Eastern Question" 47–8
Egypt and 19, 31, 32, 48–9
First World War and 123, 126
Gladstone and 111
Kab piracy and 15–16
Kuwait and 118
London Convention (1840)
    and 51–2, 72, 86, 89
Mudros Armistice (1918) 140
the Muslim world and 107
nationalist movements and 141–2
post-First World War 150–1
Russian invasion of 33
Second Egyptian-Ottoman War
    (1839–41) 52
Sykes views on 134
Taba affair (1906) 116
Ottoman-Persian War
    (1743–46) 10–11
Ottoman-Persian War
    (1775–79) 16–17
Ouseley, Sir Gore (British
    diplomat) 37

Pakistan 191
Palestine 131, 134
  Anglo-American Committee of
    Inquiry (1946) 192
  Anglo-American policies and 191–4
  anti-Zionist riots 159
  Arab League and 185–6, 194, 196

Balfour Declaration (1917)
    and 138–9, 144, 161, 162
British evacuation of 194–5
British mandate 142, 145–6, 160–1
Egypt and 159, 200–1
internal politics (1942–45)
    of 183–6
inter-war years (1918–39) 160–6
Jewish population in 137
King-Crane Commission
    and 143–4
UNSCOP plan 193–4
UN vote in favor of partition
    of 195, 200
Zionism and 143–4, 145–6
Palestine riots (1929) 164–5
Palestine Royal Commission 165–6
Palestinian Arabs 138–9
    1929 riots 164–5
    1936–39 revolt 165
    1949 "Diaspora" 197
    in Israel 195–7
    question of Arab self-rule 162–4
    rejection of British mandate 160–1
Palmerston, Henry John Temple,
        Viscount, Prime Minister of
        United Kingdom 47
    Crimean War (1853–56)
        and 65, 66
    Eastern policy of 39, 42, 46, 48, 50,
        53, 63, 71, 85, 101
    First Afghan War (1838–42)
        and 58–60
    Russian threat perception
        and 55, 56
    subjugation of Mehmet Ali 50–3,
        72, 74
    Suez Canal construction and 79,
        80
P&O. See Peninsular and Oriental
        Steamship Line
Paris Peace Conference (1919) 143
Pauncefote, Sir Julian (British
        diplomat) 91
Peel Commission. See Palestine Royal
        Commission
Peel, William Robert Peel, Earl 165
Peninsular and Oriental Steamship
        Line (P&O) 50, 52, 230 n.58

Perim Island, establishment of British
        naval base 30
Perpetual Treaty of Maritime Truce
        (1853) 46–7
Persia. See also East India Company:
        Persia and; Iran; trade
        agreements, Anglo-Persian
    1921 coup d'état 151
    Anglo-Persian Agreement
        (1919) 151
    attack on Herat, Afghanistan 56
    Britain and, during Fateh Ali Khan
        reign 37–8
    claims to Bahrain 44–5
    during eighteenth century 9–12,
        14–15
    post-First World War 151
    Russo-Persian secret treaty
        (1854) 65–6
    Russo-Persian Treaty of Friendship
        (1921) 151
    Russo-Persian War (1796) 36–7
    Russo-Persian War (1804–13) 37, 38
Persian Gulf. See also Middle East;
        Trucial Coast
    Anglo-Ottoman Convention (1913)
        and 118
    Britain's strategic domination
        of 29–30
    British withdrawal from 207–8
    East India Company and 2–12,
        16–17, 29–30, 45–6
Peter the Great, Tsar of Russia 9
Picot, François (French consul at
        Damascus) 132, 134
piracy in Persian Gulf 9, 10, 41
    East India Company and 42–3
    General Maritime Treaty of 1820
        and 43–4
    Government of (British) India
        and 43, 44
    increase in 16
    Kab tribe 14, 15–16
    Perpetual Treaty of Maritime Truce
        (1853) and 46–7
    Pirate Coast/Trucial Coast 34–5
Pitt, William, Prime Minister of
        United Kingdom 42
Poland, German invasion of 170

Popham, Sir Home, Rear-Admiral
30, 36
Portugal
1622 Anglo-Persian expedition
against 6
Indian and Gulf commercial
interests 3–4
protectorates, British
Egypt as 110–11, 124, 130, 148–9
in Persian Gulf 35–6, 49–50,
116–18, 120, 153
Prussia 64

Qajar, Fateh Ali Khan, Shah of
Persia 37–8, 44
al-Qasimi, Ibn Saqr 35, 46
al-Qasimi piracy 43
al-Qassam, Sheikh Izz al-Din (Muslim
activist) 165
Qatar 117, 118

Raffles, Sir Stamford 42
Raglan, FitzRoy Somerset, Baron 67
railroads
Berlin–Baghdad Railway 116–18,
120
in Egypt 77–8
Russian proposal for railway to
Persian Gulf 116–17
Ranjit Singh, Maharaja 56
Rashid Rida, Sheikh (pan-Islamic
leader) 132
RCC. See Revolutionary Command
Council (Egypt)
Rendel, George (British diplomat) 165
Revolutionary Command Council
(RCC) (Egypt) 201, 202
Reza Shah Pahlavi, Shah
of Iran 151, 181–2
Robert, Field-Marshal Frederick 69
Robinson, Lieutenant-Colonel 160
Roe, Sir Thomas 1, 4–5, 6–7, 8, 10,
13, 25, 39, 101, 155–6
Rome-Berlin Axis (1936) 157, 170
Rommel, Erwin, General 173, 174,
178, 179
Roosevelt, Franklin, President of
United States 176, 179, 180,
181, 185
Rossetti, Carlo de (Venetian consul) 23

Rothschild, Lionel Walter, Baron 137
Royal Navy 42, 45
gunboat diplomacy **119**, 157
Russell, John Russell, Earl of, Foreign
Secretary 65–6
Russia. *See also* Soviet Union
Battle of Tannenburg (1914) 123
and British understanding on
Ottoman Empire 63–4, 150
Brussilov Offensive 129, 140
Crimean War (1853–56) 64–8
dual entente with France 112
expansion towards Afghanistan
55–6
First World War and 122, 123, 129
intrusions into Balkans and
Middle East 86
invasion of Ottoman Empire 33
invasion of Persia 9–10
Napoleon's invasion of 38
railway line to Persian Gulf
proposal 116–17
secret treaty (1854) between Persia
and 65–6
Treaty of Brest-Litovsk and 137
Treaty of Paris and 66
Treaty of Tilsit and 34, 37
Triple Entente (1907) 115
War of the Second Coalition
(1798–1802) and 28, 29
War of the Third Coalition
(1802–07) and 33, 34
Russo-Persian Treaty of Friendship
(1921) 151
Russo-Persian War (1796) 36–7
Russo-Persian War (1804–13) 37, 38

al Sabbagh, Salah al-Din,
Colonel 175–6
Sadat, Anwar, President of Egypt 160,
172, 173, 177, 178
Sadiq, Ismail (finance minister of
Egypt) 82
al-Said, Nuri, Prime Minister of
Iraq 175, 206
Said of Egypt, Wali of Egypt and
Sudan 75, 77, 79
al-Said, Saiyid bin Sultan, Sultan of
Muscat 45
Saint-Simon, Henri de, Count 79

Salisbury, Robert Gascoyne-Cecil,
    Marquis of, Prime Minister of
    UK   83, 104, 112
Salman, Sheikh (Chief of Kab)   15–16
Samuel, Herbert Samuel, Viscount,
    High Commissioner of
    Palestine   163–4
Saudi Arabia   142–3
  creation of   139
al-Saud, Saud Ibn Abdul Aziz, Amir of
    Najd   43
Sazanov, Sergei   134
Schlieffen Plan   122
Second Anglo-Afghan War
    (1878–80)   152
Second World War
  British imperialism and   187
  in East Africa   174
  in Egypt   172–4, 176–8
  end of   186–7
  in Europe   174–5
  global conflict (1942–45)   178–81
  imperial defense   **174**
  in Middle East   171–9
  in North Africa   171, 174, 175, 179
  origins and progress of   169–71
  Second Front   181
Selim III, Sultan of Ottoman
    Empire   22, 32, 34
Sepoy Mutiny (1857)   68–9
Serbia   122
Sergeants affair (1947)   194
Seton, David, Captain   35
Seymour, Frederick Beauchamp Paget,
    Admiral   95, 97, 98, 99
Shah Hussain, Shah of Persia   9, 10
Shah Shujah, Amir of Afghanistan   56,
    58–9, 60
Sherif Pasha, Mohammed (Prime
    Minister of Egypt)   87, 88, 92
Sicily   181
Sidki, Ismail, Prime Minister of
    Egypt   199–200
Siege of Kut (1915–16)   129
Sinai and Palestinian Campaign
    (1917–18)   126, 137
Sirri, Hussein, Prime Minister of
    Egypt   172, 173
slave trade
  Britain's role in eradication of   45–7

Congress of Vienna provisions   42, 44
General Maritime Treaty of 1820
    and   45
Soine, W., Commander   230 n.66
Soviet Union. *See also* Russia
  Afghanistan and   153
  Atlantic Charter (1941)   179
  German invasion of   175, 179
  Middle East and   151
  Non-Aggression Pact (1939)   170
  Suez Crisis (1956) and   205
  Tehran Conference (1943)   181
Spain   5
  Civil War (1936–39)   170
  Peninsular War (1808)   38
Stack, Sir Lee, Governor-General of
    Sudan   156
Stalin, Joseph, General Secretary
    of CCCP of Soviet
    Union   180, 181
steamship network of Britain   **76**, 77,
    229 n.57
Stern Gang (Zionist extremist
    organization)   184, 193,
    195, 196
Stevens, George   77
Steward, William, General   34
Stilwell, Joseph, General   180–1
Stone, Charles Pomeroy, General
    (chief of staff Egyptian
    army)   87, 94, 98
Sudan   48
  Anglo-Egyptian Treaty of 1936
    and   157
  Battle of El Obeid and   107–9
  Battle of Tel el-Kabir and   106
  British re-conquest (Battle of
    Omburman) of   112–14
  Egypt's claim to   198, 199–200, 202
  independence   202
Suez Canal
  Anglo-Egyptian Treaty of 1936
    and   157, 200
  Britain's control of   100, 199
  Britain's objections to   79, 80
  Britain's purchase of shares   82
  British occupation of Canal
    zone   200
  construction of   78, 79, 80
  First World War and   126

Gladstone's support of   79–80
  inauguration of   80–1
  nationalization of   203
  Second World War and   174
Suez Canal Convention (1888)   202
Suez Crisis (1956)   203–5
Sufi, Shah of Persia   7
Supreme Muslim Council   163
Surat   4, 5, 6
Sykes-Picot Agreement (1916)   123,
    132–4, 143, 150
Sykes, Sir Mark   132–4, 137, 148
Syria   49, 51, 131
  Feisal I and   142, 143, 144
  French mandate   142, 161
  independence   185
  King-Crane Commission and   143
  Second World War in   176, 179

Taba affair (1906)   116
Tahmasp, Shah of Persia   2
Tehran Conference (1943)   181, 182
telegraphic communications   90
terrorism. See also Irgun (Zionist
    paramilitary organization)
  in Egypt   156
Tewfiq Pasha, Khedive of Egypt
    and Sudan   83, 84, 86, 87–8,
    92, 95
textile industry, Egyptian   73
Third Anglo-Afghan War
    (1919)   153
Townshend, Charles, General   129
trade agreements, Anglo-Indian
    under Mughals   4–5, 6–7
trade agreements, Anglo-Ottoman
    1618   17
trade agreements, Anglo-Persian   5
  during Karim Khan reign   14–15
  during Shah Abbas I reign   5, 6–7
  during Shah Abbas II reign   8
  during Shah Sufi reign   7
  evolution of   1–2
Trans-Jordan
  Abdulla I and   145, 148
  Arab Legion   176
  British mandate   142, 154, 155
  Feisal I and   142, 144
  Feisal I capture of   135, 137

Second World War and   176
  separation of Palestine and   161
Treaty of Amiens (1802)   31
Treaty of Berlin (1878)   117
Treaty of Brest-Litovsk (1918)   137
Treaty of Lausanne (1923)   151
Treaty of Paris (1856)   66
Treaty of Rawalpindi (1919)   153
Treaty of Sèvres (1920)   151
Treaty of Tilsit (1807)   34, 37
Treaty of Unkiar-Skelessi (1833)   63
Treaty of Versailles (1918)   141, 157
Tripartite Pact (1940)   179
Triple Alliance (1882)   111, 112, 121
Triple Entente (1907)   115, 121
Trucial Coast   34–5. See also
    Persian Gulf
  Britain's strategic protection
    of   35–6
  General Maritime Treaty of
    1820   43–5
  Perpetual Treaty of Maritime Truce
    (1853)   46–7
  Ten Year Maritime Truce   46
Truguet, Laurent (French
    admiral)   22–3
Truman, Harry S., President of United
    States   185, 192, 193
Tunis, French occupation
    of   88, 89, 91
Turkey. See also Ottoman Empire
  birth of the Republic   124, 151
  Treaty of Lausanne (1923) and   151

United Company of the Merchants
    of England Trading in the
    East Indies   8–9. See also
    East India Company
United Nations   180, 185
  creation of   179
  Egyptian case (1947)   200
  Iran membership   182
  Palestine case   193–4, 195, 200
  see also League of Nations
United Nations Special Committee
    on Palestine (UNSCOP)   193–4
United States
  aid to Britain   179
  Atlantic Charter (1941)   179

British imperialism and 180–1, 190
Cairo Conference (1943) 180–1
Casablanca Conference (1943) 180
Egypt and 200
First World War and 142
occupation of Germany 190
Palestine and 191–4
Second World War and 178–81
Suez Crisis (1956) and 205
Tehran Conference (1943) 181
Zionism and 185
UNSCOP. *See* United Nations Special
Committee on Palestine
Urabi, Ahmed (Egyptian
nationalist) 81, 105, 106–7
exile of 100
Islamic Union and 106
Ottoman declaration as Pasha 94
revolt 87–8, 91–8

Victoria, Queen of United Kingdom 60,
66, 109, 114, 115
Vienna Note 64

Wafd party (Egypt) 150, 156, 157,
158, 201
Wahhabis 43, 139, 142–3
Wali Khan, Mohammed (Afghan
representative) 153
Wallace, MacKenzie (*Times*
correspondent) 105
War Office (Britain) 93, 116, 124,
159, 172, 173
War of the Second Coalition
(1798–1802) 28–9, 31
War of the Third Coalition
(1802–07) 31–3
Wauchope, Patrick, General 34
Wauchope, Sir Arthur,
High Commissioner of
Palestine 165
Wavell, Archibald, General Officer
Commanding-in-Chief of Middle
East Command 160, 172,
173–4, 175, 176
Webb, Sidney, Colonial
Secretary 164–5

Weizman, Chaim, President of
Israel 137, 138–9, 144,
145, 164, 186, 193
Wellesley, Richard Wellesley, Marquis
of, Governor-General of
Bengal 42
Wellington, Arthur Wellesley,
Duke of 38, 60
Willoughby, Sir Hugh 1
Wilson, A. T. 148
Wilson, Sir Arthur, Admiral 99
Wilson, Sir Charles Rivers 82, 83, 91
Wilson, Woodrow, President of United
States 142, 143
Fourteen Points 142
Wingate, Sir Reginald, High
Commissioner of Egypt 137,
139, 148
Wolseley, Garnet, General 69, 100,
109, *110*
World Zionist Conference (1945,
London) 186
World Zionist Organization 161–2

Yemen 207. *See also* Aden
Young Turks (political reform
movement) 132, 133
Yugoslavia 175

Zaghlul, Said, Prime Minister of
Egypt 116, 127, 132–3, 148, 157
campaign for Egyptian
independence 149–50, 156
Zionism
Balfour Declaration and 137–40,
144
British policy towards 162, 163–5,
166, 171, 183–5, 191
critique of 186
Haganah 176, 183–4, 193, 195
Irgun 184, 193, 194–5
Palestine and 143–4, 145–6
1918–39 160–6
1942–45 183–6
Stern Gang 184, 193, 195, 196
Zionist Biltmore Conference
(1942) 185